To Dr. Botbol, Hope you enjoy the crazy stories. Rick

LIFE'S LESSONS

"A Successful Collection of Failures"

Written by
Ted Fearnley and Rick Fearnley

www.lifeslessons.ca

4th Floor Press, Inc.

ALL RIGHTS RESERVED. NO PART OF THIS PUBLICATION MAY BE REPRODUCED IN ANY FORM OR BY ANY MEANS WITHOUT THE EXPRESS PRIOR WRITTEN CONSENT OF THE AUTHORS.

THIS BOOK IS A COMBINATION OF THE AUTHORS' PERSONAL MEMORIES, REFLECTIONS, AND OPINIONS. SOME OF THE DATES, NAMES, AND LOCATIONS ARE INTENTIONALLY NOT SPECIFIC TO PROTECT THE IDENTITIES OF THOSE INVOLVED.

Life's Lessons: A Successful Collection of Failures/Written by Edward (Ted) Fearnley and Richard (Rick) Fearnley

Fearnley, Ted, 1932-
Life's lessons : a successful collection of failures / written by Ted Fearnley and Rick Fearnley.

Includes index.
ISBN 978-1-897530-06-1 (bound)
ISBN 978-1-897530-05-4 (pbk.)

1. Fearnley, Ted, 1932-. 2. Fearnley, Rick, 1961-. 3. Ontario--Biography. 4. Family--Humor. 5. Canadian wit and humor (English). I. Fearnley, Rick, 1961- II. Title. III. Title: Father and son share their life's lessons.

FC3077.1.F43A3 2008   971.3'04092   C2008-906148-9

Published by 4th Floor Press, Inc.
www.4thfloorpress.com
1st Printing 2008
Printed in Canada

This book is dedicated to our families, who put up with the long hours of solitude we lavished upon them as we regularly neglected our relationships with them to fulfill our own lifelong dream. We wish to thank everyone who has contributed to this book by being a memorable part of our lives—especially the poor souls we occasionally refer to in our public apologies.

"Humorous stories that brought back many fond memories of my youth."
—Wes Jarvis, Retired NHL Hockey Player

"This road map to family life includes all the happy disasters and fortunate detours that eventually lead us back home."
—Serafin LaRiviere, Journalist and Musician

"Extremely funny...without a single lecture or a word of preaching this book is filled with insightful lessons that people of all ages will enjoy."
—Phil Demetro, Mastering Engineer, The Lacquer Channel

"These treasured tales are humorous lessons that have relevance to readers of all ages and point to the preciousness of family life."
—Dr. Susan Joyce

"I laughed out loud many times and, like any good book, it left me wanting more. It is a rainy day pick-me-up book for sure."
—Lesly Taylor, Badge #88417 Toronto Police Service

"It has been more than entertaining to read about the Fearnley family. Each story gave me a certain warmth. Some reminded me of my childhood...stimulating fond memories of growing up and recognizing that life truly is a series of lessons."
—Gord Wilson, President, Wilson Niblett Motors Limited, Canada's #1 Corvette Dealer

Acknowledgements

In the past, some of our more memorable life experiences have been enjoyed time and again by sharing them with our family. Many times we were asked to recount them for the enjoyment of others. We wish to thank all of those who, upon hearing a story or two from our past, suggested that we "write a book."

Writing the stories was a major undertaking. We wish to point out that no one other than the authors was willing to sacrifice their cash flow, give up meals, delay needed rest, or spend days on end closeted in underground bunkers formatting our adventures into book form, tapping the way to victory. Nevertheless, this book would never have become what it is without significant contributions from many others.

We would like to thank our family for being the characters they were, are, and are yet to be. Ted's sister, Lynn Coleman, helped enormously by challenging the author's depictions of nearly every story involving the older generation siblings. On the other hand, Ted's brother, Greg Fearnley, made his mark by adding colour to these childhood memories.

Our ongoing thanks is extended to our wives for their patience and continuous proofreading efforts, and to Dave Fearnley for setting up and maintaining our website. We also wish to thank Wendy Drobiasko and Dy Curran for providing helpful editorial input, and Tim Zub for being a good friend and an avid supporter of our work.

Thanks are also extended to Josh Sera for his ongoing and insightful legal advice. We would like to thank Jaymz Bee for always being available to listen, advise, and encourage, regardless of how busy he was. We appreciate Lynne Truss and the timely publication of her book on punctuation, *Eats, Shoots and Leaves*.

Thanks are also offered to Tony Robbins for his practical motivating CDs, tapes, and books, and his words of inspiration contained therein. Typically, his work proved to be the spark needed to begin this life-changing adventure and provided the energy necessary to complete our book. We are truly grateful to our Literary Agent, Johanna Bates, who took the dream of publishing our book and turned it into a reality.

The team at 4th Floor Press consists of many fine professionals who helped transform our family memories into the book you now hold. We have benefited from the editing skills of Wendy Lukasiewicz, who has become a permanent entry on our contacts list. If Johanna Bates is this team's coach, Anne Bougie is most certainly the captain. She has proved to be more than an asset in just about every aspect of publishing.

We also wish to acknowledge all of the characters we refer to in our collection of narratives for willingly meeting with us and reviewing our stories for accuracy. All offered sincere, helpful, and insightful suggestions, thereby providing the endorsements necessary to present our recollections in a version that is less likely to incite lawsuits.

In addition to the many fine people involved with this project, we wish to thank you…our reader…for buying this book and requiring our publisher to furnish us with a charitable stipend.

Preface

This book contains many of our family's stories. Our family members from all sides, both distant and close, have commented over the years on the predominance of two major characters: Ted and Rick. Some have said, "like father, like son" but this cliché does not give justice to their uncanny ability to find themselves in some sort of trouble—together and on their own. We are the authors of this book.

Although we have both been known to be impatient at times, we did not start writing until Ted had had a health scare. In October of 1992, he was diagnosed with skin cancer. Concerns for his health were compounded when it was discovered that a dermatologist had repeatedly misdiagnosed the melanoma and Ted had been living with this condition unnecessarily for two years. The lesion was removed from the back of his leg, but in 1998, doctors advised him that the cancer had returned and spread to his lymph nodes in his upper left thigh. Ted was scheduled for an operation to test and remove all cancerous lymph nodes within this area.

The situation was grave and it motivated Ted to consider the various unique heirlooms he had inherited over the years from the estates of earlier generations. He wanted to be involved in the process of distributing them to his family. Being the closest geographically, Rick, the oldest of three sons, was the first to learn of Ted's intentions. Despite most of the items being valuable antiques, Rick was not willing to store such "junk." And, citing their lack of practical use, declined the offer.

Some time later, after the concerns for Ted's health had lessened, Rick approached Ted at his home and announced, "I've figured out what you can leave me." Ted, delighted with Rick's apparent change of heart, sat in anticipation and admired the cherished family keepsakes around the room. He was anxious to divest himself of the many special articles that littered his new downsized home, but Rick responded, "I want your stories." It was time to write the book.

Although both of us have been known to offer the long version of any event we are asked to recount, almost everyone who has heard either of us recite a family story or two has encouraged us to write a book. At times, our efforts to educate thoroughly have been mistakenly viewed as a selfish opportunity to boast, rather than a willingness to share. Regrettably, this perception is reinforced when a spirited desire to be understood manifests itself in the form of otherwise unnecessary details. However, we each blame the previous generation, believing that we came by this honestly…this is who we are.

In some cases our stories will read more like a documentary or a report rather than a narrative. This is because this book was first intended to serve merely as chronicles for our families. It was not until the later stages of the project that the possibility of publishing them was considered. However, once we started working, we both enjoyed spending this extra time together, and later, writing our book became an obsession.

We suggest that reading it should be enjoyed like strong drink. Massive quantities taken in one night may prove to be too much, too quick—and altogether overwhelming. If you begin to feel your senses numbing, we suggest you take a break. Digesting relatively smaller doses of our seemingly unbelievable foolhardiness may help make your reading experience that much more pleasurable.

Many of the stories that follow were quite painful at the time. Although we can laugh at ourselves, the recalling of some still penetrates our core, causing us to relive the pain. Our book consists solely of true stories. However, we have sought out the humour in each situation and have told them in this vein. In fact, the writing of this book has proven to be cathartic and therapeutic for both of us. Hence, there has been no need for embellishment, nor have we succumbed to such a temptation.

We both knew that we had learned much from the various escapades of our younger years. But, well before the stories were written, we recognised that even just listing them together tended to paint a different picture. Both of us appeared to be meandering through life as if we were a couple of imbeciles. Our problem was that all of these stories were true. (They still are.)

In addition, we felt that every tale begged justification—

especially in its written form. So, after each one, we added a tag line to reflect what our father-and-son team feel is the moral of the story. We call them our *Life's Lessons*.

Our main difficulty was not so much recording the incidents, but rather having some sort of flow from one story to the next. In the past, we could sit around the dinner table casually telling one after the other, and it was easy to tie one major problem into the next. However, in written form, jumping from one time period to another is confusing. Also, our family and friends would only need a slight introduction to the tale before we could begin, primarily because they were all familiar with our family members and many a previous story.

You, however, are at a disadvantage. It can be difficult to grasp the significance of a given situation when you were not at our last family dinner. Therefore, in an effort to share our *Life's Lessons* publicly, we decided to do what many dinner guests have requested: "Just start at the beginning."

For this reason, we have structured the material primarily in chronological order. As patriarch, Ted's stories compose Part One, and Rick's those of Part Two. Various time periods in both of their lives each become a chapter in their part of the book. Hence, Ted's stories begin in his childhood and continue through his marriage and fatherhood, and then into his second marriage. Then, Rick relates stories from his early childhood, adolescence, and fatherhood.

You cannot tell the players without a program. So, for your assistance we have devised a simplified visual aid in the form of a Fearnley family-tree, commencing with Thomas Fearnley, Ted's father. You will note that the last arrow falls to Rick's son, Andrew Fearnley, who is currently displaying the behavioural traits characteristic of the mutant gene needed for creating enough material for the next book in this series.

FEARNLEY FAMILY TREE
(Tracing the Mutant Gene)

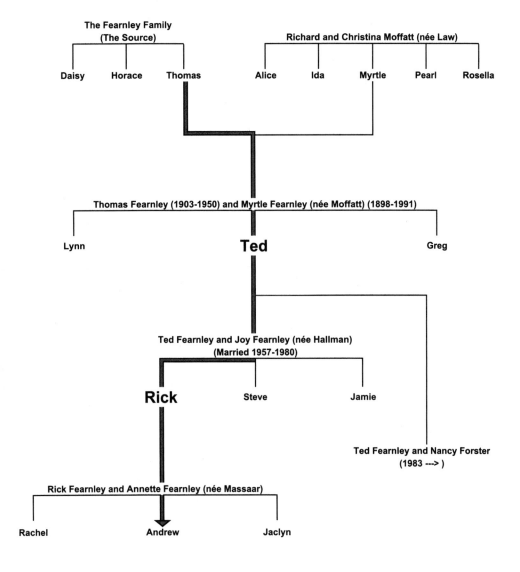

TABLE OF CONTENTS

Acknowledgements v
Preface vii
Fearnley Family Tree xi

PART ONE - TED AND HIS FAMILY

1. LIFE WITH MY PARENTS 1
Time for "R" Dessert 4
Customer Loyalty 6
New Pets 8
Food for the Hungry Mathematicians 10
Christmas Cake 11
Small Treasures 12
Renovating the Garage 14
Home Improvements 17
A Serious Talk 19
Mother on Vacation 21
Slipping Away 23

2. AT HOME WITH MY SIBLINGS 27
Greg and Ted's Vacation 29
Eyes in the Dark 31
Tunnel Vision 33
Ashes to Ashes, Dust to Dust 36
Parachuting 39
Flying Lessons 42
Tomatoes at Stake 44
Planning Dinner 46
A Trip to Toronto Island 47
Telephone Tale 49
Upgrades (Not Scholastic) 50
Only Eight Lives to Go 53
Pumpkin Pie 55
Lynn's Horse 56

Table Talk 58
Seventh Heaven 60

3. AT THE LODGE 63
Working Like a Dog 65
Another St. Bernard 68
Hand Lawnmowers 70
The Algonquin 72
The Race 74
The Garden 78
The Golf Club 80

4. CAMPING 83
Mother Needs to Know 86
The Proper Use of a Headband 88
Finding Our Way 91
Night Attire 93
Protection in the Wild 95
Amphibians 97
The General Store 98
Cold Feet 100

5. ON THE ROAD 103
Memories 105
Courting 106
Clear Lake 107
Waterskiing 109

6. FRIENDS AND FAMILY 113
Cottage Bliss 115
Pie in the Sky 119
Short Visit 121
Port Dover 124
Small Talk Anyone? 127
Ted's Favourite Pie 129
Fruit Stand 130

7. MY THREE SONS 135
Richard 137
Milkman 140
Sunday Dinner 142
Easter Celebrations 144
Richard Be Nimble, Steven Be Quick 146
The Go-cart 148
The Contest 151
Steven 155
Safely Hidden 159
The Wager 162
The Facts of Life 164
The Naturalist 166
The Fire Within 170
A Study of Dynamics 174
The Dad Who Knew Too Much 178
Steven Buys a Pizza 182
Steven Rents a Video 184
Jamie 187
I Spy 190
Buried Treasure 192
Playing Games 194
The Collector 197
Jamie the Philosopher 199

8. MORE PEOPLE, MORE PETS 201
A Decent Proposal 204
Fun in the Sun 206
Blown Away 209
Cheese Grinder 214
Intuition 216
Soup 218
Chocolates 220
Bread Pudding 222

9. CLOSING: PART ONE 225

PART TWO - RICK AND HIS FAMILY

1. LIFE WITH MY SIBLINGS ... 233
Monsters Under the Bed ... 235
Passing the Time ... 238
Three's the Limit! ... 241
Table Tennis ... 243
Faster! Faster! ... 245
Out of Gas ... 252

2. MY FRIENDS ... 257
The Picnic ... 259
A Hot Time at Home ... 261
Counting Traffic ... 264

3. THE AMAZING RICK FEARNLEY ... 267
Egg Salad Telethons ... 271
Under the Canvas ... 275
Midnight Madness ... 281
Carrey On ... 291
The Trial ... 298
Vertigo and Vomit ... 303
Flight for Pride ... 308

4. LIFE AFTER THE ENTERTAINMENT BUSINESS ... 317
Egg Nog ... 319
Could You Give Me a Push? ... 323
The Chandelier ... 328
Neon Lights ... 335
Fit for a King ... 339
The Laser Show ... 343
Concert Time ... 352
The Dimmer ... 356
Rush Hour ... 361
Belts in the Bush ... 366
Night Service ... 372

5. FAMILY AND FRIENDS 379
A Tale of Two Ties 382
New Clothes 384
Cottage Road 388
A Shot in the Dark 393
Tennis Anyone? 397
Call Waiting 403
The Life Preserver 405
The Birthday Party 412
The Laundromat 415

6. MY THREE CHILDREN 419
Rachel 421
The Milk Train 424
The Cutting Edge 426
Listen to Your Mommy 430
The Move 432
Andrew 435
Gone Fishing 438
Bumping Heads 442
Tuberboy 444
Hooked on Fishing 447
Jaclyn 451
Mother Beware 453
Table for Ten 455

7. CLOSING: PART TWO 457

EPILOGUE 461

INDEX OF LIFE LESSONS 465

PART ONE

TED AND HIS FAMILY

LIFE WITH MY PARENTS

Thomas and Myrtle Fearnley had three children. My sister, Lynn, was the oldest, then me, then my brother Greg. While the three of us were growing up, life was different from today. My dad was a salesman on the road and there were fewer distractions when he came home from work. Families tended to spend more time together than we typically do now. There was no TV. Sunday evening in our home was spent listening to radio shows like Charlie McCarthy (and Mortimer Snerd).

Then, on the heels of the Great Depression, Dad volunteered for army duty in the early fall of 1939, just after Canada joined World War II. Training for action at the front, being overseas for several years, and being assigned to Camp Borden as a member of the Interim Army, made his impact on our family during these times more like that of a special guest than that of a father who should discipline his children. Weekend passes and short visits with him while he was in Canada reinforced this both before and after the war.

In the mid-forties, it was government policy that before being transferred into the permanent Army, each soldier required a physical examination after one year in the Interim Army. The army doctor who was scheduled to do Dad's examination was absent in the last week of Dad's Interim Army stint. Since transferring into the Permanent Army was effected immediately after one year in the Interim Army, Dad had become a member of the Permanent Army automatically.

A few days later, just after the medical examinations had been completed, the doctor was filling out forms when he asked my father, "So what are you going to do on 'civie' street?" Dad replied, "As of last week, I'm a member of the Permanent Army." At this point, the doctor tore up the discharge papers he had been preparing and instead sent Dad to Chorely Park Military Hospital.

Apparently Dad had become infected with Tuberculosis. Becoming a member of the Permanent Army only days before his illness was officially diagnosed meant that he was entitled to all his medical treatment under government care. Dad had narrowly escaped discharge, thereby allowing his family to benefit from a full army pension upon his death.

From Chorely Park Hospital, Dad began a series of sporadic hospitalizations and treatments between Christie Street Hospital, the Weston Sanatorium, and Sunnybrook Hospital. He endured constant releases and re-confinements until 1950, the year he died. All of my stories about my dad took place while 'on release' during his visits home, rebuilding the relationship with his wife and children in the late 1940s. My mother went from being a single mom while Dad was overseas to a single mom helping our family cope with grief after he died.

The first chapter is entitled "Life with My Parents." We chose to begin here, primarily to create some insights as to what my parents were like. In this way, we hope that the stories that follow in subsequent chapters where my parents are not the prime focus, will have greater meaning if the way my parents approached life is understood. After all, they are responsible for the genes the authors now carry.

Friends would frequently suggest that Mom move on and ask, "Have you ever thought of getting married again?" Mom's reply would simply be, "If I got married again I'd have to marry someone my age, and who wants to marry an old geezer like that?"

∞ Time for "R" Dessert ∞

Mom wasn't feeling very well and was resting one evening in her bedroom in our house on Dundas Street in Islington, Ontario. My mom's youngest sister, Rosella, was preparing dinner. We called her Aunt Babe and she had a dessert that she felt sure my mother would appreciate. I was around three or four years old and ran upstairs to tell my mom about it. I thought it would be fun if I made her guess what it was.

Willingly, Mom agreed but wanted a hint, so I told her it begins with the sound wuh. She guessed and guessed until she gave up and begged me to tell her what it was. Eventually I gave in and exclaimed, "It's Wubahb! Don't you love Wubahb, Mom?" I recall her taking me in her arms as she lovingly said, "Teddy, rhubarb starts with an R."

I had trouble with my Rs. Not with reading, writing, and arithmetic, but with pronouncing the letter R. Until that time I thought I was saying my Rs correctly. Her willingness to amuse me by repeatedly guessing was a heartfelt response to her little boy.

Throughout my childhood this problem with Rs followed me. When I was a bit older, I can remember rushing upstairs to get something, and then calling downstairs a few minutes later, "Mothah, what ah I up heah fauh?"

Eventually, Mom took me to a doctor in an effort to cure me of this minor speech defect. He listened to me in his office for a few minutes. His remedy was to snip the connecting ligature between the bottom of my tongue and the floor of my mouth. I can remember not only the sharp pain but also the sound of the snip. Later, my mother worked patiently with me as I followed the doctor's orders. He had prescribed a rhyme for me to recite: "Round and round the ragged rocks the ragged rabbit ran." In addition, he asked that I repeat it with rolled Rs, which made me sound like a young Scottish actor rehearsing for a part as Robbie Burns: "Rrrround and rrrround the rrrragged rrrrocks the rrrragged rrrrabbit rrrran."

This phrase was repeated as many times as I could each

day with my mom listening and correcting me until my speech improved. I can now pronounce my Rs with distinct articulation. I do not know whether I was cured or whether I just became used to the sound of my own voice over time. It is also possible that I simply did not want to return for yet another snip.

Sometimes it helps to listen with more than your ears.

∞ Customer Loyalty ∞

Dad was overseas fighting in World War II. While trying to raise a family on her own, Mom was working full time, plus, like everyone else at the time, one half day on Saturdays. At times, Mom was quite a good cook. Depending on the amount of time available, she would cook anything from fried eggs for breakfast to a full roast beef dinner.

Unfortunately, my mother's approach to fried eggs was different than most. Upon finding that she had slept in and could be late for work, she would rush downstairs to slap the cast iron frying pan onto the stove, turning the element to full heat. She would then race upstairs to comb her hair and apply makeup. Then she would race back down, crack eggs into the red-hot frying pan and once again race back upstairs to get dressed. Soon after, she would tear down the stairs to flip the eggs, which would result in thoroughly searing both sides. She would serve them to us "barked" to such an extent that a shoemaker could have used them for half-soles. Despite our pleas, she performed this rite a few times a week.

Roast beef on Sunday was a completely different matter. The very best cut of meat (T-bone steak as a roast) would have been purchased from Gibson's Meat Market on Mount Pleasant Road, potatoes peeled and set around the meat in the roasting pan, along with carefully prepared vegetables. It was always a delicious meal and leftovers went to the stew pot.

I remember when I was around nine years old. Since Mom was not home much before dinnertime, Lynn and I (and to a much lesser extent, Greg) had to shop for and prepare the family dinners through the week. Having no imagination whatsoever—perhaps something that is common amongst most young men when it comes to food preparation—I fried sausages, peeled potatoes, and set them on the stove to cook while I opened a can of peas. It was a great Monday night dinner. I was so proud of myself.

Mom was thankful it was not another pot of burnt stew. Burnt stew was the usual result from three kids rushing home after school to throw an enamel pot of Mother's pre-cooked stew on the stove, turning the burner on high, and running out to play. Like anything in life, you get out what you put in—meals included.

The next day I felt there was no need to tamper with success. I returned to Gibson's Meat Market, where I was the day before, to purchase the sausages and asked Mrs. Gibson for another pound of the same. I gleefully prepared another round of sausages, potatoes, and canned peas. Second time around it was still better than burnt stew. However, by Thursday evening my special meal had lost most of its appeal and certain members of the family were in open revolt. Still, I was just as proud. By Friday late afternoon, faced with the option of a fifth serving of my special dinner, Mother had a choice of lovingly encouraging me to develop my culinary skills or carping to the butcher. She chose the latter.

Mom phoned the butcher shop and threatened Mrs. Gibson, saying, "If you give Teddy another pound of sausages tonight, I'll take my business elsewhere." In Mom's case, her 'business' was a considerable debt to Mr. and Mrs. Gibson, and the thought of such an option more than likely pleased the owners. In truth, the butchers likely would have welcomed this from us or any other customer of theirs who were struggling on the home front during the war.

Sausages were not seen at our house for quite a long time.

A threat misses its mark if the person being threatened welcomes the suggestion.

∞ New Pets ∞

Greg and I had a one-time friend who we were visiting one Saturday. He suggested we purchase two new pets from him. So, with money we earned from our paper routes, we paid our so-called friend handsomely for a couple of white rats.

With some foreboding, Greg and I felt that our parents would not necessarily treat these critters as welcome additions to the family. However, we did expect that news of their residence with us would be accepted gradually. The garage was chosen as the best location to keep our new pets, since our plan included hiding them at first.

For what we anticipated would be a brief stay in the garage, we constructed a delightful rats' nest made of an old cardboard box with a luxurious collection of carefully torn paper. We interlocked the flaps of the box and placed it in a far corner of the garage to ensure that our pets would be secure in their new home. We imagined the rats' accommodations could be gradually upgraded from garage to basement, then into the kitchen or dining room, where the entire family could learn to enjoy them, or to the bedroom that Greg and I shared, where they could be given the most love and affection.

The next day, while Dad was having his coffee after Sunday brunch, he looked out of the window in the back door and shouted, "What in tarnation is that?" 'That' was a white rat who had just squeezed under the garage door and was running around in the driveway. Greg and I prepared to explain all the details about our new pets and our dream-plan for their integration into our family. Unfortunately, the time allotted for this process was shortened with one brief statement from Dad: "Get rid of them—now!" From this point on, it was mostly a one-way conversation in which we were instructed—without options—to take them back to their former owner regardless of how much we paid for them.

Later lectures revealed that, as a child, Dad apparently had to clean his father's stables. During the course of his regular chores at Fearnley and Son's Roofing Company, he once used a pitchfork to clear rats (not the white variety) out of the oat bin where they were gorging themselves on the horses' feed. The process was basic in concept. Open the oat bin and stab repeatedly with the pitchfork to frighten the rats away. Unfortunately, one rather stubborn rat, who enjoyed his life the way it was, decided to fight for his foraging rights. While Dad was poking into the oat bin, the rat jumped up and bit him on the lower lip, and didn't let go. Dad shook his head from side to side, but the clamping critter remained a part of his face for an excruciating length of time. Although I was not able to fully appreciate his pain at the time, I now understand that sustaining such significant trauma to the lip is classified in modern medical terms as "bleeding painful."

I believe if you poke your nose into someone else's life, you must be prepared for the fork-in consequences. That same day, our pet rats (the white variety) were returned with neither argument nor refund, and to this day I have no idea how many times my former friend resold them.

Sometimes childhood fears return to haunt us through our children.

∞ Food for the Hungry ∞ Mathematicians

Like all soldiers, Dad had to adjust to home life when he returned to his family after the war. While at home, he shared in the cooking, cleaning, laundry, and all other family duties, including the disciplining of his three children.

My siblings and I were not eating as well as he thought we should be—except for dessert. Determined to change this, he devised a ploy that he felt would encourage us to develop good eating habits. His plan was simple: Offer us a full helping of dessert for every main course we could eat. He felt the desserts we loved so much would be all the motivation we needed. We couldn't believe our luck. With a promise like that we challenged Dad to make sure there was no trick. He assured us not only was there no trick, but also there was no limit to the number of desserts that could be earned. We couldn't wait for dinner.

Dad prepared plenty of veggies, meat, and potatoes. More importantly, he prepared more than one type of dessert. Throughout his preparations, the excitement amongst the three of us was palpable. We all arrived at the dinner table with great anticipation and ready for the main event. Never in our household were all three of us more excited about eating dinner.

I ate three helpings of the first course. Greg had the same. Cumulatively, with Lynn's efforts, we had earned more than eight servings of our favourite desserts. About halfway through my third serving of the first course, I began to feel a sense of fullness. I suspected that the others were experiencing something similar.

Dad broke into my thoughts: "Now, who's for a piece of apple pie?" he asked with a grin. "Or would you prefer cake and ice cream?" The three of us looked at him with sullen eyes; our hands patted our bloated bellies. "I'm too full," I replied. Greg and Lynn nodded glumly. Unfortunately, excitement had given way to reality, and dessert would have to wait.

What you sow, you can't always eat.

∞ Christmas Cake ∞

While on release, Dad maintained his sense of humour and his love for cooking. One of the things he most enjoyed was light Christmas cake; that is, in contrast to my mother's heavy, dark Christmas cake. Both types take a comparatively long time to prepare in relation to some other holiday treats. In either case, one must chop nuts, halve the red and green cherries, slice the candied fruit peel, prepare the batter, mix in the peel, and bake. After baking, it is set to cool on a rack.

One day close to Christmas, in his favourite room, Dad had done all of this. To ice the cake, he wished to transfer it from the baking rack to a plate. Since the kitchen table had a porcelain-like top, he first slid the cake off the rack and onto the smooth tabletop. Then while holding a plate under the table's edge, he tried to slip the cake onto the plate. Both the plate and cake crashed to the floor during the transition. The plate survived but the cake broke into a multitude of various-sized pieces, all of which were too small to be glued together with icing.

As Dad surveyed the mess, questions arose. How to pick up the pieces? Then, what to do with them? Dad had the answer:

Pat-a-cake, pat-a-cake
Baker's man
I'll make you a cake
But not as planned.
Wrap the pieces in cheesecloth,
Tie 'em in a ball,
Steam 'em in a pot,
Christmas pudding for all!
With white sauce it was delicious.

The best recipe for success is one that has room for failures along the way.

∽ **Small Treasures** ∾

One spring day, my dad hollered up the stairs, "Let's go, guys, we have to clean out the garage." Although we were both young teenagers at the time, it didn't matter to Greg or I since neither of us had plans for the day. In truth, Greg and I always enjoyed working around the house with Dad since we had so little time with him. The three of us adjourned to the garage, where our first task was to sort out what should be thrown away and what should be saved.

In a far corner of the garage, I remember Dad rummaging amongst a series of boxes. He suddenly stood up holding a full package of premium cigarettes. I had already been given permission to smoke at home. I had no need to hide them and knew instantly that they had to be Greg's, even though he was not allowed to smoke. Just who belonged to the newfound cigarettes was immediately apparent to my dad as well, but he did not let on. Instead, we could not resist a playful banter between us as we teased Greg about the obvious. In a knowing voice, Dad asked, "Are these yours, Ted?"

"Not mine, Dad."

"I wonder whose they are."

"Not mine."

"I wonder who bought these cigarettes. Are you sure you didn't, Ted?"

"Not me, Dad."

"Would you like to have a cigarette, Ted?"

"Don't mind if I do, Dad."

This exchange was repeated several times throughout the clean-up and well into the early evening until all of Greg's cigarettes were gone. Greg showed greater and greater disdain towards our dialogue as the number of cigarettes dwindled with each succeeding offer. In contrast, Dad and I became more and more enthusiastic with each repetition of our well-rehearsed act. Greg's overall clean-up effort in the garage was of an unexpected efficiency since he spoke precious little.

The combination of Greg's industry and the well-motivated

pair of my dad and I with our constant 'incentive sticks' made for an afternoon of fun. We actually got a lot more work done than planned.

I gave up smoking over forty years ago. Greg was barely a teen when this happened, but even though he is now in his seventies, he is still sent to the garage for his smokes.

Every smoker's life is reduced by at least one life lesson.

∞ Renovating the Garage ∞

Once again, Greg and I found ourselves helping Dad in the garage. This time we were on hand to help construct a lift door. A luxury, or at very least a set of doors much better than the conventional side-swing doors we had at the time. I said "swing," but in reality they often had to be dragged or scraped along the ground to effect access to the garage. Snow was no friend of our swing doors.

Dad had an idea. He wanted to fasten the two existing doors together and hang a track from the roof stringers so that the newly-formed oversized door could be opened and closed. He designed a sophisticated pulley and ballast system, which incorporated a clothesline arrangement and two long and thin galvanized buckets filled with sand to use as counterweights. In theory, Dad believed opening and closing his primitive overhead door would be easier than doing double duty with the two original side-hinged doors.

Unfortunately, in 1947, there was no such thing as a power tool. Even simple fasteners like screws were hard to work with in those days. To reduce associated blisters, Dad had a strategy that seemed to work well, especially when it came to large screws. His technique was to take the screw and jab it into a large bar of Fells Naphtha soap. Upon removal, the threads would be covered in soap, which would act as a lubricant in a hole pre-drilled by hand. Dad used to call this soap 'Beeswax' as in, "Pass me the Beeswax."

Final touches for the new door included fastening a closing strip to the doorframe using finishing nails. Dad's habit was to tap a finishing nail gently once or twice with the hammer until it was steady, then with one hard blow, smash the nail home. Tip, tip, WHAM…Tip, tip, WHAM without ever damaging the closing strip!

With our job nearly complete, Dad went into the house to refill his coffee cup. The same mischievous thought struck both Greg and I simultaneously. "What if we put Beeswax on the face of the hammer?" We weighed the thought. Was the risk of getting Dad upset worth the fun we would have before he figured it out? Would he be mad or laugh along with us? Was Greg going to rat me out before I could assure Dad it was all Greg's idea? How would we get out of it? Or, preferably, how could I get out of it and enjoy Dad blaming it on Greg? Our minds were racing but time was running out. Dad would soon return.

We put a great deal of thought into our scheme. After three full seconds of deliberation, we began our sabotage. We had about the same amount of time to effect our plan. I handed Greg the hammer and he wiped the face of it with the Beeswax, careful to remove any excess to avoid detection. Greg quickly handed me the specially lubricated hammer, and I replaced it in exactly the same location and position in which Dad had casually laid it aside. I completed the final step of our manoeuvre just as Dad came out of the house.

Dad grabbed the very first nail, expecting to pick up exactly where he left off. Tip, tip, SMASH! The nail lay embedded lengthwise horizontally in the wooden closing strip. Greg, behind Dad, nearly exploded trying not to laugh.

Dad tried again. Tip, tip, SMASH. This time the nail lay embedded in the closing strip but nearly vertically on approximately a north by northeast bearing. I was out of sight behind him so that I could observe the action, unnoticed. I knew he was holding a straight face the entire time, which made it all the more difficult not to burst out laughing.

Dad tried one last time, with similar results. He then looked at the hammer, muttered "Beeswax," and wiped the face of it on the leg of his work pants. Dad then carried on without incident or comment.

Greg and I slowly came to the realization that our dad was not going to give us the satisfaction of acknowledging himself as the butt of our joke. Time proved that he had no intention of ever saying anything about this.

Any harmless practical joke can be funny for the prankster. However, if the victim never shows their real feelings, they can get the upper hand. The more time passed, the more we realized that this form of one-upmanship can often be the best way to stop an antagonist from hammering his point home.

Dad died without ever mentioning this particular prank of ours.

He who laughs last, laughs best…but he who laughs inwardly can laugh longer.

∽ Home Improvements ∽

Some time ago, I read a humorous excerpt regarding an accident. An insurance company quoted a driver from a police report in which the driver stated, "In an attempt to kill a fly, I drove into a telephone pole." I found the above statement funny because it created a picture of a madman driving ferociously towards a fly with the intent of squishing it between the front bumper of his car and the telephone pole.

My mental picture of this scene is not far from the unnecessary vigour with which some people attack insects. I'm sure most of us have experienced the fear of losing a prized possession as someone else flails around yielding any item within arm's reach that could be used as a weapon for insect eradication. In some cases the bug is annoying, but in other cases it is just there.

One of our family's infamous make-work projects began with the simple and unassuming act of my father attempting to kill a fly. It was buzzing against the bathroom window one fall day in 1948. The window had been carefully constructed high in the wall behind the sink. To reach the pest in the far corner of the window, Dad opted to extend his reach by standing on the toilet. The plan was simple: step up onto our rock solid American Standard toilet, squish the fly that was bugging him, then go for a cup of coffee and enjoy the afternoon with his family. This was not to be.

With his first heartfelt swing, Dad slipped. As he twisted to regain his balance, he pushed the toilet seat downward and to the side and split the cheap thing in two places. His initial reaction was simply to buy a new one. Although the price of a new toilet seat was much greater than that of a flyswatter, it seemed that Dad was content to absorb the cost of the new acquisition. In just over two hours, Dad had purchased, unwrapped, and installed a splendid new toilet seat. He was thrilled with the new seat because it had a "shiny pearl finish" and represented the latest in toilet seat technology.

The house had been constructed in 1928. The bathroom was replete with hot water radiator, wall-hung sink with standard taps, claw-foot bathtub with separate hot and cold faucets—all in the company of painted walls, linoleum floor, and an aged toilet, which unfortunately boasted a seat with a shiny pearl finish that looked, "just a tad out of place."

Within two days, a decision was made to purchase a new toilet. Dad called, explained, and negotiated a contract with a plumber to install a toilet to match the new seat (with the shiny pearl finish). After installation, the plumber pointed out that the sink just to the left of our new toilet (or to the right, from the seated position) now appeared "just a tad out of place." He went on to explain that, for a small extension to the contract, he would be pleased to install a shiny new sink with state-of-the-art taps next to our slick new toilet. The new toilet seat with the shiny pearl finish had somehow led to a new toilet and a new sink.

Later, in the midst of admiring the shiny new toilet and its complementary new sink, our helpful plumber suggested a new radiator. It would be narrower and taller and would distribute heat more efficiently. For yet another extension to the original contract, he would be pleased to install the radiator.

Eventually, plans were made for a full renovation, including a new—and more efficient—radiator, new tub and shower, new flooring, new wall tile, a built-in medicine cabinet, and fresh paint. Throughout the construction, we reflected upon how small incidents could lead to bigger things—even before the invention of power tools. For a time we contemplated keeping the newly renovated state-of-the-art bathroom locked and out of sight for fear that the rest of the house would look "just a tad out of place."

Dad's new American Standard became…don't kill bugs.

There is always an opportunity to change when something is broken—especially for people.

∞ A Serious Talk ∞

Throughout my childhood, my dad referred to my older sister, Lynn, as "Princess." On one memorable occasion when Lynn was a young adult, she had upset Dad. He felt that he had to have a talk with her concerning her attitude. He considered this a serious matter that required his intervention. From Dad's perspective, his talk did not last long enough. From Lynn's viewpoint, it took far too long.

Only moments after, Princess was sniffling and snorting. Although the sounds were coming from her upstairs bedroom, they could be heard throughout the house. It sounded as if she might be severely depressed or experiencing prolonged suffering.

Dad's only objective had been for her to recognize that a change of attitude was required. I could tell that Dad felt badly because he made comments about how he thought he might have been "too hard on her." His genuine feelings of remorse were apparent. Although he was confident that his stern talk was necessary, it did not take long before he headed up the stairs to apologize.

There were not many things any of us could do that would keep Dad angry for very long. He was not interested in having his Princess suffer any longer, so he quietly knocked and opened the door to her bedroom. I think Dad expected to have a short exchange of soft-spoken words to reinforce his earlier message. To his surprise, he found that the sounds he heard of sniffling and snorting were Lynn's attempts to suppress her laughter. Apparently she had either taken to heart what Dad had said and changed her attitude very quickly—or perhaps and maybe the more likely of the two—she decided to forget about whatever he was lecturing her about and go have some fun.

For most children, being sentenced to your bedroom for an unspecified period of time is never an enjoyable punishment. Lynn had adapted quite well by simply deciding to read a humorous book. She was reading a copy of a very funny book entitled, *Three Men in a Boat*—the American version. The humour in that book (matching that of Jerome K. Jerome's) more than compensated for the stern lecture about changing her attitude du jour. Future outbursts proved it was easier for Lynn to cope with a lecture rather than its inherent issues.

When Lynn ignored the implication of her actions, she lost the meaning of the lesson and its value was reduced from a serious talk to a boring lecture.

Inasmuch as our children often underestimate the value of our words, we, as parents, often overestimate them.

∞ **Mother on Vacation** ∞

Many years after her "serious talk," Lynn grew up. She had trained in New Jersey, worked in Toronto, moved to California, married, and divorced, before she met her present husband, Neil Coleman.

In 1969, Lynn and Neil had just celebrated their second anniversary. Mom had driven her two sisters, my aunt Ida and aunt Babe all the way from Toronto to relax and enjoy some time with Lynn and Neil. As a pastor, Neil was well versed at giving directions to The Glass Chapel, which Mom was keen on visiting. During one of Mom's visits, Neil was pointing the way to the chapel along freeways and roads on the local map when Mom asked, "Why can't I take that black highway? It seems to go straight where I want to go and it's shorter." Neil replied, "Because, Mom, that is the county line, not a road."

Mom had her own version of getting to the church on time and her opinion about maps was not common. Although it has been said that one's journey can be just as important as one's final destination, at times, Mom's destination was more of a target…and her journey better likened to that of taking aim with her vehicle. For her, a map tended to be somewhat unnecessary, especially in cases where her destination was "well in sight." At no time did Mom ever sport the bumper sticker, which reads, "If you don't like my driving—stay off the sidewalk." But, it is possible that the author of this one-liner may have been motivated to write this after witnessing someone with driving skills similar to those of my mother.

As she got older, it became more and more apparent (not to her) that her driving skills were deteriorating. Driving on the wrong side of the road, going through stop signs, and driving at half or three times the speed limit were all minor variances in Mom's driving world.

On one occasion, she was driving out to see Lynn and Neil in their new place in Claremont, California, for the first time. Shortly after arriving, Mom was describing her trip through the downtown parts of Los Angeles and onto the San Bernardino

Freeway. (I'm not sure why she was coming from that direction, and to this day it still remains somewhat of a mystery, but that's another story, I'm sure.) Anyway, about halfway through her story, Mom mentioned rather casually that she had gotten onto the wrong freeway by mistake, but in her words noticed her error, *"Just in time to back up and go onto the right one!"*

After Neil picked himself up off the floor, he said, "You did WHAT? Not only could you have been killed, but if you had been caught, they would have locked you up and thrown away the key." When Neil tells this story, the most humorous part for me is when he states with renewed amazement at each telling, that, "Mom backed up from the busiest highway in California to get onto the second busiest one!"

Mom's initial response was a placid reply of, "But I had to do that. If not, I would have become hopelessly lost and would never have found my way back to that point to take the correct freeway." It appeared that she had become so focused on getting onto the right highway, she ignored the potential problems associated with her alternative plan. Without the use of a good map, her 'plain view doctrine' was later shared as being perfectly logical with anyone who would listen.

Justifying something to yourself does not make it right.

∞ Slipping Away ∞

It saddened me to watch my mom's driving skills decline in her later years. In her prime she was a very competent person with a work ethic born of the Depression in the 1930s. However, there was a stark contrast between her actual driving and her official driving record. For example, there were no collisions on her official record—primarily because she was often able to persuade her victims to refrain from reporting an accident and instead accept reimbursement from her for all damages.

In one unique case, she wrote off another driver's vehicle that she had T-boned on its way to the junkyard. Her good fortune also allowed her to wiggle out of a collision involving a brand new car, again through gentleness, sincerity, and her cheque book.

The most memorable time she escaped scarring her official driving record occurred on "a dark and stormy night." Ironically, this incident was the highest insurance claim she had ever made. Much to the insurance company's detriment, it was not the last—especially because they insisted on reinstating her insurance with no increase in premium despite my objections to the contrary.

On that stormy night, Mom was at home sick with the flu. Her driveway was in need of shovelling after a significant snowfall. As had been her custom, a neighbour's young son was hired to clear the snow. Unfortunately, Mom's car was parked in her typical casual fashion in front of her house on Hillsdale Avenue in North Toronto. The rear of the vehicle was overhanging the driveway. It only needed to be moved about three feet or so, to allow the boy to finish clearing the snow. When asked to move her car, Mother, suffering from the flu, suggested that he do it since she could not bear the thought of suiting up just to move the car a few feet.

Her willing helper eagerly agreed. He had always been interested in cars. He was enthusiastic about driving and many times prior had talked glowingly about car trips with his family. Sadly, he had never driven. This nineteen year old did not have a driver's licence. In fact, he never would be able to drive, because unknown to my mother, his mental capacity was that of a twelve year old. Inasmuch as his excitement about the opportunity far exceeded his skill level, it also encouraged Mom to make a serious error in judgment. Mom gave her car keys to him and expected their return within a few minutes.

The first clue that something might be amiss was that the snow remained and the vehicle was gone. True, only an hour had passed since she had given him the keys, but Mom reassured herself that all was well because she recalled the boy reminiscing about his drives with his family. Unfortunately, she did not realize her self-assurances were false, missing the fact that her helper had always been a passenger in any motor vehicle. That is…until now.

The keys were returned about two hours after first being entrusted to her snow shoveller. As noted earlier, this night was stormy. It was also snowing, cold, and slippery—all factors that eventually would take their toll on the insurance payout.

It wasn't long after the keys were returned that the police were knocking on Mom's door. Being genuinely concerned for the young lad, Mom asked the officer if he had been in an accident. I am not sure exactly what the officer's response was, but *technically*, the answer was no. The truth was he had been in many.

Apparently, the boy's only driving experience had been in his dreams. On this night he had logged over a mile before he managed to bring the vehicle to its first full stop. Although the car looked nothing like it once had, it was later confirmed to be Mom's car. A confusing conundrum, since the attending traffic cop had accepted Mom's claims of being at home, in bed, with the flu.

Although not pieced together at the time, the police investigative team would later reveal:
- The lad had started off eastbound rather poorly by failing to stop for the posted sign at Cleveland Street,
- One or two parked cars on the residential street of Hillsdale Avenue had been sideswiped,
- One car was badly damaged during an attempt at a three-point turn,
- Before he turned onto a main arterial street called Bayview Avenue, he had knocked down a stop sign,

- While southbound on Bayview Avenue, other cars were treated similarly to those on Hillsdale Avenue,
- He managed to make a right turn to head west on Manor Road with only minor damage to an eastbound car waiting at the light,
- Proceeding westerly without incident for nearly 200 feet, a car parked on the south side of the street by a somewhat optimistic motorist sustained significant front end damage,
- After extricating himself from this particular collision, our driver continued west straight past Cleveland Street without regard for the stop sign,
- Evidence of his passage through this intersection was the relatively minor damage to the stop sign post,
- Continuing west on Manor Road, only a couple of vehicles parked on the street were damaged,
- At Forman Avenue, the driver, now feeling somewhat more confident, executed a right hand turn without incident,
- His unblemished new record, now 300 feet of accident-free driving, was shattered along with a small truck he hit on Forman Avenue,
- As he turned onto Hillsdale Avenue, two vehicles on opposite sides of the street restricted the travelled way, and with ploughed snow, the available room to pass was further reduced. Rising to a 'thread-the-needle' challenge, his forward motion resulted in an otherwise successful carom manoeuvre as he bounced between the parked vehicles, and
- Once eastbound on Hillsdale Avenue, our 'driver' managed to continue the final half-block without incident. He came to rest straddling the southbound lanes of Cleveland Street, where he once again had been unable to effect any braking action at the stop sign. Surprisingly, he was only a short distance east of his original starting point, serving only to confuse the pending investigation.

- The greatest amount of damage occurred to a Chevrolet Corvette. The proud owner had carefully positioned the car halfway up his driveway on Hillsdale Avenue to ensure no damage could be caused by an errant vehicle. Apparently, our errant driver, suddenly aware that he had made a serious error driving my mom's car in the first place, made a desperate attempt to return to his shovelling duties. Unfortunately, his very first attempt at a three-point turn failed to exclude this beloved sports car from the carnage. The only thing on this block that had not been 'taken out' was the last three feet of snow required to complete the task he had set out to do two hours before.

It is possible that a few of the accidents stemming from this particular incident have slipped my memory. Although Mom was not even in her car, I am certain that this was her greatest insurance claim. It is a shame that the entire episode could have been avoided had she not been home sick that day with the flu.

It has been more than twenty-five years since, and we have still not heard that the traffic cop has completed all of the necessary paperwork. No charges were ever laid.

No one has a fond memory of the flu.

AT HOME WITH MY SIBLINGS

In the 1940s, things were quite different than today. While Dad was overseas, Mom worked about fifty hours a week. This was not unusual for any mother of three children while her husband was at war. In our home, money was scarce and there were few options when it came to our lifestyle.

My siblings and I all had chores that were required to run the household. It was commonplace to expect pre-teens to cook meals for the family and shop for groceries. The house simply did not run itself. With my mom working full time, and my dad at home only sporadically, our chores were more than a form of developing responsibility—they were a necessary part of our family's daily life.

Although my life as a young boy involved chores and quibbling with my brother and sister, it was not void of entertainment. With no TV, a child's entertainment could not be obtained instantly with the flick of a switch. So, Greg and I usually made our own fun.

The life of any boy as he grows to maturity is usually filled with at least a few acts of mischief along the way. In many cases, mischief is what a child sets out to accomplish. However, in other cases, at least for my younger brother and me, the trouble we got ourselves into was often simply the result of attempts to entertain ourselves.

The more we lacked the necessary forethought or consideration for others, the more trouble we ended up in. Fortunately, the more trouble we got ourselves into, the funnier the story reads fifty years later.

Time is a good healer, and for my family, half a century seems to have been enough time to have the pain and frustration give way to laughter and lessons.

This chapter reflects some of the more memorable times in my childhood while at home with my siblings.

∞ Greg and Ted's Vacation ∞

Children generally enjoy being at home alone without their parents for brief periods of time. When I was younger, my siblings and I were on our own for about a half hour in the morning and again for another two hours each weekday afternoon. This was a regular occurrence because Mom would leave for work before we left for school. She never saw us off but would always say goodbye as she headed out the door each morning on her way to work.

Her working hours were 9:00 a.m. until 5:00 p.m., and we all looked forward to greeting her by 6:00 p.m. every weekday, if she wasn't working overtime. On Saturday, a half day for work, she would leave at the same time but get in a little earlier.

On a typical day, Mom could count on the three of us leaving for school together within thirty minutes or so after she left for work. Unlike Lynn, Greg and I enjoyed strolling to school through the puddles, playing marbles, and experimenting with any other recreational activity we could find along the way. For us, the best part of a school day was getting home a full two hours or so before Mom arrived.

At the tender ages of six and eight, Greg and I realized that Mom's absence created a wonderful opportunity for us to make the most of our time. We decided to play hooky and take the entire day off. The food already laid out on the kitchen table for our school lunch break was easily packed into brown paper bags. We had a wonderful time playing all day in a nearby swamp at the northwest corner of Bayview and Eglinton, known as Wilson's Bush. No one found out.

The next day, feeling somewhat confident with our last adventure, we decided to try it again. This time, after packing our lunch with a couple of Mother's chocolates in each, our day was spent observing toads, frogs, salamanders, and odd-shaped sticks. The second day, and neither Mom nor Lynn was even suspicious.

Marvelling at our extraordinary luck, we decided to try it again. With a few pieces of Mother's silk cloth remnants, we made ourselves capes and masks and played as superheroes all day in the bush. We played so enthusiastically, a couple of young strangers came running up to us late in the day and excitedly told us how they thought we were *real*! The third day…and our luck still held.

With our confidence showing no signs of waning, we tried our luck again for the fourth time with similar good fortune. Greg and I had begun to really enjoy spreading our wings to the fullest. Our mistake, aside from planning to play hooky in the first place, was thinking this could go on for the rest of our lives without anyone catching on.

Consistent with modern day children stories, but in stark contrast to a typical superhero's lifestyle, our plans were foiled by a meddling school secretary who chose to phone our mother. I'm not sure if the secretary was inquiring about our health or if she was just acting on reports of two superheroes spotted in Wilson's Bush. Either way, in the end, everyone found out.

Mother was furious. She was so mad that she spanked us both with the back of her elephant tusk hairbrush. My only consolation was that Greg received his full lashing, whereas mine was stopped short when Mom's weapon broke—on my backside.

If you're going to play hooky, don't do it for a full week.

∞ Eyes in the Dark ∞

As young boys, Greg and I were both fond of toads. We liked all different kinds but our favourites were the ones that came in pairs. This species could be found in the same places as others but there was always a small one on top of a larger one. They would always be facing the same way and it was difficult to get them to jump or separate them from each other.

One day just before returning home from Wilson's Bush, we found a small old dishpan near the pond where these toads lived. We picked it up and took it home with us after we had filled it with 'paired' toads. This pan was substituted as a miniature pond for more than a dozen coupled toads.

As we got closer to home, we began to realize that our pets would need protection from others in the house. When we arrived, we settled on keeping the toads in the unfinished basement, feeling this to be far superior to our original idea of hiding them under our bed. However, where in the basement remained a question. We slipped in the side door because it had easy access to the basement. Our epiphany was to keep the special toads in the coal bin—another relic from an earlier age that helps illustrate the differences between then and now.

Coal was needed for heating the home and it was stored in the coal bin. This made a coal bin a necessary part of every home in those days. It was usually located in one corner of the basement where the outside walls formed one end and one side of the bin, and interior wooden walls formed the balance of a five foot by ten foot storage box. With two-by-four studs and tongue and groove wooden slats fastened horizontally to hold the coal in the corner of the basement, it was very sturdy. An excellent place to keep toads.

We sat the dishpan full of toads on top of the coal, not expecting them to move. Later that evening, Mom went down to shovel the last load of coal on the fire for the night. As she stooped over and scraped the shovel along the floor to scoop up the coal, she came face to face with a large toad. I can still hear her scream. Greg and I had a suspicion as to what had happened. Within a few seconds of Mom asking us why there were toads in the coal bin, we had to come up with an explanation. We informed Mom that they were our pets.

Over the next few weeks, each time Mom or Lynn was confronted with yet another *pet*, Mom would ask how many we had brought home. We only admitted to having as many as had been discovered. In truth, we had no idea how many there were. We hadn't bothered to count.

Since bringing them home and ensconcing them in the coal bin, each of the toads had managed to migrate to their own special place in the basement in which they could find some sense of security. Mother had the misfortune of discovering them beside the laundry tubs, under the stairs, in the hole in the floor where the water service came into the house, and other nooks in the basement.

Obviously, Mom asked the same question many times. I can still remember her frustration as she inquired well into the next season, "Teddy" or "Gregory," depending on who was close at hand, "Are you sure that's the last one?" To which we always answered a convincing, "Yes."

Every pet deserves a special place in your home.

∞ **Tunnel Vision** ∞

In this story I was working on my own, without Greg or Lynn. I did however have the help of my friend who lived directly across the street. I was in grade seven at the time; my buddy in grade eight. My project with him could well be considered as one of my earliest engineering works as it took place almost twenty years before I graduated in Civil Engineering from the University of Toronto in 1960. My work with my buddy contrasts with that which I performed as a Professional Engineer. I believe it could serve as an example to any seventh grader about the importance of a secondary education.

One day we were playing and talking about all the fun we had each time we got together. The discussion included how we would be lifelong friends and our mutual commitment to each other as to how we could maintain our friendship. To facilitate our visits, we envisioned a tunnel between my house and his, and thought it would be a good idea to build one. Besides, we both felt it would be really neat to have access to a tunnel under the street. We knew that the best place to start would be in the basement.

Since we were already at my house on the day in question, we thought it easier to begin there and dig towards his house. We reasoned that the basement walls would not allow us to go directly from one basement to the other because the layout of the road was somewhat depressed between our homes. I still believe that our decision to first dig down and then across was brilliant. No other turns would have to be negotiated until it became time to dig up into my buddy's basement, which by our estimation would be somewhat later that afternoon. At the time this was a bit naïve, since neither of us had the education to understand that the road bed could hold potential obstacles such as buried telephone cable, storm and sanitary sewers, catch basins, and various electrical cables.

Deconstruction of the existing basement floor began immediately and with great enthusiasm. We were proud of our progress when, in an area roughly less than two feet square, we smashed through the two inches of concrete in no time. The brittle concrete was no match for my dad's eight-pound sledge. Our efforts continued with vigour as we removed the chunks of concrete exposing a layer of crushed stone—the next hurdle in the making of our tunnel.

Once the gravel had been excavated, the earth was a welcome sight at the bottom of our now six inch deep hole. Only the packed earth from the home's original excavation remained, and we continued with a renewed spirit until we had removed at least six inches of that packed soil. Never once did we feel we had bitten off more than we could chew. The only time we began to rethink our steps was when we found ourselves surrounded by copious amounts of loose dirt.

For some reason, the height of the excavated material we were piling up in the basement was rising faster than the hole was gaining in depth. It seemed that for every inch of earth we removed from the hole, we had two inches of dirt in the basement. Ignorant of the laws of physics, we did not know that packed earth will often take up to twice its original volume in an unpacked state. This is why when anyone digs a hole in the ground and then fills it back up, it always ends up with a hump.

With the basement now housing a significant pile of dirt, and our tunnel barely more than a foot deep, we took a break to plan how and where we could dispose of the onslaught of more filth.

Our common goal and keen interest in my first engineering feat never allowed us to consider abandoning the project—that is until my mom got home and immediately issued a stop work order. There were other orders but I cannot include them here in a family book.

If our excitement had been reduced when we recognized the problem of disposing the loose fill, it was annihilated when my mom told us what she thought of our endeavour. The speed at which the construction crew ceased production would make any building inspector envious. The hole was soon refilled, but the hump of dirt that remained in the middle of the basement served for many years as a reminder to my siblings, and to my friend when he dared to visit, that my mom did not like tunnels.

It was not until some time after Dad returned from the war

that the hole in the floor was finally rectified. A level floor had to be constructed when Dad decided to build a recreation room in the area of the basement where evidence of our tunnel still remained. Now the only evidence of my first engineering project, begun more than sixty years ago, is a house with a basement ceiling height four inches less than any other house on the street—or at least four inches less than that of my buddy's.

> ***If you are going to build a tunnel to your friend's place—START THERE.***

∞ Ashes to Ashes, Dust to Dust ∞

In the 1940s, very few people had enough money to afford waste of any kind. Even remnant pieces of coal were sifted out of piles of ash from the furnace. It was a simple concept but hard work. It entailed shovelling large amounts of ash out of a compartment in the bottom of the furnace into a two-part receptacle. The upper part was a square, galvanized metal box about 18" x 24" and 5" deep. It had a screen bottom with large holes designed to catch the reusable pieces of coal. The ash was aggressively sifted through to the lower part, a container with a rounded bottom. The bottom of the lower portion was outfitted with two rockers to facilitate the necessary end-to-end rocking motion required to separate the ash from the salvageable coal.

When the task was executed correctly, the top part held the reusable coal but with various clumps of ash attached. This material was dumped into the coal bin and mixed with the good coal to be burned again. The bottom part—the ash can filled with the unusable portion—would be taken to the curb for pickup by the city dump truck. It was heavy. As the oldest boy in the family, it was one of my household chores. Sifting the ash for coal was a messy job at best. Each time I did this, I felt as if I had eaten a bowl of dust.

I was old enough to know that most chores I delayed grew from small jobs into large jobs. On one occasion, I ignored this coal cleaning responsibility of mine long enough for it to become a huge undertaking. On this particular Saturday morning, Mother had insisted that my work be finished before she returned home from the office around 1:00 p.m. Mom's edict did not motivate me to the extent she had intended.

I began to think about how I could make this tedious job more interesting. Dad was overseas and the whole family had access to his hand tools and workbench while he was away. Dad's rule of putting them back when we were done was clearly understood by all, but rarely exercised by any.

There was a blower fan mixed up amongst other tools on the bench. We had different uses for this implement. It was handy for removing spiders from hard-to-reach corners or annihilating anthills with one blast. We also found many other uses for it, including anything mischievous young boys could imagine.

I should have been sifting through ash and dust for reusable pieces of coal, but instead I was sifting through Dad's workshop looking for this wonder tool that I felt sure could help me accomplish my chore with great speed. I found the quarter horsepower electric blower and wondered how I could use it for the task at hand. After much thought, I had an idea. I'd suck a piece of coal into the rotating cylinder of the fan blades at full speed, and the force of the air would blow the unwanted ash from the half burnt coal as it swirled around.

Holding my fingers gingerly above the motor's cylindrical fan I dropped in a small piece. Success! The fan was blowing off the ash and dust at record speed. I then tried a bigger piece. I admired the perfectly clean coal. This was much more fun than sifting for remnant pieces of coal like a desperate gold digger. The job now took far longer but the coal was virtually spotless and void of ash. I had revolutionized the relatively new household product known as a vacuum, except mine didn't have a bag. If only I had patented it before James Dyson was credited with inventing a bagless vacuum thirty years later.

Mother's arrival home from work is often a pivotal point in many of my stories. This was no exception. She failed to appreciate my ingenious device, perhaps because she couldn't see it through the dust. In fact, she couldn't see anything clearly. No one could. The ash and dust had travelled into every room and onto every possible surface throughout the house. This was quite an experience—especially for my mother.

I had created a vastly disproportionate amount of unnecessary clean-up work in exchange for the thrill of having four hours of fun in the basement on a Saturday morning. Unfortunately, the upper two floors of the house displayed a scene in sharp contrast to the cleaner look that Mom had been expecting. I still find it amazing that no surface in the house escaped a covering of soot. It was as if it had been snowing dust indoors for the entire time Mom was at work. In truth, it had been, and it was all my fault.

Mother was truly not pleased…again. I was forbidden from experimenting further with my coal-cleaning contraption, and to make matters worse, I had inherited more dusting chores than ever before. Although this was not as bad as Pompeii, it was a few weeks before the smaller pieces of ash reached their final settling point, and then a couple more for the dust to settle completely. To Mom's credit, her demeanour improved long before the mess had been fully cleaned up.

Vacuums without a dust bag really just suck.

∞ Parachuting ∞

Both Greg and I had our own morning paper routes. We shared another by splitting the list of customers between us. So, technically, we were each responsible for a paper route and a half. There were a few hundred names between the three lists and this translated into more than one bag full of newspapers for both of us, six days a week.

Unfortunately, carrying them never gave me a muscular build. The size of the daily newspapers were not comparable to those of today. The only body modification I received was one shoulder sitting lower than the other. I carried the weight of two hundred plus newspapers on my right shoulder from my elementary school days through to my early high school years.

Collecting payment from the weekly subscribers was usually done on a Saturday. Customers paid about eighteen cents a week for delivery. Of this, carriers received about three cents a week. Times were tough enough that both Greg and I understood a good part of our earnings would have to be spent on clothing and school supplies. We spent our money on socks, gloves, hats, and other needs. Fortunately, such items were much cheaper in the good old days. We both felt that necessities such as blocks of chocolate and treats from the local five-and-dime store should not be neglected. In addition, I accepted large ice cream sundaes at a local Greek restaurant as full payment for their weekly subscription.

One of our more important expenditures was the purchasing of desirable pets, such as white rats ("New Pets," Chapter One), turtles, and tropical fish. This did not preclude us from obtaining other cuddly pets for free when the opportunity arose. On occasion, we captured local wildlife such as the special toads referred to in the story "Eyes in the Dark."

In this account, turtles take centre stage. Greg and I had each purchased a painted turtle. They were our constant pals. We took them with us in a pant's pocket, or for those longer trips such as to school, in a small matchbox. One spring they were our regular travelling companions for several weeks. We included the turtles in everything we did.

One Saturday, Greg and I were somewhat bored and made efforts to entertain ourselves by having a competition involving homemade parachutes. We tied string onto the four corners of our good linen hankies. A weight was necessary for the parachute to unfold and remain open during its descent. Typically, a rock or other small dense object would be tied to the support cords and rolled up into the handkerchief before launching into the blue spring sky. We had spent our time earlier in the afternoon building various parachutes and competing to see whose could stay in the air longest. Naturally, we soon devised a way to include our pet turtles, believing they might like a parachute ride.

Substituting a turtle for a rock, we faced two unique problems. One was that we required a special carrier to hold the turtle under the linen hanky. As well, we needed to throw them high enough into the air to ensure the parachute would open and provide a safe descent. Since a turtle's smooth shell is not conducive to tying things to, we resolved to create a basket-like contraption.

The drawer from our matchbox carriers solved the carrier problem. After all, these were familiar to them since they spent many hours inside the matchboxes when they were not in their aquarium or man-made puddles. The second issue was resolved by Greg's brilliant suggestion of going to our upstairs bedroom window and releasing them with the parachute already partially opened. This plan worked well for a couple of hours, on into the afternoon. Greg and I expended a lot of energy running down the stairs to retrieve our pets, and running back up to re-release them on their parachute rides. We never complained because as far as we could tell, our turtles enjoyed their afternoon.

Mother returned from work late Saturday afternoon. As you may have already guessed, she was not pleased. She was mollified when we explained exactly how much care we had taken to keep our turtles safe—despite that they would have been much safer had we just left them alone.

I cannot remember if the time period in which this occurred was when Greg and I were beginning to take less notice of our pets, but I am sure that I have no other memories of these pets beyond this point. I wonder if they knew how much we enjoyed their company and liked playing with them. At the same time, I believe the reverse is true—animals notice the lack of attention as a child's interest inevitably dwindles. In any case, I wish to emphasize that no animals were injured during our experimenting, competition, or in the writing of this story.

Even animals have to account for their ups and downs.

☙ Flying Lessons ❧

All the time I was in elementary school, Wilson's Bush remained a natural preserve. It was near our home and immediately to its east was a large grassy hill from which much of Toronto could be seen. This was partly because there was not much of Toronto at that time, as Bayview Avenue stopped at Eglinton Avenue, which in turn did not continue past Laird Drive. Standing on top of this hill, I often noticed a strong updraft that flattened the grass and other vegetation on the south slope.

Being of an experimental nature, I concluded that this environment would be an ideal setting from which to launch a manned glider, with myself as pilot. I had a keen interest in gliders and wanted to enjoy the thrill of soaring with eagles. Despite having no formal training or even an informal education with regard to the theory of flight, I embarked on a quest to build such a glider.

I enlisted the help of my tunnel-building buddy, whose qualifications in aerodynamics could be considered on par with his tunnel-digging abilities. He thought this ground-breaking endeavour was a great idea, and agreed to help me on one condition. The agreement was for me to teach him the piloting skills I acquired from my first flight. Then, after his flying lesson, he would be the second pilot to fly our soon-to-be-built glider.

I looked up to my grade eight mentor because he theoretically possessed significantly greater engineering and structural planning skills. Our sum total of aviation experience was substantially less than our tunnel building capabilities. However, we were in a hurry to get started, so the planning and designing stage was overlooked. We knew what we wanted and we knew how to get it.

In our minds it was a relatively simple task. We only needed a frame with two wings and some covering. A broken kitchen chair residing in the garage had already been chosen for the pilot's seat. This propelled us into phase two. We had to search for material suitable for the frame.

Ideally, a lightweight metal with high strength should have

been chosen. We knew that bends were essential for completing the wing tips and for other curved areas. We would need a common metal that came with various off-the-shelf options of 90 degree and 45 degree bends in the form of pre-made elbows to produce the various configurations we required. All I needed to do was to determine the necessary dimensions for the straight pieces, which could then be cut to size and threaded into the joints.

In addition to lacking the basic intelligence required, we did not have a budget for such a project. This would have discouraged lesser folk. We, however, pushed forward, settling for the first metal that was readily available and met most of our criteria. As project engineer, I chose common household plumbing pipe since it could be purchased at any nearby hardware store. We even had two or three elbow joints lying around Dad's workshop area in the basement.

I had seen movies of the Wright brothers' initial flight at Kitty Hawk, North Carolina, and from the structure of their aeroplane it appeared to me that their frame had been made from some sort of piping. In my mind, they were the world's most famous plumbers. My buddy and I set to work rummaging through piles of plumbing pipe. We could barely control our giddiness at the thought of our glider actually flying.

We were lifting some of the many eight-foot lengths of lead pipe when reality struck. Our arms strained under the weight. In disgust, we dropped the heavy pipes and let go of our hopes. Foiled again. Our pipe dream faded away as we realized that our glider would never feel the wind beneath its wings.

Breaking wind on the hill near Wilson's Bush was the closest my buddy and I ever came to being pilots.

Not every great idea will get off the ground.

∞ Tomatoes at Stake ∞

In my earliest years, getting on with something was more important than understanding what needed to be done. My failure to plan the tasks required for building a glider properly seems to have set me on a lifelong course as a planning junkie. I grew to enjoy the process rather than be frustrated by the supposed delays associated with developing a good plan.

Shortly after the glider debacle, I began to develop an uncontrollable urge to sketch, draw, draft, develop strategies, and share my plans with all who would listen. I gradually learned that planning is an important part of almost anything worth doing. Planning became a personal policy for me, for even the simplest of undertakings. This has served me well but occasionally frustrates different members of my family for various reasons.

Mom loved to work in her garden. The flowers and the caring of them proved to be therapeutic for her. The garden was situated in the backyard of our home on Hillsdale Avenue, and the view from the dining room window at the rear of our house served as a favourite place of hers from which to admire the greenery.

By no means was Mom a horticulturalist. The forsythia was overgrown, a striking white rose bush had not been trimmed since it had been planted, and other plants, including tomatoes, were interspersed with the flowers. However, our walnut tree was growing well and the beauty of the peonies was spectacular. In simple terms, the garden was a welcoming place for all.

One time when Mom and Greg were standing in the dining room looking out into the garden, they were discussing its status. Mom remarked that the tomato plants were in need of support and suggested they be "staked up." This practice was common and the term refers to the simple action of hammering a stake into the ground beside the tomato plant. Then, using strips of torn sheets, the weak stem of the plant is tied to the stake for support. Greg's deadpan response was, "Don't tell Ted, he'll have to draw a plan."

Despite his sarcasm, such comments did not discourage me from planning, nor did they lessen my belief in the need to do so. I agree with the old adage, "Failing to plan is like planning to fail." For me, they became words to live by. In fact, four years after graduation, this compulsion of mine manifested itself into a job where I was carrying out professional traffic and roadway planning, eventually becoming a private consultant for such work. Since retiring, I have wondered if my career in planning was somewhat predestined. However, I'm now inclined to think the reverse may also be true.

Our passion shapes our destiny.

∞ **Planning Dinner** ∞

Our family had an arrangement. The first person home from school prepared dinner for the whole family. However, arriving home first after school was not without its advantages. You got to retrieve the mail, decide what was for dinner, and have the house to yourself for a while.

One day, Greg arrived home first and began the routine. I am not sure if he received this honour because he hurried home on this particular day, or because Lynn and I better understood we could enjoy the fruits of Greg's labour if we chose to dilly-dally with friends after school.

After going through the mail, he frowned, then called Mom at work to discuss dinner. He excitedly suggested something out of the ordinary. He wanted to treat the family to a meal cooked over an open fire. He would willingly season the meat for grilling, prepare potatoes for baking, and select the finest vegetable from our supply of canned goods. He even suggested that we eat in the living room by the light of the fire and burning candles.

Mom agreed that it would be a wonderful change. "Whatever made you think of that?" she asked. Greg responded, "They just shut off the electricity."

The truth was that the power had been out for the entire conversation. A letter from the electrical company explained that our electricity would be shut off for non-payment. Apparently, the electrical company did not send any other warnings after the pink one. Mom learned that, unlike all of the previous colourful 'reminders', ignoring the pink one had greater consequences.

Despite the lack of electrical energy, dinner was delicious and the ambiance sublime. It was a good thing that the phone company had only sent us a yellow reminder.

Making the best of any situation creates warm memories.

∞ A Trip to Toronto Island ∞

Mom did little complaining throughout the times she was left to raise our family on her own. She often dealt with such challenges by soliciting the help of others. She had four sisters, three of which enjoyed helping Mom throughout their relatively long lives. On other occasions, the YMCA proved to be a form of entertainment for Greg and me, while acting as a means of responsible care for us while Mom was at work.

Most of the time, 'day camp' at the YMCA was fun. Although Greg and I got into our share of trouble, we enjoyed the swimming, crafts, and other activities provided. Our favourite activity was going on field trips. The day we went to Toronto Island was one of mixed adventures.

An early morning start was necessary since the group was taking public transit to the lakeshore and then a ferry boat to the island. Lunches, towels, swimsuits, and treats for both of us were packed into a shopping bag. Greg and I took turns carrying the shopping bag. It was a bit of a bother because the counsellors had arranged for various team races and games to be played during our outing. We decided to leave the bag and all of its contents some place safe until we went home.

In our minds, slipping the bag under a slightly overhanging bush was prime security. The fact that it could be seen from afar was immaterial. We viewed this as added security. We reasoned that we could keep an eye on it while we played, and if someone took it, we would immediately notice it was gone. Not a wise choice.

The afternoon was filled with play, and for a brief time we were allowed to explore. We had to meet back with the counsellors at the dock by a certain time. We missed the little bit about 'a certain time'. I'm not sure what time it was, but it was definitely almost evening, and not one member of our group could be found upon our return to the dock. We missed the boat—literally.

In our haste to catch the next ferry, we forgot about the shopping bag full of our belongings. Unlike *E.T.*, we phoned home, and eventually met up with Mom. I willingly confessed that Greg forgot our clothes. Greg maintained that it was solely my fault. Being the older brother, I was sure Mom would take my account over Greg's, but she was more worried about something of greater importance—getting them back.

Without arguing about whose fault it was, she simply asked if we thought the bag could still be there. Since we didn't know one way or the other, Mom decided it was worth a try to return to the island and find out. For the second time that day, Greg and I headed off towards Toronto Island. This time, we had Mom and a helpful sister of hers, Aunt Babe, with us.

We all travelled to the ferry dock and back to the island. It was a lovely summer evening and we made good time on our second trip with most of the crowd headed the opposite direction. We found the clothes and our mother breathed a sigh of relief. Our mission had been accomplished. With clothes in hand, we arrived home late in the evening, about four hours after our originally scheduled return. We could have been home much sooner, but once we were on the island, we all chose to relax and enjoy the sunset.

Mother's patience and non-accusatory attitude meant that even the second trip to the island was an enjoyable sundown experience that we still treasure.

Two day trips are better than one—even on the same day.

∞ Telephone Tale ∞

On another day when Greg was the first one home from school, he again reviewed the mail—bills, bills, and more bills. For fun, he chose to call Mom on the phone and razz her while she was at work. While disguising his voice and pretending to be the bank manager, he scolded her for being behind on making her payments.

When he told her of one overdue bill, Mom's question was, "Is it pink?" Mom had learned to balance her books according to the colour of paper used for the warning notices. She now knew that harshly worded yellow reminders could be overlooked, whereas weakly stated pink warnings required her immediate attention.

Greg was surprised that Mom had not discovered his ruse. Anticipating that she would soon catch on to his prank, Greg decided to fess up. Her creative financial solutions were not always endorsed by others, but they were nevertheless able to bridge the inevitable awkward gaps between "now overdue" and "thank you for your payment."

The art of survival calls for creative strategies.

∞ Upgrades (Not Scholastic) ∞

Mom decided to go on a well-deserved holiday when Lynn, Greg, and I were all in high school. She left the three of us in charge of the house, but alone for the first time. Mom didn't think we could get into too much trouble—or perhaps she just did not think. After entrusting the house to our care, she happily drove away with a couple of her sisters and a cousin on a two week trip to Peggy's Cove.

Mom had left strict instructions for Lynn to "Keep the boys out of trouble." After all, Lynn was the oldest, and Mom felt that boys are generally not as well self-disciplined as girls at that age. Perhaps this is not a fair statement about other males in high school, but it was spot on for Greg and me. For no other reason than because "Everybody else was doing it," Greg and I had decided to renovate the living room and dining room while Mom was away.

Won't Mom be surprised, we thought, to come home to new picture windows, a new archway where the French doors had been, specially-designed shelving, freshly painted walls, and new furniture.

Deconstruction started immediately. Before Mom and her clan were on the highway, Greg and I had already removed some of the windows. Our diamond glazed leaded windows from the front of the house were broken into small pieces to facilitate disposal. The unwanted parts of the frames were knocked out. Our neighbours stood on the sidewalk, gawking. No cheering—just worried looks.

What the passers-by could not see was that inside, Greg and I had already taken out the French doors and were removing their framework to prepare for plastering the archway. Furniture that Greg and I considered old was readied for sale. Tearing things down took very little time and was thoroughly enjoyed by both of us. Lynn, on the other hand, was not as enthusiastic. Her lack of approval was so distinct she left the house for most of the time that Mom was away.

Like most home projects, the working time had been

underestimated. Our hope had been to have the renovations finished and ready for Mom's approval upon her arrival. Unfortunately, every swing of the hammer during our deconstruction phase resulted in a ton of repair work later. Regrettably, this is true for any renovation. However, Greg and I did not realize this until well into the work. By this time, although we were making progress, Mom was on her way home.

All-nighters were now essential to finish the project on time; however, major problems had begun to surface. Strangely, this occurs almost instantaneously upon realizing one is definitely unable to meet an intended deadline. It is almost as if the project itself speaks and says, "You haven't got a hope, and even if you did, look what else I've got for ya." I do not believe that Greg and I were the first to discover this. I wish contractors could speak "project."

Mom would be home in a couple of days and we still had to install the glass for the windows, hire a plasterer to finish off the archway, purchase the lumber for the shelving (the china cabinet had been sold), patch the walls, and paint. At one point during our final stretch, we were so tired that Greg fell asleep while holding the other end of a board I was sawing. With the fear of Mom finding our home in total disarray, Greg and I continued our efforts with even greater focus.

When Mother arrived home, nobody was there to greet her—not even the original front window or her dining room furniture. It was the first time in her life she had been early for anything. Lynn was not there by choice. I may have been out trying to reorder the paint, which, for some reason, was not as good a match on the wall as it was on the swatch in the store. For the most part, the renovation was done. Perhaps only because renovations really never get finished, they just get to the point where one can live with the unfinished parts.

Greg and I had succeeded in at least one thing—surprising Mom. Despite her regret over some of our choices, she was very polite and supportive. She soon purchased a matching rug and re-covered the furniture in a dark colour that matched the new paint inside the open china cabinet Greg and I had just constructed.

Even Lynn helped out by shopping for some patterned vinyl and re-upholstered the new dining room chairs—perhaps out of sympathy for the would-be contractors.

Greg and I had bitten off more than we could chew. We spent the next few weeks helping Mom. However, we were thankful that she decided to concentrate her efforts on redecorating the house, rather than punishing the wayward contractors. Immediately after the work was completed, Greg and I retired from the renovating business.

***Contractors are rarely finished on time,
even when YOU are the contractor.***

∽ Only Eight Lives to Go ∾

Over the years we had many pets. Some of our cutest ones were kittens that we had brought home from my aunt Pearl and uncle Ted's lodge in Huntsville. But these kittens turned into cats. It's a natural occurrence.

One such cat had grown up and become a mother. Our family was dealing with the consequences of a moment of madness with a nearby stray. There were seven kittens in total. They too were all very cute, but apparently not cute enough for Mom to approve of keeping them.

It was late fall. Days were becoming shorter and Halloween was approaching. Things were different then. For example, parents rarely felt the need to accompany their children on such a night. It was not until much later that it became commonplace to escort young children on Halloween rounds. Greg and I were past the age of shelling out, or trick-or-treating as it is now called. We were more interested in staying home to give out candy, homemade toffee apples, and other treats to the younger children. It was entertaining and we enjoyed eating the leftover toffee.

Preparations for the evening included separating the candy from the chocolate bars and setting out our toffee apples. The goodies were placed by the front door in anticipation of the many children who were expected. Part of the job entailed keeping the family pets away from the treats.

We were having a lot of fun with the rush of children who called on us. About halfway through the evening, I was in need of a bathroom break. Leaving Greg in charge, I disappeared upstairs. When I returned, I was astonished to see one of our confused kittens being lowered into a child's treat bag. Trick or treat indeed. I laughed and asked Greg what he was doing. "Giving out treats," he replied. Still laughing, I said, "It seems more like a trick." I pressed him to think this through. What was he going to say to their parents when they returned the kittens? "The kids won't tell them," he said. Greg's response, however unorthodox, was ideal—at least for us. We were virtually untraceable.

Greg felt, and I later came to agree with him, that anything goes when getting rid of a pet, as long as it will be safe. Perhaps the kids refused to reveal where they got them, but in any case, only one was returned.

***Finding a simple solution is the trick to
resolving difficult problems.***

∞ Pumpkin Pie ∞

It was mid morning on a Saturday. Greg and I had completed our paper routes and I was resting upstairs. Greg decided that he would like to bake a pumpkin pie. So, with much noise, Greg set the Mixmaster up on the kitchen table and got ready to go.

Despite the appearance of the kitchen each time he finished baking, Greg was a good pastry maker. On one occasion, when he was around eight, he won a prize for his butter-less butter tarts. I think the judges appreciated his creativity during our awkward times throughout the war.

Upstairs in my room, I could follow his every move. He dropped the eggs, spilled the sugar, slopped the milk, and mixed the filling in the Mixmaster. Setting that task aside, he then started on the pastry.

I could tell he was getting close to the end of this chore when I heard him cutting the excess dough from around the edge of the metal pie plate. At the point when I envisioned him pouring the filling into the pie crust, there was a loud crash, followed by an even louder expletive. I guessed there would be no pie.

Greg's final 'ingredients' were stomping to the front door, yanking it open, and slamming it shut as he left. He did not return until mid afternoon after the movie matinee. In true brotherly form, I had unsympathetically left the mess for him to clean up upon his return.

It has been said that taking a break from a frustrating job can prove to be beneficial. This, however, is based on the premise that one returns to complete the original assignment. In Greg's case, he felt better abandoning this job, returning only to clean up once he had finished swearing and having purged himself of the frustration.

This incident proved to be an anomaly of sorts as Greg's skills quickly returned to their prize-winning level. He has proven to be a baker of note, and I have since enjoyed wolfing down many of his pastry creations.

Taking a break helps to provide a fresh perspective.

⚭ Lynn's Horse ⚭

Of the many animals that graced our home, not all were pets. Lynn had developed a love for horses. We all knew that it was impossible for us to care for a real one at home and we couldn't afford to keep one stabled anywhere else. This did not dampen Lynn's interest in them.

There's something about girls and horses that I have never quite understood. There seems to be a connection of some sort that bonds the majestic strength and regal beauty of many of these creatures to most females. From black stallions to snow-white mares to Native American Pintos, Lynn loved them all.

Lynn also loved to ride horses, but only had the chance to do so on rare occasions when she helped out as a stable hand for a children's camp. She fuelled her passion for them by collecting tiny replicas of her favourite animal in fine china and treasured them as she did our family pets—rats excepted.

On her sixteenth birthday, oh sweet sixteen, Greg bought Lynn a horse for her collection. It was not made of the best china or even of a cheap ceramic. It was not composed of anything stately. The poor beast had an enormous snout from which two elongated and oversized nostrils flared, shoulder blades and a pelvic bone as sharp as a butter knife, and a hump back so ridiculously deformed that it made my own back hurt just looking at it. It was moulded to a dull green slab of a stand. If this base represented a pasture, it was one to which the horse had clearly been banished a long time ago. This objet d'art was grotesque and looked like nothing more than a consolation prize from a travelling carnival midway.

Greg had picked it up from the joke shop in the arcade on Yonge Street near Adelaide, where he was known to visit. This horse was not a welcome part of Lynn's fine collection. Lynn despised it. Greg and I loved it. Her disgust has spurred Greg and me into uncontrollable gut wrenching laughter each time we reminisce about her reaction. Lynn, on the other hand, took many years to see any humour in the gift.

To everyone's surprise—including Lynn's—it eventually became her favourite. She can now smile wanly at our reminiscing, recalling the incident with fondness. Over fifty years later, it is the only one of her once-prized collection that is still in her possession.

Humour is like a life lesson…it can only be enjoyed after it is understood.

❧ Table Talk ❧

As a young man still in high school, my weekends were often spent hanging out with friends. On one evening, five or six of the regular group planned to meet at my house before departing for the nightlife. Mom was sewing in the dining room, using the table for laying out her pattern and cutting the material.

When everyone arrived, a rambling conversation covering all sorts of topics progressed. Eventually, the talk came around to dreams that startle us just before we fall into a deep sleep. Some were *very* different. When it was my turn, I told the group what startled me when I drifted to sleep.

In my case, I would often dream of lying on our large eight-sided oak dining room table and rolling off one of the small chamfered corners. My arms and legs would convulse, rudely waking me just at "lift off." This always caused me to jump to the extent that I would awaken from my partial slumber instantly. As my friends laughed, Mom listened attentively.

She had been enjoying the discussion and our laughter but was shocked by my story. She explained that when I was "too young to roll over," this had really happened. It was obviously a long time in the past but apparently I was regularly reliving the memory of the mishap. It was a great surprise to my mom that I knew of this occurrence. For me, her story was a spooky revelation.

Sometimes dreams affect us in unknown ways and perhaps they're more real than understood. If dreams have meanings hidden in the subconscious, then talking about them may expose their elements to the conscious mind. I know that understanding my re-occurring dream helped me to sleep better, perhaps because I learned more about myself.

A friendly psychologist later explained why this was so. Apparently, my situation of not understanding my dream is technically known as being in a covert state—a condition in which my brain was trying to sort out a past or present experience. This manifested itself in the form of my re-occurring dream. My mother's revelation allowed me to understand that what I was dreaming about had been an actual physical experience. This created what is known as a gestalt moment, a technical term used to describe a quantum jump of understanding, commonly referred to as "the light coming on."

Once I had been able, mentally, to piece together the parts of the puzzle, I was instantly transported into an overt state, wherein the problem had been resolved. My mind had been cleared. My once re-occurring dream has never been experienced again.

Understanding is a medicine that cures.

✢ Seventh Heaven ✢

My dad died mid summer in 1950, when I was seventeen and Greg was only fifteen. Lynn and I were both working at the time but Greg was not. Mom didn't want to leave Greg alone at home and she felt he needed time to reflect on our loss in the company of family.

Her aunt Ede and uncle Fred lived in Kemptville, Ontario. Aunt Ede's two sisters and two brothers ran a farm at Miller's Corners, while many other relatives of ours were living in rural areas nearby that spanned from Perth to Ottawa to the north shore of the St. Lawrence River.

Mom was looking for a place for Greg to spend the rest of the summer, and this branch of our family was asked for their assistance. Cousin George, who lived and farmed with his family near Williamsburg, was suggested. Mom's request came at a perfect time since Cousin George needed assistance with a new farm they had recently purchased. Greg stayed there for the balance of that summer.

Cousin George's new farm came complete with livestock, all of which needed to be transferred to the farm where he lived. While Greg was helping out, he met a friendly neighbour who by some unknown stroke of serendipity had the first name of Fearnley. After quickly becoming friends, Greg spent a lot of time during his month-long trip with this new friend.

While overseeing the work of transferring the animals from the new farm, Greg found a small black dog chained up in a barn. Apparently, she stole eggs from the chicken coop and was known as an "egg sucker." This was why she had been restrained. She was left there without even a dish of water. Greg was horrified.

Being a dog lover, he resolved not to return home without the leash in his hand and the dog in tow. Cousin George had received the lands and chattels with his purchase of the new farm. The small black dog was part of these acquisitions. He had his own dog and did not need a second, let alone an egg sucker. So he allowed Greg to take ownership of the unwanted farm animal. Greg rescued her and named her Cindy.

On his trip back home to Toronto, Cindy was sick in the car, much to the chagrin of the driver. I had been anticipating Greg's arrival and looked forward to seeing him and sharing the stories of our adventures while apart. Even teenage brothers that fight start to miss their sparring partner after they have been separated for a few weeks.

Once home, Cindy was introduced to the rest of the family. After Greg and I had played with her for a couple of hours, she disappeared. We were devastated. Together we searched various parts of our neighbourhood, in different directions, with ever-increasing perimeters. Some considerable time later, we both returned and in sadness remarked that we had had a pet, but only for a very short time. We were grief stricken.

We adjourned to the backyard to commiserate. We sat on the porch and were astounded soon afterwards when we found Cindy resting comfortably underneath. To this day I have difficulty imagining how a dog could possess the skills necessary to return to a strange new home to which it had just been introduced. Nevertheless, Greg and I were overjoyed.

Earlier that summer Mom had agreed that the family needed a pet. She had hoped it would divert our attention away from our dad's recent death, so she allowed Greg to keep Cindy. Oddly enough, Mom had already brought home a kitten from her sister's lodge. So, now there were two pets. In addition, we had no idea that Cindy came with accessories—as revealed in the following rhyme:

Roses are red, violets are blue.
We now have a cat and a black dog too.
Greg took the dog, and I took the cat,
And Cindy was pregnant—how about that!

Cindy always enjoyed the cat's company. She would transport the cat from room to room using an unorthodox method; carrying the cat around by one of its hind legs. It was obvious to everyone in the house that Cindy was practicing for the arrival of her expected pups. Nobody seemed to care—except the cat.

A few weeks later, Lynn returned from her job in New Jersey. When she arrived, Greg and I were tending to Cindy. At 2:30 a.m., four pups had been born. We went to bed. In the morning there were five pups…oops. I guess we weren't very good veterinarians. Now there were seven pets.

Halloween was far away, so we couldn't invoke Greg's give-away program for the new pups. We would have to find homes for all of them through conventional means. Four went to good homes. The fifth pup had decided that she was not going to leave, not as a pup anyway. Several months later, Greg and I could walk to Bayview Avenue each with a dog on a leash beside us.

In hindsight, our family should have communicated with each other prior to bringing the pets home, but none of us ever regretted having an abundance of dogs…or the cat. Mom's suggestion of having a pet around to help us cope with the loss of our dad was an insightful and loving decision.

All of our pets have since gone to meet their maker and are perhaps resting with my dad who left me so long ago. But I still cherish my memories of them in my heart, and I miss them all.

The life lesson found below is a direct quote from my wonderful mom's words of wisdom that served to comfort us through those difficult times. They are engraved on my father's tombstone and will forever be written on my heart.

To live in the hearts of those we love is not to die.

AT THE LODGE

Most of the stories in this chapter, took place prior to my dad's death. With Mom working and Dad overseas, the thought of leaving three pre-teen children on their own for lengthy periods of time was a serious concern for Mom. The summer months when school was out created a break in our family's daily routine and gave rise to this problem.

We had few options. Fortunately, my mom received an offer no mother in her position could refuse. Her sister and brother-in-law, my aunt Pearl and uncle Ted, were unable to have children of their own but had a gracious love for their extended family. They lived and worked at their home on Fairy Lake in Muskoka, Ontario, where they ran a resort known as Puck's Lodge. Puck was a fictitious resident of Pook's Hill in Rudyard Kipling's writings and also a character in the Shakespearean play *A Midsummer Night's Dream*. They both loved these classic authors. Since the lodge was situated at the foot of a steep hill and its busiest season was mid summer, the name was most appropriate.

Aunt Pearl and Uncle Ted's offer was to have the three of us spend the summer at their lodge while we weren't in school. This would allow Mom to work without leaving us unsupervised and also give her a bit of a break when she wasn't working. Aunt Pearl and Uncle Ted would have three more helpers around the small lodge at their busiest time. Lynn, Greg, and I were fond of them and in earlier times had enjoyed visiting them at their cottage before they purchased the lodge. Everybody viewed a summer with them as a win-win situation. Our labour was offset by room and board. However, Aunt Pearl and Uncle Ted never failed to send us home after each summer ended with a cash stipend gleaned from guests' tips and a little of their own money added for good measure.

Aunt Pearl and Uncle Ted's suggestion was a kind offer which our whole family readily accepted for several years. However, not having had children of their own, my aunt and uncle probably didn't know exactly what to expect. Upon the arrival of three children ranging from seven to twelve years of age, they were suddenly 'blessed' with an instant family. They only needed to add water to complete the recipe. Lake water made for a more seasoned dish.

Aunt Pearl and Uncle Ted both proved to be wonderful, loving relatives who cared for my family, and helped me discover the life lessons found in this chapter.

∞ Working Like a Dog ∞

Aunt Pearl and Uncle Ted had owned their lodge for a few years before we had been invited to stay with them in the summers. While we lived there, they shared many of their experiences with us. They had guests all year long, and they had to carry supplies over the frozen lake in earlier years when there was no road access in the winter. When the lodge was purchased, it came complete with a garage across the lake on Cookson's Bay (also known as Fairy Bay), where a car could be parked in the winter months. The garage has since been converted into a small cottage on the bay.

To solve the problem of transporting the long term supplies over the lake, they purchased a St. Bernard and a large sleigh with proper harnessing. Ideally, the dog, whom they named Peter, was to pull the sled loaded with supplies across the lake to the lodge on the opposite shore. The plan boasted many benefits: there would be no need to carry heavy groceries in paper bags, the trip would be faster and more efficient, and the dog would receive its needed exercise.

The frozen lake was covered with snow more often than not. This complicated the trip. Peter was a black dog who did not tolerate discomfort. Within a few hundred metres or so into the mile-long trip, the hair between his toes collected sufficient snow to bother him to the extent that he would stop in his tracks to remove it. Unfortunately, his method of removal was to lick the snow from his paws. However, his saliva only compounded the problem by making it easier for the snow to accumulate between his toes. This resulted in more and more frequent stops and greatly extended the crossing as his problem literally snowballed.

Aunt Pearl and Uncle Ted were exposed to the prevailing west wind that constantly whistled around them during the trip. Also, the cold temperature bothered them as the winter elements prevailed for far longer than had they pulled the sleigh themselves.

Technically, the trip itself never proved to be a shore too far for their St. Bernard. The journey across the lake was always well within his tolerance. However, this was not the case for my aunt and uncle. Each time they relayed various "Peter the pooch" narratives, they concluded with a quip that made him that much more memorable.

When Lynn, Greg, and I began to spend our summers at the lodge, Aunt Pearl and Uncle Ted viewed our presence as yet another convenience. And, although we all had assigned chores, we were never made to work as hard as Peter. Lynn's were somewhat more structured than those handed out to Greg and me. She had to assist other staff members as they made up the rooms each day, beginning immediately after the guests arrived for breakfast. Later, she would help prepare meals and clean up afterwards.

Aunt Pearl's understanding of what could be expected from small boys was refined within a day of our arrival. Greg and I were given our first project after our first breakfast. The task was to pick wild strawberries for fresh pies for the guests at dinner that night. We were told to go to the top of the hill where there was a large grass meadow—the closest strawberry field. We were asked to pick the small strawberries without the hull, because the wild berries are so tiny that it would be difficult to remove the hulls after the fruit had been picked. We gathered them until it was time to head back for lunch.

Upon entering the kitchen, we presented my aunt with enough wild strawberries to barely make a tart. She was aghast. She required—and had been expecting—one quart of fruit for each of the six pies she was planning to make.

Immediately after lunch, Aunt Pearl organized a charge into the berry field, this time leading a few strange guests who actually professed a love for such a chore. Greg and I humbly followed and helped as much as we could. We watched as they picked their quota in only a couple hours. Everyone, including Greg and me, enjoyed the pie for dessert. Aunt Pearl, through her persistence, met her goal, and recovered from her disappointment in us.

Unlike Aunt Pearl, Uncle Ted had been a young boy. He had experienced and understood the fine line between adventure and mischief. On one occasion, Greg and I were told that we could borrow Uncle Ted's old cedar canoe he had kept since his childhood. It was the one he had used in his youth to learn his paddling skills. Greg and I were excited as we looked forward to the evening. That is, when our chores were done. Uncle Ted was to give us our first paddling lesson, after which we would be allowed to set out in the canoe on our own.

On this evening, after our instruction, Greg and I left the main dock but stayed nearby until Uncle Ted felt comfortable enough to leave us on our own. The guests sitting on the dock watched. As soon as his feet left the dock, we immediately headed straight across Fairy Lake towards Cookson's Bay, still well marked by Grandview Inn. Eventually, we rounded the eastern point and headed into a marshy area that we thoroughly enjoyed paddling through.

Aunt Pearl returned from a meeting in town and her sense of responsibility caused her to fret about us as we were out of sight. Knowing that we were in a craft that required considerable competence to operate safely, she became more and more worried—especially since we had learned only a few basic skills. We felt in control, but Aunt Pearl came closer to losing hers with each passing moment. We returned to find her standing on the dock with arms crossed and toes tapping. She was not amused and in her disgust restricted us from ever going out in a canoe again. Within a week of arriving, we had been forbidden to use a canoe "for life."

Greg and I were not providing as much help as Aunt Pearl had anticipated. Fortunately, a couple of days later, Uncle Ted dropped by while Greg and I were cleaning the guests' freshly caught fish. He said, "Don't worry, kids, I was a boy myself once. Your aunt will get over her fright and you'll soon be able to go canoeing again." It was a turning point in my life to know that an adult could understand and empathize with energetic, carefree young kids.

__Some conveniences are inconvenient.__

∞ Another St. Bernard ∞

Aunt Pearl and Uncle Ted were the caring owners not only for Peter, but also for Sheba and Cleo, the second and third in a line of St. Bernards. Sheba was black and white, whereas Cleo, who was named after Cleopatra, had predominantly black hair.

Cleo was following in Peter's footsteps when it came to protecting the lodge. However, in her time, she never had to cross the ice. She had no plans to 'work like a dog' as her predecessor Peter once had. Cleo's entire life was spent as a welcomed pet. She was always receptive to a pat on the head from a guest or anyone who bothered to show her some affection.

This training left her ill equipped for the task Greg and I saddled her with one summer afternoon. We had been asked to mow the croquet lawn for the guests and felt that a dog the size of a small pony would be better suited to do the work. Of course we had to persuade her. However, we felt that our effort was well worth the time if Cleo could be motivated to cut the lawn.

Peter's harness had been hanging in the garage since his last winter expedition. It would be ideal to connect Cleo to the reel-styled lawnmower. After fitting Cleo with the collar, Greg and I tied the straps of the harness to the metal handle of our manual cutting machine. We reasoned that Cleo could pull it more easily than either of us could push it. The dog was not pleased with being tied up, nor responsive to our enthusiastic commands. We tried to convince her that it was in her best interest to do so. This was not an easy task. An incentive was needed.

We believed that dog biscuits would provide sufficient motivation. Cleo polished off about two or three pounds of biscuits at a progressive rate of approximately one foot per biscuit. At this rate, the lawn could safely be completed and Cleo would not have needed to be fed for over a month. Our fearless dog managed to mow only one full row of grass before upchucking all previous incentives. At this point we tried others. Nothing was working—including us.

We spent a great deal of energy avoiding the task at hand before we gave up. I'm sure that we could have cut the croquet lawn and trimmed every blade of grass on the property in the time we spent training Cleo.

It took a lengthy and unnecessary amount of time to clean up Cleo's contribution and finish cutting the lawn. The convenience of having a large dog at hand to assist in our afternoon chore had cost us our swim time. We learned that some conveniences are *really* inconvenient.

Not every St. Bernard is a work dog.

∞ Hand Lawnmowers ∞

Nan, a golden brown St. Bernard, was another pet my aunt Pearl and uncle Ted owned in the succession of such dogs at the lodge. Greg and I learned that Nan, like Cleo, also refused to pull the lawnmower. Our failed efforts to avoid work, through the help of the dogs at the lodge, did not discourage us from including them in our play.

Nan loved the game called Monkey in the Middle. We would throw a football to each other and watch as she ran between us attentively chasing the ball. She was always eager to join in but not as anxious to follow the rules. Each time Greg or I fumbled the ball and ran to retrieve it, Nan would take part in the chase. She displayed her understanding for the game by repeatedly tackling us as we raced for the ball. She was also well versed in the illegal art of clipping.

One day Greg and I chose to ignore our responsibility to cut the croquet lawn. Instead, we decided to entertain ourselves by building a racing cart. We thought it would be more fun spending the afternoon taking turns riding on our new contraption. We decided that a four-wheeled cart could best be created by utilizing various items around the yard that already had wheels. So we turned two reel-styled lawnmowers upside down and tightly tied their handles together. Behold: a four-wheeled racing cart.

We hoped to use Nan for the necessary horsepower, but, like Cleo, she was not interested and flatly refused. Greg and I elected not to use the cookie incentive this time. We decided to provide the motive power ourselves. As we admired our contraption, we invoked a sophisticated process for establishing who would ride first. I lost the toss. Greg took the more favourable position, and he now sat astride the two bound lawnmower handles contentedly waiting for propulsion.

Steering was limited to the initial position we set the vehicle in. We aligned our invention at the top of a small hill to provide the straightest and longest ride. Unlike Wilbur and Orville Wright, I was Greg's propeller and readied myself near the rear set of wheels with my hands on the lawnmower's strike plate. If

I had been half as sharp as the blades, I wouldn't have attempted to push such a dangerous vehicle with my bare hands. My right hand was cut badly during the first push as the fully-exposed blades began to rotate. Their shearing action cut deeply into the meaty part of my thumb.

More than sixty years later, my scars still show, and to the best of my knowledge the croquet lawn is still badly in need of cutting. It was a good thing Greg decided to sit amidship.

***People not as sharp as their implements
are often considered tools.***

∞ The Algonquin ∞

Throughout the 1940s, the MV Algonquin was a large passenger ship that was used by many visitors travelling between three linked lakes known as Vernon, Fairy, and Peninsula, in the northern Muskoka area. This craft was a sister ship to the HMS Seguin that still plies the waters of other larger lakes in the lower Muskoka district. The Algonquin stopped at the docks of various resorts on its trips through the lakes—provided that there were adequate docking facilities, water deep enough for a ship of its size, and the docking flag was up.

The helmsman of the Algonquin never ceased to amaze his passengers as he manoeuvred a ship of that size through the narrow canal between Fairy Lake and Peninsula Lake. On one occasion, I was a passenger standing on the upper deck close to the bow as the ship passed through the channel. One of the curves was so tight that the protruding bowsprit got caught in the branches of a large overhanging tree. Only skilled manoeuvring allowed us to reverse and later proceed without incident.

Puck's Lodge was not a stop on the regular route of this ship. The closest it got to the lodge was when it passed by at full speed in the middle of the lake. Even though full speed was barely over a few knots, it created a large rounded wake—the result of a heavy boat travelling at a slow speed on its approach to the canal. At times it travelled closer to our south shore than others.

One day Greg and I had a whimsical idea. Along with our sister, Lynn, and two or three friendly young guests, we thought it would be fun to paddle out into the middle of the lake to meet this grand ship. The fastest boat to get us there was the cedar canoe Greg and I had once been banned from using. It was the tipsiest canoe at the lodge. We quickly headed out into the middle of the lake to get a close look at the Algonquin and "catch the waves."

We were excited as we paddled feverishly towards the Algonquin but soon realized that ships get bigger the closer you get to them. With several of us inside the small canoe, our group was riding with the gunwales no more than a few inches above the surface of the water. The waves also appeared to get larger the closer we got to the vessel. I was too embarrassed to admit my misgivings, and no one suggested that we turn back, so we paddled on. I felt a bit like David going out to meet Goliath. Who knows what the others were thinking as we bounced over the large waves.

Aunt Pearl *always* arrived at the worst possible time. She would usually yodel to call us back to the lodge when we were a fair distance away. On this day, like many others, that yodel was spine chilling. We began to think about our actions. Only then did I see our adventure as a collision course with a larger ship whose manoeuvrability was much more limited than ours. We exhausted ourselves on repeated attempts to navigate our overloaded canoe into the most risky of waves close to the ship—without any margin of safety. Also, our inexperience led us to believe that we had not needed to bring our floating safety cushions simply because we were all good swimmers.

Until then, our inexperience had allowed us to view these hazards as the exciting parts of the trip. With my aunt on shore in an all too familiar militaristic stance, we paddled back. It was a long trip to the dock. Our voyage home gave us time to think about the potential danger we had escaped. There was also another precarious situation we had not considered—the impending danger we faced at our inevitable meeting with Aunt Pearl.

Without experience, danger can be mistaken for adventure.

∞ **The Race** ∞

In the mid 1940s, Greg and I were fooling around on a windy day at Puck's Lodge. We both thought of ourselves as masters of the water. We had rowed the rowboats, paddled the cedar canoe, and had even jousted with padded poles while standing on the bow and stern of the craft. We expended much energy. It was time for a change. On this wonderful breezy day in the summer, perhaps like some ancient caveman long before, our thoughts turned to the wind and how we could harness its power.

Our first try using umbrellas did not quite cut it. Obviously other equipment was required. We knew that to sail the seas, one must first have a mast and a means of holding the sail at the top. With pictures of earlier ships in our minds, we opted to use a design that incorporated a square mainsail. We thought this would be easier than a modern triangular shape.

We searched for something to use as a mast at a point on our shoreline where guests typically sat to watch the setting of the sun. It was a shaded area in a natural state with pine needles and leaves from nearby cedars carpeting the ground. Many of the cedar trees were small enough to cut down but still tall enough to be used as a mast for our small craft.

Uncle Ted had scraps of kiln-dried hardwood stored in a woodshed for use as kindling. The wood stove in the kitchen, the fireplace in the living room, and outside bonfires were all dependent on this supply. To call this material hardwood was an understatement for those who had to work with it. Perhaps it would have been best named *harder* wood. After rummaging through the woodshed, we came up with a piece that was large enough to hold a sail. All we needed to do was fasten it to the round cedar mast. This was done with great difficulty. It took much effort and time to get the crossbeam fixed in place.

The lodge itself was a large building with three floors. The attic was on the upper floor where there were two bedrooms, each with storage cupboards along the eaves. It was in these storage areas that Greg and I found a material that would make perfect sails. This fabric was rectangular in shape and just wide enough to fit the crossbeam, which had been nailed to the trunk of the cedar tree. We folded the material several times where it was to be nailed to the hardwood crossbeam. As we pounded the nails through the folded material and into the beam, the mast rolled back and forth with each strike of the hammer. Nevertheless, we persevered and eventually felt that the sail was ready to take the pull and tug of the wind.

We were eager to launch, but we still had to figure out how to hold the mast in place, hold the sail against the wind, and steer. All of these necessary functions needed to be operated from the rear half of the boat and required at least two hands each. Unfortunately, with the mast in its optimum position, there wasn't enough room in our canoe to carry the crew needed for this concept. A re-design was essential and undertaken immediately.

Back with the boards in the woodshed, we managed to find a near match to our hardwood crossbeam. By fastening this second piece of hardwood to the lower part of the mast and nailing the material to the new lower crossbeam, we eliminated the need for one crew member. This new design meant that Greg and I could now take turns holding the mast while the other used a paddle to steer.

We got ready to try it out. At first, the mast was difficult to hold on such a breezy day. We decided to lash it to the central thwart to stabilize it. This provided much needed leverage for the person elected to be the 'mast-holder'. We paddled out into the middle of the lake in hopes of sailing back to the lodge. This worked fairly well. We even improved our efficiency when we discovered that our sails captured the wind better after soaking them in lake water. With this new improvement, we were able to enjoy longer and longer trips. It was the only canoe on the lake with a sail—but it was the fastest one of its kind.

After Lynn and her friends noticed how much fun Greg and I were having with our new invention, they decided to copy us and have some fun of their own. I can't remember what materials they used for their sailing canoe, or how it was assembled. In our minds, it didn't really matter since Greg and I had the faster craft. We were sure of this, but Lynn and her friends became cocky.

They were certain that they would develop better skills within a short time. Later, Lynn and her friends challenged Greg and me to a race.

As various guests discussed our homemade sailboat at mealtime, Aunt Pearl's interest grew. She asked to see our latest contraption. We proudly displayed our sail still dripping wet from the afternoon's fun. Aunt Pearl was not pleased. Many high quality sails are made of linen. Apparently, ours were close—they were made of Aunt Pearl's linen curtains. She had saved these curtains in the attic storage cupboards of the lodge since first moving there in 1938. Why her distinguished drapes had been stored instead of being displayed in all their supposed splendour is a mystery on par with the enigmatic circumstances surrounding the building of the great Pyramids.

As we learned the reason our sail was working so well, Aunt Pearl experienced a range of emotion that was clearly discernible from her facial expressions. She coursed through denial, disappointment, anger, depression, and finally acceptance. Gradually, Aunt Pearl had become almost immune to life with little boys, accepting to the point of giving up, and she decided to re-hem her curtains later. She even supported Lynn's challenge to a race and suggested that it take place at the lodge's next weekly picnic.

Two guests volunteered to judge the race and determine the winner. Another couple offered to act as starters. Greg and I were Team One, Lynn and a friend Team Two. The picnic was typically held close to the entrance of the canal on a nearby friend's property, which had a large beach. On the day of the race there was a steady westerly breeze. The judges and participants had established a finish line that was defined by an imaginary line between a boathouse near the picnic area and a highly identifiable object on the opposite shore of the bay.

From the middle of the lake, a considerable distance back from the well-established finish line, we began our race towards the cheering guests upon the starters' signal. Both canoes were travelling at a good clip early into the race. Team One was moving quickly, but on a course not directly towards the centre of the bay.

We were veering off into a direction that was not at right angles to the predetermined finish line. Team Two was travelling straight towards the guests on the shore, but at a slower rate.

Greg and I knew that changing course to a more direct route towards the *closest point* of the finish line would ensure we would lose valuable time during the manoeuvre and risk losing the race. Neither Greg nor I could accept such a loss—especially to our big sister. We continued on our course towards the far side of the finish line, believing that our faster speed would more than compensate for the greater distance we needed to travel.

Greg and I were officially judged as crossing the finish line first—despite not crossing it at a ninety-degree angle. Lynn and her teammate contested the official result. Lynn still disputes the judges' findings. Sixty years later, Greg and I still refuse to hear her appeal.

As in all great moments in sport, only the winning team readily accepts the decision of the judges.

∞ The Garden ∞

In total, Lynn, Greg, and I visited our aunt Pearl and uncle Ted at Puck's Lodge for about five or six summers. In one of the latter years, Greg suggested to me, during our trip to Huntsville, that we carry out our chores with a greater sense of responsibility. I agreed. If we took our weeding job seriously at the start and diligently worked for the first couple of weeks, then the garden would be in good shape and we would have less work to do maintaining it for the balance of the summer. As we discussed this, we felt that such an effort was likely to be the best way to have our new attitude recognized, as the garden would be a visual record of our commitment.

For us, working in the garden had always been a chore from which we gained no real pleasure or sense of accomplishment. Aunt Pearl and Uncle Ted, on the other hand, liked to advertise the home-cooked meals and the garden fresh vegetables they served to their guests. They took pleasure from hearing that their guests enjoyed the meals they served. In her gracious acceptance of their compliments, she would reply, "Hunger is a great appetizer." This was a favourite saying of hers that I believe she got from her mother—my grandmother. I don't know where the saying originated.

That year Greg and I weeded the garden with a vengeance on our very first day. We felt Aunt Pearl deserved this simple treat, if only because we had given her so much trouble in the past.

In previous years we had always been burdened with an ongoing problem. The stubborn pasture grass would creep past the surrounding post and wire fence, into the garden, and smother all the different herbs that Aunt Pearl liked to plant around the perimeter. It was difficult to weed once it got to that state. This year, Greg and I had resolved that it would never reach that condition again.

On this first day, we planned to attack and prevent the field grass from moving into the garden. We diligently worked for the entire morning removing the bothersome greenery from the entire perimeter. We felt we had done an excellent job—especially where the grass had been in nice neat rows. This was the only task at the lodge we had completed without having to be asked first.

Aunt Pearl was pleased when she heard about our initiatives. After lunch we proudly showed her the results of our handiwork. She quickly became dismayed. Apparently, Greg and I had thoroughly removed every stock of corn she had planted well before our arrival. Our actions had excluded garden-fresh corn from the menu. Neither the guests nor the gardeners enjoyed home-grown corn that year.

Although it appeared as if we were growing up, it seemed as if we would make just as many mistakes this summer. However, this time we were well ahead of schedule. We learned that there is no such thing as a dumb question. Much to Aunt Pearl's chagrin, the variety of problems we presented her with ensured that she was always two or three steps behind us. We could argue we were improving. We were still making the same mistakes, but we weren't making them for the same reasons.

It is unwise to start any project without approval from the appropriate authority.

∞ **The Golf Club** ∞

At the top of the hill at the back of Puck's Lodge there was a large field. It was there Uncle Ted taught Greg and me to drive his 1920 Dodge quarter-ton pickup truck. The advantage of learning in this field was that its borders always seemed far away, and this gave us plenty of room for error and to turn around as required. I remember Uncle Ted being a good teacher and how he explained the way to shift gears. He did so with such relevant detail and kindness that we both learned quickly. I don't remember even grinding the gears. His teaching skills were such that he never exhausted his patience on us.

Aunt Pearl was just as kind. She taught us to drive a golf ball by letting us practice with her set of golf clubs. The first few times we played, Greg and I used the croquet lawn as a putting green, later graduating to the field as a driving range. In those days, the drivers all had wooden heads—true woods—reinforced with a metal plate on the bottom. The bag was not as elaborate as we use today, although it had been the latest design in the 1930s. It had a place for a few tees and golf balls, both of which looked similar to those we use today. Aunt Pearl and Uncle Ted both enjoyed the game, but Greg and I were only allowed to use our aunt's set of golf clubs.

One day Greg and I were playing golf in the field and making up our own rules as we went along. I was out of tees, so for one shot I used a small nearby rock about four inches square and a couple inches tall. I teed my ball up by setting it on this convenient piece of the Precambrian shield. I swung and missed. The head of Aunt Pearl's best driver smashed into the granite at full force.

I looked at the club and noticed that the impact had severely rippled the brass plate that was inset into the bottom of the club's wooden head. It was now completely unusable. Aunt Pearl had taught me that honesty is always the best policy, but I was too scared to show it to her in that condition, so I decided to fix it. After all, Uncle Ted had a cellar full of tools including a vice, and I was sure I could repair the disfigured club.

I started by removing the screws that fastened the plate to the underside of the club. It came off easily and I was soon smashing it flat with Uncle Ted's ball-peen hammer. It was somewhat difficult to hold at the same time but I managed. When I finished flattening the plate, I placed it back into the inset in the bottom of the club. Careful to use the same screws in their original holes, I fastened it in place. It was screwed on…but screwed up.

For some unusual reason, the alignment was askew. The edge of the brass plate that should have fitted tightly to the face of the wooden club was at a slight angle. My perfectly hammered flat brass plate was re-affixed to the bottom of the club but refused to align itself into its initial position. How this came to be still remains a mystery to me. I decided the best option now was to sand the face of the club to the point that it would match the edge of the brass plate.

When I was done sanding, I realized that its next user, namely Aunt Pearl, would readily notice the unvarnished face of the wooden club. It needed some colouring to match the rest of the stained wood. There was no stain handy and none of the available paint remnants were even close to the needed colour. The only thing I could think of using was the brown shoe polish conveniently located in my uncle's old wooden shoebox at the top of the stairs. With a small piece of cloth I sparingly applied the shoe polish until I achieved the desired colour. It was a fairly good match and I actually hoped that the extreme effort I had put into this repair would improve the club's performance.

I placed the club back into Aunt Pearl's golf bag without feeling it necessary to acquaint her with my recent upgrades. It certainly appeared to be in good shape—at least from a cosmetic standpoint.

On Aunt Pearl's next and only drive with the 'improved' club, the ball was sent into an unpredictable direction, on an unorthodox path. She produced a sharper slice than any veggie dicer advertised in an infomercial. The ball actually made a whirring sound as it spun out of control and out of sight. Unfortunately, the well-groomed appearance of the wood lulled me into a false sense of security, to the extent that I never thought it necessary to test it. I had lost track of my goal to repair the club somewhere between the hammering and polishing. I should have been trying to make it work—rather than look—like it once did.

The brown shoe polish acted as a lubricant, creating less purchase than one ought to have when swinging such a weapon. Sanding the carefully engineered face of the club to fit the repaired base plate had been a major mistake. Even without the lubricating brown shoe polish, the new angle of the striking face on the club would have made a straight drive impossible. The misaligned plate ensured that the club could never be restored to a useable state.

Aunt Pearl never used the club again but did ask me what I had done to it. After explaining my actions, her face was blank. She seemed to have become further reconciled to life with young boys. I learned that great effort does not always ensure great results and that goals can often be lost through a lack of focus.

Sometimes the better things look, the less likely they are to meet your expectations.

CAMPING

In addition to his many responsibilities at the lodge, from Chief Financial Officer to Supervisor of Septic Tank Cleanouts, Uncle Ted had always been involved with various organizations in and around his hometown of Huntsville, Ontario. His time away from the lodge was devoted to The Rotary Club, The Legion, and the Chamber of Commerce. He never missed his business luncheons at the Rotary Club and was always busy helping at the Legion, which organized the summer lacrosse, and some time later, winter hockey leagues for youth in the area.

As one of the businessmen associated with the Chamber of Commerce, Uncle Ted helped initiate the Muskoka Cavalcade of Colour, which is to this day an annual celebratory tour of fall colours in the Muskoka area. Despite his hectic schedule, he often included us in his activities and took us to see the summer lacrosse games on days when he was responsible for operating the box office at the arena.

Aunt Pearl continued with her many daily chores around the

lodge as General Manager, Master Chef, Chief of Staff, and Head of Housekeeping. I think both Aunt Pearl and Uncle Ted enjoyed the mature satisfaction that comes from pleasing others. Their long standing customers illustrated their success in the hospitality trade. Many had first visited at the opening of the lodge in 1938 and were still visiting annually well into the 1960s. Then, Uncle Ted became ill and Puck's Lodge was forced to close.

In the last chapter, Lynn, Greg, and I were all still spending our summer-long breaks from school at the lodge. One of the reasons we continued for many years was because it helped Mom so much by reducing the worries of caring for her three children on their summer holidays while she worked full time. Nevertheless, Lynn, Greg, and I all enjoyed helping out at the lodge during these years, but we were growing up and gradually our summer trips were replaced with other interests. In the years that followed, we came to participate in different activities both close to and far away from the lodge.

Lynn was interested in going to a camp in Bracebridge, just south of Huntsville. Greg was in the Reserve Navy and took time in the summer to go on various tours of duty throughout parts of the Atlantic Ocean. I worked at the local A&P grocery store in Huntsville, and later, throughout the school year, with the same company at a Toronto location. During these times we still remained close as a family.

In between other summer adventures, Lynn, Greg, and I returned to the lodge but only for one or two weeks at a time. Unlike previous visits where we travelled together and stayed for the entire summer, we were now travelling to the lodge and visiting other members of our family there on our own. We did so around the many other activities we had planned for ourselves during the summers that followed. For example, once, after having worked in British Columbia for most of the summer, I was hitchhiking back to Toronto and dropped in to see Aunt Pearl and Uncle Ted at Puck's Lodge. I found that the staff had left them alone for the busy Labour Day weekend. So, Aunt Pearl and I worked together as a team throughout that weekend cooking all of the guests' meals and doing the necessary housekeeping. My stipend for this weekend was a large chef's knife that I had fancied and used for all of the food preparations on those four days. I still use it.

To this day, Lynn, Greg, and I still remember our times at Puck's with Aunt Pearl and Uncle Ted as wonderful years in our youth. After they closed the lodge it was the end of an era, but we continued to visit with them and still cherish these memories. They had both helped bring the three of us into our adolescent years.

This chapter involves a series of shorter chronicles that journal a single camping trip that began at Puck's Lodge. Greg and I had ventured into Algonquin Park near Huntsville, Ontario, while we were in our late teens. The first anecdote describes some of the preparations for this coming-of-age trip. The other accounts are of the trip itself before we returned to the lodge. This proved to be a time to gain greater wisdom through an eclectic gathering of new life lessons.

∽ Mother Needs to Know ∽

Greg and I had decided to go camping for a week or so in the deep interior of Algonquin Park—one of the province's largest wilderness reserves. Uncle Ted offered us the use of one of his canoes for the trip. We were to start at Puck's Lodge, travel through the canal to North Portage at the far end of Peninsula Lake, carry our equipment to South Portage on the shores of Lake of Bays, cross that lake, and continue by following the Oxtongue River deep into the park. Later, we expected to simply retrace our route for the trip home. The smallest operating train in the world had been running between North and South Portage and would have made this journey easier, but it had ceased operations shortly before we embarked on our adventure.

Planning for the trip was relatively basic. We made preparations to bring food, clothing, and camping equipment. The equipment consisted of a tent, backpacks, hatchets, hunting knives, and some new fishing equipment including fishing rods. For apparel we packed swimsuits, footwear, pyjamas, and newly purchased togs. We planned many of our meals, including some conveniences like French's powdered potatoes and Bisquick, along with all of the necessary cooking utensils. We also included a few treats like a side of smoked bacon and twenty-four tins of canned baked beans. Greg and I had put a great deal of thought into our preparations and were very excited about our upcoming trip.

One evening while having an after dinner cup of tea, Mother was concerned about our ability to organize the trip. She challenged our planning and organizational skills. She asked us to explain what we planned to pack, where we were planning to go, when we were leaving, and how we hoped to survive. We had discussed all of this with her before, and Greg and I felt that we had addressed her concerns already. In Mom's defence, we had discussed different aspects of our trip but had done so at different times. This time, she wanted to be assured that we were taking enough of the necessary provisions. We were confident, but also recognized the need to address her concerns in detail.

To lay out the basics, Greg and I started to itemize our

equipment, food, and clothing by alternately rhyming off our various pieces of gear. We began with serious responses in our desire to have Mom appreciate our comprehensive planning abilities. Typically, Mom's concentration waned as Greg and I droned on. We quickly detected this but didn't let her know. We chose to continue listing items in response to her original question, but we deviated from the actual items we planned to take.

Instead, Greg mentioned an item that to any attentive listener would have appeared somewhat unnecessary. He spoke of bows and arrows. I followed up with a 22-calibre rifle. The list continued with each of us alternately detailing a 12-gauge shotgun, a 303 rifle, bazookas, dynamite, and depth charges (for fishing). The one-sided conversation continued as we graduated from listing illogical items, to detailing equipment needed for excessive use of force, to an extensive cataloguing of artillery and defence arsenals.

It wasn't until Greg voiced his supposed intent to include three 40-millimetre ack-ack guns on our excursion that Mom woke up. All of the previously recorded items of overkill had failed to register with her. I never got a chance to mention the highlight of my list—Sherman tanks. We all had a good laugh at Mom's unwillingness to listen to our response. The conversation concluded when Greg turned to me with a deadpan expression on his face and sarcastically relayed her latest concern. "She wants postcards."

If you ask a question, take the time to listen to the answer.

Life's Lessons: A Successful Collection of Failures

∞ **The Proper Use of a Headband** ∞

While preparing for our camping trip, Greg and I were cramming the food into our backpacks and trying to balance the loads. We were faced with having to carry a great deal of equipment, clothes, food, and a canoe across significant portages and wanted to ensure two things. First, we needed to know that we could actually carry our fully loaded backpacks into the bush. It was unrealistic to expect either of us to lighten any excess load through extreme gluttony at our first meal. Second, we wanted each of our loads to be equal so that in case of collapse it would happen to both of us at the same time, and hopefully, in a place suitable for setting up camp.

With respect to easing the burden of carrying the load, I had noticed earlier in a couple of history books that when Native Canadians 'camped' they carried huge backpacks. One of the things that enabled them to carry such large and heavy loads was a special headband attached near the top of each pack. I made an executive decision that Greg and I should have the same benefit. After all, Greg should have welcomed anything that would have helped us carry twenty-four tins of baked beans. He agreed.

Before completing our packing, we cut strips of canvas-like material. Mother sewed them together and into loops at the top of our packsacks. Once this was completed, we finished our packing and were ready to go.

With Mom and her youngest sister, Aunt Babe, we travelled to Puck's Lodge and were surprised to find out that we would not be allowed to fish in the park unless both Greg and I had fishing licences. That night, we made a rushed trip to the park gate to obtain said licences since we were anxious to leave after breakfast early the next morning. We hurried back to the lodge as Mom had been hoping to drop us off and return home later that night. There was no need for the family car to be at the lodge while Greg and I leisurely paddled through the park.

The next morning, after we finished breakfast, we were ready to commence our journey. We had the blessings of our family, everything packed, and a beautiful sunny day beckoning us. The problem at this point was that our upcoming expedition to tough it out in the bush was sharply contrasted by the cozy, tranquil, familiar atmosphere at the lodge. It took us almost two hours to have breakfast and get into the boat.

Carefree and light-hearted, we paddled through the canal and Peninsula Lake to North Portage. We now had to portage for about a mile and a half to Lake of Bays. After strapping our paddles to the thwarts of the canoe and struggling into our packsacks, we heaved the canoe up onto our shoulders and started walking. We stumbled our way up our first hill where we rested. At the halfway point of our portage, we were much more than half spent.

We were resting for the second time, only a couple of hours into our two week trip, when Greg suggested that it was "high time" to ease our load through the use of our new headbands. He asked me to lift the weight of the packsack so that he could loop the headband from his pack onto his forehead and thereby lessen his burden. His pack, like mine, was the heaviest it would be during our trip, but I did so willingly as I would require the same 'help' from him once he was loaded up.

The moment he gave me the signal that it was in place, I let go. Before I had a chance to move away, he was screaming, "Take it off!" The exact same words were repeated in a series of three progressively intensifying calls of despair. The first of which had been a reasonably intense statement possibly made in an attempt to hide the pain that was increasing at an alarming rate. His second cry for help more accurately reflected his panicked state. This was quickly followed by his third and final yell, which was more of a loud screaming demand for immediate action as the apparent risk of snapping his neck seemed imminent. All this before I had taken a step away from him. Greg had gone from enjoying a leisurely camping trip to the pain of self-inflicted whiplash in only a few seconds. It was a good thing that we had opted for powdered potatoes.

My design had failed to dissipate the weight as intended. Instead, it efficiently concentrated the entire load onto one of the weakest parts of the body—the neck. The muscles in the back of Greg's neck did not return to their normal position until I had lifted his backpack high enough for him to remove the headband. Just like my 'repair' to Aunt Pearl's favourite golf club, my design of the headband looked—but did not work—as its originators had intended.

My design for the headband looped from one side to the other with sufficient room to maim anyone who had not read my owner's manual. Had I written one without testing this handy device, I am sure I would have emphasized a disclaimer to "Use only as directed." But, I'm not sure this would have saved the first poor soul who tried it on. Please do not try this at home.

Looking back on this incident, I'm sure that the failure occurred because I hadn't planned it as carefully as I could have. No drawings had been prepared—the strap was merely my mental picture of what it should look like—and there had been no consideration for load balancing. All in all, insufficient work had preceded the design, and failure had been assured from the start.

Don't tell Greg.

If you are going to try emulating Native Canadians, talk to one first.

∾ Finding Our Way ∾

I learned from an inveterate hiker that when hiking or camping, the way to separate the wheat from the chaff is to pile everything you think you need on the floor, in the middle of a room. Decrease this pile by one half, then take a break for at least twenty-four hours. Go back to the pile again and reduce it by another half. Now you have the necessities.

The first portage of our camping trip was more than a mile along a gravel road. By the time Greg and I reached the dock on Lake of Bays at South Portage, we were wishing we had followed the advice of our seasoned hiker friend. We were now only three hours into a two week trip and both of us were sweating, out of breath, hungry, and in need of another rest.

Deciding to push on after a brief moment to catch our breath, we re-launched the canoe, stowed our freight, and headed out into Lake of Bays. Our destination was the mouth of the Oxtongue River, which flowed into Lake of Bays near Dwight, Ontario. I had taken up a position in the rear of the canoe and was responsible for steering and keeping us on course. To help with this, my equipment included a compass, firmly attached to the front of my belt. A second navigating tool was a contour map of the area stored in my hip pocket.

As we paddled along on this bright sunny afternoon on our way to the mouth of the Oxtongue River, something was amiss. The map indicated that the mouth of the river should have been at the end of a bay. The compass was pointing me into a bay that did not look large enough to match the one illustrated on the map. No matter which way I held the map, I couldn't reconcile it to the shoreline in my view. Either someone had moved the Oxtongue River or the compass was wrong.

I was becoming more and more concerned. I told Greg that we needed to ask for directions. We stopped at a cottage where we had seen people moving about. The sounds of meal preparation were emanating. Knocking on the door, we asked for directions as we explained our conundrum. They pointed out a simple truth—the compass was right and I was wrong.

Apparently, our destination was in the bay directly across from their cottage—exactly the area to which the compass had been, and was still, pointing. I expected a look of disgust from Greg. After all, if you're not going to believe your compass, why bring it? However, the fact that I had landed us in the middle of a family's dinner—a family that had two good-looking daughters our age—greatly ameliorated Greg's assessment of my error. The invitation to join them for dinner was readily accepted but embarrassing for me, as we ate with our destination in full view.

Over dinner, Greg and I exchanged looks that made me think he was contemplating revising our schedule as our minds wandered into fantasies of how the evening might unfold with our new-found friends. There was more than a bounce in their step as they ran down the stairs and excitedly encouraged us to make 'camp' with them that night. Greg wanted to stay, but for some reason I was focussed on setting up our tent before sundown. Unfortunately for Greg, I was on a mission.

Sadly, our evening visit came to an uneventful end. We set out from the dock and waved goodbye from our canoe. Greg's pain and frustration was channelled into each forceful stroke of his paddle. Ironically, this helped keep us on schedule as we paddled away from our new female friends—pushing onward in our quest for the mouth of the Oxtongue River.

Learn to take direction from your instruments.

✦ Night Attire ✦

The camping expedition with my brother continued with our search for the mouth of the Oxtongue River. There it was. Lately arrived at and in time for setting up camp, what could be better than an evening campfire followed by a sleep on the beach? Greg gave me another look.

This was our first night 'out' and we were both determined to make it a comfortable one. We picked a flat location on the beach on which to pitch the tent, unpacked, and laid out our sleeping bags. It only took two hours of fumbling to make a fire and set up our tea caddy over the campfire before we got into our pyjamas and retired for the night.

It was cold, damp, uncomfortable, and a far cry from our missed opportunities. It was too cold even to fantasize about them. We only slept for brief moments at a time throughout the foggy night. These short intervals of rest were interrupted by long, awkward efforts to reposition ourselves in our clammy sleeping bags.

For some reason, we never got up to change out of our pyjamas and into something warmer. Instead, with foolish optimism, we continued to hope we would fall asleep in the same conditions that woke us up in the first place. We even tried to get comfortable by burrowing into the ground, hoping to mould the sandy foundation into a shape that would match that of our bodies. Unfortunately, this only brought us closer to the water table and made for a much colder and damper bed.

The next morning we arose quite stiff. We set a fire and had breakfast at sunrise. Although we began our activities quite early that morning, we shivered until noon. Our next stop was scheduled near Marshs Falls, which was a short distance away but required portage around the falls—necessary before we could travel farther along the river to set up our next camp.

This second night was spent ashore in the middle of Oxtongue Lake. It was not on some cold beach. It was on the only thing capable of harnessing more dampness, cold, and discomfort—an island. To keep warm, we chose to dress for bed in every article of clothing that we had worn in the last day or so. Our campsite's unforgiving foundation—Precambrian granite—was no match for our fatigue and we snoozed through the night looking like a couple of overdressed mannequins. Although we acknowledged that our night attire looked ridiculous, we didn't care. Our concern was to stay warm so that we could get a good night's sleep. We knew it would be better to rest and look peculiar than to lie awake all night in fashion.

Appearances are secondary.

∽ Protection in the Wild ∽

Greg and I always had fun fishing together. It was our hope to enjoy fresh fish for more than a few meals during our excursion into Algonquin Park. Beyond Oxtongue Lake, there was a warden's cabin a few miles up river. We stopped for a chat with the warden, who told us that bears were a great problem that year. He cautioned us not to leave any food out at night, as this would attract them and could create a dangerous situation for us. He also explained that we needed to keep all of our food high off the ground to discourage their interest.

We continued on our way as I mulled over the official warnings. I felt fairly safe since I had been careful to pack my handy new nine inch hunting knife. Greg felt that a single swipe would be enough to bring any bear from a state of curiosity into full-fledged fury and ensure we both suffered the consequences.

We made camp that night in a picturesque area. We gathered fallen needles from various evergreens and piled them so they would act as mattresses for our sleeping bags. Then we pitched our bottomless tent over top of our makeshift beds. We set up our tea caddy and prepared our supper. Later that evening, after finishing our meal, we poured ourselves our first cup of tea. It had been on the fire for hours and was well steeped. In fact, it was blacker than the night and more acrid than the smoke from the campfire.

The nearby logs made for pleasant seating as we lounged, chatted, and sipped our bitter drink until early morning. I was dressed in my brand new khaki shorts, comfy shirt, and moccasins. I felt as if I was meant to live in the wild. We got undressed and were resting inside our sleeping bags when a thought came to me. "What would I do if a bear *did* come into our tent?" I pondered the possibilities. Greg fell asleep, obviously less concerned about the bear situation.

Despite Greg's attitude, I felt I needed to have a weapon close at hand to use for an encounter with a bear. I sat up in the darkness to get my hunting knife that was near my feet just inside the tent, and placed it within arm's reach. I wanted to keep it close at hand so that if needed, I could retrieve it in an instant and thereby be prepared to fight off any impending danger.

Continuing with my plan, I laid back down in the position I typically slept. While holding the handle in my right hand, I swung the knife over my head and stabbed it into the earth just beyond my head. I tried a few times to grab it quickly. Each time I wasn't able to do so, I repositioned it by repeatedly swinging and stabbing it into a better position. After I was content that it was in an ideal location for retrieval, I continued to practice these actions to prove to myself that I could reach my weapon from virtually any sleeping position.

Locating the knife in this way gave me a feeling of greater security and allowed me to drift off. I awoke peacefully to birds singing early the next morning. I arose to dress in my special camping outfit and found my favourite shorts pinned to the earth with the blade of my nine inch hunting knife. Once freed, I noticed that the rear end had been pierced seventeen times with the blade. The vigour with which I practiced my skilful manoeuvres ensured that the holes went straight through all folds of material in the garment, thereby multiplying the damage.

My best shorts had been mutilated to the extent that I could never wear them again. Attempts to 'protect' myself in the wild by destroying the very thing that made me feel as if I belonged there, was ironic…and kept Greg laughing well into the next day.

Life in the wild is fraught with surprises.

∞ Amphibians ∞

One of the 'treats' Greg and I looked forward to on our trip into Algonquin Park was having frogs' legs for dinner. Just above Marshs Falls, Greg had taken out his fishing rod and baited the hook with a small piece of red cloth. This was a method we used to catch bullfrogs. Our experience had been that no frog could resist this type of lure.

As the red cloth got close, every one of them would attempt to bring the red 'insect' into its mouth, thereby making them an easy catch. On our way to the next campsite, they would be stored in front of Greg in the bow of our canoe. Later, once we had stopped, they would be cleaned and readied for our frying pan.

The frog's legs that Greg and I used to eat were prepared differently than those one might get in a restaurant today. We had found that the two front legs joined at the breastbone could provide an amount of meat roughly equivalent to one of the rear legs. These parts were salvaged and fried in butter along with the traditional crop of back legs.

We ate them with Bisquick cooked in a stone oven we made over our campfire, accompanied by powdered potatoes, which like the Bisquick, had been reconstituted by just adding water. At dinner we discussed how resourceful we had been by living off the land, and we continued to 'fish' for frogs throughout our trip upstream. This provided us with many delicious meals.

Later, as we travelled home, we continued fishing for them on our way downstream. Greg and I would spot them with their heads just above water resting in the shallows. We would approach them quietly, but as Greg brought out the fishing rod with the red cloth, they would quickly dive. Ploop, and they were gone. Not a single frog would bite on our entire return trip downstream.

I have changed considerably since those days. Now, as an animal lover and vegetarian, I feel remorse each time I recall this story or any other in which I was so cruel. I have included this occurrence in our book because I feel it illustrates a point.

Bad news travels fast…even amongst small animals.

Life's Lessons: A Successful Collection of Failures

∽ **The General Store** ∾

We were more than a week into our camping trip and on our way home when we both had a hankering for real potatoes. Baked, fried, or boiled, we longed for the taste of a real potato.

We decided to deviate from our original plan of staying away from civilization. We now wanted to get to a country store and buy some fresh potatoes. We knew that there was a general store on Highway 60 south of our planned route. If we walked from a nearby campsite and left all of our gear behind, we could reach the store in a couple of hours.

Our time in the wild was coming to a close but after living off the land without any modern conveniences, both Greg and I felt a true sense of achievement and independence. We found a camping spot on the north shore of Oxtongue Lake, where Highway 60 crosses the Oxtongue River. After lunch we set up camp. This was earlier than we had typically done during the last week or so of our trip. We set up early because we had a long walk to the store. Also, we wanted to return to our campsite in time to prepare our dinner with the fresh potatoes.

The meat for the night was thick slices of smoked bacon with the mould carefully removed. After a week with no refrigeration, the bacon had succumbed to the natural degradation in the intense heat of the summer days. Our special dinner would be rounded off with our last can of beans.

Surprisingly, we were looking forward to this gourmet meal. With great anticipation, we left camp and headed off along the shoulder of the highway for the general store. It was a long walk. We entered the store and began to look around. The only potatoes we could find were canned ones. Our anticipation was such that we decided canned was still much better than reconstituted. I looked around for sales staff to help me find other items we were hoping to buy. As I approached a salesgirl, Greg said something that distracted me. When I turned around again, she was nowhere to be found.

Greg spotted another girl working in the far corner of the store. As he approached her for help, she casually faded to the right and exited into the "employees only" section. In fact, after the sales help left, the customers followed, leaving Greg and me alone in the store. He turned to me and when our eyes met we instantly came to the same conclusion. We were not liked. Although we felt like two rugged, seasoned campers, we appeared more like a couple of vagrants, each of us with ten day old beards, an overall scruffy appearance, and a distinct need for a strong deodorant.

By consistently ringing the bell for service on the countertop near the entrance to the store, we were able to encourage one brave soul to enter our area of influence and collect the payment for our groceries. Once back at camp, we enjoyed our meal, but we both looked forward to returning home to civilization and real potatoes.

For faster service, shower before ringing bell.

∞ Cold Feet ∞

The dictionary definition of a "soaker" is "a downpour, deluge, or rainstorm." Throughout our childhood, Greg and I understood it to be soaking your foot by stepping in a puddle, river, or lake. This occurred frequently on our memorable camping trip in our teens. In all, our trip 'deep' into Algonquin Park only brought us to the edge. We reached just inside what is commonly depicted on most maps as the shaded border.

One of the inconveniences of camping is being plagued by wet feet. On this trip, as a result of many soakers, my feet felt as if they had been wet forever. I had had enough and decided to dry out my leather moccasins while enjoying our last campfire dinner. Since the fire was already burning, I felt that the heat could be used to speed the drying process. I set my footwear carefully side-by-side next to the fire and left them there for the entire night.

By morning, the heat from the fire had reduced my right moccasin to a size five. My left moccasin, a little farther away from the fire, but well sheltered from its mate, remained soaking wet but fortunately still fit my size nine foot. Our last day in the bush was spent enduring the worst of both worlds. I was forced to wear my right moccasin as a 'semi-sandal' and hobbled around in it whenever we were out of the canoe. It was uncomfortable but dry. On the other hand (read foot), I was forced to wear my left moccasin in a contrasting fashion. It fitted perfectly but it was still soaking wet, and cold.

A pessimist could argue both my feet were uncomfortable—either wet or ill-fitted. A statistician could claim that, on average, my feet were comfy.

Fortunately, I had an idea to improve my sorry state. I could resize the smaller moccasin by reversing the shrinking process. However, to do this, I had to soak my only dry moccasin and stretch it onto my only dry foot. It took the remaining part of the trip to force the leather back into a shape that would accommodate my right foot.

All of the stories in this chapter occurred over a couple weeks in one summer, but we arrived home shortly after to the safety and warmth of the lodge. This was the last episode of my memorable camping trip with my brother Greg.

Ironically, I finished our camping trip with feet that were wet, damp, and cold, because my shoes were placed too close to a fire. I liken this lesson to the old adage, "Too much of anything is not good for you." Now back at the lodge, Greg and I were enjoying all of the modern conveniences Aunt Pearl and Uncle Ted could provide. Here, we were willing to take our chances.

The longer away from the comforts of home, the more they're appreciated upon return.

ON THE ROAD

My maternal grandmother's maiden name was Law. My grandmother, Christina, married Richard Moffatt. Other members of the Law family had settled in the Kemptville area a few miles south of Ottawa, Ontario. One of Christina's sisters was named Edith, but we called her Aunt Ede. She was my mom's aunt and my great aunt. Her husband came from a local family with the name of Robinson, and together they settled in the town of Kemptville on Highway 16—the main street.

As kids we loved visiting Aunt Ede and Uncle Fred. When Lynn, Greg, and I were young, we loved to play "catch me if you can" because their house had a back staircase perfect for this game.

Later we came to enjoy the fresh produce from Uncle Fred's garden. He always picked the vegetables when they were very young and sweet. Boiled with little water, they were food fit for angels. Also, Aunt Ede had her special way with pies. After spending a few weeks with her one summer, I returned home and insisted that when Mother made her pies, she had to use exactly the same lard as Aunt Ede.

Our love for Aunt Ede and Uncle Fred extended late into our adolescence when Greg and I would travel many hours to visit them in Kemptville even on short two day weekends.

The four narratives in this chapter are about brief memories Greg and I experienced on the road once we were old enough to drive. The first two take place visiting family in and around Kemptville, and the last two follow us to a shared cottage on Clear Lake.

∞ **Memories** ∞

It was Aunt Ede and Uncle Fred's 45th wedding anniversary, and the entire family was visiting for the celebration. Greg and I were wheeling around the Kemptville countryside with Uncle Fred on our way to purchase the celebratory turkey from a nearby farm.

Uncle Fred was at the incredibly old age of seventy-two. Greg and I were in our early teens. As we drove along through the dairy farming community, Uncle Fred casually mentioned a fond memory of his. It was obviously a gem from his past. Pointing to an old farmhouse and recollecting fondly, he said, "An old girlfriend of mine used to live there…she was a little loose at both ends."

Greg and I were at an age at which we understood the context and were able to appreciate Uncle Fred's sense of humour. The contrast of such a spirited comment coming from an elderly relative made us feel accepted as adult members of the family. We have never tired of sharing his punchy comment and the circumstances that led up to it.

The memory of this story became a gem for Greg and me as we recited it for others many times in the years that followed.

Some old gems never lose their lustre—they are preserved by being shared.

∽ **Courting** ∽

On one of our visits to Kemptville, Greg and I were sitting with Aunt Ede in her living room as she reminisced about her life. She was talking about the good old days of yesteryear before it was commonplace to own a car. Back then, people travelled using a horse drawn buggy, surrey, phaeton, or wagon.

Unlike the automobile, the driving power of these vehicles had brains. They frequently got used to the common routes their owners would take. Often, because they knew their stable and where the oats were stored, they wouldn't require direction or guidance on the way home. In fact, this is one instance where 'sleeping at the wheel' could be beneficial. After working late on any given day, you were at liberty to fall asleep while the horse took you home. Stopping at the stable usually woke the 'driver' up. Talk about a Global Positioning System.

Aunt Ede went on to recount a story of one such horse. It took place during the time Uncle Fred was courting her. He had a wonderful horse that, as Aunt Ede described it, could find its way home without anyone having to handle the reins. Greg innocently asked, "What did Uncle Fred do with his hands, Auntie?" She did not answer the question, she just blushed demurely.

Later, Uncle Fred answered Greg's awkward question in an indirect way. He told us that he was dating *another* girl around the same time he was courting Aunt Ede. He took this other girl out, travelling in the same buggy, and hitched to the same "wonderful little horse." On the way 'home' it trotted straight to Aunt Ede's house and up the driveway without Uncle Fred or his date noticing the mistake. In truth, it was not fair to consider the horse's action as being a mistake, since it was only doing what came naturally.

Apparently, so was Uncle Fred. Obviously he had made amends with Aunt Ede as she laughed each time he told this story.

Nature will find a way—even at the most awkward of times.

◈ Clear Lake ◈

Many people opt to spend their weekends in the city with a heartfelt desire to visit bars and restaurants, and experience new shows…sometimes in search of romance. Others prefer spending time at a slower pace, relaxing, and experiencing the many other benefits of life in the big city. I enjoy filling my weekends with casual dining and mingling with family, especially at the water's edge.

Many people I know have a second home by a lake, on a river, or somewhere away from the big smoke. For many families, a visit to a summer home is a weekly occurrence. Some make the trip to cottage country in every season—regardless of the weather.

In some cases, people refer to their getaway as a 'cabin' in the woods, or their 'camp', when in actual fact the building is an elegant lakefront house. I have heard others refer to their lake house or cottage to describe a structure not fit to store firewood. Hence, there is simply no way of determining how stylish or rugged someone's seasonal residence is, based solely on their terminology. Large rooms and comfy beds are other terms misused by such intelligentsia.

Regardless of such confusion, I feel there is one thing that all of these getaways reflect—a general love for the great outdoors. To me, any rural retreat has some sort of magical relief from the common urban stress that typically builds to a boiling point on most of my Fridays around mid afternoon.

In my opinion the terms tent, cabin, cottage, and lake house all refer not only to dwellings, but also to different types of experiences. A tent or cabin is not a poor man's version of spending the weekend at a cottage or lake house. It is simply a different experience, whether by a lake, on a river…or in the middle of a swamp.

In truth, there are many other terms commonly used to describe temporary housing for getaways, such as rooming in a lodge, hotel, or resort. This is too confusing to discuss here in the middle of my story…so I won't.

In the summer of 1961, Greg and I rented a cottage at a small resort on Clear Lake in Southern Ontario. It was a bright sunny day when we arrived. I was so anxious to relax in the serene lakeside setting, I hastily grabbed Greg's fishing rod, which was already outfitted with a lure. I headed to the dock for a couple of casts before unpacking. At the end of the dock, I made my first cast of the weekend. Unfortunately, Greg had failed to fasten the reel securely to the rod. It took off in a slightly different direction than the lure and ended up at the bottom of the lake.

    I figured that I could retrieve it easily. I simply rolled up my pant legs and jumped in next to the sunken reel. Somewhere between the water's surface passing above my knees and coming to rest just below my nipples, I realized Clear Lake had been aptly named. I might well have continued for more than twenty feet. I believe the other guests soaking up the afternoon sun at the water edge were quite amused. As I fully submerged myself to pick up Greg's reel, their entertainment continued. I finished the show by clambering onto the dock and trying to rescue the important documents from my soggy wallet.

    Obviously the lake was clearer than my thoughts on that day. I was well behind. I needed to change my clothes before I unpacked the car, and Greg insisted I clean out his reel as soon as we had prepared and eaten our late lunch. I was so far behind I had to hurry in order to have time to relax.

You need not rush to enjoy the slow pace of reel life in the great outdoors.

∞ Waterskiing ∞

Greg and I had the opportunity to go waterskiing, for a nominal charge. It had been a few days since I managed to dry out Greg's fishing reel during our stay at Clear Lake. I believed learning to water-ski would be too much fun to pass up.

We left the dock and I managed to get up on my first try. Like Greg, I enjoyed a couple of laps around the lake before my time was up. In only a few runs, I learned how to veer to the right and left (both are important) and later cross the wake. On my last run I recognized the value of learning to stop. Until this time letting go was sufficient.

The significance of my last run was that I was anxious (there's that word again) to impress other guests with my newly acquired skills. Busy sunning themselves on the beach for a few days—non-stop—they were quite lethargic from their hard work. They had been mildly entertained by my opening act a few days earlier. I believe they were now anticipating further amusement.

I had already learned to cross over the wake and felt a surge of pride when I managed to complete a series of continual crossovers on my second near twenty minute run. Although not ready for much more than this, in my mind, I was certain that in a short time my waterskiing abilities would allow me to successfully execute many trickier manoeuvres. I did not know just how little time would pass before I was given the chance.

With each subsequent turn, my confidence increased. I whipped through an "S" pattern of crossovers behind the ski boat while it sped up to accommodate my newfound confidence. Unknowingly, I had reached a point at which my speed was far greater than my judgment. I believed I had an opportunity for one more crisscross before letting go and slowly sinking into the water as my last run took me past the people on the beach. Like any smug novice, I decided to "go for it."

It was a bad decision. I had been at a point of no return, but in my cockiness I had failed to recognize it as such. With overconfidence as my best friend, I pressed on. Crossing the wake to the left, I completed the first of my two turns. I had crissed.

Life's Lessons: A Successful Collection of Failures

Now I had to cross. Within less than a second of completing my final turn, my confidence began to decrease—rapidly. It was now necessary to fulfill my goal in much less space and at a much greater speed. I was headed straight for the beach. At that moment I realized that somehow, I must stop…and soon. But how?

I later learned that there was not enough space or time for even a seasoned water-skier to successfully complete such an undertaking. It was a conclusion that all of those watching from shore had already reached.

As the shore rushed to greet me, my options reduced significantly, and I fell back on my natural skills. I knew that to decrease my unwanted velocity, I needed to get a greater part of my body into the water and hope that the drag would slow me down in time to avoid parting the seers on the beach and giving new meaning to the name Clear Lake. I feared falling to my side might well have reacquainted me with the dock in a painful way—so I sat down.

This natural but rather speedy self-induced enema was not the sort of drag I was looking for. Nor was it anticipated as the last trick in the final pass of my impromptu ski show by my gallery of fellow guests. In a unique demonstration of a three-point stance, my finalé became waterskiing on land.

The resort had provided several Muskoka (Adirondack) chairs, and had set them out for their guests to use by the beach. They were filled with people enjoying the quiet afternoon. That is, until I interrupted their peace. They stared in amazement as I approached. Some scattered quickly as I skidded up the beach toward them. The more astute observers were already standing and chose to utilize this time to move away from the star of the show. Many eyes were wide with apprehension.

With my feet rammed further into the bindings of the skis, I slid up the beach on my rump. I was too stunned to stand up and wore out the rear end of my bathing suit faster than any manufacturer's endurance test could. One helpful guest ran to my aid, suggesting I sit down and take it easy. I refused, saying, "No thanks, I already have." I have always been thankful that I hadn't arrived a few feet to the left, as this would have taken me straight through a group of springy saplings that surely would have whipped me unmercifully.

Later I realized I could have skied up the gentle slope of the sandy shoreline and remained upright with my knees bent to maintain my balance. In this way, I could have stepped out of the skis and bowed to the crowd, turned around, and saluted the driver of the boat. Or better still, I could have simply elected to not to be so daring. Hindsight is clearly 20-20.

Cockiness is the point at which we stop learning.

Life's Lessons: A Successful Collection of Failures

FRIENDS AND FAMILY

I was studying at the University of Toronto and married my first wife, Joy, in 1957. During my "skule" years I was earning some money by working during the summer breaks. This income was only enough to cover the tuition fees and other costs related to my studies. Since we got married while I was still a student, the money Joy earned as a legal secretary covered all of our other living expenses. If not for her willingness to continue her financial contributions to the E. Fearnley Benevolent Fund, I would not have been able to stay focused on my education and graduate by 1960. Our teamwork continued until shortly after my graduation, when I began my career as a Civil Engineer.

Within a year of starting my new profession, we were expecting our first child, whom we named Richard. Later, we added two others, Steven and Jamie. As my family grew, I continued to share my memories around the dinner table, especially those from my childhood while at the lodge with Aunt Pearl and Uncle Ted.

I have remained close to, and have fond memories of, our

entire extended family. Visiting with my mom and her sisters on Christmas Day is still vivid in my memory—especially our raucous games of six-handed euchre. Time passes and we tend to lose the older members of our family. Eras come and go. I lost my namesake and a mentor when my uncle Ted died in the late 1960s, just before our third son, Jamie, was born. In fact I lost much more. I lost a close friend.

Joy and I separated after twenty-three years of marriage. However, I would not have chosen a different life path because the one I did choose provided us with three sons, all of whom I consider to be my best friends. This chapter deals primarily with friends and family, and my learning curve in parenting while helping to raise three young boys.

∞ **Cottage Bliss** ∞

I have always enjoyed spending time away from the big city. Staying near the water adds to the experience. When friends are around to share, this is best of all. With this in mind, Joy and I asked friends of ours if they would like to share a cottage in Muskoka for a holiday. Their two children were similar in age to ours, and the four of them all got along well at family visits. (Jamie had not been thought of yet. In fact, he was a surprise that would come a few years later.)

Joy and I agreed to search for a cottage that was suitable for both of our families. We planned to take an entire day, tour Muskoka, and return with a confirmed booking. We were prepared to put a deposit on a property to secure it for our highly anticipated one week vacation. We started out very early one Saturday morning with hopes of completing our search by early afternoon. Unfortunately, it became apparent that most of the decent cottages had already been rented. The ones we were viewing had obviously been left over from the early scramble for cottage rentals. There was no internet or email back then to aid in the exchange of pictures, so we had to use newspaper ads as our source of possibilities. Rather than select a place sight unseen, we chose to drive from one advertised place to the next, until we found something that would accommodate both of our families.

By late afternoon, our standards had deteriorated to the extent that any lakefront beach with a shed and a toilet would do. Rooms such as a kitchen and dining room were now considered luxuries. Most did not have a phone and in those days of yesteryear there were no cell phones to discuss our findings with the other couple. Richard was getting carsick from all of the travel and this added to our internal pressure to find a place soon.

We settled on a shack located on the shores of Ril Lake and parted with a significant amount of hard-earned cash to ensure it would be our vacation home for a full week in the coming summer. We reasoned that the lack of amenities would be overlooked by the other family since the shallow waterfront area was ideal for children and we did not plan on spending a great deal of our time indoors. A boat had been included in the rental. When we shared the news of our find with our friends, we highlighted the fun our children could have at the beach, as well as in and on the water, and looked forward to our time together.

It was a beautiful day when we arrived. We all unpacked and loaded our stuff into the six hundred square-foot structure that would house our two families for the next seven days and nights. It was quaint at best, and provided little room for adults once the children's toys had been distributed throughout the four-room retreat. It did not take long before we were settled in and starting to prepare our first meal together.

It was not "cozy" like the ad in the paper had claimed. Depending on what room the group was in, we each had less than twenty square feet to call our own. Nevertheless, this would have been ample space in which to dress, eat, sleep, and navigate around the various pieces of furniture and appliances, but something dreadful happened. It rained.

All week.

Occasionally, the sun would appear in a fleecy sky, but only long enough to tease us. Once, it stopped long enough for the older two children to try their hand at fishing. Up until this point, although the boat that had come with the cottage was floating in the water, it had not been tested for seaworthiness. I had assumed the water that nearly filled it was from the rain. It turned out to be demonstrating a unique state of equilibrium between lake water and rain. Luckily, it floated for a while once it was emptied of water. We got a few brief moments to fish, making use of the leeches in the lake as bait and the bait bucket for bailing. The leeches were in such abundance that had it warmed up enough to swim, they would have prevented us from doing so. Exiting the water tattooed with fat slimy bloodsuckers was not a welcomed thought.

The first evening we had a difficult task. Getting our four children to sleep was a major challenge. The adults could not play cards or even talk because the bedroom walls were only eight-foot partitions that didn't even extend to the ceiling. Even the wall between the two bedrooms was more of a divider than anything else. Any noise we made kept the restless four from dozing off. We decided to read until they fell asleep, but our silence was broken by giggles coming from their rooms. We noticed flying teddy bears being tossed aggressively over the dividing partition between the bedrooms. Their laughter, although somewhat suppressed, did not escape our attention. In addition to this, they could hear themselves talking and laughing. Eventually we had had enough. I stormed into Richard and Steven's room, catching them in full wind-up mode. Our efforts prevailed, and eventually they fell asleep…only six more days to go.

Because of the leeches and the rain, most of the playtime took place inside. Our friend's eldest child loved to play in the water. However, she was more than content to play indoors, since she chose to pour, puddle, splash, and make bubbles…in the toilet.

It was an enormous frustration for her father, who, for some time, had been trying to break her from this uncommon childish fixation with toilet water. Her toy was always easy to find, and somewhat difficult for her father to remove from her environment. Eventually her intense approach to her hobby made her ill. She joined the balance of the sickened troops who were also plagued with various symptoms of the common cold.

My youngest son, Steven, enjoyed the water as well. Whenever our children's activities inside the cottage had exasperated us, we collectively lowered our parenting standards and encouraged them to play outside in the rain. Steven enjoyed this the most. He haphazardly tinkered around the dock, focusing his time on uncovering various bugs, spiders, and other small creatures, until he fell in the lake.

Every day.

Halfway through our 'holiday' we were all ready to go home. All of us were helping to prepare lunch in the kitchen area of our living/dining room. Steven had been whining from the moment we arrived. He now showed advanced symptoms of the cold he had been nursing to this point, and continued to snivel and whine about wanting to go outside and play. His whimpering whittled away at what was left of the adults' patience. It was lunchtime and Steven began to complain about not being allowed to go outside to play (and fall in the lake, again). The only other man along for this ride was at a bit of a disadvantage. This was not his child.

He was content to stand at the counter and diffuse his tension by focusing on chopping the "veg" for our salad. As Steven pressed further, the chopping became more and more vigorous, until the slicer and dicer screamed. He turned around and was visibly struggling to contain himself as his hands appeared to be desperately fighting for control of the knife. He screamed, "*Go*, in God's name, *GO!*" Steven obediently went.

After lunch an announcement was made. The other family could not handle any more of their 'vacation' with the Fearnleys. With a daughter still sick, and the rain still falling, the veg chopper knew he could not make it to the end of the week. He took his family and left. I was sympathetic towards his actions and considered trying to dissuade him as he stood in the doorway. I thought for a brief moment…twice the space, half the tumult, no toilet issues, and a bedroom of my own without any kids. So, like a good friend, I waved goodbye.

If you're going to lose your temper, put the knife down.

∞ Pie in the Sky ∞

The same family that shared a cottage with us on Ril Lake were friends of ours for many years. Joy still visits their whole family. The relationship began with the women becoming the best of friends early in their childhood and they remain close to this day. The antics of our children during the times our families got together tended to produce memorable occasions.

Their youngest child survived on a constant diet of peanut butter. Typically he would eat peanut butter and banana on toast for breakfast, peanut butter and jam sandwiches for lunch, and peanut butter on a dinner roll for supper. In his mind, these were three distinctly different meals, and he considered them to have enough variety to constitute a well-balanced and nutritious diet.

One evening Joy and I and our two children were entertaining the four of them over a Thanksgiving dinner. The peanut butter kid was always allowed to have dessert if he ate his first course, which in this case he did. He was about seven years old and as rambunctious as they come. A special dessert had been prepared to complement our celebratory meal. As a treat, Joy had made a traditional homemade apple pie. Her apple pies were delicious. (They still are.) All of us were looking forward to it.

As we finished our main course, the excitement over dessert increased, especially amongst the children. The pie was carried from the kitchen into the dining room and had to pass by the two visiting children. Joy alerted them to her arrival by cautioning, "Heads up."

For fun, the seven year old obeyed by taking it upon himself to carry out her order literally. He was sitting with his back to her as she entered the dining room. Coincidentally, he jumped up precisely at the moment she carried the pie over him and his actions resulted in his head coming straight up into the bottom of the pie plate. The force of his head sent the dessert into a graceful arc from the top of his head to the middle of the dining room table—upside down.

There was a stunned silence for a moment. Then gradually a new attitude focused on salvaging the dessert. This led to discussions (read heated disputes) as to which would be the best way to rescue the upside down pie and keep it intact.

Some suggested simply removing the pie plate and encouraging all of us to dig in to the remnants with our forks. I had a more elegant solution. With the aid of steel flippers and various other kitchen tools, I suggested we slide them in between the upper pie crust and the tablecloth, thereby providing a means to support the pie. By lifting the pie with the use of the flippers, the entire mass could be turned over. In this way, the bottom of the pie plate could be returned to the top of the table with the pie resting in its intended position for cutting up and providing each diner with their fair serving.

We did this flawlessly. Well, almost. Some bits and pieces of the crust remained on the table and were gobbled up by the diners, thereby giving those who supported the earlier but lame suggestion an opportunity to illustrate their theory. With fork at the ready, I willingly participated. The pie was devoured in no time.

Every problem has more than one solution.

∞ Short Visit ∞

One summer day, Joy went to visit her mother in Oshawa, Ontario, and took our children with her. They called her their "Grandma Short." She had just been released from the hospital after being treated for a heart condition and was at home to rest following the doctor's orders. Joy's good friend was along for the visit with her youngest child, the peanut butter boy. They had known each other since grade school, and my mother-in-law welcomed the opportunity to visit with both of them and their children.

The peanut butter boy and my sons, Richard and Steven, were playing outside in the tiny backyard of my mother-in-law's property. There wasn't much in the way of toys, but the frame garage with its unpaved floor and open studs, provided an area in which a variety of leftover boxes and materials were stored. This environment was more than enough to keep the average little boy, or boys, entertained for a day.

The 'boystress' antics of these three children playing in and out of the garage gave rise to a memorable game of hide and seek. As Richard counted from inside the somewhat rundown, openly-shared garage, Steven and his friend ran to hide. Their travels took them to a place previously forbidden by the moms—the neighbour's backyard.

In an attempt to arrive 'home' and shout "home free" before the counter, Steven and his partner in crime ran into the garage through a hole in the wall on the neighbour's side. They had to duck under the neighbour's tree that was partially blocking the rotted opening. Steven lowered his head to go under a branch and got through the makeshift entrance of the metal clad wall in quick order. Unfortunately, another wooden hurdle—the cross support bridging between the studs—was unforeseen and well intact. While following close behind, the youngest participant of the game discovered this structural feature of the garage as his forehead smashed into the unforgiving wooden bridging as he darted into the garage behind Steven. The game came to an equally abrupt close, only moments after it had begun.

The flow of blood was horrendous. However, our little friend remained conscious as he staggered around the tiny backyard like a drunken soldier holding his head. His efforts did not contain the flow of blood, which continued to spurt through his fingers and drizzle all over his face and into his eyes. Not seeing or thinking clearly, the three of them agreed, as most children do when fearing reprisal, to act in a cooperative manner to prevent their mothers from learning of their predicament.

The plan, as they later explained, was simply to clean up the blood. This was a challenging task as the injured party initially refused to stand still for his accomplices as he danced in pain. Later, he became most cooperative when my two boys explained they were helping him keep the news of his injury from his mother.

Presumably, Richard and Steven felt that the blood could be cleaned up and that somehow, later, the problem would go away. They asked for paper towel from the adults in the kitchen, and each time returned to the scene of the crime to mop up. My children took turns requesting the necessary wipes. The injured one did not dare go inside. Instead, he remained content to hide behind the garage and peak around the corner while awaiting the next delivery of paper rags.

Soon, Steven had to make further requests for more paper towelling, and Richard agreed to go inside to talk to the others in hopes of distracting them. Gradually, the identical call for "a couple pieces of paper towel" triggered a different response from those in the kitchen. This time, despite Steven's appeal being relayed in the same casual manner, it was not granted. All three mothers asked, "What do you need all this paper towel for?"

Steven made a lame attempt to protect his bleeding buddy (and himself). He simply responded, "For the blood." This instantly transformed casual interest into an alarmed concern. With fading hope in their voices, they questioned further. "Whose blood?"

Steven continued to be evasive and responded with, "It's okay, it's almost all cleaned up." This did little to alleviate the growing concern. Stunned, Richard sat at the table unable to change the subject again. As the mothers looked around the small room, it soon became apparent that all of the visitors were accounted for except one. There was a rush to the door.

The sight of the numerous blood-soaked paper towels would have sent the average mom into a tizzy. Fortunately, peanut butter boy's mom was somewhat used to the sight of his blood, the circumstances of which often took them to the Hospital for Sick Children, close to where they lived in Toronto. In fairness, their need to seek medical attention frequently involved contributions from our family. As Joy gathered up the makeshift rags the injured child's mom did what should have been done immediately—she stopped the bleeding.

Unlike most of their previous trips to the emergency ward, in Oshawa the mothers were asked to accompany the injured child while he was repaired. Being forced to witness the stitching up process only added to their uneasiness. During the trip home, all of the children received a lecture. The subject of which was that any wound where the bone is visible should be reported to parents or other authorities, regardless of what the Fearnley boys say.

This episode did little to help my mother-in-law who was at home to relax her strained ticker. The visit was intended to be calm, restful, and enjoyable. Instead it had been cut short and Grandma Short was left to deal with additional worry on her own. I can picture her waving goodbye, her hand over her heart, her face pale with concern, hustling her visitors out the door on their way to the hospital.

If by accident you expose your friend's skull, take the time to tell his mother.

∞ Port Dover ∞

When my children were younger, we had an aquarium in the recreation room of our home. The large room was decorated in Olde English décor, had a magnificent stone fireplace, and a convenient walkout to the backyard patio. We commonly referred to the aquarium as our "hundred gallon tank." There was a lot of water to maintain as it was about three feet long, two feet wide, and two feet deep. Serving as a focal point in the open area of the room, it was big enough to accommodate fish larger than the traditional tropical miniatures. The entire family took pleasure in selecting and stocking the tank with fish large enough to see and appreciate from a distance and throughout the lower level of the home.

Our collection of fish consisted of many creatures of beauty from domestic waters. We set driftwood and plants into the gravel bottom and added floating weeds in the tank. At times, the algae was allowed to grow for the benefit of smaller fish. However, many of my friends and family were not impressed with our focus on achieving a natural habitat for our swimming guests. Some felt the aquarium looked dirty and unkempt. Public perception forced me to clean the glass from time to time—especially just before parties.

I had always felt that the Ontario sunfish with its bright orange belly, blue and green back, and other vibrant coloured markings, were every bit as striking as any tropical fish. We stocked our tank with many other members of the piscatorial family. More than one sample of the bass, trout, and pickerel families were often included. We had catfish, whose calm bottom feeding nature helped keep the water clean, and fish that were not fish at all, like crayfish and fresh water muscles who were also 'invited' to make it their home. These, along with the continual aeration filter, were included to create a self-contained ecosystem.

Our family enjoyed fishing together. Rods, reels, and watertight buckets stored in the trunk of the family car were staples on any outing—which more often than not turned into fishing trips. The combination of having the buckets on hand

and the aquarium at home allowed me to respond positively to my sons' frequent requests of, "Can we keep him, Daddy?" Almost anything they caught, regardless of its make, model, or year, was considered for transport back to the house. In fact, because we were often fishing to stock our aquarium, we practiced a relatively unusual routine of throwing the big ones back.

Our water world was designed to be an educational benefit to all. I wanted my boys to understand the rules and regulations of angling and what types of fish could be legally kept, and why. This environment was created to teach the children a few things about fish. However, I learned a few facts myself.

One belief my family had was that a fish would die if it swallowed a hook. I explained that this is not so. I demonstrated this by setting an unlucky sunfish free in our aquarium with the line cut away and the swallowed hook left in place. It took a few days for the acid in its digestive system to dissolve the barb on the end of the hook so that the fish could spit out the unwanted remaining metal. My sons understood from firsthand experience how a fish could be saved by using this procedure.

We also learned many other helpful facts regarding the fish we caught. Our first trip home taught us that most fish need oxygen. Another trip demonstrated that well water has very little oxygen. Subsequent trips illustrated that some fish need more oxygen than others. We also discovered that no matter how many healthy fish you have in your aquarium, natural driftwood can be infested with dreadful parasites that can kill every living thing in your tank within a week.

Other interesting points worth noting were that every aquarium has a bully, and that getting rid of one bully only promotes another. Perhaps the most disturbing fact of all was that big fish *always* eat smaller fish. Consequently, there was a continuous need for fishing trips to replace our bloodthirsty creatures of beauty.

One time when the population of our aquarium had been significantly depleted, we headed for the Lake Erie watershed. This was an area known as a habitat for several types of fish not readily available nearby. We wanted to add variety to our aquarium, so we decided to go on a day trip and fish in Port Dover, near Ontario's Long Point Provincial Park on the north shore of Lake Erie. This area is known for its large commercial fishery. Local merchants typically sell fresh fish and other seafood from their stores. Many have large tanks—some even larger than ours—with live fish for sale, which I intended to exploit to enhance the stock of our aquarium.

In one store we visited, I tasted various samples of their products from those offered on the counter displaying fish that were no longer swimming. As we were leaving the fish morgue, I was asked to try some of their smoked salmon, which the owners considered one of their specialties. It had a crumbly texture that melted in your mouth, with meat that was delicate but full of flavour. Obviously it had been smoked by a master and was the best I had ever tasted.

Curious, I inquired as to how it had been prepared. The young woman serving me stated in a straightforward way, "We use corn cobs for the smoking process." I was amazed at how creative and resourceful this was, and asked, "Where on earth did you get that idea?" She answered, "Well, my mother is Native Canadian." I guessed from her matter-of-fact reaction that her family had been doing this for hundreds of years, long before my ancestors had even learned about her country.

Sometimes the best discoveries are those that are re-discovered.

∞ Small Talk Anyone? ∞

At the beginning of this book we indicated that our memories are often recounted over the course of a Sunday dinner—often sharing them with others. In the past, throughout a normal week, our daily life experiences were shared with each other at mealtime. It was a habit for our family to sit down and eat together, a custom that appears to be long gone. I believe that today, people tend to prioritize family time around their own schedules instead of families meeting together to schedule their priorities.

At our family meals, we were able to apprise each other of our activities, whether they concerned our attendance at various school functions, visits to grandparents, or other family outings. Mealtime became an opportunity for us to ask about each other, provide advice, and encourage one another.

I found some of my children's plans and requests shocking, but likely no more so than that which any other parent receives. I learned of their trials and challenges by a continuous flow of information inspired by their active and imaginative young minds. Unfortunately, we were usually advised about their more impulsive acts after the police showed up. Other enforcement agencies also came to know our family in a formal sense.

Typically we had sedate discussions during our meals, but we always had fun sharing our lives. Over the years I had heard of many mind-boggling schemes that were being hatched.

Mealtime was ideal for coordinating events that involved the entire family. Our children were encouraged to participate in the decision making process. One night, we had agreed on a date and time that we could all get together with another family without interfering with any of our individual plans. While finishing our dinner with the rest of my family still sitting around the table, I telephoned our friends to finalize these arrangements. I had assumed that my friend Henry had already worked things out with his family.

He was not home. When the lady of the house answered, I politely began talking about mundane everyday topics. We discussed the weather, current events, the actions of local politicians, and how our kids were doing at school. We talked for several minutes, but I was anxious to speak to her husband to finalize the arrangement for our visit. The trite conversation ended when I asked, "Is Henry home?"

Hesitantly, she asked, "…Who's…Henry?" Equally puzzled I asked another question, "Who's this?" I learned that it was someone who did not know Henry. Unbeknownst to me, I had dialled the wrong number.

We both signed off abruptly with an apology from me and shared embarrassment over our mindless chatter. Although it was a sincere effort on my part, I'm sure she didn't believe this to be the case since the other four members of my family were hooting with uncontrollable laughter in the background.

If you're going to have a chat, take the time to find out who you're talking to.

∞ Ted's Favourite Pie ∞

At the lodge, my aunt Pearl often served sour cream pie. As a youngster, I enjoyed it immensely and sour cream pie became my favourite pie for many years. In essence, it was like eating a giant butter tart.

Following my uncle Ted's death, my aunt Pearl lived on her own, and when I visited, she made my favourite pie with pride. She would always ask if I wanted more, in a confident tone that clearly indicated her anticipation of a resounding "yes." My reply was always, "Oh, I'll have a second piece." And, when I was a child, I would add "just to be polite" as a jocular ending, since anyone present knew that I would have eaten the entire pie if given the chance.

Much later, I realized that dosing oneself with as much sugar as was in Aunt Pearl's sour cream pie was not healthy. In fact, over time I had consistently decreased the amount of sugar in my diet to the point where I could just barely consume a sliver of it.

However, after my change of heart, I still repeated the same closing words to Aunt Pearl, but they now had a new meaning—the truth. So as not to hurt her feelings, I continued relaying them as if nothing had changed. And I would often eat two large pieces of lovingly prepared sour cream pie.

In truth, I have always enjoyed all of her other pies. Her fruit pies were delicious, from deep plum to gooseberry and back again, including the all-time North American favourite, apple pie. She was always anxious to please others and I have never forgotten her customary desire to please me. I chose to maintain my charade to honour her until the day she died on October 21, 1995.

Love is…swallowing your pride for the sake of others.

∞ Fruit Stand ∞

As a Transportation Planning Consultant, I worked on many large projects—in earlier times as a member of a large team and later as a chief planner. One of the jobs of which I am especially proud was a project in Windsor, Ontario. It was the re-design of Huron Church Road, a major arterial road linking Highway 401 to the Ambassador Bridge International Crossing through the City of Windsor.

In 1979, this route had a nasty reputation with many Windsor residents in the west end. They preferred to forgo the traffic hassle, primarily leaving the route for tourists headed to and from the USA.

Because of the many motels, gas stations, fruit stands, and tourist attractions, the city was concerned that they would face a barrage of lawsuits for lost revenue if the re-design of the road were to prevent left turns into any of these individual businesses. One of the city councillors could not believe that the project should be a priority. He was taken out on a trip to illustrate the typical traffic problems on Huron Church Road. The highway engineer in charge of the project, who understood the need for the road's improvement, gleefully recounted their experience. The councillor was very nearly physically sick within a few minutes. The entourage missed several close calls with other vehicles. It was reported that when they finally turned off the roadway, the councillor's face had a distinctly greenish pallor.

I suggested a time-lapse photography study to record the turning traffic and to support these findings with interview surveys that would establish travel patterns and typical expenditures made by those using Huron Church Road. I pointed out that we would be creating a foundation from which the extent of business could be assessed for any that felt they had been adversely affected by the city's new construction. The data would provide a base that could assist with legitimate claims while discouraging frivolous ones. The city agreed and authorized my time-lapse study.

It was quite a project. With the assistance of a bucket truck, eight time-lapse cameras had to be fastened high in the air on streetlight arms or telephone poles, and focused on commercial driveways along the road on both the east and west sides. Eight-millimetre film was used and set to snap one frame every two seconds, which meant that a single reel could encapsulate two hours of roadway and driveway action. This also meant that the timing for removing and replacing film, restarting the camera, and identifying the location by means of a clapper, had to be completed for all eight cameras in about two hours (or fifteen minutes per camera). One reloading cycle of the study area took exactly two hours. We spent the seventy-five hours of time-lapse work driving the study area in continuous circles from 7:00 a.m. to 10:00 p.m. over the five consecutive-day study period.

Starting at Prince Road, we would go south to Fred's Fruit Stand to reset the first four cameras, then loop back northbound to Totten Road, performing the same functions for the balance of them. In addition, 2500 interview surveys to assess travel patterns and purchase costs at various establishments had been planned to support the time-lapse work.

Before any of this took place, I had to determine a location for each of the cameras. As a courtesy, prior to the official start of the surveys, I approached several property owners and renters to explain my reasons for being there. Although in most cases I was on city property and did not need their permission to install a camera, I preferred to ask for it anyway. I did this as a means of introducing the study and my corresponding responsibilities. This gave those occupying a property a chance to ask questions and offered me an opportunity to gain additional information from them.

Because of the nature of the bucket truck tasks, I was not dressed in my usual business attire. I had traded in my three-piece suit for casual business wear. This dress code was better suited for the work I was doing and the casual discussions associated with it. The process of contacting business owners prior to venturing close to their property usually prevented misunderstandings. In fact, I made some friends. I still visit Fred, a friendly fruit stand owner from the area. However, in one instance trouble arose.

As I approached a different fruit stand owner, I remarked sympathetically that it must be tough trying to make a living selling fruits and vegetables. This was a sincere comment as I have always had sympathy for farmers and their plight when a new highway threatens to cut through farms or cut off established farming patterns. Unfortunately, in this case, the owner exploded into a tirade of just how much money he was earning and that he "…had more money in the bank than I would ever see." As he ranted on, I tried to apologize. This angered him further. He ratcheted up his invective to a new level. By this time I figured that if he ever settled down it was very unlikely that I would be able to install a camera at this ideal location.

Then my adversary challenged me and I made a serious mistake. Somehow he got onto the subject of who had more money in their wallet, and by this time I was seriously annoyed. I had considerable cash on hand for the study staff payroll. So, I responded. I laid a wad of cash onto a handy nearby orange crate. This was neither smart nor a thoughtful move. I was immediately subjected to a rain of gravel he picked up from the shoulder of the road. I barely managed to grab the staff's wages before retreating as he continued to fling stones at my retreating back. Next, he ran to his house to unchain a rather large German shepherd dog that appeared to me to be at least as angry as his owner. The speed of my retreat increased.

A couple of hours later, while my staff and I were setting up a camera on the adjacent property to the south (focused on the angry owner area), we heard the scream of police sirens and to our surprise the cruisers came to a stop in front and to the rear of our bucket truck—effectively eliminating any chance for a high-speed escape. Actually we did not have any idea as to why they were there so an escape was not even considered. They asked for "the guy in charge" and I walked over to see what the problem was. I was told that I was being arrested for something but his words were so ambiguous I was not sure for what or why.

In an attempt to explain my reason for being there, I referred to some of those involved in the study. I gave him the name of the Director of Public works, the City of Windsor's senior road engineer who was in charge of the project, and the names of the consultants for whom I was doing the work. Unfortunately, although these were my business contacts—at seven o'clock in the evening—they were not available. I later learned that the arresting officer viewed my references as name-dropping in an attempt to avoid arrest. He was half right—I had no time for being arrested. The cameras were still ticking. After listening to more police gobbledygook, I ended up with handcuffs on my wrists and a non-too-gentle forced ride in the officer's cruiser to a downtown police station.

There, I was told by the sergeant in charge that a complaint had been made about my "threat to blow up a fruit stand." This was unbelievable news. I just stood there and gaped in astonishment at the officers. I was left alone to stew in my confused state for some time. Upon their return, they seemed to be dithering about whether or not to charge me. The cameras were still snapping away, which helped bring my patience to an end. I too snapped and finally told them to get on with charging me properly so that I could get back to my fieldwork and institute my false arrest lawsuit immediately thereafter. In hindsight, I did not pass the attitude test. But, I was released and driven back to the site once they had decided not to lay any formal charges.

Shortly thereafter, I contacted a lawyer who made a formal complaint to the police on my behalf. The local police department responded by calling for an official inquiry. Later, I learned from my lawyer and others that my angry fruit stand owner was—and had always been—known to the police as one of the local crackpots. This was something my lawyer emphasized at the inquiry. During one exchange, the arresting officer justified his vague reasons for the arrest. Obscurity was his personal policy. This gave him sufficient latitude to increase the severity, and possibly the number of charges, once he arrived at the station.

Throughout the hearing, this police officer stressed again and again the seriousness of my "bomb threat." It appeared as if he felt the accusation justified his actions. My lawyer allowed him to babble on for some time elaborating on his concerns and the importance of his report. To which my lawyer asked one simple question in front of the high-ranking officials and the panel of senior officers: "And what did you do with this extremely important information?" The response came softly and in a hesitant tone, "Uh...I um...put it in my sergeant's in-basket." My lawyer had no further questions. In truth, his question and the officer's subsequent sheepish response made it clear that there had been no need for the Keystone Cops run-around.

I had learned early in my career that the difference between a good survey and a bad one is how it is executed. If preconceived notions are maintained throughout the process, they become influential and consequently taint the results, making them of little use. To be a good researcher one must put aside any preconceived beliefs. Otherwise, any information that supports their preconceptions is readily accepted and data that would logically lead to different conclusions tends to be ignored. This practice can become especially dangerous in police work.

As for my situation, the arresting police officer failed to put aside his prejudiced beliefs. This was not tunnel vision. It was worse. In his case there was a cognizant dismissal of relevant facts.

Like anything else, there is good and bad in everything, including police forces. My experience has taught me that the best investigators refrain from the temptation to prematurely answer the question "Who dun it?"

Now, more than twenty-five years later, each time I am in Windsor, I still make a point of stopping to visit my friend Fred. In contrast, I now make a point of passing two things—the location of my least favourite fruit stand operator, and subsequent attitude tests.

Making a point is not worth making an enemy.

MY THREE SONS

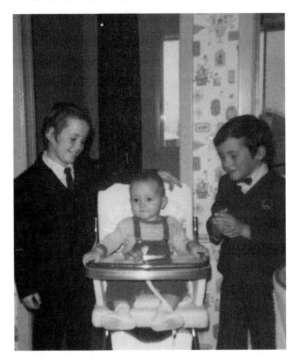

In the early part of 1980, Joy and I parted ways after nearly twenty-three years of a marriage that, among other things, produced three children: Richard, Steven, and Jamie. When we separated, Richard was eighteen, Steven fifteen, and Jamie was almost ten. The breakup was painful, but we both understood that the well-being of our children should be our uppermost concern.

Although there were some hard times for both of us, Joy and I have managed to remain civil and have avoided the rancour, acrimony, and outright malice that many divorced couples and their families are forced to endure. In the interests of our sons, we kept our emotions in check during the times it was necessary to communicate with each other, and perhaps more importantly, during our conversations with our children. To this day we are able to converse amicably.

Our three sons stayed with me for a short while after the separation, but Jamie soon announced that he wished to live with his mother. Arrangements were made, and within a week she was looking after him. Later, as part of our separation agreement, I purchased a townhouse for them. They lived there together for many years.

This chapter deals with my three sons from my first family, broken into three sections—one for each son. The sections are consistent with other chapters in this book. Individually, the stories in each of the sections are in chronological order but not necessarily from one section to the next.

Consequently, the first section of this chapter focuses on Richard, the second on Steven, and the last on Jamie. Although each section is devoted to a specific son, other family members, by necessity, intrude as a part of each story.

Also, because they are *my* sons, they are referred to with their given names of Richard, Steven, and Jamie. Later, in Part Two, Richard and Steven are referred to with the names they chose for themselves in adulthood: Rick and Steve. And, as for my youngest, Jamie…will always be Jamie.

SECTION ONE: RICHARD

Richard is my first born. He is more than the co-author of this book—he was the driving force behind it. If left to work on it alone, my approach would have been to find years of 'necessary' work that "had to be done," before spending time writing any family chronicle for posterity.

When I was growing up, I was credited as the 'star' in a number of eccentric escapades. However, from my perspective, Richard has exceeded my hard work by several degrees. It is often said that the student will surpass the master. But, since Richard was not around when my brother and I were confounding my parents, this could not be the case. This tends to support his theory: there may be a mutant gene in the Fearnley lineage responsible for our idiosyncrasies. I refuse to accept this, believing it to be too convenient an excuse. Everyone knows you should blame your troubles on your mom—not your dad. Besides, I think my first born is far worse than me.

In truth, he could hardly be thought of as a student of

mine. Until he entered the national labour force, he never was a committed student. After all, what can you say of a lad who in grade six English class wrote a book report about a famous hockey coach's autobiography, refused to consider editing his first draft, and then resubmitted the project every year up to grade twelve as his annual book report.

In addition, he took various excerpts from it in unmodified large chunks and unceremoniously hacked them into other essays to support every other subject except gym class. Such notable titles included: "The *History* of Hockey," "The *Mathematics* of Hockey," "The *Geography* of Hockey," and even "A *Social Study* on the Cultural Effects of Hockey." In fact, the originally submitted manuscript may be still hovering around somewhere in his home…"just in case."

Richard's education has come from the school of hard knocks, learning from his own mistakes and from those of his associates—the good, the bad, and the truly nasty. Richard's intelligence grew when his desire to read increased. This book is evidence of his transformation.

Today, I marvel at the guy who sat beside me throughout the writing of this book and would not let go of a single sentence until, in his mind, we could do no better. Then after returning to his daily routine, would revise a couple of words that he felt could have been worded just a little better. He now has a keen interest in words, their meanings, synonyms, and antonyms. With his study of punctuation, ably assisted with a small book on the subject by a successful British author, he has become a "stickler" for the art. Fortunately, this has assisted us enormously in the preparation of this book—our greatest writing challenge to date.

I have learned many things while writing this book with him. Partially because I had resolved long ago to accept advice from all of my sons as they grew into adulthood—mainly because my elders would not. Once, when I was leaving a restaurant after stopping for coffee on a trip to Kemptville, my mother reminded me to "Go to the bathroom." I was in my forties. I resolved then and there never to be condescending toward any children—especially if they were over thirty-five. Early on, I realized that even the very young can make contributions to one's learning. Unfortunately, we miss these opportunities if we have not embraced such a concept. This is not to say that I always achieve this somewhat lofty goal—but I try.

∞ Milkman ∞

Richard was always eager to help, whether in the workshop with me or in the kitchen with his mother. I remember setting an unopened one-gallon can of paint on the workbench so that he could sit and watch as I tinkered. He would lean towards me to ask questions and discuss the projects at hand, being careful to keep his bum on the lid. It's such a fond memory for me.

In the kitchen, Richard loved to help his mom when she prepared her own jam or baked fresh pastries. He had learned that doing so almost certainly gave him the chance to lick a spoon or sneak pieces of fresh apple before they made it into her pie. Cleaning out any filling that remained in the mixing bowl was every bit as pleasurable for him as eating the finished product.

Sometime in 1964, when Richard was between two and three years old, my family, along with Joy's parents, were having a roast beef dinner in the kitchen. The menu consisted of roast beef, potatoes cooked around the meat in the same pan, and garden vegetables. We were having one of my favourite desserts—fresh berries.

My mother-in-law, "Grandma Short," preferred her berries with cream. Our family was well prepared for her after dinner request of said topping. In fact, we had ensured that a full pint of cream was in the house. Richard had been told to leave it alone so that there would be plenty for his grandmother to enjoy at dinnertime.

As our main course came to a close, and the berries were placed on the table, Richard's grandma asked if we had any cream. When she made her request, Richard proudly exclaimed, "I'll get it for you Gamma."

When Richard ran to the refrigerator to get his grandmother the pint of cream, he opened the door, reached for the carton, tucked it under his arm, and triumphantly strutted back to the table. Cries of alarm immediately arose on his return because he was carrying the container with the open end down. He was inadvertently pouring cream onto the floor behind him.

When Richard swung around to see what the excitement was

about, he forced the cream to spew out in an extended arc, which added to the trails of cream between him and the fridge. Everybody in the room was trying to get his attention, but the subsequent motion of his abrupt back-and-forth turns in an attempt to see what was causing the glugging sound, caused him to slip and fall into one of his self-made puddles.

I jumped up to get him, grabbed the carton of cream, and righted it. With Richard standing by my side, I illustrated the fact that the carton was open by tipping the final ounce out onto the floor for added effect. As I did this, I said, "Richard, the carton was open. Look at the floor." My actions brought the audience to a greater emotional peak but I was not concerned. The milk store was only a few minutes away.

Leaving the women to wipe up, I headed out for more cream after changing the milkman's clothes. The oily mess was in its final stage of clean-up when we returned. And, it seemed as if Grandma Short's efforts to help served to increase her appetite for berries and cream.

Help comes in many forms.

∞ Sunday Dinner ∞

Family stories aren't the only topics discussed at family dinners (though it might seem that way). Early in my fathering apprenticeship, every dinner was a chance for me to discover things that my children had done. Sometimes I would learn about what they had achieved on that day, while on other occasions I would learn of their adventures long after the fact. In most cases, these events from the past denied me the opportunity to influence the outcome. By the time "Dad found out," it was usually too late for him to do anything about it.

Normally, a mother-in-law or two and various aunts attended our Sunday dinners. On one particular occasion, the dinner party consisted of our family, my mother, Grandma Short, and three of our favourite aunts. The average age of our visitors gathered around the table was about sixty-six. Everyone was enjoying their meal and the dinner conversation, which was providing a forum for childhood stories as it had so many times before.

Richard was about five years old and made a bold attempt to break into the conversation by asking, "Daddy, where do babies come from?" There was a deafening silence. Suddenly, all eyes—accompanied by knowing smiles—focused on me. Everyone was anticipating my answer.

I wasn't worried. Richard had a special knack for obtaining enough information to satisfy his curiosity. Previously, he had startled his nursery school teacher with a drawing. The children in the class had been given a chance to colour and allowed to draw anything they wanted. Drawing a tree, the sun, a house, some clouds, a dog or pet, a lake or campground, or even a group of people such as their family, would have been acceptable. Instead, Richard chose to draw his penis, which he always called his "toilet." He did this with alarming regularity. Once when a polite educator encouraged him to draw "something else," he drew another bigger penis next to the first one and offered his explanation. "This is my toilet and that is Daddy's toilet."

When this was first brought to my attention, I did what every responsible parent would do when faced with such an awkward situation. I ignored the problem. I was simply too embarrassed to attempt justifying his 'art'. I'm sure this did little to comfort the teacher's concerns as to how our children were being raised. Perhaps I should have at least said goodbye.

Now, sitting at the dinner table, I knew Richard's curiosity had to be addressed. I sat there feeling as if I was on stage performing a monologue at a theatre-in-the-round. My relatives, my audience.

In my best talk-to-a-five-year-old voice, I explained about the animals. For a baby to be born, I said, there had to be both a male and female present at conception. Everybody else at the table could see that Richard's mind was digesting this news and knew it would lead to other questions. It did. He soon asked, "Daddy, do you have to be married to have a baby?" I fell back to my 'animal' instincts and said, "No, it only takes a man and a woman." There was a very long pause.

Although I had maintained a serious tone throughout these general explanations, I did not dare look at anyone else as I was on the verge of losing my composure and breaking into hurls of laughter. All eyes were on me, still gleaming with anticipation. No one was quite sure if Richard was satisfied. A hint of laughter and snickering echoed beside me. I chose to keep silent, hoping that the next question would be about hockey or anything other than procreation. But knowing Richard as well as we did, he wouldn't stop until he fully understood. I worried about how this might manifest itself in Richard's next piece of art.

Richard cleared his throat. We all leaned forward. His next pronouncement was, "Well…you would have to be awfully good friends."

When the tension broke, each of us disappeared into other rooms for a muffled but well-needed laugh.

Even young children have an instinctive desire to understand where we come from.

∞ Easter Celebrations ∞

One Easter, Joy and I had hidden a number of chocolate eggs around the house for the traditional egg hunt. Richard and his younger brother were both in public school and loved the annual search for Easter eggs. Typically, we each made efforts to help the son who was falling behind in the count. To even things up, I would often sneak one from Richard's collecting bowl and drop it into his brother's.

At times I would grab a few of the found eggs and re-hide them to prolong the excitement. Both of our children could have played well into the afternoon, but eventually we would all have to stop and account for every one of the sweet treasures. Each year we would finish the hunt by counting all of the cheap treats that had been found, and thereby avoid coming across a lost one many months later. I dreaded the thought of finding a chocolate egg melted into the carpet on a hot summer's day.

One year, Richard got the idea of drawing out the morning hunt by taking turns with his brother hiding the eggs. The plan, as I understood it, was that Richard would hide the eggs for his brother to find, and then later they would reverse roles. This worked well for the better part of the afternoon while I was able to provide some suggestions. Later, with dinner guests arriving, I allowed them to continue on their own with a specific number of eggs.

Most of the good hiding spots in the house had been used a few times already, and Richard had become somewhat challenged finding new ones. His younger brother was getting tired of the game and becoming more interested in a nap. Oddly enough, this provided Richard with an idea. The object of which was not brought to my attention until sometime after. For reasons known only to Richard, when my youngest fell asleep on his side, Richard placed a small chocolate Easter egg into his brother's ear.

As we worked away in the kitchen and prepared for our guests, the warmth of an ear melted away one of our holiday eggs. I am not sure what Richard was doing at the time I discovered this, but I do know it ended abruptly.

"What in God's name were you thinking?" I asked. In the past, Richard had been creative when it came to getting into trouble, but I usually had a relevant response. This time I was completely lost for words as I stood dumbfounded next to my chocolate covered son. It had melted so deeply into his ear I thought we might have to consult a brain specialist. Maybe I should have insisted on it and negotiated a group rate to include examining Richard's head as well.

Doctors in the emergency ward of the local hospital echoed my sentiments. Their looks of disapproval, however, were directed at me, not my first born. Profoundly logical statements were made. Things like, "Don't put anything smaller than your elbow in your ear" and "Keep chocolate in the cupboard." Believing that some people need instructions for anything, they jokingly suggested that "If not used correctly, chocolate Easter eggs can be dangerous."

I was not the one that needed a lecture. The one who desperately required correcting was Richard, but he was not on hand to provide sheepish looks as evidence of the truth. Instead he was at home 'celebrating' Easter with his mother—who was taking her turn in our bout of tag-team scolding. Unfortunately, there are few holidays from parenting.

__Not every trouble melts away.__

∞ Richard Be Nimble, ∞ Steven Be Quick

One spring day when I was getting ready to take my family out for dinner, I asked Richard and his brother to busy themselves while their parents got dressed. The boys decided to go outside and look for things to occupy their minds for the ten minutes or so that I said it would take. For them, like most kids in junior high school, ten full minutes without someone or something to entertain them would definitely make for a gruelling experience.

Not wanting to be faced with the depressing task of sitting still, they sought out adventure on their own. Looking around on our side lawn, they noted a consistent pattern of wasps entering a small hole in the ground. In days gone by, they had stomped on various wasp nests and then quickly ran for cover. They would wait a few minutes and then return to amuse themselves watching the fury of activity amongst their flying friends.

On this day, there were wasps flying in and out of an opening in the ground at the rear of the garage near the side door of our house. Understanding that the flying insects would react by stinging at least one of them, Richard carried on with his usual lack of forethought. He suggested to his younger brother that they throw dirt into the entrance of the nest and then run away. This time, they planned to watch the reaction from a distance. Richard then plugged the hole, to see what would happen.

Together they watched one wasp land and wander over the area where the entrance to the nest had been. It appeared to be somewhat confused, as if having received poor directions. Others arrived, exhibiting similar perplexity but made more aggressive efforts to reacquaint themselves with the access that up until a few moments ago had been fully operational. Still others turned up, and with each successive arrival, the group became increasingly agitated, working themselves into a fury. After a few minutes it appeared as if half of the occupants were trapped outside refusing to accept that they were unable to get in. The other half could be heard buzzing about inside the nest as if they were discussing a plan of action with those on the outside.

The wasps were obviously confused about what caused their predicament, when it had occurred, or why. Yet Richard was amazed at their uncanny instinctive ability to know *who* had caused their troubles. They had a short meeting before they attacked their enemies—my sons. It appeared to Richard and his brother that the swarm of angry critters had a strategic goal that could likely be summed up as "Let's get 'em."

Both of my sons ran for the car, but neither made it inside without a few souvenirs in the form of small penetrating needles of venom. Richard was stung in one ear a number of times. It had swollen to the extent that it was noticeably larger than its mate. They were both in obvious pain and discomfort, but Richard had received significantly more venom. While recounting this adventure, one where they clearly knew the risks, I asked, "Then why did you do it?"

No answer worth committing to memory was uttered. Meanwhile, my youngest was enjoying the fact that my eldest was in extreme pain. Perhaps it was some ironic twist of fate that evened the score after Richard had 'hidden' a chocolate Easter egg in his younger brother's ear, only a few years earlier.

If you know the consequences, why bear the pain proving the point?

∞ The Go-cart ∞

Richard was taking auto mechanics in high school and actually became quite proficient in motor repair—especially with small gas engines. His grandma Short was visiting from Oshawa and her car, a Datsun B210, sat in the driveway. Richard decided that, for practice, and as a favour to his grandmother, he would tune-up her car. With only a few parts left over and with little recollection as to how they fitted back together, her car had to be towed to a mechanic's shop so that Richard's tune-up could be rectified. Apparently, unknown to Richard, the motor had an unusual vacuum advance mechanism—specific only to Datsun.

Later, as his skills developed, he purchased and sold a couple of vehicles using our concrete driveway as a grease pit. He learned that a one hundred dollar car, with six hundred dollars spent on parts, allowed no markup for profit when sold for seven hundred dollars. It would have been better to have purchased a seven hundred dollar car that did not need repairs and sell it for exactly the same amount, because at least his time repairing it would not have been wasted. However, the process helped him understand that time is a valuable commodity.

Caveat emptor was his motto for the cars he sold. No need to trouble oneself about the angry calls from recent purchasers. Then came the Go-cart. Richard had decided to pursue his love of small gasoline engines. The unannounced purchase of this off-road vehicle caught me by surprise, but I made sure that Richard understood he could not drive it on the neighbourhood streets. I wanted him to get rid of it and told him that I felt it would be "too tempting" not to drive it on the road. His response was "But Dad…I promise I won't." Later, I realized that the entire conversation had been an exercise in wasted breath.

He worked on the motor and had it running smoothly before he decided to fix the rear axle, which had a kink in it. Richard decided that my best steel carpenter hammer would be the perfect tool for the job. His plan was simply to bash the axle until it was straight. When this failed to do anything but create a loud ringing in his ears, he smashed the axle with the shaft of the hammer. His approach must have shown some promise. He continued until the shaft of my hammer was badly bent and the head severely out of line. The axle, however, remained unscathed. Any handyman will appreciate the sort of challenge I faced each time I tried to hammer in nails with a hammer whose head was at forty degrees to the handle. Today, I only use screws.

Shortly after my hammer's passing, I was finishing a cup of tea when there was a knock at the door. The police were responding to a complaint. Richard had been out on the street, around the corner and out of sight, roaring around in the go-cart. Children had been begging for rides. It was obvious that Richard had succumbed to the temptation of experiencing some instant pleasure instead of focussing on the possible lasting repercussions of his actions.

He was nowhere to be found at this particular moment and the police wanted to speak to him. In a spirit of helpfulness, I got into the cruiser with the two constables to help search for Richard. I toured the entire neighbourhood from the back seat of the cruiser. Judging by the looks I was receiving, it was apparent that everyone thought I had been arrested. In an effort to assist the police find my son, I had inadvertently subjected myself to unprecedented neighbourhood gossip.

Near the end of my tour, upon smelling the odour of burnt leaves, my guides stopped behind the local library to investigate a group of school children that were smoking there. As the officers walked over to the group, I spotted my second oldest child, who was playing nearby on his bike but had stopped to see what the commotion at the library was about. I was able to catch his attention by pounding on the cruiser window and shouting, *"Get me out of here!"* With wide eyes and in a stunned state, he came to my rescue. He opened the door from the outside (cruisers, I found out, do not have handles on the inside of the rear doors) and I returned home on foot. My neighbours were either confident in the knowledge that I had not done anything to cause my arrest, or, near panic thinking that I had now escaped and was an even greater threat to the neighbourhood.

Just after I arrived back home, Richard showed up. The

police constables followed within a minute or two. We all sat down in the living room to 'discuss' the situation. The officers and I were trying to explain to Richard that he could not ride a motorized vehicle on public streets without insurance. In frustration, he cried out, "If they'd give me insurance, I'd buy it!"

Apparently, he had phoned various companies to inquire about purchasing insurance before venturing onto the tarmac. Equally frustrated (or perhaps more so than Richard), I remonstrated, "If the insurance companies *wanted* people to drive go-carts on the street, then they would have insurance for it."

Richard's response was a simple. "Oh." At last, he had begun to understand and accept the reasons for police concern. I suggested that Richard expand his used car salesmanship to include go-carts. Thankfully, the police officers who had been very understanding throughout the hunt, agreed.

Yielding to temptation can be a dead end on the road of life.

∞ **The Contest** ∞

When Richard was in high school, he bought yet another seventy-five dollar car. This time it was for delivering pizzas. It was one of his ideas for making money. Regrettably, keeping the thing running sucked up a considerable amount of his earnings. Richard remained dedicated to his business plan despite the constant repair costs. The concept had been to pay off the car with the money he earned from the delivery charges and tips, but the continuous maintenance expenses stretched the commitment of a casual job into a part-time occupation.

Instead of working a few nights during the week to earn his own money for the weekend, he ended up working Friday and Saturday nights as well—just to pay for vehicle repairs. Plagued with ongoing breakdowns, his first car became a re-occurring liability rather than a worthwhile asset. Still, Richard's tenacity kept him plugging away. Gradually, the earn-to-repair cycle frustrated him more and more, and with my encouragement, he began to look for different ways to make extra money.

I never expected him to come up with his get-rich-quick scheme of collecting milk bottle caps from the prevalent three quart jugs of milk typically sold at any food or variety store. Supposedly, for reasons known only to Richard, he thought that one day there would be a contest in which the caps from these milk jugs would be required in much the same way promotions encouraged customers to collect pictures of rock stars from cans of pop. I remember Richard saving bottoms of 7UP pop tins in an effort to collect pictures of all the band members from the popular rock group *Lighthouse*. All this in an effort to win a prize.

I believe the milk-bottle-top plan he conjured up had two major flaws. First, in the mid 1970s, the dairy industry was not known for excessive spending on aggressive marketing campaigns. Executives from various pop, soda, and other beverage companies, yes, but not dairy farmers. They've always had more important things on their mind. Generally, people drank milk as a habit, and there was barely a need for advertising such a product. Second, any company that promoted their product by means of a contest would use "specially marked" items to identify winners and control the number of contestants and chances to win. Therefore, the hoarding and stockpiling of unmarked milk bottle tops was nothing more than an exercise in futility.

Regardless, Richard plugged on. He filled his bedroom with various containers full of useless circular pieces of cardboard. Luckily, they had the word "Milk" printed on the top, which served to fuel his ridiculous unfounded hopes to being one up on everyone in the 'soon-to-be-announced' milk bottle top contest.

Although it has been said that anything can be a "collector's item," if ever there was not a collectors' item, I humbly suggest that this would be it. I repeatedly asked Richard, "When are you going to throw those dam' things out?" By the mid 1980s, I was still waiting. Some fads take a year or two to pass, but Richard's can last more than a decade.

I nagged Richard many times trying to force-feed him some intelligence during those years. I suggested, "If you're going to stock up for an event, try to assess the chances of the event occurring." In hopes of turning a light on from a different approach, I tried, "If you want to look for a needle in a haystack, take the time to find the right haystack." And finally, just before giving up, "If you're going to collect items for a promotion, why not wait for the contest to be announced." All of this was to no avail.

I have always believed the importance of a collection is in the eye of the beholder. For every collectable item there is at least one collector. Also, my experience indicates that for every collector there is at least an equal and opposite number of anti-collectors who consider such collectables nothing more than junk. Unfortunately, opposites attract and collectors have even been known to marry anti-collectors.

Having inherited a few objects over the past fifteen years, I have hung onto a variety of miscellaneous items from the estates of several members of my family. I've been accused of being a pack rat, but I prefer to consider myself a collector. As well, since I'm self-employed and have worked from a home office for more than thirty years, I haven't had any business requirement to "clear my desk" during this time.

Until some of my thirty-year-old newspaper articles *need* to be removed, I'm quite content to keep them where they are, for now, or if need be, for another couple of decades, thank you very much. Recently, I have seriously considered leaving my 'collections' for my children. If they want my desk cleared, *they* can clean it up.

The above account from Richard's adolescent years indicates that he might appreciate such a windfall. However, this is not the case. Our roles have reversed. Richard has come full circle and lovingly became a nagging pain in the butt, and my worst anti-collector. He habitually complained about the alleged "clutter" on my desk and the "mess" in my home office nearly every time we sat down to write this book. As you read this, he is probably still moaning and groaning.

One can treasure what others long to throw out.

SECTION TWO: STEVEN

Steven, my middle child, was born at Wellesley Street Hospital in Toronto after a panicky ride from the northern part of the city. He was my special gift for Father's Day in 1964. Steven has been larger than Richard for most of his life. This is possibly my fault. Not because of genetic disposition but rather because of a typo.

Upon the death of my father-in-law, Joy and I went to Oshawa to care for her mother. Two of my mom's sisters—my aunt Ida and aunt Babe—had offered to take care of our new baby, while we were away.

My aunts were both in their sixties and had lived together on their own without children since the death of their parents. To ease their workload, I provided them with specific instructions about caring for our infant. In the rush, I gave my aunts the wrong proportions for Steven's baby formula. The recipe called for two parts water to one part of the enriched powdered milk. In my haste, I inverted the ratio as I scribbled a number of instructions for them on our way out the door. They took care of him at our house for a full week.

When we got home, there was a blob of fat sitting on the chesterfield that was welcoming us upon our return. He was hard to recognize despite the fact that he was the only infant in the house. It was a good thing we had not been away for a month.

Throughout most of Steven's school years, he seemed to be growing faster (and became larger) than other children his age. I have always wondered if my mistake on the formula somehow provided a greater impetus for early growth.

Possibly because of his size, Steven had a penchant for fighting his schoolmates. Once, after being contacted by the principal, I explained to Steven that he had to control his temper—just as my aunt Pearl said to me at the lodge, when I was about twelve years of age. I explained that, next time, he should count to ten and his anger would dissipate somewhat and he would be better able to exercise self-discipline. He responded, "Okay, I'll count to ten and then hit him."

Eventually, he progressed to the extent that he actually broke up fights. One of my proudest moments occurred when Steven told me that his Chinese buddy and an African chum were fighting a lot. In my usual support for racial tolerance, I exclaimed that the fighting was very unfortunate—especially here in Canada. Steven replied, "It's okay, Dad. I told them if they wanted to be my friends they would have to stop fighting." They did.

Throughout high school, Steven assisted me with my professional work in my home office. He understood trigonometry and since he was well versed in mathematics, he was soon helping with drawings, travel analyses, and traffic distribution problems. However, although he expressed a great desire to continue working with me "for life," I explained in my best fatherly tone, that if I became ill in the future, he would not have any recognized skill to fall back on. He would need a formal education to continue working in the engineering field. Also, I felt that my line of work was quite limited and for many, only provided a livelihood that was barely comfortable. I wanted more for him, and all of my sons.

Once, when Steven was reminding me how much he wanted to stay at home and work with me, I explained that it is a parent's responsibility to encourage their children to develop skills so that eventually they can fend for themselves. He was somewhat disappointed with my comment, so to cheer him up I told him that I would cry a lot when he left but preparing him for adult life was something that I had to do for *him*.

Steven and I often pursued other common interests. His attraction to rocks and minerals paralleled mine. Upon completion of high school he soon left me on my own for the better part of a year to attend the Gemological Institute of America (GIA), in Santa Monica, California.

He did well. So much so that his instructors at the GIA believed (for a time) that he had to be cheating to obtain the marks he was receiving. As part of the final exams, students had to identify three separate trays of gems that had been studied during the course. Each tray would have a number of different precious and semi-precious stones. The course required that the students identify all of them correctly—on their own—in order to graduate. Since there was a rumour that Steven had cheated throughout the course, the instructors forced him to identify a group of additional gems. Three more trays were prepared specifically for him.

This made the number of identifications required for his graduation double that of any other student in his class. He breezed through the first five trays, but on one of the extra samples in the last tray he was stumped. He determined that the 'precious stone' had no other distinguishing characteristics than glass. Discouraged, he reluctantly labelled it as such and left the examination room.

It was a trick. There was supposed to be only samples of precious gems, semi-precious stones, and common materials like the glass that had been studied in the classroom. The school authorities had surreptitiously included a finished piece of glass with a lead content that was outside the range of the optical and physical properties that had been taught and studied in class.

Correctly identifying all of the unexpected pieces in their experiment proved he had *not* been cheating. They were convinced he would misidentify their impromptu inclusion and provide evidence for their unfounded beliefs—but their deceptive ploy failed. In fact, it was not long before someone from the GIA suggested Steven pursue a job opening as an instructor in their New York school. I believe it was simply his previous knowledge in trigonometry and a love for math and gems that helped keep him ahead of the pack.

Steven's trip to California took another unexpected turn when he met a young girl from upstate New York. He planned to move there to live with her after graduation. They married a short time later and gave me two grandchildren named Emily and Alex.

For the most part, the next chapter consists of memorable accounts from Steven's childhood in Toronto, Canada. These days, I hear less about his daily activities since he has lived most of his adult life in the United States. To date, living in different countries and the fact that he has a busy schedule has made it impractical to consider writing a book with him. Besides, no one could nag me to "get it done" as much as his older brother. Steven is now a full-fledged US citizen, and appears to be content to spend his life as a Graduate Gemologist and jeweller in Atlanta, Georgia.

∞ Safely Hidden ∞

Steven disliked vegetables. It was always a chore for me to get him to eat them. His older brother, on the other hand, begged for broccoli. It was Richard's favourite and I can still remember him asking for "More bwockidi pwease."

Steven hated broccoli from his earliest years. It topped his "yucky" list and was followed closely by cauliflower and peas. I remember one evening at our home in Burlington, Ontario, when Steven was about three years of age. Joy was serving dinner and had called everyone to the table. Steven had been playing outside in the backyard and came into the house through the kitchen door. Regrettably, the most direct route to the bathroom for a much needed clean-up paralleled the counter at which Joy was busy dishing up fresh vegetables. As he came into the kitchen, the aroma of cooked broccoli was vividly evident. The first step he took was accompanied by a loud and unpleasant regurgitative noise, which manifested itself into a series of repeated involuntary gags concurrent with each successive stride.

Gagging is a close cousin to vomiting. I am a sympathetic vomiter. It took Steven about a dozen steps to walk across the kitchen floor. Although I was very hungry when he entered the house, by the time he reached the bathroom I had lost my appetite. The retching sounds that he was unable to suppress became the focus of my attention. They continued for as long as the broccoli was on the table. Such dinner music did not add to my dining experience.

Soon after, our family moved back to Toronto. The change of scenery and another two years of challenging meals did little to improve our eating environment. The move had done nothing to reduce Steven's antipathy towards vegetables. Luckily, Steven had learned a few coping skills. For example, when it came to eating peas, he found that he could place a few on his tongue and hold them there for a moment while he drank large gulps of milk to wash them down. In this way he was able to swallow them whole and thereby eliminate any need to chew or taste them.

He developed this strategy into an extreme level of proficiency until he was able to stomach large spoonfuls of peas at a time. Unbeknownst to him, I had caught on to his ploy, and one evening waited until he stuffed his mouth with three spoonfuls of cooked, warm, mushy peas. When he reached for his ever present oversized glass of milk, I grabbed his wrist and prevented him from raising the drink to his mouth and simultaneously ordered him to "Eat 'em!"

He was unable to communicate any verbal appeal with his mouth so full. The stunned look on his face gradually turned to one of fear (from actually tasting one of the peas) and then agony as he struggled to swallow them—one at a time. I had had enough. Steven was instructed to finish his dinner in the next few minutes. I stipulated that if it were not done within this time period, he would have to take the remainder of his meal, along with his utensils, to the laundry room. Eventually his time ran out and he was ordered to eat the balance of his entrée in the basement. Then and only then could the rest of my family enjoy our dessert in the kitchen.

It was not until a few years later that I discovered the extent of distress I had put Steven through. It was zilch. My punishment should have been focused on correcting the problem. I needed to motivate Steven to rethink his position. Sadly, all I did was provide a way for him to escape the issue at hand. In truth, he was hiding his cheerful feelings from the entire family by acting marginally disappointed each time I relegated him to 'fine dining' in the laundry room. He had embraced my punishment for many years and I did not discover why until the day our washing machine broke down.

I was preparing for the serviceman by pulling the washer and dryer out from the basement wall for easy access. I instantly realized that sentencing Steven to eat in the laundry room only served to provide him with a unique opportunity. It appeared as if he passed his time by making a game of throwing vegetables through the open legs that supported the laundry tubs. There was a disturbing amount of accrued garden produce distributed against the hidden portion of the wall behind and under the laundry tubs. Also, it was apparent that he had consistently disposed of any unwanted vegetables by inconspicuously dropping them behind the washer and dryer. As I removed each of the appliances from their long term positions, I recognized an alarming mixture of vegetables now well dehydrated and partially mummified from their dry home over the previous few years.

Steven's trick had worked many times because I was focused on my problem rather than his. In hindsight, I should have given him incentives to eat his food rather than simply disciplining him for ruining our meals. In my haste, I was focused only on my own concerns, and failed to see how the prescribed punishment could give rise to a different dilemma. I have since realized that fatherly care should always be dispensed with a spirit of helpfulness. Unfortunately, I did not understand this at the time and did not apply this principle in my efforts to solve the immediate problem. Treating the symptom rarely solves the problem. Any solution is only worthwhile if it constructively improves the overall situation.

By the way, Steven now enjoys all vegetables in his adult life. Ironically, believe it or not, broccoli has become his veggie of choice. Through some sort of happenstance, I must have done something worthwhile in his childhood. Either that or the laundry rooms at his favourite restaurants are absolutely unbearable.

Sometimes resolving one problem makes another one worse.

∞ The Wager ∞

Steven has a unique characteristic that was most prevalent in his younger years. He has been referred to as clumsy, awkward, maladroit, graceless, and uncoordinated. As one of *my* children, I prefer to think of him as merely somewhat ungainly. In my mind this sounds so much better. However, he is unquestionably the most accident-prone of the lot.

Steven has always been ready to lend a hand around the house from the time he was just starting school, and was especially helpful to his mom in the kitchen. In those days, the dairy industry was transitioning their packaging from the customary three quart jug of milk to flexible soft plastic bags. Some families had made the switch when the bags were first introduced, but our family preferred to use the traditional three quart jugs since we consumed so much milk.

Our family was having dinner at a friend's house, and in his usual spirit of helpfulness, Steven offered to help set the table. This family, like many others in this era, drank milk regularly. As a result, part of setting the table in their home was to ensure that there was lots of milk handy. Steven was somewhat unfamiliar with bagged milk.

Typically, there are only two simple steps to prepare the bags for use. One bag of milk would be placed in a slightly larger hard plastic container, which had a handle for pouring. A small snip at the exposed corner of the bag, once it was in the container, provided a makeshift spout so that the milk could be easily dispensed into a glass or cup.

Steven carried the bag of milk from the fridge to the counter, where he laid it on its side, snipped the corner, and turned away to retrieve the necessary container. Mistakenly, he had inverted the simple two-step process. The milk spewed out and puddled on the kitchen floor, causing our hosts much grief. His attempts to save them some time cost us all a warm meal.

Ironically, another milk story occurred not much later, with the same family. This time they were at our home for dinner with us. They also had a son who exhibited somewhat graceless traits, similar to those of Steven. In the centre of our dinner table (unlike theirs) was a large lightweight plastic pitcher of milk that we filled from our still-available traditional three quart jugs. During the meal, the pitcher needed refilling and the two ungainly sons offered help. The offer was quickly refused by both sets of parents. As the father of the other boy returned from the fridge and filled the pitcher, he explained his reasons for doing so. "If my son doesn't spill it, Steven will."

Miffed at this comment, Steven instinctively reacted. "Wanna bet!" He quickly and forcefully extended his arm to invoke the handshake necessary to seal the wager and knocked over the full pitcher of milk in the process.

A frustrated mutter of "I rest my case" was heard as several of us scrambled for paper towelling. Steven had outdone himself once again. His impetuous move had reinforced his reputation.

Slow down; impulsive acts reveal our true selves.

❧ The Facts of Life ❧

When my children were young they had many favourite television shows. One of them was *The Partridge Family*, a single parent family who all played different instruments in their family's band. My boys, and probably several million other young lads throughout North America, found the eldest daughter very attractive. She was a wholesome and slender young woman, and as in most sitcoms, she took turns being the main character with the other members of the show.

One episode of particular interest to Steven was about this young girl buying her first brassiere. She often wrote about her daily life in her diary, recording both her thoughts and her actions. After recording the life-changing shopping trip in her diary, she misplaced it and discovered that one of her brothers had helped himself to her comments. This controversy provided sufficient material to fill the thirty minute show. Steven was enraptured.

At the end of the show, Steven asked me some awkward questions. I have always felt that a parent should not sit a child down to have a sex talk. Instead, I believe, at least when it came to my own children, that the most appropriate way to deal with the subject of sex was to simply answer their questions—when they were posed—as directly and discreetly as possible.

Earlier, with Steven's older brother, I treated each question asked of me with a concerted effort to address not only the question, but also the underlying motivation. I used proper names for body parts and maintained a serious tone during my responses. The time had come to answer some of Steven's questions.

His first inquiry led to many others, and before long he had received his official talk about the birds and the bees. I have always felt that adults tend to forget children are content with short responses. So I kept my answers succinct. I steered the conversation to systematically cover the series of changes a girl experiences as she becomes a woman.

I told him there would be things he would notice when a female evolves in this way. I added that there were other things occurring at the same time that would not be as apparent, such as hair growing in new places on her body as she matured. I explained how the discomfort associated with having her periods was necessary for her to conceive babies. I made a point of warning Steven about how this time of transition can be uncomfortable, explaining how this can be emotionally difficult for many. I reinforced that he should always be considerate to others, but even more so towards any young lady during such awkward times. I closed my thorough message by reminding him that he was welcome to ask me further questions if he wanted.

Although Steven had listened attentively during our discussions, he did have one question after I finished. He immediately asked, "What do the boys do…just sit around and wait?"

I thought the lesson had been complete, but his question reminded me that I had failed to include any information about boys becoming men. Our discussion began concerning females and did not venture from this because I maintained my policy of answering only what was asked. In doing so, I failed to relate the information to Steven in a tangible way.

Boys need facts about themselves too. The conversation continued. This time I relaxed my strategy of answering only what was asked. Interestingly, we both learned something worthwhile by the time we had finished our talk about "the facts of life." Steven's question taught me something worth noting.

No lesson is complete unless we learn something about ourselves.

∽ **The Naturalist** ∾

In the rush before Christmas in 1972, I wanted to do something very special for my family. The previous year in my transportation planning business had been a prosperous one. As a surprise, I decided to fulfill my long standing desire to visit Trinidad and Tobago. I packaged it as a once-in-a-lifetime vacation for the whole family to enjoy. How to wrap it?

I arranged for a two week journey that was to begin in Trinidad, take us to Tobago for a full week of sightseeing and fun, and then back to Trinidad for a couple days to relax before we flew home to Toronto. I planned this through a travel agent, who, in response to my special request, typed individual letters and addressed them to each member of my family. These form letters simply explained that accommodations had been reserved for our family holiday in the spring of the following year.

Then, I thought, this special type of present deserved a special type of delivery. I did not want to advise my family in what I believed to be a cool manner by simply handing them each an envelope on Christmas morning. So, I decided to devise a paper chase for the children. This was something that my aunt Pearl had done when my sister, brother, and I visited her in the winter holidays of our youth.

Each clue was written as a short four-line poetic riddle that had to be solved in order to find the next one. The hunt started out with an envelope on the Christmas tree in the family room, went upstairs into their bedrooms, outside into the garage, downstairs into the workroom, and then finally back to the Christmas tree on which there were three special packets. The packages included personalized form letters and tickets—one for each of our children.

By the time the kids returned to the Christmas tree, they were so excited they were bouncing up and down from the thrill of the chase. When the boys opened the letters and read what the tickets were for, they were ecstatic.

As the New Year dawned, a new calendar was placed on the wall and my sons took turns crossing off the passing days prior to our departure. On the day we left, the taxi arrived, our luggage was loaded, and the entire family packed into the cab. But, just as the driver pulled away from the curb, Richard called out, "Stop... I've forgotten something!" He jumped out of the car and ran to the house, with me following in a hurried state to unlock the door for him. Once inside, Richard ran to the kitchen, disappeared around the corner, and put the last "X" on the calendar. We were on our way.

However, there was a small incident as we waited in the lounge area inside the secured part of the airport. Steven had inadvertently added a new dimension of excitement for all of those eagerly waiting to board our aircraft and begin their Caribbean vacation. He had brought some toys from home to play with, and to pass the time in the waiting area he pulled one of them out. He chose to entertain himself with his plastic water pistol—a detailed replica of a German Luger.

Any child playing with a gun is enough to set off a panic. At the airport it can be complete pandemonium. I was standing nearby when the startled girls assisting the boarding passengers approached Steven. There was a slight delay while Steven was stripped of his war-like toys as we sorted things out with security.

Eventually, I was able to thoroughly enjoy exploring the islands, swimming in the surf, playing in the swimming pools, deep sea fishing, and hunting for land crabs. These experiences are still fond memories for all of us, especially since we spent it together. Ironically, one of the most memorable parts of the trip took place at the airport in Tobago on the way back to Trinidad. We were in the process of being checked in for our flight.

At the airport, I noticed that Steven's hair was quite messy. He was wearing a blue captain's hat but his locks were still noticeably dishevelled. Like a typical father concerned about appearances, I whacked the peak of his hat in an effort to remove it so that he could straighten his hair. When I did this, a full deck of souvenir playing cards were thrust into the air and fell all over the floor, surprising everyone in the small island airport, except Steven. The look on my face was one of confusion.

I was perplexed. He was holding what I thought was the deck of cards. I could clearly see a card container in his right hand. We had purchased this deck of cards for Steven earlier, because they were circular and had caught his fancy. They came complete with a round plastic case about three inches in diameter.

The bottom of the case was made of a coloured plastic. Its mate was a clear lid that was in a cylindrical shape with an edge about a half an inch deep that helped hold the special cards securely when it was on. It appeared as if the cards were well packed inside this container. However, a couple of playing cards on Steven's head and the balance of about fifty others spread about the floor, contrasted my assumption…and that of all the security guards who looked on with even greater interest. I was just curious, but they seemed more concerned.

As Steven hustled to pick up the cards, he was avoiding eye contact with me—fearing the obvious question, "What's in the card case?" Realizing he would be unable to answer the question in any acceptable way, Steven, rather sheepishly, removed the top of the case and the lone card that was underneath the lid. Inside was the largest beetle I have ever seen in my life. The hard-shelled wings were huge, its pincers enormous, and it had legs so long that they had to be scrunched up for it to fit into the cardholder.

I asked him why he would do such a thing. To which, at the tender age of eight, he replied, "I wanted to smuggle it through customs." I explained we were travelling within the same country and customs did not enforce imports between two parts of the same country. However, I did caution him that transporting a beetle from one island to another—even within the same country—could cause serious environmental damage. After Steven (et al) had picked up the cards, I spent the next few moments of my relaxing vacation stressed to the nines answering 'pointed' questions from the nice men with *real* guns.

Later, the airport officials agreed that the 'naturalist' could take his friend to Trinidad but not home to Canada. Steven demonstrated his love for small animals by gently playing with the enormous critter during the flight from Tobago to Trinidad.

Although I was upset with him at the time, I did not want to end our family's special holiday on a bad note. I chose to leave his embarrassment as punishment enough. Besides, I sympathized with him since his efforts to conceal his would-be pet seemed to parallel my initial struggle to keep the trip a secret.

The bigger the secret, the harder it is to keep under your hat.

∞ The Fire Within ∞

We once lived on a quiet residential street in North York, Ontario. The property was high on a hill and although our lot was only about one hundred and twenty feet deep, there were four distinct levels. The front curb to the back of the garage was one level. The entrances on both sides of the house were three steps down on a second level. From there, about a dozen steps down led to a third level, and the final level another five steps lower.

All of the stairs were made out of concrete, except for the ones that separated the two lowest levels. This last set of stairs was made of railway ties, giant pieces of eight inch by eight inch solid oak that are usually soaked in creosote to preserve them for a longer life in the field. After the ties are no longer suitable for their heavy-duty railway function, they are frequently recycled for use in other applications, such as commercial and residential landscaping.

In our split-level backyard, a retaining wall separated the third and fourth level and it was also made of used railway ties. They were weathered and nearing the end of their useful life as structural units of our dividing wall. Aiding in their deterioration were a number of different ant colonies all busily carving out their nests as the wood was extremely dry and quite pulpy in places.

The retaining wall held the earth in place with successive rows of used railway ties that had been staggered over top of one another. Each row was offset by about two inches from the one below. This design exposed ledges that offered visible evidence of the many ant colonies present. When Steven was about ten years old, the ants scurrying along these ledges intrigued him.

One hot summer's day, he had been using a magnifying glass to study his little friends. Somewhere along the line his love for bugs turned from that of observation and admiration, to one of being subjects for his entertainment. Steven noticed that the ants retreated abruptly when they were exposed to the rays of the sun through the magnifying glass. The more he concentrated the sunlight through the glass, the more violently the ants reacted.

He also discovered that the beam of sunlight could be

focused to such an extent that the intensity of the heat generated could stop them dead on contact. In fact, on the day in question, Steven perfected his art to the point that he could kill any little critter with ease. He would simply maintain a sharply focused beam on the railway ties, and wait for his next unsuspecting victim to pass along the exposed ledges, and into the spotlight.

Instead of playing with the creatures, as he was accustomed, Steven spent the better part of the morning practicing his newfound talent. He was zapping ants with alarming dexterity, when he was surprised to notice a small wisp of smoke. His interest increased. He decided to try this again in another location on the wall. This time he chose to keep the beam focused on an exposed piece of the dry wood. He did so until he had created another wisp of smoke. He continued decorating the wood with small burn marks—well into the afternoon.

Steven finally tired of this and decided to leave and play with one of his friends. While they were playing, Steven gave little thought to his previous actions. Eventually, he returned to the scene. The few wisps of gray smoke that had dissipated quickly had changed into numerous plumes of dark little clouds spiralling up into the air from the railway ties. Something had to be done immediately. Steven knew he had to act quickly to prevent the worst possible outcome—getting in trouble with Dad.

Steven went to the garden hose on the second level of the property, unwound it, and dragged it towards the smoking railway ties. He turned the water on and doused the wooden wall for several minutes until there was no sign of smoke. So as not to attract any undue attention, he was careful to rewind the hose and replace it in its original position. This may well have been the first time he ever put any of my tools back after using them. Steven then went off to play again. This was the second time that day he had tried to solve a problem by running away from it.

Around dinnertime, I came home from a business meeting. My meeting had not gone as well as I had hoped. However, that was consistent with how my day had been unfolding up to that point. We had a spectacular view because the house had been built on a hill and we could see downtown Toronto from this

Life's Lessons: A Successful Collection of Failures

part of our North York home. After dinner, I was trying to recuperate from my business setbacks and walked into the living room to relax and enjoy a fresh cup of tea.

I sat down to doze by the window and began to admire the cityscape. As I started to unwind, I noticed a hint of gray smoke. With my cup in one hand and the saucer in the other, I rose casually to investigate. I gazed about and my attention was drawn to the retaining wall—which was now smoking from more than one location. My immediate reaction was "What the heck is that?" I suddenly realized our backyard was on fire!

I rushed to the garden hose, which for the first time in history had been neatly rolled up by the previous user. I was puzzled by this but quickly moved on, recognizing that "where there's smoke, there's fire." I ran towards the smoke, calling for Richard and Steven to come and help before the retaining wall burst into flames. I was seriously concerned that the fire department would have to be called if we couldn't put it out ourselves. Steven was slow to arrive.

It didn't take long to understand what had happened. I discovered Steven's magnifying glass lying on top of the burning retaining wall just around the time he showed up. I was about to lose my cool, but I suppressed my anger for a moment. I was forced to deal with the danger at hand instead of acting on my compulsion to throttle Steven.

It took a great deal of time to snuff out the stubborn fire, which had been smouldering in the depths of the railway ties for the better part of the day. I rammed the garden hose into every hole in the rotting wooden ties in an effort to stop them from burning. The somewhat picturesque waterfall over the exposed edges of the railway ties did little to calm me down. I had drenched myself in the process of thoroughly spraying and soaking every piece of wood in the backyard. I was winning the struggle with the smouldering railway ties but losing the battle with the fire that was raging inside me.

I lost my temper. In my fury, I grabbed the magnifying glass, then Steven, and headed for my workbench inside. I went berserk and looked for a strong base upon which to smash Steven's fire starter. I selected the vice in the workroom, made of tempered steel. It was perfect. I held the handle of the magnifying glass positioning the glass portion on top of the vice and began hitting it with a hammer. I smashed it to smithereens while simultaneously subjecting Steven to the balance of a much needed lecture. I recall demanding that he fetch the vacuum cleaner and clean up the mess I had created during my tantrum.

Before I sat down to write this story, I asked Steven for his input. He confessed that most of the happenings of this day are relatively vague in his mind after the point in which I discovered the cause of the fire. He was quick to add that the only thing he remembers clearly from that point on, is a memory of standing next to the work bench and thinking, "There's a whole lotta smashing goin' on around here."

The neighbours typically did not give much thought to what the Fearnley children were up to (until it concerned their property). If I had been home during Steven's escapades, I am sure that I would have noticed something as peculiar as smoke rising from the backyard and addressed the problem much earlier. I am embarrassed to put this account of my rash actions towards my son in this book because they represent poor fatherly behaviour. In addition, my remorse compels me to apologize formally for putting my son through such an experience. However, it is included here for two reasons—Richard and Steven.

First, from Richard's perspective, he wants to keep the memory "alive" because it was one instance in which *everything* was Steven's fault. In his mind, forgetting such important parts of family history would simply be unfair. Second, Steven insisted that his recollection of the numerous pieces of flying debris—and the number of unnecessary strikes of the hammer used to destroy his tiny toy—needed to be recorded so that the memory of my actions would not fade with time.

As painful as it is for me to recall, I agreed to include my moment of weakness because I have since become much more likely to control my anger, especially at this stage in my life.

Tempered self is stronger than tempered steel.

∞ A Study of Dynamics ∞

We had our 100 gallon aquarium for about twelve years, but we were still learning about aquaculture and discovering more about life in nature. For example, we found that placing shiners in the tank was not a great move—despite the expected brilliant flashes of silver as they turned near the vertical lights at the ends of the tank. One time I dumped about two dozen shiners into the aquarium before lunchtime, and when I checked them immediately after my meal, only two still had eyes. The others remained able to swim but were clearly dying.

The sunfish had been more cruel than I could ever have suspected. They had gone after the shiners and rather than eating them, only tore the eyeballs out of their sockets. I thought I had understood that life in nature could be rough, but I was not prepared for the sheer brutality exhibited by the same sweet little fish that our children loved to catch. Nor was I prepared for another instance of live-in nature.

We had decided that our aquarium should represent life in a typical lake of southern Ontario. To this end, we captured several crawfish (or crayfish if you prefer), some freshwater muscles, snails, and other small denizens of the deep. We released them all into the tank to live together. The crawfish preyed on sunfish and other occupants. To catch a fish, their modus operandi was to climb up the large piece of driftwood that acted as a centrepiece for our seascape. As a fish approached, the crawfish would float down through the water and onto the back of the fish. Because the crayfish have claws for feet, they could manoeuvre themselves down to the fish's abdomen area, and while clinging to the fish with their main pincers, tear open the abdomen to feast on the entrails. No fish could survive such an attack. The remainder could then be consumed at the crawfish's leisure, interrupted only by a few dozen or so others that would fight for their share of the carcass. Again, this provided an ugly display of life in the raw.

The aquarium was set at eye level in the bar—a part of the recreation room typically frequented by our 'thirsty' guests. At parties, these snippets of life could be viewed at our leisure while refilling one's glass or sipping the usual alcoholic refreshers. The family room was a large area that had an enormous fieldstone fireplace. To recreate the look of Olde English pubs, I purchased many smoothly-planed cedar planks from the local building depot. I hacked at them with a traditional one-sided hatchet to achieve a hand-hewn appearance. They were then stained a dark brown to simulate three centuries of smoke and dirt that typically would be found in a real English pub. (I gave myself a dose of tennis elbow that lasted over a year from my repeated methodical hacking.) The family room was used for a great number of diverse activities and games—traditional ones, and ones that had been made up by my imaginative sons.

One notable day, Richard and Steven were each taking turns trying to hit the other with marbles they had recently received for Christmas. There were a few cardboard tubes that had held wrapping paper still lying around in the sewing cupboard attached to the family room. Richard showed Steven how the speed of the marble could be greatly increased by placing it in the hand-held part of a tube and then whipping the tube in an over-the-shoulder rotating motion. The marble would explode out of the free end of the tube with a velocity just short of the speed of light.

This produced a much more satisfactory yelp from other participants when one's opponent was hit by the exiting missile during such games. This led to a modification of the game—ducking. You did not dare stand still if a marble was coming your way.

It was late in the afternoon when Richard and Steven were called to the dinner table and we all sat down to enjoy the food. Halfway through the first course there was an extremely loud *CRAAAACK*. I was the only one who instantly knew what had happened. Just recently I had cleaned the aquarium and had replaced its three-eighths-inch front glass panel (three feet by two feet) by gluing it into place with silicone. The only thing that could have made such a sound was another one of the glass panels that made up our large aquarium.

In a panic, I dashed downstairs, calling for Richard and Steven to follow my lead and help. I was not looking forward to picking up twenty or so fish, several crayfish, plants, and gravel. This is to say nothing of the chore it would have been to mop up the one hundred gallons of water that I envisioned spewing out all over the family room floor. (Let's see now…one hundred US gallons, at about twelve cubic feet…equals one family room floor of four hundred square feet with about half an inch of water on top. Or perhaps a little less, allowing for the soaking action of our rugs and their under pads.)

However, as I rushed into the room, I could see that the water had not yet burst out of the aquarium but rather was leaking profusely from a crack that ran diagonally from the lower left to the upper right corner of the front glass panel I had just replaced. The water pressure was sufficient to be spurting out the lower part of the tank and only dribbling out at the part nearest the top. There was no time to explain the reasons for the unbalanced flow of exiting water with a lesson in fluid mechanics. It was a rather striking 'waterfall' on display as our crew flew into action.

I was hollering at the top of my lungs. "Steven! Grab all the buckets you can." "Richard! Fill up the laundry tubs for the fish." "Someone get towels and newspaper." "Where the (beep) is the net?"

Spurred on by my far-from-calm instructions, our bucket brigade removed much of the water without too much slopping onto the floor. The laundry tubs and several of the buckets served as holding tanks for the fish as we helped reduce the water level in the aquarium. Finally, with buckets full of water, the laundry tubs full of fish, and every towel in the house spread out soaking up any spilled water, I stood back to take a breath and assess the damage to the glass. For a brief moment, I reflected on the situation at hand. Then…I noticed a small but distinct conchoidal fracture about the size of a marble. Hmmm.

In my shock, and with utmost confusion, I enlightened my helpers. "Look…this glass has been hit!" I then noticed Richard and Steven sidling towards the stairs. I called them back. Under my pressure, they eventually cracked and confessed to me that one of them had flung the shooter marble at the other with phenomenal speed but had missed their intended target. The other had managed to duck in time to avoid almost certain death. They were about to receive a lecture, which would include the study of dynamics.

During fact-finding sessions while writing this book, all of those involved in each memorable occasion were asked for their account of each story in hopes of obtaining an unprejudiced endorsement of the recollections. The goal was to have every account as truthfully accurate as those who were involved could recall. Every other story in this book has been subject to such a process and received this type of confirmation. Oddly enough, for this chronicle, Richard maintains that it was Steven who broke the glass, while Steven insists that Richard was the shooter. Except for this minor detail, they are in complete agreement with my record of this event.

While I replaced the glass in the aquarium, I had the opportunity to reflect on the situation. Specifically, I evaluated my response and realized that cracking under pressure is not limited to an aquarium. I realized that everyone always has a choice of acting instead of *re*acting.

Anything or anybody can snap under enough stress.

∾ The Dad Who Knew Too Much ∾

There's a time when all siblings tend to fight with each other. In some cases there is a distinct rivalry in terms of ownership of their toys. In others, there is an ongoing struggle for the greatest attention from their parents. Some siblings insist on equality and fairness in every aspect of their lives—including both generosity and discipline. Even simple things like bedtimes can turn into major issues between them.

From my earliest days of fatherhood, I was prepared for my children to be no better than those in any other family and fully expected to experience such conflicts. Unfortunately, I was forced to endure this stage of their lives from the moment Steven was born until all of my children were young adults.

Every problem always has two basic aspects: the immediate concern and the steps that should be taken to prevent it from happening again in the future. In our house, I usually tried to focus more on the future aspect of our conflicts. In other words, I was more concerned that my children did not make the same mistakes twice. I believe that discipline is only needed to motivate someone enough to change. If I believed that my children were not going to repeat their actions, I was content to forgo any punishment.

For many years, I was required to play the role of family mediator. However, at times, when senseless disputes between my children produced no means of meting out discipline, I resorted to punishing the lot of them. Such favourite major issues as "he's looking at me" only served to erode my patience. Silly, petty retorts of "he started it" nearly drove me berserk.

On occasion, in severe cases where one of them was clearly in the wrong, I would spank them with a wooden spoon. Steven maintains that I once broke one on his backside. Although I honestly cannot remember this happening, I know my punishments could have been improved on. However, I believe that my actions were not excessive. If for no other reason than the fact that throughout these times, all of my children would still come to me for fatherly advice.

On one such occasion, Steven did not know how to refuse

a particular dessert that was a family favourite. Steven did not like it. Knowing that I took pleasure in maintaining the harmony amongst our family members, he came to me searching for a diplomatic way to avoid having to eat his 'favourite' dessert. I suggested to Steven that he could avoid hurting his mother's feelings and also achieve his goal simply by asking for a substitute dessert—preferably fresh fruit.

For the next few weeks or so, each time the unwanted dessert was offered to him he replied, "No thanks, Mom, I'd rather have an orange." Steven learned that an orange a day could keep Mom's dessert at bay. Eventually she caught on and we all had a good laugh.

This was reasonably successful because, unlike conflicts with his siblings, Steven wanted to solve the problem. In his childhood, all of us referred to him as "Even Steven." He tested me many times by whining about getting an equal portion of everything his older brother received. I'm not suggesting that Steven never wanted to resolve issues with his siblings, because he did—once.

One meal when we were all eating in the kitchen, Steven was fighting about yet another inconsequential issue with his older brother. I don't remember who started it, but I do remember sending both of them to separate rooms in my disgust. As I escorted them to their solitary confinement, I made a comment to each of them before shutting the bedroom doors. I was fed up trying to sort out "who dun it." I wanted them to tell the truth about what had just happened. With this hope, I threatened both of them, promising some sort of penalty if they did not both have exactly the same story when I returned. I thought they understood.

Immediately after shutting the two bedroom doors, I went downstairs to my workroom and heard them talking to each other in faint but clear voices. I wondered how this could be. I returned upstairs to the hallway that joined the two rooms, and both doors were still shut. From this vantage point I couldn't hear anything so I returned to the workroom. Upon my return, I once again heard muttering and scheming. Another trip to the upstairs hall still did not provide an explanation to the mystery. What was going on?

Their voices would stop and start, but in time became less

sporadic and more conversational. It took a few minutes before I was able to determine what was happening. They were talking to each other from separate bedrooms through the heating vents. Since the plenum on the furnace was immediately behind me when I stood at the workbench, I had a natural receiver for their broadcast. I had sent them to separate areas of the home to ensure that they would logically conclude that their only way "out"—of both trouble and the rooms—would be to tell the truth.

Unfortunately, they had circumvented my intentions by daring to meld their versions of the past. Had they simply been making an effort to ensure they got their stories straight, this would have been acceptable, and perhaps even considered shrewd. But instead, after each of my sons had ranted to the other about their feelings concerning what had happened, they began to negotiate some of the issues between them. "I'll admit to…if you confess to…" I heard one of them say. Through their conniving, they agreed that they would both downplay each other's actions to soften the impact of their disagreement and thereby lessen their pending reward.

They were running through various scenarios—three or four different ones—all of which appeared to have various shades of truth. As I listened, I felt the need to intervene, but I had to gather my thoughts. There were a number of things I wanted to address. First, I wanted them to understand that despite some of my previous actions, their dad was no dummy. Second, I wanted them to know that just because they both agreed on something, did not make it the truth. And finally, because I had some time to think about this, I was hoping they would realize the importance of the lesson so that I would not have to effect a punishment.

After listening for some time and receiving new insights as to how children think, I decided what I was going to do. They were commenting on the pros and cons of their top three variations of the truth, when I abruptly interjected through a nearby vent. As they were debating the merits of their third creative option, I made a casual suggestion that they should stick with "the previous one." The use of the bedroom heat vents for communication had just been expanded to include the downstairs workroom.

My comment came straight from the heart. They were stunned and in a state of shock. Their immediate silence told me that they both knew that it was my voice and they realized I had heard far too much. They had learned a valuable point: if you're trying to get your stories straight, don't include your inquisitor.

To this day, Steven believes that my actions were based purely on the fact that we were running out of wooden spoons. I vehemently deny this. I distinctly recall seizing this opportunity to resolve the issue in a manner that did not hurt anyone's feelings— or backside. In any event, I believe they got the point because they both still remember this incident vividly.

Venting is communication from the soul.

∞ Steven Buys a Pizza ∞

Steven has two children, a daughter, Emily, and a son, Alex. Emily has proven to be just as picky an eater as Steven was in his childhood. One unusual example is that she does not like tomato sauce on her pizza.

In her childhood, pizza night at their house would go something like this:

"Would you like pepperoni?"

"No thank you."

"Would you like any meat?"

"Nope."

"Would you like any vegetables?"

"No way."

"Would you like any pineapple?"

"Don't be ridiculous...just cheese please."

All she ever wanted for a pizza was dough and cheese. If that wasn't enough, she always insisted on double cheese. In my mind this does not a pizza make.

Like any married couple, Steven and his wife at the time had experienced a few conflicts in the years of their marriage. One night, in an effort to resolve an earlier argument, they went out to dinner. The plan was to start the evening with a few happy hour drinks at a local establishment to reminisce over happier times. Then Steven was to pick up pizzas for Emily and her younger brother and deliver them to his children at home, before returning to the restaurant to have a romantic dinner with his wife.

The problems of the day combined with the tension of the evening helped contribute to Steven mixing up the pizza order. The first two stressors were both considerable challenges and the drinking helped make ordering Emily's pizza a third. For some reason Steven mixed up the order. He did remember something about doubling down. He placed an order for pizza with double sauce and nothing else.

Upon arrival at the pizza emporium, Steven ordered a small salad for his peckish wife but was confronted by a confused employee. When questioned about his order, Steven exclaimed,

"Don't argue with me, it's the way my kids like it." He picked up the pizzas and headed home but not without incident. In his rush the entire meal package was dropped on the way to the car.

En route, he didn't recognize the extent of the damage since he had not bothered to open the boxes until he arrived home. Once in the kitchen, he opened the first pizza box with flair, and presented it to Emily. When the leaking box was opened, Steven remembers the pizza as resembling a "murder scene." It looked as though there was nothing more than blood in a box.

The salad was soaked, both pizzas inedible, and the evening ruined. One indication of Steven's stress level around this time is that he screwed up a simple task of ordering a couple of pizzas for his kids. His relationship with Emily was strained further that night. Too much sauce had turned a hopeful evening into an awkward night with a hungry family. The rest of Steven's family chose to get something else to eat, whereas Steven opted for a few more drinks—this time, to forget.

If you're drinking to forget, remember—too much sauce can ruin anything.

Life's Lessons: A Successful Collection of Failures

∽ Steven Rents a Video ∾

Steven and his son, Alex, are both avid golfers. When Alex was about nine years old, the two of them were invited to go to England and watch the British Open with another father-and-son pair of golf fans. The other boy was Alex's schoolmate and this boy's dad was a friend of one of the pros on tour who was competing in this world class golf tournament. It was to take place at Royal Lytham and St. Anne's Golf Course. Steven and Alex stayed with their friends in a nearby hotel.

One night, after an enjoyable day of watching professional golfers display their talents, the boys wanted to watch a movie. The hotel staff gave the boys permission to use the TV and videotape machine in the lobby.

Not far from their small hotel was a local video rental store. Steven made his way there and asked if they had the movie the boys wanted to watch. Delighted, Steven looked forward to renting the movie and spending a relaxing evening watching it with the boys. Unfortunately, this was not to be.

The rental clerk refused to rent Steven the video because he was not from England. They also refused to let Steven purchase it. Steven offered to provide the store with a deposit that was large enough to replace the movie and buy half a dozen more with the balance if he failed to return it after the rental period. He made a number of other creative suggestions involving a credit card that clearly addressed all of management's concerns, but none of them were accepted. The answer remained a phlegmatic "no." Then as if to tease Steven, the store clerk asked, "Could you get a letter from the hotel?"

Steven didn't understand how a letter from the local hotel would provide any form of security. However, he agreed to go back and get one if for no other reason than to appease the 'management' at the video store. Besides, there was no need to understand the rationale behind the request. Steven's only goal was to treat the boys to a movie.

Once back at the hotel, the boys welcomed Steven excitedly. He explained that there would be no show unless he could obtain a letter of reference from the hotel. In addition, it had to be on their letterhead. To this end, a request was made to the young woman minding the front desk. She indicated that it would take a few minutes. Steven, Alex, and their friends all waited... and waited...and waited some more.

Upset with the time it was taking to draft such a simple letter, Steven went to the front desk to ask if it was ready. This time the young lady was slightly less friendly, but offered further assurances that it would soon be completed. By the time a third inquiry was made, any moviegoer in Canada would have had time to watch the movie and return it. This became apparent to Steven and he realized that the young lady was not about to help him—despite her declarations to the contrary. Besides, while passing the time waiting for her to write the all-important letter, Steven discovered that the videotape machine in the lobby was broken. The clerk had been too lazy to volunteer this information when Steven first inquired about using their equipment. There would be no movie that night.

After the golf tournament, Steven and Alex headed to Manchester where the four of them stayed for a short while with their host's mother. Luckily there was another video rental store nearby. Once again, Steven set off to rent the movie the young boys had been asking for all week.

This time, although it was a completely different company, Steven was confronted with another series of similar lame excuses disqualifying him from renting a video. In his frustration, Steven solicited the help of his friend, who has a strong British accent, but the owner requested that he provide a reference. After explaining that he was only staying with his mother for a short while, the owner made another illogical suggestion. "Could you get a letter from your mom?" Steven turned to his friend and asked, "What is it with the letters?" In a sincere tone, Steven's friend apologized and said, "In England, they're not exactly big on service."

When Steven or Alex recounts this, neither of them remembers the name of the movie as easily as the struggle to rent it.

In England, always carry a letter from your mom.

Life's Lessons: A Successful Collection of Failures

SECTION THREE: JAMIE

Jamie, my youngest son, became part of our family on April 15, 1970. Earlier in 1969, Joy and I had been so shocked to discover that 'we' were pregnant that we decided to keep her condition a secret until she began to "show." He was one of the few things I helped bring about in this world without a plan.

We kept him a secret until a close friend phoned and announced that she was "pregnant again." So, there was no longer any reason to keep Jamie's presence quiet. Now, there were two in our engineering social group expecting a birth around the same time.

At the time of Jamie's birth, I was coaching two hockey teams, one for each of his older brothers. I looked forward to doing the same for Jamie one day. I mentioned this to his mother, who felt that to carry on with such responsibilities and add a third team would be too much. However, I told her that by the time Jamie had learned to skate, both of his older brothers would be able to help. I thought it would be great to have them as my official assistants. I noted that they would likely be dating and driving by that time so the situation wouldn't be that bad. This did little to comfort her, and only served to give her something else to worry about. In fairness, I have to admit it was a little hectic coaching three hockey teams at the same time, especially when their playoffs overlapped with their baseball season.

Jamie played hockey well into his adult life and for a while, with Richard, in an industrial league. On one team, their linemate was their cousin Dave. The three of them made up an entire forward line. I remember one time I snuck into one of their games. I wanted to see how they were doing. I was a little late, but the score was four to zip for their team. The Fearnley line had combined for a total of twelve points—two assists and a goal every time one of them had scored. They were doing very well and having a blast at the same time. So was I.

After high school Jamie wanted to continue his education. He was accepted at The University of Waterloo, and the search for accommodation was on. I bought a detached house in the same town near the school and entered Jamie's name as the owner so that he could rent to the maximum number of boarders. After all, the mortgage had to be paid. There were some frustrating moments for him while he was at university, just as there had been for me when I was in university.

It was not until Jamie was attending the University of Waterloo, and living on his own, that he had a fundamental revelation. He was asked about some of the things he was learning at school and shared one particularly eye-opening experience. As if in a spirit of helpfulness, he told us, "When you leave a shirt on the floor, it stays there." He made the remark as if it was a profound discovery, but his statement only served to amuse the balance of our family. Once his renters began dumping on him, Jamie began to have a greater appreciation for his mother.

I remember an incident when he was completing an assignment and complaining that the computer printer I had bought him at an auction was not working well. In fact, it was not working at all. He complained bitterly that the thing had worked perfectly at first but had lulled him into a false sense of security. Apparently, he had finished an assignment with just enough time to print out his term paper and hand it in, but the printer stopped working—just when he needed it most.

Later, when he relayed this to me, I told him not to worry. I would get him another printer for his computer but asked him to save me the broken one. I wanted to use the parts for future repairs to my office printer since it was the exact same make and model. He tried to talk me out of this but when I insisted, he confessed that he had taken a hammer to the "dam' thing." It was now in many pieces, all over his room. So much for spare parts.

I think names of any computer component are actually acronyms that all secretly mean "something that will stop working just when you need it the most"—unlike family, who is supposed to be there for you no matter what. I'm not sure who first said "Children need our love the most when they deserve it the least"...but I agree. Ironically, one of Jamie's most satisfying moments in the four year computer course had occurred over the span of a few minutes when he chose to fulfill a noble dream and smash the crap out of a computer part that desperately deserved it. I laughed for days.

Despite this, he has managed to reconcile his frustrations with electronic devices and focus his attention on fixing them. Originally, Jamie wanted to become a computer programmer. However, after an enjoyable co-op stint in a support role that involved working with people and their computer issues, he switched from his programming path to one that would help him apply his problem-solving skills in the computer world. Now, after graduating with an Honours Co-op Bachelor of Mathematics Degree, he is comfortably established in Toronto, solving network problems for various professional firms. He enjoys a busy career helping others—especially people with computer problems. He will never be out of work.

The next chapter primarily consists of accounts from Jamie's childhood when we were a family of five. Now, despite living the closest to me geographically, I hear less about his daily adult life than from either of his older brothers. I blame the computer industry.

∞ I Spy ∞

When our children were little and our family drove to visit relatives, we played various games in the car to pass the time. This avoided most of the "Are we there yet?" queries as we travelled throughout southern Ontario. A favourite game of ours was "I spy."

The rules of the game were simple. After stating the introduction by rote, "I spy with my little eye something that begins with…" we would give the initials for the object. Anything that could be seen from our car was acceptable—even a memory of something from earlier in the drive.

I remember being stumped by some of my children's simple items: "G" for grass, "C" for clouds, "SS" for speed signs, and even "K" for knife. I would retaliate with such selections as: "SF" for snake fences, "OSF" for old snake fences, and "LS" for lane striping.

From the start, the group would bombard the 'spy' with a barrage of questions to determine what had been seen. Richard would always demand that we keep questioning until the item had been discovered.

When Jamie was old enough to join in, he would take his turn with relish. Once, while heading to Oshawa to visit my mother-in-law, young Jamie did his "I spy" routine and gave us the first letter as "B." The drive usually took about thirty minutes and because of his tender age, Jamie had been given first turn. As we approached Oshawa, all of us had spent the entire trip trying to guess Jamie's "I spy" word to no avail. Everybody had given up, and we begged Richard to do so as well. We all desperately wanted to understand what Jamie had spotted.

As I turned off the highway, Richard finally succumbed to the pressure from all of the other guessers in the car. For once in his life, Richard had conceded defeat. So, almost in unison we asked, "Okay Jamie, what did you spy?"

With tender pride, he emphatically revealed his answer to the riddle: "Bolkswagon!" Despite some hearty groans from you-know-who, the rest of us laughed and explained to Jamie that the word for that make of car was Volkswagen, and the first letter was "V." Jamie joined us in our laughter. His faux pas had helped the entire family feel that the trip had been shorter than usual.

Spelling always counts.

∞ **Buried Treasure** ∞

Jamie followed in Steven's footsteps with regard to liking, or more accurately stated, disliking vegetables—cooked or raw. On our family's holiday trip to Trinidad and Tobago, and despite the fact that I had paid for a complete package of children's meals for Jamie, he would eat nothing but peanut butter throughout the entire two week trip. Regardless of the quality of a hotel's fare, he would adamantly insist on peanut butter—usually with a "bread roll." I feared that he was turning into another 'peanut butter kid'.

For the most part, despite the frustration, we gave in to his demands because we were on vacation. Once while we were having a picnic in Tobago, we had brought food that I was sure Jamie would eat. He would have none of it. As I returned to our picnic site from the tiny roadside stand where I had purchased a very small bottle of name brand peanut butter, I realized that I had paid more for it than we did in Toronto for a jar four times its size. Well, at least, I reasoned, he wouldn't go hungry.

At home, Jamie's hatred for vegetables manifested itself in other distinct ways. By this time we had discovered Steven's dehydrated store of unused vegetables in the laundry room, so this was not an option for Jamie. However, he later came to show more interest in his veggies soon after the Tobago food fiasco. In fact, he was cleaning his plate regularly and both his mother and I relaxed our vigilance.

At this time he was quite small and could not sit at the table without having a lift from a booster chair or something that was similar in height. We had somehow managed to lose his booster seat, so instead of buying another, we simply used an old four-inch-thick Toronto telephone book.

One day, Jamie's mother needed to get the number and address of a local merchant. For some reason it was not listed in the current edition so she elected to try an older one, which was conveniently located on Jamie's chair at our kitchen table. As she flipped open the pages, a shower of dried peas and carrots deluged her. Jamie had *not* been eating his vegetables.

The phone book was an ideal storing place because Jamie could slip numerous veggies between any two pages in the thousand or so that made up the phone book. In truth, he cherished the phone book that pressed his unwanted food like wild roses and allowed him to sit on his secrets for quite some time.

Richard's habit of begging for broccoli and other greens, from his youngest of years, lulled us into an unrealistic hope that his younger brothers would follow his lead. The battle to get Jamie to eat his vegetables continued until one day when his otherwise reserved mother took some rather unprecedented action. We had both become totally fed up with our continuous struggle to get our youngest two children to eat their veggies. With Jamie around nine years old, and Steven older than fifteen, we had both put up with this strain for over a decade and a half.

I had mistakenly believed that she had become inured to our struggle. When she snapped, Jamie had been diddling with his vegetables for an entire meal, despite them being re-buttered and re-heated a number of times. She had finally had enough. She dragged Jamie from his seat and placed him on his back in the middle of our kitchen floor. The rest of us sat dumbfounded. This was so unlike her. No one dared move.

No action on Jamie's part could divert her from her seemingly appointed task. He twisted and turned his head in disgust and fought nobly in his quest to avoid the taste of a single carrot. However, his efforts were no match for his mother.

I do not know who was more surprised. Joy, the day she discovered the phone book full of vegetables, or Jamie when his otherwise non-confrontational and loving mother pinned him to the kitchen floor, sat astride his chest, and forced his allotted serving of cold cooked carrots into his mouth and down his throat.

Now, in his thirties, Jamie is finally eating his veg. In fact, he is regularly upgrading his vegetable repertoire at a rate of about one new garden delight per year. However, for some strange reason, he still does not like carrots.

There's only so much a parent can do.

✣ **Playing Games** ✣

Richard and Steven, along with some neighbouring friends, liked to play a game on their knees with a soft sponge ball. Goals were set up, usually against a room's walls with the object being to slap the sponge ball into the opponent's goal. Whoever had the most goals won the game. I am not sure whether this new sport of knee-hockey was an official version of some other sport or if it had been invented by the neighbours, or Richard and Steven, or some combination of them all.

In any case, it was not long before Richard and Steven had figured out some further variations that would enhance their play. Like most kids their age, their imagination was such that even games that were well thought out by major toy manufacturers and came with detailed instructions, were varied in some way. For example, they had to reverse and explore new ways to play a traditional board game that normally required travelling up ladders and down snakes.

One of my sons' modifications to their unique version of knee-hockey was to use a ping-pong ball rather than the soft foam plastic ball. This quickened the pace of the game and sharpened their reflexes to the extent that they would have distinct advantages when playing the original game with others. Coincidently, they would welcome a stinging blow as the ping-pong ball whizzed around the room because this gave them licence to strike back. Both considered themselves the best shooter and looked forward to smacking the ball and stinging their opponent. It was understood that if you played this game you would inevitably be hit at some point, even playing in the largest room of the house—the recreation room.

Jamie wanted to play. Despite the fact that it would mean playing two against one, the one with the extra 'help' felt he would be handicapped. Since neither Richard nor Steven wanted Jamie in their game, they tried to discourage him and explained that he could get hurt from being hit by the ball. They each took time to demonstrate the action and explain how the ball would sting if he were to be struck by it. Jamie was adamant: he wanted to play.

Before being let into the big boys club, he was told that neither crying nor screaming would be acceptable regardless of how badly he might be hurt. Also, the bigger boys played rough and tumble, and if Jamie was squeezed or crushed in one of their attacking plays, no whimpering would be tolerated. If he accepted these conditions, he could join them. Against all anticipation, Jamie decided that he would still like to play. Richard and Steven evened the odds by taking turns with their handicap.

Anyone who has read even one story from the previous two chapters is likely to know what happened next. Within less than three minutes, Jamie was rolling around the floor in pain. He was howling loudly at his two older, but unsympathetic, brothers. They explained that he had accepted the rules of engagement and refused to offer any compassion. Noticing that no sympathy was forthcoming, Jamie gave up his histrionics and continued to play—this time with a firsthand understanding of his older brothers' warnings.

He quickly dried his tears and joined his older brothers with a vengeance and a renewed desire to smack the ball at his opponent, regardless of who it might be. Winning seemed less important. After all, it's not if you win or lose, it's *how* you play the game. They were all engaged in a riotous game for the next couple of hours, which ended, without incident, upon their mother's arrival.

Jamie immediately got up to welcome her home…or so his older brothers thought. Richard and Steven both took a needed break from their spirited game and rested. Jamie ran to the foot of the stairs and began to cry uncontrollably. Puzzled, his older brothers listened attentively in hopes of learning what he had done to become so upset. He continued to wail loudly enough for all to hear but did not stop snivelling until he reached his mother on the stairway landing.

Apparently, she was advised of the terrible mistreatment Jamie had been subjected to earlier by his two older brothers. This astonished both Richard and Steven, but to their amazement Joy readily accepted their explanation—much to Jamie's surprise. Perhaps because this marked the first instance in which both of

Jamie's older brothers had told the exact same story of the events in question upon cross-examination.

I believe their mother sensed that Richard and Steven were telling the truth (perhaps another first) when Jamie admitted that the incident had occurred much earlier. Nevertheless, despite realizing that Jamie was just playing games, his mom offered her sympathy. This was in stark contrast to the attitude of Jamie's older brothers, who dismissed his pleas for pity and returned to the games room.

Later is better than never, but on time is better than ever.

∞ The Collector ∞

Jamie had broken his leg in a skiing accident, which contributed to him having problems completing his school assignments. He was living with his mother in North York during this time—his first years at junior high school. As a result, his marks deteriorated to a point much lower than his mother and I knew he was capable of achieving. Richard, although finished high school, had still not learned how to be a good student so he certainly was not qualified to teach Jamie good study habits. Steven was unavailable because he was in California studying to be a gemologist at the time.

Eventually, his mother and I managed to purchase a computer for Jamie, to help with his studies. His grades began to improve, partly because his homework was being submitted in a much neater format. He even went on to win a school-wide science fair competition. We were very proud.

During his school years, we noticed an assortment of fancy valve stem caps sitting on his dresser, accessories typically used to decorate expensive mag wheels on sporty cars. I thought that it was an interesting hobby, until I found out that he was not purchasing them. He was taking them from parked cars in the area, and installing them on his bicycle tires since they fitted both types of valve stems. He had an extensive collection. His mother and I were appalled.

In a stern lecture, I pointed out that this was stealing, and that he would be in court if caught. I noted that he must immediately stop taking them. During this conversation, Jamie attempted to downplay his involvement in the theft by mentioning that he was having his friends do his "collecting." Several younger children were working for him and all he did was "buy them a little treat" or provide small "cash payments" for each valve stem cap that they supplied. Under further cross-examination, he made another lame attempt to justify his actions: he wasn't keeping them for himself; he was selling them to friends. In my mind, his network of suppliers and customers constituted a miniature crime ring. I was stunned.

So I did what I and many other parents have done before. I

had a tantrum—what my mother's family would have described as a "conniption fit." It took some time for me to settle down. Ultimately, when I finally felt that I could curb my temper sufficiently to discuss the problem in a calm manner, I continued my 'talk' with Jamie. This time, in addition to repeating the same lecture, I tried to emphasize my cautions about the serious consequences associated with such activity.

I expanded on my previous explanations and warnings, reinforcing that what Jamie was doing was still against the law. I pointed out that the police and the courts would be less likely to cut him any slack because he was offering others enticements to commit crimes. I likened his action to drug barons that provided the wherewithal for others to carry out their dirty work.

I believe this explanation helped Jamie to understand, because he assured both his mother and I that he would never collect valve stem caps again and immediately promised to stop his 'incentive' buying.

Parents should be cogs in the wheels of justice.

∞ Jamie the Philosopher ∞

To lessen the effect of the separation on our children, Joy and I had resolved that our sons could visit back and forth with merely a phone call to announce their intentions. Generally speaking, my two oldest sons lived with me, and Jamie lived with his mother.

One evening, eight years after I had been separated, Jamie arranged to come over for supper. I cannot recall the exact reason why we were getting together, but I think it may have involved his upcoming sojourn to the University of Waterloo. After finishing supper, Jamie and I were washing the dishes. I didn't mind because it added extra time to our visits. This time, Jamie was washing and I was drying. Dirty dishes were stacked to his left, and I stood on his right prepared to dry.

We continued our dinner discussion at the sink and our conversation was in full flower. Then Jamie handed me a plate from the sudsy water, its bottom surface covered in food. I guess when only one side is used, the other is often forgotten. I returned it to him and said, "Jamie, there are two sides to a plate."

Without any more than a caustic comment, Jamie washed the plate properly and handed it back to me.

Several years later, when Jamie was at university, he and some of his friends went on a fishing trip for the weekend. They treated themselves to a great meal of fresh fish—fried in butter of course. The group enjoyed themselves immensely.

After dinner one evening, two of them were cleaning up. Jamie was drying the dishes while a friend was washing. When handed an unclean plate—exactly as I had been, several years prior—Jamie returned the dish to his friend and said, "There are two sides to *every* plate." Upon hearing this, his friend instantly exclaimed, "Jamie! That's *very* philosophical."

Although not discussed at the time, my son and I had sensed that there was a greater meaning to our simple statement. However, with Jamie's slight modification, his friend immediately focused on the philosophical implications. We have since come to realize that a line or phrase someone casually throws out can be another's profundity.

Although Jamie had made this statement informally, I believe he had only understood its intrinsic value. He did not appreciate the deeper abstract meaning until the statement had been shared. Initially, neither Jamie nor I were wowed by the statement. However, over time, we have both come to appreciate it in a more profound sense. In fact, we still often joke to family or friends disputing a point, interjecting that, "There are two sides to every plate."

Anything shared increases in value; those who share increase in worth.

MORE PEOPLE, MORE PETS

After about three years of living on my own as a single parent, I was ready for a change. On Labour Day weekend in 1983, I went to a "Parents without Partners" dance held in North Toronto. I looked over the crowd in the same manner in which I had at other single parent dances. My routine was to observe first and act later. In other words, I would watch to see whether a woman was accepting or rejecting those that asked her to dance. There is nothing more embarrassing than struggling through a maze of other tables crowded with singles, all of whom have just witnessed your humiliation after the object of your desire has denied your request to dance with an abrupt "No." I came to refer to this walk as the "death walk."

I spotted someone who caught my eye. She seemed to be enjoying herself and the dance. I felt that her attitude indicated a desire for fun, and I figured that my chances of avoiding the death walk were pretty good. I asked her to dance. She responded with an enthusiastic "Sure!" During one of our first dances, I mentioned to her that I was interested in long term relationships. Through our discussions that night, I found out she was a dog lover like me. Over twenty years later, Nancy and I are married and still enjoying life together—at least to my knowledge, anyway.

On the night after our first dance, I met her two sons: David and Greg. Unexpectedly, they were both excited about their mother's first date since her official separation. With Dave being fourteen and Greg, twelve, they fitted nicely between the ages of my youngest two sons, Steven and Jamie. For the most part, all five children get along well with each other. The closest bond has been between the two youngest. Now, in their adult lives, Jamie and Greg get together socially and remain close friends.

On one occasion, a few years back, Jamie was telling Greg the story of my arrest in Windsor. Greg knew of my deep love for fresh fruit and vegetables. In truth, he views it as more of an obsession. This may help to explain why he understood my predicament to be self-inflicted. Jamie was unsure as to what exactly had precipitated one fruit stand owner's outburst and subsequent fabricated accusations. Mistakenly, Greg thought that I had threatened to blow up the owner's makeshift building over the inexcusable absence of fresh tropical fruit.

Much later, after Greg's inaccurate assumption had been corrected, Nancy, Greg, and I were having a conversation over dinner. Since I was not around until David and Greg were in their teens, I often related experiences from my past around their dinner table in much the same way I used to with my first wife and our three children. As I began to speak, Nancy was listening attentively but Greg interrupted. He asked abruptly, "Is this another Ted Story?" Nancy and I both laughed because his classification of my many previous awkward predicaments was so apt. Greg's taxonomy has stood the test of time. To this day, my second family will refer to my narratives as yet another "Ted Story." Members of both families all credit Greg with coining the phase.

Now in the latter part of my life, Nancy and I live alone. All of our sons have flown the coop. In doing so, they have presented us with a total of eight grandchildren. And they *are* grand.

In her retirement from the teaching profession, Nancy continues to attend school, but now from the other side of the educator's desk. She busies herself attending numerous lectures and classes while staying healthy with regular physical fitness. My life has changed as well. I no longer practice as a Transportation Planning Consultant, having retired from the profession recently. However, I do keep busy as the Canadian representative for an innovative line of roadway safety equipment. Some people, when they retire, are concerned that they won't have anything to do. Anyone worried about such a problem is welcome to spend a day or two with Nancy or me and see if they can keep up.

This next chapter is focused on my new life with my new wife. These records are consistent with other chapters in the book, in that they are in their own chronological order. However they are not as outrageous in nature, as most of the previous anecdotes. Not that Nancy and I have led a boring life together. In fact, it's quite the opposite. But the lack of crazy stories in this chapter is a testament to her calming influence and reserved demeanour.

I am now in my seventies and cherish the quieter times I spend with Nancy in our empty nest. We have learned to enjoy life together. However, I still slip from time to time and drag her into difficult situations when I forget the lessons of yesteryear and revert to habits more characteristic of my youth. My natural children are quick to claim that my behaviour is undeniable proof that I am the carrier of the mutant Fearnley gene, and I am the *only* one responsible for passing it on to them.

Life has begun to quieten for me, and my evening conversations with just Nancy and myself at the dinner table have given me a peaceful but strange feeling. Instead of being the only one telling and retelling the memorable episodes to my own family, I now often listen and learn. Perhaps because I didn't meet David or Greg until they were young men, I get to hear wonderful stories of the challenges they put Nancy through in their youth. I knowingly chuckle to myself when I hear them, believing my life as a storyteller to have come full circle.

∞ A Decent Proposal ∞

As indicated in the introduction to this chapter, Nancy and I had met one day at an evening dance on Labour Day weekend in 1983. I was committed to Nancy from our first dance, and our courtship took off from there. I will always remember our first date—dinner and a movie. I liked a unique restaurant in downtown Toronto that served shrimp baked in a butter sauce as one of their specialties. I felt that Nancy would really enjoy a dinner like that.

I enjoyed the butter sauce so much that when I saw that Nancy was not finishing hers, I asked if she would mind if I ate it. I finished off both dishes of melted butter, sopping it up with fresh homemade rolls. Nancy didn't mind because she prefers to leave room for dessert. Looking back, I cringe when I recall my bad manners. However, I have learned to accept this because Nancy has since enjoyed telling anyone who would listen.

We had some time after Nancy had finished her dessert and before the movie started, so we went for a walk. We rested on a park bench. It was there that I stole my first kiss.

Then, contrary to her friend's advice, Nancy and I went to a movie with sexual overtones. From the moment the romantic movie ended, things had changed. Our emotions had been stirred and we were definitely on a path much different than before.

At Christmas, I was invited out for dinner at her sister and brother-in-law's home in Scarborough. Nancy severely cautioned me on the way over. She said I was not to "talk about politics." Yet the conversation at the dinner table immediately turned to politics. With great self-control, I avoided joining in. The discussion was heating up and I could tell that the participants would not have welcomed my opinion.

Later that evening, I showed our hostess a necklace that I had bought as Nancy's Christmas gift. She remarked how nice it was. I thanked her for dinner and said, "You know I love Nancy a lot." I then realized something. "Perhaps I should tell Nancy."

I know that I was not a man free of a past, but I felt that I was a decent catch despite my baggage. I proposed to Nancy shortly thereafter. The response was not exactly what I had been hoping for. Nancy was concerned about committing to another relationship, since the last one she had been in had broken down. Besides, she said it was too soon after her separation. I accepted her comments and did not raise the issue for some time. In fact, every time I brought it up, Nancy reinforced her position. After a few months, I stopped asking and resolved to let it be. After being together for over two years, I moved in with Nancy and we carried on with our lives...together.

More than five years later, as we sat down to watch TV one evening, she said, "Well...when *are* we getting married?" Surprised, I said, "Let's do it this spring." So, on May 11, 1991, we were married in the hallway of our new home with many of our friends and family present. Greg, who was at university taking a music course, played his guitar from an overlook in the vast main hall. My brother-in-law, Lynn's husband, Neil, a pastor from Oregon, presided. Well, nearly. Because of a misunderstanding with a doctor's prescription, our pastor took his medicine shortly before drinking wine for the toasts. Just after the ceremony, he presided over the spare room, asleep on the bed. No one expected the pastor to pass out on our special day.

Earlier, Nancy had given me a plaque with the words of Elizabeth Barrett Browning: "Come grow old along with me, the best is yet to be." It became a keepsake of mine because Nancy had whispered these words to me early in our relationship.

I had first suggested including these poetic words for our wedding when we were planning our ceremony, but Nancy said, "If you do that, I'll cry." With some encouragement, she consented, and together we agreed to recite them to each other during the official proceedings. When the time came for us to repeat these treasured words, Nancy was fine...*but I cried*.

On our wedding day, in front of our witnesses, Nancy officially said "yes" to the question I had asked many years prior. My proposal had taken over seven years to get the response I was first hoping for, but it was well worth the wait.

Patience is more than a virtue; sometimes it is a necessity.

∞ Fun in the Sun ∞

Nancy is a committed teacher. She taught for several years both before her children were born and after raising them. Her specialty was guidance, and when she retired, she was Head of Guidance at the high school where she had worked for several years. Since Nancy and I met, we have travelled together many times—generally to the south and to Caribbean shores—but always at the busiest times of the year for air travel.

I had diligently worked to become a self-employed consultant so that I could take holidays at the more relaxed off-peak parts of the year. Only to fall in love with someone who could only travel at the most popular and congested times of the year.

Nancy needed respite from her students. Like many other teachers, she used the holidays to regenerate her enthusiasm and love for her job. Plans had to be made weeks and sometimes months in advance, or we would be completely out of luck if we planned to get away—especially in the midwinter break. In addition to Florida, our favourite spots included St. Kitts, Barbados, Cuba, and other islands in the Caribbean.

A couple of times we went to Florida because Nancy's relatives owned a mobile home in one of the dedicated parks near Clearwater. Once, as a treat, we suggested that the two younger boys come with us for a bit of their own fun near Indian Rocks beach. We had reserved a condominium with a balcony on the shoreline so we could watch the sun set over the Caribbean. Originally, I was looking forward to some romantic times with Nancy, but Greg and Jamie were keen to travel with us, and Steven and his children planned to visit as well. I relaxed my initial hopes, rationalizing that we could all have our own fun in the sun.

As a seasoned traveller, I never forget more than two or three crucial items. I undertook to plan our trip and the packing. I suggested that everybody take a carry-on suitcase with them so that they would have a swimsuit and a change of clothes in case anything happened to their other luggage. I guess I sounded like the "Accidental Tourist" because I was razzed by all of my travelling companions. A torrent of abuse carried on in my direction, but it could be summed up to one succinct statement: "Who needs to go to that sort of trouble?" At that point, I continued with my own preparations for my carry-on and other luggage, giving little thought to what the others packed.

The Saturday flight was uneventful until we went to claim our luggage. I had my carry-on in hand. Every other piece of luggage I had packed showed up on the carousel. However, no other suitcases bore the names of my detractors. There they were, three of them, looking somewhat despondent…sans swimsuits, toiletries, clothes, patience, and without any defence for their predicament. Three quarters of our group were a sorry looking bunch as we picked up our rental car. They did not appreciate my remark about an unplanned advantage of mine—lots of room for my bags in the car's trunk.

Since the condominium had been rented from Sunday afternoon to Sunday morning, we needed a place to stay for the first Saturday night when we arrived. We knew this before we left and decided on a local motel. Being crammed together with little privacy, Nancy had to sleep in her street clothes. Greg and Jamie did the same.

Early in the evening, long before we were likely to nod off, I discovered colonies of several different peculiar looking bugs in the bathroom who welcomed us to the tropics. I hung my luggage up to avoid bug infestation. In the morning, I took our complaints to the front desk. During my protest, several prospective guests decided to leave. We, in turn, vowed never to go back.

That evening I enjoyed my dip in the sea while others watched in envy. The next day, we visited the mobile home owners, and Nancy was able to borrow a swimsuit from a niece who was visiting. Greg and Jamie opted not to do the same. They had to wait a little longer. That is, until their luggage arrived later that night. Jamie declared never to fly anywhere without his essentials packed into his carry-on luggage. He has remained true to his vow to this day.

Every minute they waited in the spectacular sunshine helped to reinforce the lesson I had tried to share with them back in

Toronto. Actually, I was hoping that they'd have a few more days to 'sweat it out' before their stuff showed up. That's a little too vindictive, so I prefer to remember things this way…we were all having our *own* fun in the sun.

Consequences are the rewards for our mistakes.

∞ **Blown Away** ∞

Once, Nancy and I went on a dream vacation to the Island of St. Kitts in the Caribbean. Our destination was Banana Bay, and we were pleasantly surprised with the resort and the accommodations. It was not the usual multi-storied hotel, owned by an American or European conglomerate, such as those usually seen along the Caribbean shorelines. Several of these types of hotels seem to have been built around a gambling concept with a stylish casino in the building where people can entertain themselves and never see the sun. That sort of holiday is greatly removed from the type Nancy and I like to take.

At Banana Bay, our building was different. It was a single story, motel-like structure that accommodated no more than a dozen rooms. Our room had a kitchen, a large bedroom with a walkout to a covered patio, and a garden—which ended about thirty feet out at a cliff to the sea. Our temporary home had been built on a shelf of land about eight feet up from the surface of the azure water. Facing east, the rising sun would awaken us, and many times, Nancy or I would go for a swim before breakfast.

The gourmet meals were spectacular. They were served in a large house that appeared to be a small but original estate mansion. The chef was Swiss, and although we found out he was casting about for a different venue, one would never have known it from the sensation he created with each meal.

Immediately to the south of the Island known as St. Kitts lies its companion—the Island of Nevis. They are separated by a channel a few hundred feet wide. The two islands share a beach in an unorthodox way. After each storm, one island would have a surplus of sand while the other one would have lost an equal and opposite amount. The storms seemed to make sure that the shifts were equalized, because historically, the gain and loss of beach sand seemed to alternate with each storm. It was de rigueur for the owner of a resort on the south shore of St. Kitts to phone a kindred soul on the shores of Nevis and enquire, "Have you seen our beach?" The query would then be returned northward after the next storm.

Despite this minor inconvenience, Banana Bay was, and I hope still is, an idyllic place. There was a bar on a large dock. The three buildings that made up the resort were widely separated with little chance of party noise disturbing residents of any other building. Nightlife was restricted to reading in bed and sleep. Nancy and I welcomed this because one of our passions is reading, and reading in bed is a favourite way for us to end our day.

While we were there, we prepared to do some snorkelling. Nancy and I had borrowed masks and snorkels from family back home. However, since Nancy had borrowed one that belonged to one of her children, it was rather small. One evening, we decided that we would snorkel the next day, so we tried on our gear in our room. Nancy put on her borrowed mask and asked what I thought. I could hardly answer the question. Her nose seemed to be squished against the glass panel and she looked pained. I fell back laughing onto the bed and then felt something digging into my back. It was Nancy's glasses, which she had dropped on the bed so that she could try out the snorkelling mask. They were now in three pieces and the tiny little plastic strap that held the lenses in place had snapped under the pressure of my weight. This ensured that Nancy could no longer see well enough to read for the balance of the trip.

Nancy was a little fed up with me. There was no optometrist in the area and it was doubtful if there was even one in Basseterre, the capital of St. Kitts. What could I do? I did what any loving friend would do. I read Nancy's book to her—every night—prior to retiring. I even tried to change my voice to fit my impression of each character. I cannot remember whether or not we finished the book together. It was a new experience for both of us; reading a bedtime story to an adult. I was also called on to perform similar readings at other times of the day, such as on the beach after swimming.

Our hotel was located on a rounded corner of the island. Its shoreline curved into Banana Bay from the channel between Nevis and St. Kitts. One could swim at either of these two beaches. We could choose the quiet of the bay, or the more raucous sounds from the bar on the south shore facing Nevis. Since our room overlooked the bay, we had only to walk a short distance to the Banana Bay beach to enjoy a tranquil swim.

We made the acquaintance of several friends—the first of which were a swarm of stinging ants that objected to me leaning against *their* tree. At the time the ants attacked, I was questioning the person who was in charge of the boat rentals about the costs, and if there were any time limits. A minute or so after I had stepped away from the tree, all assault on my person ceased. Apparently, these ants do not hold grudges.

After finding out that there was no charge for taking out a sailboat, I asked Nancy if she would like to go sailing. Come on, I said, "It'll be exciting." Her response was a timorous, "Yes." She loves boats but prefers the kind that do not tip. I had done some sailing before and the type of dinghy that was available to us on this day appeared to be quite manageable. After the usual routine preparations, we set out.

As we moved out into the strait between the two islands, the wind picked up considerably and became quite gusty. This didn't bother me because I knew how to compensate for the effect of a gust by quickly letting out the mainsail so that the wind could escape and its pressure would not tip the boat. Even with ideal conditions, this is not Nancy's favourite way to travel. Unfortunately, on this morning, the wind had a nasty spirit that continually rocked our small craft from side to side with a series of rapid gusts. As each one approached, I had to sit out far on the gunwale then scramble back to the centre after it had passed. Repeat, and repeat again. Although I was accustomed to "riding the gunwale," I knew that this was going to be somewhat more difficult for Nancy.

Suddenly, a very strong gust hit the sail. I let out the mainsheet but was dismayed to find that some gormless twit had obviously needed a piece of rope before we had taken the boat out. He had cut his piece of rope from the mainsheet and *tied a knot in the end of the remaining rope so that it would not slide through its stays on the boom.* This thoughtless idiot could not have been a seaman. Such careless actions eliminated any way for me or any other sailor to relieve the sporadic gusting of the wind by simply letting go of the mainsheet. A moment after I discovered the shortened mainsheet with the knot in it, Nancy and I were swimming. Not pausing to curse, I righted the craft and helped Nancy to climb aboard.

Oh well, what's a dump in the water? It was at least refreshing. Then just as suddenly as before, another strong gust hit, and Nancy and I went for another swim. Now I was mad. I *again* righted the sailboat. We travelled some distance before a third and more powerful gust hit. This time, after being dumped for the third time, I could not get the sodden sail up out of the water.

The fact that I had ruined Nancy's glasses earlier meant that she was experiencing all of this with blurred vision. This added to her 'excitement'. Also, we found ourselves drifting in a rapid current assisted by a strong wind in the same direction. We were forced to float in the strait for some time until someone noticed that we needed assistance and came to help. This added to our stress considerably. I was truly worried. If no one had come, we could have ended up in the middle of that broad expanse of water, leaving our families to hear about how we had been blown away into the vast Caribbean Sea.

Spurred on by spectators on the beach, the man in charge of the boats at our hotel finally arrived in a launch to help us. Unfortunately, he was more interested in saving the boat. He towed it home and left Nancy and I to swim to land on our own and walk back along the shore to our room. How embarrassing. To make matters worse, once we arrived back at the dock, we were told that there was an emergency. A hurricane was rapidly approaching the Island of Nevis and all the residents at Banana Bay had to be evacuated to Basseterre. No wonder it had been so gusty.

However, I know that even as blustery as it was, had the mainsheet not been tampered with, I could have sailed without dumping Nancy into the drink. Well...maybe not three times anyway.

Our trip to Basseterre was by motorized launch because there were no roads connecting the bay to the capital. Despite the concern about the hurricane, we enjoyed the trip. However, we did not enjoy spending three days of our supposedly idyllic trip in town, as opposed to the rather tranquil Banana Bay Hotel. We eventually returned to the bay to enjoy the remainder of our vacation. However, Nancy has never gone sailing with me since.

Recently, my son Jamie spoke to me about being interested in learning to sail. When he asked about this, he was wondering if I felt we should take an introductory or an intermediate course together. I suggested that we take beginners' lessons.

Perhaps Jamie will dump me into the drink and help me understand exactly how Nancy felt when she was thrown overboard after one of my 'skilled' manoeuvres.

Few things improve when you get to the end of your rope.

∞ Cheese Grinder ∞

Nancy's dog, Casey, was a spitting image of the little pooch that my brother had brought from the Kemptville area when we were in our teens. Both of these dogs seemed to pop up, or out, when a Cocker Spaniel has had a moment of madness with some other breed. We called Casey a Black English Water Spaniel 'type'.

Casey only stole my food once. At three-thirty one morning when I was preparing for a fishing trip, I left my cereal on the table for a moment. When I came back, Casey was sitting on the chair enjoying it.

His successor was Felix, a large Golden Labrador Retriever. Felix had done this sort of thing many times. The last five stories in this chapter comprise a sample of his relentless efforts to feed himself people food—regardless of our continued efforts to prevent him from doing so.

Once, when I had been home alone for dinner, I had prepared spaghetti for myself. Rather than dish up the pasta mixed with preserved ginger and curry powder as I had once sampled in a Chinese restaurant, I had decided to 'go traditional'. I had a fine recipe for tomato sauce and with several additions of my own, plus some homemade bread, I settled down for a great meal. I even had some special Parmesan cheese—purchased in the renowned Kensington Market—and a new plastic cheese grinder that Nancy had given me as one of my Christmas presents. For me, it makes a major difference to the flavour of a pasta meal when one grates fresh Parmesan cheese onto the tomato sauce just before dining.

I cleaned up after my dinner and placed the dishes in the dishwasher. When I came to the grinder, it had only a few tiny fragments of cheese left on it. I mulled over what I should do. I could have put it in the dishwasher but because it was a bit of a pain to dry, I elected to brush the cheese off without giving it a proper washing. I reasoned that I would clean it properly after lunch the next day, when I intended to eat the last of the pasta.

The next morning at breakfast, while sitting at the kitchen table and perusing the newspaper, I noticed funny looking small white bits of plastic on the kitchen floor. I was perplexed. These 'bits' weren't there the night before. Further investigation produced funny looking small white plastic bits ground into the dining room rug as well.

There was also a trail of funny looking small white plastic bits on the living room floor. And there I found the remains of a cheese grinder incapable of ever being used again. It was now clear. Our dog, Felix, was the culprit.

I was amazed at the dog's fortitude. Just a few miniscule fragments of cheese had inspired Felix to devise a plan, open the drawer, remove the grinder, take it to the front of the living room, and satisfy his urges with such intensity that *he* ground my Christmas present to pieces. Later, I tried to remember not to leave as much as a morsel of food in any drawer less than seven feet above the floor.

Dogs will find a way.

∞ Intuition ∞

Generally, it would be safe to say that my relationship with Felix cost me several meals. Although he was not supposed to be as smart as me, he continually proved otherwise when it came to gathering foodstuffs for his gut. For example, I love to bake fresh homemade bread. Unfortunately, that was one of Felix's favourites. I used to answer the phone with a fresh loaf on the stove still cooling. However, even this short time would be enough to allow Felix to scarf the bread. So, over the years, I learned that if you have a large dog that likes homemade bread, don't answer the telephone after leaving a freshly baked loaf to cool on anything lower than the top of your fridge.

Another time, I had purchased several slices of my specialized pizza from a place in Kensington Market—to the tune of twenty-five dollars. When I got home, I intended to wrap each slice individually and put them in the freezer in separate packages. I wanted to ration these expensive but delectable squared slices until I had time to revisit my favourite downtown pizzeria.

On this occasion, someone called me from upstairs and I was sidetracked. I left the pizza in a large box on the kitchen counter, only because I expected to be away from it for less than a minute. Typically, the minute stretched into about ten. As I returned to the kitchen, I passed Felix on the stairs. He was coughing on something. I wanted to get back to my wrapping…but there were no pizza slices left on the counter. The entire box had been cleaned out in the short time I was gone.

I rushed back to the stairs to get Felix, and when I turned on the light I noticed funny little black bits. Evidence! It was chewed up black olives from my pizza, but I still hadn't caught Felix in the act. In this case, I learned that if you have a large dog like Felix who likes to feed himself, do not leave pizza anywhere lower than seven feet above the floor.

Gradually, as I learned his tricks, I felt I could anticipate his intentions. On one evening, I had prepared a cheese omelette for dinner using my large chef's knife to slice the cheese and other ingredients. I had enjoyed my omelette and it was time to clean up. However, I had wanted to watch a particular documentary that was to be televised that evening. So, I switched on the TV and started watching the show. With all of the food safely stored, I figured that I could clean up the kitchen when the program was over.

I settled in to enjoy the program with Felix lying beside me. Throughout the show I continually reminded myself to clean up the kitchen. Suddenly the chef's knife clattered to the floor. I had become so engrossed in the documentary that my mental vigilance over the clean-up had been compromised. A moment later, Felix experienced an uncharacteristic slip when he tried to lift my chef's knife off the counter. His persistence got the better of me again!

After reflecting on the situation, I realized that I had stopped thinking about the chef's knife only a few seconds before it fell to the floor. It was as if Felix had been reading my mind and secretly waiting for me to stop thinking about the knife. The fact that he seized the opportunity to snatch my knife—within a few seconds of my mind drifting—still causes me to wonder how he was so intuitive.

I don't know how this could be. Perhaps man's best friends are able to detect micro mannerisms of ours and interpret them to their benefit. Or, maybe Felix simply recognized my concentration lessening as I began to relax. Either way, I am sure of one thing— I should have cleaned everything up before I left the kitchen.

Although a dog is man's best friend, it is possible he is working as a double agent.

Life's Lessons: A Successful Collection of Failures

∞ Soup ∞

I come from a family where my father loved to cook. After he had returned from the war, I always enjoyed watching him in the kitchen and learning about his use of herbs and spices. I remember observing one day in 1948 in which he wished to perfect a recipe that he had just discovered in a magazine. This new dish was called Pizza.

Since those days, I continually make efforts to update my skills as various cuisines come to the fore. After years of watching my mother and father cook, combined with two formal classes about cooking East Indian food, and another dealing with vegetarian food—I can confidently whip up a meal of scrambled eggs in no time. This reasonable grounding in the art of cookery has allowed even my fried egg sandwiches, and my egg salad sandwiches, to be acclaimed.

It was in the vegetarian food course where I learned how to make green lentil salad. I decided to make a batch for supper. As is often the case, I made too much. After having servings for nearly a week, I decided that I needed to do something different. So, after some creative thought, I decided to venture into uncharted territory and make soup out of the salad.

I felt as if my imagination was in full flower when I was working on my soup. My ingenuity was at its greatest heights. After dinner with some potato water, a bit of this, a bit of that, some ground coriander, a batch of onion sautéed in butter, some fried mushrooms with their juice, two large whole red chillies, chopped fresh coriander, black mustard seeds, turmeric, fenugreek, and a soupçon of asafoetida I continued to concoct my creation. I felt as if I was on my way to preparing a soup for the gods.

It was late by the time the soup had finished simmering. I tried a small sample. It was delicious. My robust but delightfully tasty soup was more like a work of genius. Since it took me almost a full evening to prepare, I did not have a complete record of the ingredients used. However, I knew that I would be able to taste and identify most of them after having a large bowl or two at lunch the next day. I could hardly wait.

I retired for the night and left the soup to mellow in a three quart pot on a back burner of the stove with the heat off. I was eagerly anticipating an early lunch of homemade soup with fresh bread for the morrow.

I was working from my home office, where I would typically put in a few hours before my first meal of the day. When I sat down to eat breakfast, I noticed that my soup was not on the stove and nowhere to be found. Nancy had already left for work, so I thought that she had put my soup in the refrigerator. It wasn't there. Since it was winter, and we sometimes used the cold solarium for leftovers, I thought that perhaps Nancy had stored my soup there. Nothing. Where was my soup?

Then, I discovered the pot at the far end of the living room— licked clean. There was no trace of soup in the pot, no marks on the light-coloured rug, and no spills anywhere between the pot and the stove, some forty feet away. Not even sticky little spots from spills on the kitchen floor. I doubt a forensic scientist could have traced the route. Obviously the soup had been greatly appreciated. Felix had done it again. But how?

I am still baffled as to how Felix managed to carry the three quart pot by the rounded side handle, balance it full of liquid, and relocate it for convenient consumption…all without spilling a drop.

To this day, with the exception of my lentil salad, I have no idea what proportions of herbs and spices were used for that special soup.

The power of positive thinking works—even for dogs.

∽ **Chocolates** ∽

Some of our friends don't think that Felix was a very intelligent pooch. Like many other Labs, he had a small peak on the back of his skull. I referred to this bony protrusion as the place where his brains were. Unfortunately, Richard and I made up our minds that our book should not stray from the truth. The articles had to be honest—at least insofar as our memories are concerned. So, in the spirit of total honesty, I have to admit that Felix continued to outsmart me.

One evening, Nancy and I had to leave Felix on his own at our new home. By this time, we felt we had learned how to make all food inaccessible to him. Before leaving, we carefully placed an open box of chocolates out of his reach on the top of the china cabinet—a perch over six feet high; seventy-three inches, to be exact. We know this because we measured it during the editing of this book. At the time, we were sure that the chocolates would be safe.

We've all heard different opinions about how safe it is for dogs to eat chocolate. Is it absolute poison or a diet staple? As a precaution, we have always made sure that no chocolate was left loosely hanging about on counters, tables, or anywhere else within Felix's reach.

Later that evening, Nancy and I arrived home to a house liberally sprayed with dark brown vomit. Felix had outsmarted us again. Considering how many chocolates he had eaten, and despite the mess, Felix was only slightly sick. Luckily, being such a large dog, his size worked in his favour. He stayed in a drained condition for only a couple of days. I have since joked with others about his vulnerable state, saying, "Felix had been weakened for the weekend."

He was soon up and about and searching for more goodies. To this day, Nancy and I are still amazed at what he had done. We still wonder how Felix managed to knock the box of chocolates off the top of the china cabinet without breaking either of Nancy's prized figurines.

Actually, the two miniature replicas—Michelangelo's David

and the Greek goddess Aphrodite—were not even disturbed. However, earlier, the figure of David had had his head knocked off, but by Mena, an Irish Setter—one of Nancy's other dogs who had been a member of the family long before I was.

Being a perplexed engineer ("At first I couldn't spell it, now I are one"), I think I have finally figured out part of the puzzle. Nancy remembers placing the box on the top of the china cabinet slightly overhanging so as to make it easier for *her* to reach. However, two sets of legs about twenty-two inches long, plus a body that added twenty more, totals one big dog within a foot of a prized treat. With the treasure so close, a little stretching and a short hop was all Felix needed to knock the chocolates off the top of the cabinet with a whap from his paws which he tended to use as hands.

How he did so, without even moving the figurines, remains a mystery. I doubt Felix ever forgot how sick he became after eating so many chocolates.

No passion for poison ever has a happy ending.

∞ Bread Pudding ∞

I had been busy preparing a favourite dessert of mine—bread pudding. As a treat, I was planning to serve it to some guests after returning from a night out for dinner. I can whip this specialty up in twenty minutes—including cooking time in the microwave. I leave out the sugar but stack it with nutmeg, currants, or raisins, to compensate. In this way I have a bread pudding that is not too sweet and just perfect for my taste.

I figured that my guests could add sugar if they wanted, sprinkle it with powdered cinnamon, place gobs of ice cream on it, or even leave it the way it was if they so desired. I cook it my way and welcome the creative trimmings of others. On this occasion, I had prepared a considerable amount. I did so because it had been some time since I had tasted any and I wanted to be prepared for anyone asking for seconds.

In the rush to arrive at the restaurant on time for our dinner reservations, we hurried out the door and I left the large shallow bowl of pudding on top of the microwave where it had been placed to cool. The bowl had been handmade and presented as a family Christmas gift some time ago. It was smooth, white, thick china, about four inches deep by twelve inches in diameter, and had dark blue writing on the side saying, "Fearnley's Fancy Fixins." I used this large serving dish for everything from scalloped potatoes to fruit salad.

At the East Indian restaurant we had a very spicy dinner. As we returned home after the meal and burst through our front door, I headed straight for the kitchen to dish up the bread pudding. It wasn't there.

By now I had learned that situations like this offered little hope for a happy ending. Just then, someone called out from the living room. "I think you'd better see this."

"Fearnley's Fancy Fixins" was on our new rug in the middle of the living room—empty. *Five pounds of bread pudding gone!* The special dessert that I was so anxious to share had become merely a part of Felix's memory. My interest quickly changed from enjoying a sweet dessert to being more concerned about the possibilities of Felix once again repainting the house with a mass of regurgitated people food.

The heavy serving dish had been taken from its place on the microwave and somehow carried across the ceramic kitchen floor to one of his favourite spots—the middle of our new and expensive Egyptian rug. Nearby, Felix was found unsettled with a look on his face that seemed to say, "I can't believe I ate the whole thing."

I have given up trying to figure out these conundrums. However, as if by some ironic twist, I have since realized that Felix's need for people food may have been preordained. One time, after becoming very ill and near death, his veterinarian indicated that Felix should no longer eat dog food and prescribed a medicine to be taken along with a special carbohydrate diet composed solely of people food. Since his diagnosis, Nancy and I diligently followed the doctor's orders.

To our sincere delight, Felix became healthy enough to continue his pursuit of my food. Sadly, although he recovered enough to keep me on my guard for a couple more years, he died after one final evening walk on Saturday, May 27, 2006.

Recovery is a sweet gift for more than the one who was sick.

Life's Lessons: A Successful Collection of Failures

CLOSING: PART ONE

My dad died on July 26, 1950, at the age of forty-seven. It devastated our entire family. For a long time, we were all severely stressed and disheartened. Nevertheless, it did not stop us from recollecting our time with him. As painful as it was, our reminiscing helped us to cope. It still does.

Grief is such a personal experience. My initial thoughts were a complex mix of shock and anger. Over time, my feelings of frustration have lessened, giving way to sorrow and regret. But I still wonder.

Why was it that after his absence during World War II, we still had to live for years with only sporadic visits, and then—just as his TB was coming under control—be forever robbed of his presence? How could it be that Dad, Greg, and I would never again work together on another home project? What Sunday afternoon would ever be the same without him 'in concert' playing the piano while Mom prepared dinner? I ached each time I habitually returned from the store and unpacked the groceries, only to watch the rest of my family deflate when they saw that I had purchased enough for the entire family—including Dad.

My mom had her own agonies. Dad died during the year Mom described as her happiest since their wedding. With the exception of two short interludes of her husband's company—just before and after World War II—her life typified a single mom. I am reluctant to comment on Mom's feelings about my dad's death. I feel that I would be doing Mom a disservice trying to describe her innermost thoughts. However, I know that regardless of Dad's many absences, Mom felt his death acutely.

As far as Lynn and Greg are concerned, I respect their personal feelings as well, so I feel that they are not mine to share. However, Lynn, Greg, and I all agree that we are fortunate to have had Mom focus her attention on the future as she quietly maintained the responsibilities to her family and full time job.

Sadly, our mother died on May 26, 1991, shortly after Nancy and I had been married. Mom's passing was an enormous loss to the remainder of the Fearnley family, but she left many fond memories behind. At her funeral, we chose not to focus on her health problems prior to her death, but rather on her long life and its richness. Those present were invited to come forward after the formal portion of the service was over. Anyone wishing to relate an anecdote from their relationship with my mom was welcome to share it with the others.

Many of her family and friends spoke. She had been retired for almost a decade, but some of the people from her work still felt the desire to share their memories. No one who spoke was able to recite a story about my mother without some humorous element. Grievers from adjacent rooms must have wondered what all the laughter was about, but it helped to relieve the tension. These personal recollections made this celebration of her life that much more memorable. Mom would have enjoyed it since she had the grace and courage to laugh at herself.

Her last few years while she was bedridden had been in stark contrast to her joy for life. She loved all that life could offer, including her work, which she refused to retire from until she was forced to do so at the age of eighty-four. I will always miss her.

CLOSING: PART ONE

Both of my parents contributed largely to my sense of humour and I honour their approach towards life by following their lead. I believe that humour is the release valve that empowers us to deal with our innermost being, and that laughter is the lubricant that can help expel most of our unwanted emotions. This is especially true when we consciously choose to celebrate what we have gained, rather than dwell on what we have lost. I feel this philosophy has helped me cope with some of my life's most difficult challenges.

Earlier, I spoke of my uncle Ted—my namesake—and of my love for him. His death left my aunt Pearl on her own for twenty-five years. When she died in 1995, four years after my mom, the life of a generation came to a close but our family memories live on.

My siblings are as far away from Toronto as they could get and still be on the same continent. Unfortunately, we are unable to see each other often.

After I moved in with Nancy, she was always a loyal supporter of my elderly relatives—my mom and my aunts: Ida, Babe, and Pearl. Nancy cheerfully invited them for Christmas and helped with their birthday celebrations. I needed Nancy's help to care for them in their later years. At one time, I used to say that we had four eighty-five-year-old children to care for. At times, the extra care disrupted Nancy's family and their plans, but they accepted this willingly.

Now, I've been with Nancy for about as long as I had been with my first wife. So, I consider that my first commitment to Nancy—a long term relationship—is being fulfilled. I hope and expect it to continue. Our life together is rewarding—mostly because we have similar interests. We enjoy books, book reviews, films, travel, and general knowledge lectures at both of Toronto's major universities. One of our favourite activities is to attend the Toronto Film Festival every September—the only place where I will line up for entertainment.

Nancy and I continue to enjoy travelling together and meeting the many interesting people that cross our path. One of the most memorable people we met was during our vacation at the Banana Bay Hotel. On this holiday we met a man who owned the launch that was ferrying us out of Banana Bay to avoid the pending hurricane. On our return trip, we had a great conversation with him and discovered some of his history.

Apparently, he had left his family and friends in Britain, determined to live a carefree life as the captain of a cruise boat—a sailing craft. His brother was to join him, but at the last minute stayed home and our boat captain sailed their large cruise ship to St. Kitts on his own.

Later, as our captain explained, he set up his cruise business and stressed that he was now free of any cares. But, as the late afternoon started to turn into evening, he told us, "I've got to go. My pets need their feeding." His pets included a couple of goats, several chickens, dogs, and cats. Nancy and I were impressed with his commitment, but as he left the dock on his way home, Nancy whispered to me, "How free we seem, how fettered fast we are." Nancy's comment has remained clear in my mind since the moment it was spoken, perhaps because these words apply not only to him…but also to Nancy and me.

As of this writing Nancy and I have a new pet—a black two-year old perky miniature poodle named Letitia—named after an unknown great aunt Nancy discovered during her recent work on her family's genealogy. We call the small, active pooch Titia (pronounced Tisha) for short. And, she *is* short. Too short to steal any of our food from tables or countertops. We brought her home in October, 2006 while still grieving from the death of Felix. Nancy felt that a new companion would ease the loss of a favourite pet still fondly remembered.

Titia and I are taking agility training but in truth it is me who needs it. Titia runs faster than I can think and is smart enough to "catch on" after a few repetitions of a command *if she wants to*. She is a great companion and seems to understand that she is both welcomed and needed in our family.

Our children are now adults and well dispersed. Nancy's two sons both live within a short drive of our home. Her youngest, Greg, and his wife, Emily, are both teachers and the parents of our two youngest grandchildren, Olivia and Elliot. They regularly invite Nancy and me to their cottage in the summertime. We also visit David and his son Justin in their nearby home, often getting together for family dinners.

My youngest son, Jamie, lives in Toronto, while Steven, my middle child, resides near Atlanta, Georgia. Richard lives a short distance north of Nancy and me, with his wife, Annette, and their three children. He lives close enough to regularly "drop by" and help me with my personal and business affairs.

Recently, I have taken to visiting Richard's children once per week during the school year. I should say *trying* to visit because other things do get in the way sometimes. I like to play cribbage with his oldest daughter, Rachel, although I've only beaten her once in about six years. This is mainly because she has great skill and complements it with good luck. Richard's youngest, Jaclyn, is next on my list for teaching the game of cribbage. I expect she'll soon be competing with Rachel for most wins "against Gramps."

One of my other local efforts is to assist Richard's son Andrew with his schoolwork. The technicalities of math seldom faze him. He is a whiz at the subject but sometimes needs to be reminded to read the question so that the answer he provides will be relevant. His math skills have helped him become a great euchre player—to the extent that he was entered in a school tournament not long ago, and finished on a winning team. Andrew is also a great athlete, but not because of any special DNA from my side of the family. However…I watch him carefully for signs of the rogue gene Richard and I have written about.

Over time, I have come to believe that whoever we might see when we leave this earth will be concerned about what we've done during our lives. I feel our legacy will have a far greater and lasting effect than what religion we practiced or whether we practiced any one at all. I believe that our actions—not our beliefs—will attest to our record of following the tenet, "Do unto others as you would have them do unto you."

Life's Lessons: A Successful Collection of Failures

PART TWO

RICK AND HIS FAMILY

LIFE WITH MY SIBLINGS

Welcome to Part Two of this book. My name is Rick Fearnley and I'll be your author and guide for your ride through the next generation of our family's more memorable antics. Each story in this part is in chronological order. However, as in Part One, this holds true within each chapter but not necessarily from one chapter to the next.

As my dad and I explained in the Preface, this book is the result of a collective effort from both of us. My sense of humour came from my dad's side of the family. He's always been the one in our family who could make you laugh, if he wanted to. My brothers and I have all enjoyed this side of him. Together, the three of us presented him with many challenges over the years, and on occasion we still do. This first chapter includes some of those challenges from our younger years. My mom was also harried and tested through every one of these occurrences.

While growing up, our family lived in the "Golden Horseshoe" surrounding Toronto, Ontario, Canada. My most memorable family times occurred from when I was about eight years old, until I moved away from home at the age of eighteen. During this time, Steve and I played, fought, and got into trouble. Then, without our permission, our parents added a third brother, to the great delight of Steve and me. We all welcomed my youngest brother, Jamie, into our lives.

My mom and dad split up many years ago, but I have remained close to both of my parents, despite the grief I put them through. My dad and I had a lot of laughs and became closer over the last few years while writing this book together. However, we struggled with each other's strong will many times during this period. I prefer to think of my steadfastness as perseverance and my dad's as stubbornness. In any case, as far as life in general is concerned, we have learned to extend grace to each other for the topics on which we disagree.

One thing we have always agreed upon is that our family chronicles are worth sharing. If not for the value of the lessons we learned, then at least for the sake of others having a good laugh at our expense. My dad often described his mother as having the grace to laugh at herself. I am thankful to him for making me aware of this fact and passing it along to me. His insight and fatherly perspective have made every one of my anecdotes more entertaining than I could ever have expected to record them on my own. My hope is that each person who reads my account of the various life lessons I have learned throughout my years will benefit in some way from the experience.

I should also mention that if you happen to be one of the poor souls who have paid a price for simply crossing my path in the past, or if you simply find yourself saying, "Hey, that was me," then please accept this book as my way of offering you a formal apology.

༄ **Monsters Under the Bed** ༄

I am two and a half years older than my closest brother Steve. When Jamie was born, I was eight years old, making Steve close to six. With the arrival of our new baby brother, Steve and I had to share a bedroom while the new addition got his own. Therefore, Steve and I shared "his" bedroom, until my dad built a separate one for me in the basement.

We both enjoyed taking turns sleeping on the floor in a sleeping bag. It was a bit like having a friend visit for a sleepover. On one of the nights when I was in the sleeping bag and Steve was in the bed, I heard him stir. I remained quiet and motionless with the top of my sleeping bag over my head. It was very early and still dark outside. Steve tossed and turned.

I wondered if he was having a nightmare. He was terrified of monsters and couldn't sleep some nights for fear of them being under his bed. I'm sure he was not the only child to think such thoughts at this age. It was common knowledge with those my age that no monster could get you if you were safely under the covers of your bed. This is another reason why Steve and I always asked our parents to tuck us in every night.

Suddenly, Steve got out of bed and darted for the washroom. I had been lying in the sleeping bag all this time with my eyes open. I was used to the darkness and I could see around the bedroom clearly. I noticed a pillow under Steve's bed and thought for a moment. My mind raced, trying to think of a way to get the pillow to jump out at Steve on his way back into bed. That would be great, I thought. It would surely be scary if I could just figure out a way to have it move at my will.

Then it hit me. I would reverse the concept and use the pillow to puff up my sleeping bag so that it looked like I was still in it. This would allow me to lurk under the bed unnoticed. I quietly stuffed the pillow into my sleeping bag and moulded it to the shape I thought I was in so as not to arouse suspicion from Steve on his way back to bed.

I then crawled under his bed, being careful not to disrupt any of the clothes or other items that were scattered around the floor of the room. Once underneath, I positioned myself far enough in from the side to ensure I remained hidden.

Every kid knows that, at night, you have to be under the covers before the toilet stops flushing to be safe. Otherwise, just being tucked in would not ensure complete safety provided by the cover rule. Steve was no different. He flushed the toilet and ran into our bedroom, racing the waning sound of the flush. I had decided to grab his leg as he jumped into bed, despite the possibility of seriously injuring my wrist. I rehearsed my frightening manoeuvre a few times while he was briefly in the washroom. I felt the longer I held on to him without making a noise, the greater the effect would be. I was mindful of the fact that once he recognized my voice, he would know I wasn't in the sleeping bag and my fun would be over. I had only one shot to get this right.

As Steve burst through the bedroom door, he ran towards the bed but jumped a greater distance from it than I had expected—presumably attempting to avoid any creatures that might have been living underneath. I missed grabbing his leg but the tips of my fingers brushed his instep from his ankle to his toes on one of his feet. Steve jerked his foot and squealed. The gentle contact was subtle enough to have him wondering what it was, but strong enough to convince him that something was definitely under the bed. This was turning out better than I had planned. He knew something lurked below him but he didn't know what.

I remained motionless and kept my laughter in check. I knew that each moment I remained silent reinforced his innermost worries. This heightened my excitement. It was difficult to keep from laughing but I managed to do so for a long time—so long that the joke was almost on me. Steve stayed awake but quiet for hours without moving. He stayed like this until sunrise. I had to lie in an uncomfortable position under the bed until he finally got up. It was not until the room was partially lit by the rising sun that Steve dared to get out of bed and leave the room.

It was worth the wait. I noticed that in his rush, he stepped over my sleeping bag so as not to disturb me. This made me believe he thought I was still in it. I crawled back into the sleeping bag the moment he left and returned the pillow to its original location under Steve's bed. There I remained, and waited, until he returned so I could exit my sleeping bag with him as my witness—all this to reinforce his fears. I was such a conniver.

Later that morning, while cleaning up our bedroom, Steve bravely attempted to look under the bed. His extreme apprehension in doing so confirmed my hopes—I had executed my prank undetected. His worry about "the monster" under his bed increased dramatically that day.

I believe we are the most vulnerable when we think we are safe. Eventually, I explained my practical joke to Steve, face to face, well after I had tricked him so convincingly. Since my confession, we have both been able to laugh at this incident, although my laughter is recognizably louder than his. But then again, I've been enjoying the memory for a significantly longer time…poor guy.

Worries increase until you face your fear.

∞ Passing the Time ∞

One summer when Steve and I were still in elementary school, we became bored and looked for something to do. We were old enough to play unsupervised and would have been allowed to walk to the nearby park on our own had we suggested this to either of our parents. Both my mom and dad were home on this particular day, but they were busy and could not attend to our entertainment.

On this morning, Steve and I were discussing different games we could play. We agreed that the best activity to engage in would be one that would last all day long. Otherwise, we would be back struggling to find a cure for our boredom in short order.

I don't remember which one of us first suggested the new game, but I do remember agreeing with Steve and commenting, "We'll play spear all day." Spear was a game not yet invented. In fact, we were just making it up at the time. We decided it would be great fun to throw spears at each other, all day long.

Not once did either of us think about the dangers involved. We had seen many battles fought on TV with spears and all the important people made it to the end without any major casualty. Besides, the girls loved it if you were slightly scarred.

We found two broom handles made of hardwood that were similar to a spear but not nearly sharp enough for our liking. We dared not ask for the use of a knife, since our parents would not have approved. We weren't even allowed to use steak knives at the dinner table. Now…how could we sharpen our spears?

We tried various techniques to whittle them down. Eventually we began to file them in a primitive sanding sort of action on the square patio stones in front of our house. This graduated to pushing the wooden sticks up and down the concrete driveway until our backs began to hurt from the strain of maintaining pressure on the lower half of the broom handle. Later, we found a more efficient manner with which to craft our homemade weapons. We held them waist high and scraped them along the bricks in the breezeway between our house and the garage. It was here Steve and I manufactured our first lethal armaments.

Together we walked up and down the breezeway shaping our wooden poles. We had been able to coordinate Steve scraping his along the bricks on the outside of the house while I did the same using the garage bricks on the other side of the breezeway. Together, we continued walking up and down the pathway, first in the opposite direction, and then later in the same direction with a patterned step. This was done to facilitate friendly conversations between us while we sharpened our wooden spears, preparing them for the all day battle.

The rhythm we maintained as we marched up and down the corridor allowed us to exit the ends of the breezeway simultaneously and turn around together with such coordinated precision it felt as though we had a true militaristic flare. It is also possible we looked more like a couple idiots practicing for an audition to act as soldiers who would announce time in cuckoo-clock fashion for a local stage production.

In either case, our plan to throw sharp objects at each other—all day long—in a friendly game of spear, was creating a great bond between us. By mid morning, we had created two weapons sharp enough to pierce straight through the abdomen of any living thing. Of course, they would have to be thrust by someone foolish enough to engage in such an act. Steve and I anxiously made the preparations for precisely such an event.

We set out the rules of the game. There were no rules—this was war. Eager to bring our efforts of the morning into fruition, we decided on a battlefield: the front lawn. Fortunately, there were no neighbours outside to observe the two boneheads in action and embarrass our parents more than we had on prior occasions.

We had prepared ourselves for action like no previous sibling rivalry. But how were we to begin? Then it came to me. I could make it appear as if I was giving Steve the upper hand by letting him start us off. I asked that he count to three then say "Go." While he was busy counting, he wouldn't be ready for the first throw until a moment or so after actually saying the word "go" and I would gain the advantage. He counted slowly and I readied myself for the precise moment my arsenal could be legally released.

The instant my unsuspecting brother said, "go" I released my spear with all the strength I could muster. He barely had time to turn away from the oncoming missile before he was struck in the back. He screamed. Our all day battle was over in less than a second. Steve lay moaning on the front lawn in a pathetic state as neighbours began to come out of their houses to see what all the commotion was about.

It didn't look good for Steve. The weapon was no longer in my hand and I appeared innocent. To approaching onlookers, it appeared as if a careless child had somehow injured himself with one of the two spears that lay beside him. If not for my presence, it may have constituted one of those brainteasers in which one has only twenty questions to figure out what happened.

The look my dad gave me when he arrived at the crime scene suggested he needed less than twenty questions to figure out "who dun it." Fortunately for Steve, I had no more javelin throwing experience than any other eight year old. Poor technique on my part resulted in the spear pivoting in the air before striking Steve in the back with the blunt end as he made a desperate but noble attempt to avoid my oncoming missile. No 'significant' injuries were sustained.

After my dad had finally pieced together what had precipitated our one-second war, he promptly sent me to my room for the rest of the day. Both Steve and I ended this day just as bored as we were at the start—but at least I passed the time uninjured.

Just because your sibling lets you call the shots doesn't mean you won't get stabbed in the back.

∞ Three's the Limit! ∞

Being the oldest, I was often allowed certain privileges. A later bedtime, the first to try something, and on occasion other benefits regularly came my way. This didn't last for long. Steve and I became treated more like children of the same age once I began growing into *his* clothes. By the time we were both in middle school, he was significantly bigger.

One evening when we were all gathered around the dinner table, we were promised a greater portion of dessert if we ate all of our dinner. My mom had made her famous peanut butter cookies. They've always been my favourite cookies—even to this day. I finished my meal and began taking from the pile of freshly baked cookies. They were addictive. (They still are.) I kept helping myself to another each time the rest of the family wasn't looking.

Steve was still gagging on his vegetables and struggling to finish his meal. As soon as he did, my mom warned, "Three's the limit!" I thought it best not to let on that I had already eaten about eight—my current record. I wondered what it would be like to eat a whole dozen. I cautiously pressed on towards my new goal as the conversation around our dinner table continued.

I was lucky that everyone seated was laughing and joking around, while I continued to fill my face with yet another cookie. I brought to the table something different than my usual comic relief. I kept a steadfast and serious focus squarely on Steve and the number of cookies *he* was having.

After each joke my dad would tell, I would make a comment that caused my mom to scrutinize Steve's cookie consumption. I continued to stuff myself with Mom's delicious cookies while Dad was busy telling us his funny stories and my mom was just as busy watching Steve.

I managed to down ten before anyone caught on. The first one who did was Mom. Her attention strayed away from Steve and towards the largely diminished pile of cookies in the middle of the table. "How many have you had?" she asked loudly as she grabbed the eleventh one out of my hand in a somewhat confused state. "Ten," I said proudly as my cookie fell out of her hands and onto the floor. She was appalled and my dad was speechless.

Steve had just begun to understand my ploy. Boy, does it ever help to be a few years older. I was smiling like a cat that had just swallowed ten canaries. As I begged my mom for more, I could see Steve whimpering about my mom's decision to cut off the cookie supply for everyone at the table. In one final desperate attempt to coax more treats out of the cookie boss, I said, "But Mom, I wanted to eat a whole dozen." For some reason my plea—although not logical—persuaded her to throw one more cookie at me and say, "There, you can have this one and the one on the floor."

I got to the cookie on the ground before Steve even thought of going for it. He had mistakenly hoped our mom would respond in the same way if he made the same appeal. His lengthy but feeble effort became my dinner entertainment as I polished off the last two cookies and revelled in my accomplishment.

He whined and complained that he should get nine more, but my mother simply refused him, citing her rule—"Three's the limit!" This is not a rational statement given the circumstances. However, it has often amazed me how people can discard sound logic to justify how many cookies they should or should not eat.

Before any record is broken, a goal has been set.

❧ Table Tennis ☙

Steve and I were quite competitive in our younger years. In middle school we both managed to make the cut for different school teams in various sports. One of the games I excelled in was ping-pong. I believe this is largely due to the fact that Steve and I were very competitive and played many games trying to outdo each other.

One of the ways my dad kept us from getting mixed up in drugs was honouring his part of an agreement with us: buying a pool table for our family. In turn, Steve and I could play to our hearts' content at home, as long as we kept up our part of the agreement, which was to "Stay out of the pool halls." I faithfully honoured the arrangement well into my adult life, and I believe Steve did as well.

Our parents had purchased the tabletop accessories that went with our pool table and this allowed us to play table tennis as well. Steve and I played both games frequently. Later in high school, I represented my school in a provincial final as one of their ping-pong players, and at one time I was actually ranked as a result of participating in these competitions. I attribute much of my success in this area to the spirited games Steve engaged me in while we were younger.

In my youth I was a poor loser, and as far as winning went, not much better behaved. One day after school, Steve and I were having a mini ping-pong tournament of our own. We were in the basement playing when he did something totally unacceptable—he beat me. I lost my temper and in frustration threw my table tennis racquet at him. Both of our parents were out at the time. Funny, but I don't ever remember losing my temper in such a way with them at home.

Anyway, Steve was bleeding and I needed to attend to him if I had any hope of him stopping his whining before our mother returned. He had a deep laceration to his forehead and was bleeding profusely. Not being well trained in first aid, I headed to the laundry room. I pulled him quickly behind me to avoid staining the carpet and facilitate disposing of the blood, which was still spewing from his head. We worked together to keep the remainder of his blood from pouring out.

After getting the blood to stop (possibly because he simply ran out of it), I begged him, "Please, don't tell Mom." He looked at me with a puzzled look as if to ask how anyone could possibly keep such a large gash hidden. I encouraged him to wear a hat and not look up. This didn't have to be forever I explained…just until he healed. Even with the blood successfully cleaned up and the evidence well hidden, it was foolishly optimistic to think he could go a few weeks without ever looking our mom or dad in the eye. However, it was the only plan I could think of, so I went with it.

Fortunately, the loss of blood had slowed Steve down a little. He seemed sluggish, possibly because his body was working to replace the blood lost earlier that afternoon. His slower pace was complemented by my earlier stipulations that he not look up. I was proud of his noble attempt as he began his six week quest to avoid eye contact with our parents by continuously wearing his hat and staring at the floor.

The first wrinkle in my plan became apparent that evening when Steve wore his hat into the bathroom. This drew undue attention to his injured head. Although I cannot put my finger on exactly why, there *is* something odd about a child wearing only a towel and a hat. It wasn't long before my mom was calling out, "Ted, would you come over here and look at something for me please." When I heard this, I knew I was in for it. Hoping to stay any punishment, I immediately went into 'perfect kid' mode.

It didn't do much good. After one or two pathetic attempts to divert my mom's attention from his wound, Steve caved in and told her the truth. He left no detail out. I was actually surprised that he had managed to conceal his injury for so long. He still teases me about the day I split his head open with a ping-pong racquet, but I've learned to forgive him.

You can stop the blood, but "truth will out."

∞ Faster! Faster! ∞

Steve and I had different struggles and were truly at odds with each other until high school. Our relationship started to improve around the time we were both dating as we began to share a unique common ground—rejection. We had a rule about the girls we dated: if one of us was interested in someone we both knew, the other would shy away from her. We honoured this agreement as we spent much of our teenaged years trying to impress the various females that crossed our path.

When we weren't trying to impress young women, we were trying to impress the guys, but not for the same reasons. We both played competitive sports like baseball and hockey. Steve was more of a daredevil, and I, more of a show off.

One time when we were playing out front of our home in North York, we were both trying to outdo each other as our friends looked on. We had invented another game to keep ourselves amused. We never named it, possibly because there is no logical name that comes to mind. The game was composed of Steve and I pulling each other on a skateboard up and down the road behind my bicycle. Earlier, I had customized my ten-speed bike by putting high handlebars and a banana seat on it. On this day, we tied an old water-ski rope to the rearmost brace of my heavy-duty seat.

The speed was not to Steve's liking. My younger brother was bigger than me, and indeed more muscular. He did that bodybuilding thing and most muscles on his body were bigger and stronger than mine. This was not an easy thing to cope with during my adolescence. Things like growing into my younger brother's clothes tended to add to the already existing awkwardness of my teenage years and also to the friction between us.

On this afternoon, Steve was adding to my frustrations by teasing me in front of our mutual friends and the neighbourhood kids who had gathered around to see what trouble the Fearnley boys were getting into. I'm sure it was fun to watch an older brother pull his younger sibling on a skateboard behind a funny-looking bicycle. I believe a good portion of their entertainment was the interaction between Steve and I as we each tried to gain the upper hand in front of our friends.

Steve's daredevil challenges raised my show off tendencies to new heights. He was complaining about the speed I was pulling him not being anywhere close to the speed he was providing for my thrill rides. He was also reminding our audience that I was two and a half years his senior. Steve was heavier and only needed to stand up while peddling to achieve a greater thrust than anyone many pounds lighter—like me.

Each time it was my turn to pull, I expended so much effort that I rotated the high handlebars of the bike towards me. They always slipped into a near-horizontal position so quickly that it was difficult to pedal and I couldn't accelerate to achieve the speed I knew I was capable of reaching. In Steve's mind, my problem was merely poor technique and constituted nothing more than a lame excuse.

Slack in the rope occurred only after every rush of acceleration. The more swiftly the peddler accelerated, the more slack would be created after this energy burst. Only during this lull with slack in the rope, could the skateboard rider demonstrate his tricks. Steve continually pointed out to the gallery that I did not have the strength to accelerate quickly enough to create any slack in the rope and give *him* the opportunity to show off.

In my frustration, I announced that this was not a result of my weakness but rather that of the handlebars not being securely fastened to the bicycle. I illustrated this to the group as I tightened the nut and bolt on the handlebar holder with a socket set from our garage. I did so with pronounced upper body actions until the nut and bolt combination could not be tightened any more. I challenged Steve to tighten it further. To my sincere delight, Steve was unable to do so—despite a valiant effort on his part. Now I could peddle as fast as I could without my high handlebars bending backwards towards me and out of position. I wanted to take Steve so fast that he would cease his taunting for the afternoon and score my performance into the minds of those watching.

With each successive pull, I was able to improve my technique and increase the speed of Steve's ride. But, to my utmost disappointment, I still could not haul him along our street as fast as he could pull me. With my head down and so focused on going faster, I almost hit our mom's car parked on the street directly in front of our house. Steve continued to mock me and taunt me in front of the others.

I didn't give up. In desperation, I kept thinking. There was a small roadway directly opposite the front of our house called Petal Court. It was sloped downhill towards our home and the street that we were playing on. In fact, if the stop sign were to be ignored, one could race down the court, continue straight across our road, and into our driveway. This is precisely what I suggested.

My new plan of taking Steve *downhill* finally allowed me to give him the thrill he was seeking. I was pleased with my perseverance and revelled in my success. With this accomplished, we agreed to take turns as our helpful crowd watched for the breaks in the oncoming cars so we could blow the stop sign, and safely avoid any repercussions from breaking the law.

After only one turn each, we had another problem. Both of us almost killed ourselves transitioning up the small bump at the start of our driveway where it met the street. Steve's daredevil attitude changed our next runs into somewhat of a challenge that my show off tendencies embraced.

He suggested that after blowing the stop sign, we could turn left at the intersection and travel along our street rather than across it. This would create an opportunity to increase our speed even more as we could whip each other throughout the downhill turn. We commissioned the now somewhat larger gathering of neighbourhood friends to judge who could ride my bike the fastest, and who demonstrated the most interesting skateboarding skills. I became less focussed on my skateboarding skills as I welcomed this opportunity to show the judges that I was the fastest bike rider. Now, since we both knew that significant speeds could be reached pedaling downhill on Petal Court, we were both excited to continue the competition.

Steve got on his skateboard first. I was determined to take

him faster than he had ever gone before. He was holding on for dear life as I peddled with all my might past the stop sign, in total disregard for the laws of the land. At top speed, I turned left onto our road, which was void of any oncoming traffic. The rope was quite long so there would be a moment before he would follow my lead. I prepared to "crack the whip." Steve was yelling "Faster, faster!" in a manner as if he was whipping me verbally.

As I raced feverishly through the turn, I was careful not to hit my mom's car. I felt a slight slack in the rope but I didn't look back, fearing I would lose my chance to disgrace my brother. I peddled forward in a heated frenzy, treating this as my opportunity to win the challenge between us. Apparently, I had taken Steve well beyond his threshold for speed on a skateboard, and he, in a somewhat selfish effort, had let go of the rope.

Ordinarily this would not have mattered, save and except for the large object parked on the road in front of our home. The energy I exerted to create Steve's downhill burst tended to keep the rope in a motion at right angles to my new direction. The handle was heading towards our driveway because Steve chose to relinquish control of the rope. Without a hint of what was to come, the momentum of the handle swiftly swung behind my mom's car and the rope wedged itself under the rear driver's side tire. I had less than a few feet before I was at the end of my rope—literally! Or to put it another way, my future consisted of only a short time period in which I would remain injury free.

Since I was not aware of the impending problem—and no one chose to yell any cautionary clues in my direction—I ferociously continued. Without thinking about anything other than shaming my brother, I peddled frantically like some possessed maniac. This ambitious action on my part lasted only a second or so before the slack in the rope was reduced to absolutely nothing. The bicycle went from the highest speed I had achieved that day, to a full stop in what was later calculated to be three-quarters of an inch.

The first significant trauma I experienced was in my shoulders as my upper body re-acquainted itself with the handlebars. I immediately flew from my seated position directly forward off the now stationary bicycle. The steering device that

I had been so careful to tighten only minutes earlier was more than prepared for a good fight. Still, it was no match for my torso, which was now travelling at the same speed at which the bike had been only a split second earlier. Blowing the stop sign and ignoring the traffic laws had contributed to the extreme speed I had been able to achieve. However, there are some laws that no one can escape, such as, "An object in motion tends to stay in motion"—the law of momentum. Twice, in less than a second, this law reached out and bit me in the butt.

With absolutely no warning time to react to the situation, my hands maintained their firm grip on the handlebars. This instinctive action, combined with my entire body now travelling in a forward motion at a high rate of speed, forced the tubular configuration to rotate from their upward position to a "full down" position. The result of which, caused my head to bounce off the front wheel as I continued forward quickly in a direction more or less parallel to the ground.

The bouncing upward motion of my upper body forced my lower body downward as it teetered into the line of the two gearshifts. They pointed skyward and were now fully exposed from the handlebars being recently displaced. My lower body smashed into these knobs and my overall forward trajectory provided enough momentum to bend them with my genitals.

After being force-fed through the front end of a bicycle at something close to thirty miles per hour, the law of gravity became the next law I was unable to disassociate myself from. I was flying away from the now stationary but dilapidated bike, forward through the air, roughly parallel to the ground, but inevitably on a crash course with the pavement. Sadly, perhaps because things were happening so fast, I was still unaware of what was causing this sudden onslaught of rather unfavourable circumstances. My hands instinctively remained in front of my head as my body prepared for its next set of injuries.

I hit the ground with such force that I hyper-extended all of the fingers in both of my hands. Still, this was not enough to prevent my skull from bouncing along the roadway several times before coming to a complete stop. Between head bounces, I actually remember thinking to myself, "This should be stopping soon." It was the first time since being catapulted that my brain had had time for logical thought. Sadly, my journey was not over and I did not stop until the asphalt had filed away most of my clothes and a considerable amount of my skin.

At this point Steve was content to say I won the challenge. As the 'winner' of this event, I laid on the road helpless, confused, and in pain. In perhaps his first display of sympathy towards me, Steve encouraged the others to help pick me up and remove me from the road. This was an effort to eliminate the pending risk of being run over by a passing motorist. They dropped me only a couple times from laughing until they found a way to carry me without worsening my injuries. They eventually managed to plunk me down on my lawn.

I had been unable to catch my breath, as I remained winded from the ordeal. I struggled to get someone to blow in my face, thinking this would help. Every time someone looked in my direction all they could do was laugh. I ached in pain, as I lay on the grass in full view of our spectators.

Once I had stopped twitching, the group rolled me over and stared at my unusual set of injuries. My forehead was scraped with alarming symmetry. There were burn marks on my upper right and lower left cheeks from the bicycle's front tire. I had two identically swelling hands from chipping bones in both of them, and I was unable to stand from the excruciating pain coming from my groin.

Somebody tried to free the rope from under the tire of my mom's vehicle, but it was wedged too far underneath to yank out. Eventually, one of us opened the unlocked door, put my mom's car in neutral, and we all pushed it forward a few inches to free the rope—once I was able to breathe.

When I learned that it was Steve's action of letting go of the rope that caused my plight, I felt as if anything I had done to him in the past was more than compensated for on this day. Steve easily got me back for all of the trouble I had caused him—at least in the injury department anyway.

As I mentioned earlier we never named this new 'game' of

ours, but Steve nicknamed the cul-de-sac next to our home "Pedal Court," instead of Petal Court. He still refers to it this way when he reminds me about his view of my head repeatedly hitting the pavement as my body bounced down the road like a rag doll shot out of a cannon.

There will always be greater challenges just around the corner.

∞ Out of Gas ∞

Most of the time when I found myself in trouble, I was with Steve. I don't ever remember fighting with Jamie. Perhaps it was the age difference. Jamie was more an ally than anything else. His sweet disposition could usually be relied upon to persuade my mom into making more favourable decisions for Steve and me, when we could not accomplish the same on our own. Jamie and I got along so well in our youth, I truly have only fond memories of our childhood together. I'm not sure he can say the same about me.

I still recall a picture of Jamie at five years of age. It was a snapshot of him in full motion as he walked, dressed in a brown suit with patterned pants, and smiling from ear to ear. His obvious haste and the angle at which he had turned his head to the camera made it look as if he was a game show host acknowledging his many fans just after being introduced. He was so adorable.

Steve and Jamie had their moments but more often than not, Jamie was the one who told our mom about a conflict first. This usually worked to his advantage regarding any forthcoming judgment. It didn't matter who started a fight, Jamie always knew the right time to "tell Mom."

One Saturday morning, Jamie, Steve, and I were all at home searching for ways to amuse ourselves. Steve was inside the house while Jamie and I looked for things to do outside. I owned a small go-cart, which I kept in our garage. I thought that it would be nice to take it to the track for a day. I had hoped to persuade my mom or dad into driving me there, so I readied the machine in the event they would agree. Jamie appeared to be content watching his oldest brother tinker in the garage.

He had learned that it was far safer to watch his older siblings get into trouble than to venture into this area on his own. Unlike Steve or me, Jamie possessed no daredevil or show off attitude throughout his childhood. He wandered in and out of the garage as I began my preparations. I received his full attention when I pulled out a long hose. Without my mother's permission, I was siphoning gasoline out of her car to fill up my go-cart.

It has been said, "Better to be thought a fool and keep your mouth shut, than to open it and remove all doubt." I don't know who originally made this statement, but I do know my dad repeated this to Jamie, Steve, and me on more than one occasion during our childhood. I should have applied these words of wisdom at this time, but I felt talking with Jamie would keep him interested in my work. I explained how a siphon works and followed this up with strong inhaling to demonstrate the lesson.

This task proved to be a challenge. Commentary from me that was designed to save face, only served to embarrass me further. With my frustration building, I attempted to fill the hose with gasoline more quickly. I took repeated inward breaths on the end of the hose and was determined not to stop sucking until gasoline had started to flow out of my mom's car and into the gas tank of my nearby go-cart.

For some reason, my attention was diverted momentarily at an inopportune time. The gasoline had reached a critical point at the top of the curve and the siphoning action had begun. Unfortunately, I had failed to notice this, and just as the gasoline was about to exit my end of the hose, I took another huge breath and inhaled as hard as I could. Instantly, I swallowed what was later estimated to be about a half a cup of gasoline.

I spit out the small amount that was inside my mouth. I choked and my throat burned. The fumes from my coughing were so potent Jamie left the garage. Fortunately, he sensed it was time to "tell Mom." I feared that she would return in anger and my mind raced for some way to explain my actions without getting her upset. This concern of mine was soon dismissed in exchange for the opportunity to stage a good laugh.

My drink was so potent that it made me high. It was as if I became drunk instantly after downing an extremely strong cocktail. Steve had arrived before my mom and opted to tease me rather than laugh. Once I explained my predicament, he made a silly comment about a gallon of gasoline being comparatively cheaper than a gallon of rum. We joked back and forth a few times and we both had a few giggles at my expense before our mom arrived.

In my giddy mood, I decided to act out an old joke and run around in circles on our front lawn. I planned to wait for an opportune moment to fall on the ground and exclaim, "I'm out of gas." My mom's arrival produced such a moment. After Steve and Jamie had briefed her on my 'high' condition, she observed me running around the lawn with the coordination of a drunken sailor. In an effort to take control of the situation, my mother asked, "What's wrong?" At this point I took my cue. With my right index finger pointing straight into the air, I fell unceremoniously to the ground and exclaimed, "I'm out of gas."

Mother was not amused. Her young teenaged son was high on gasoline. Not only was I embarrassing the family on the front lawn in front of the neighbours, but I also had to be taken to the hospital to seek medical attention for my dangerous and inebriated state. Thinking I could vomit at any moment, my mom instructed me to wait near her car until she returned with something for me to throw up in.

Steve helped me get up and propped me against the vehicle. My mom returned with an empty laundry basket made of meshed plastic that had over a hundred holes in it. Each hole was large enough to place two fingers through. Steve's comments to our mom about her choice of a doggie bag were not well received. To my mom's credit, she chose to stay my punishment until the medical professionals had made their diagnosis. She pushed me into the front passenger seat of her small car and stuffed the large oval plastic container onto my lap. Her instructions to me as she forced the door shut in disgust, was, "Do not throw up unless absolutely necessary."

This was strictly for medical reasons and had nothing to do with my mom's budget for cleaning her car. She had just taken a first aid course in which she had been taught that vomiting should be avoided after ingesting any harmful liquid. Since the course did not include swallowing gasoline as one of their examples, she insisted that we get to the closest hospital for professional advice. We were both familiar with the route.

Mom called my dad from the emergency ward of the hospital. Her side of the conversation painted the picture of a rather confused father on the other end of the line. My dad arrived just as the doctor came to see me. Oddly enough, my mom's precautionary measures were the exact instructions given by the doctor in charge. With the benefit of an x-ray, the studious doctor explained his diagnosis and the reasons for his recommendations to both of my parents…and a few of the nurses who were still standing nearby in disbelief.

Evidently, I had ingested an inordinate amount of hazardous liquid. However, there was a greater risk to my throat if vomiting were to be induced, than to my stomach if we chose to allow my body to digest the toxic substance naturally. His official recommendation to *me* was, "Next time, why don't you buy a two dollar siphon pump."

He instructed my parents to "Keep him away from any open flame—even a match." Apparently, the gasoline still inside my stomach was blending with the air from my encouraged burping. This was creating a highly flammable air-fuel mixture, which if I were to be exposed to so much as a spark during my recovery, could have *ignited and literally exploded inside my abdomen.*

I was advised to thoroughly blow out the air from my lungs after every prescribed belch. This action proved to be quite disgusting for those around me in the days that followed. For example, the next day my father came to check up on me while I was recuperating in my bedroom. The fumes were so potent that he could not stand by my side or even sit in the room. In fact, the entire family kept their distance—all weekend.

Nobody is your friend when you're full of gas.

MY FRIENDS

I didn't have a lot of close friends during my years in high school. Perhaps it's difficult to imagine how anyone would want to be my friend after reading thus far and learning how I treated my brother Steve in my younger years.

There may be an element of truth in this theory. However, just having a few close friends is a blessing. It's been said that anyone can survive all of the pain and heartache this world can dish out, if one has but a single close friend with which to share all.

Only a few of the friends I made along the way are mentioned in this chapter. Others have been mentioned earlier, but many of my closest friends are not. This is partially because my dad and I chose not to deviate from our "like father, like son" theme. Also, those who are close to me know who they are, because I have told them so, and in most cases because they have heard these stories many times before.

During this chapter, I share some serious times in my past. I honour a few of those in my life who played a brief but memorable role. In each story, contributions of love and laughter helped enrich my life with one simple act of kindness. Unfortunately, I have since lost touch with most of those mentioned in the next three tributes, but I still remember them with fondness and how their actions and kind words of acceptance affected me. I doubt that they realized this at the time. They each made a day in my life a little bit better and I will never forget their kindness.

∾ The Picnic ∾

During the time my mom and dad were married, our family went on vacations and several fun day trips. We often travelled with other families for such events. I have many fond memories with my parents' friends as well as with their children. Everyone from the engineering social group got along well with each other during these times.

On one weekend getaway, a few of my dad's engineering friends and their families decided to go to a nearby park for a picnic. I was looking forward to seeing the other guys my age and spending the day with them at the waterside. We all met at the campground before lunch. Everybody was allowed to sample desserts from the other families' wares after we had finished our first course.

One friend and I had our treats on the go and left the eating area to explore. We had received strict instructions from both of our parents to stay together in case one of us got into trouble. These common words of warning were usually aimed at whomever I was with, in reference to *me* getting *them* into trouble. I think the other adults were hoping their child would not succumb to any of my negative influences.

This day was different. After some exploring, we discovered a pond that my friend thought would be good for fishing. We both went back to the picnic area to get his fishing rod and then returned to the pond. Shortly after, his lure became caught on something in the water. He couldn't pull it out.

Fearing a reprimand from his mom and dad if the lure were lost, he made up his mind to jump into the water and retrieve it. The water was very clear and looked to be a little more than a foot deep. He tightly rolled up his pants until they could not be turned any further, jumped in and sank rapidly. The bottom of the pond had a significant amount of muck and silt, which provided little purchase for his footing. The bottom half of his body disappeared, and I gaped in shock as I pictured the brown gunk swallowing him.

Thankfully, his head remained safely above the water, though he gasped for air as he sunk in. I breathed a sigh of relief when his descent stopped. Fortunately, I wouldn't have to explain to his parents how he left this world.

Spurred into action, I struggled to pull him out. Once freed, my friend gathered his composure and began to unfold his pant legs. After he finished, we had to laugh.

His head, shoulders, and upper thigh portion of his pants were relatively clean and dry. His torso and feet were covered in smelly brown gunk. He was striped like a candy cane but with two alternating horizontal stripes of brown gunk instead of Christmas red. My friend looked like an unfinished piece of work a potter had removed and thrown from his wheel after mistakenly beginning with dung instead of clay.

As we returned to our camping area, everyone who looked our way appeared puzzled. Maybe they didn't know what to ask, or where to begin their line of questioning. After all, it was impossible to determine what he had done just by looking at him. Perhaps my friend's parents had already resigned themselves to finding their son in some sort of unfit manner. Suspiciously, I was the only one who was clean.

My friend described what had happened, assuring those who were listening that *I* had not been responsible for *his* predicament. His honesty in the face of authority was sheer bravery. Most others in this situation would have opted to take the easy way out and implicate me in their mishap to soften the repercussions of their own actions. His honesty and forthrightness combined with his interest in maintaining my friendship was greatly appreciated because it gave me a lasting feeling of self-worth.

The finest compounding interest is that which we invest in others.

∽ A Hot Time at Home ∽

Our three bedroom family home in North York was situated on a residential street with very little traffic. My dad fixed most things around the house, but he wasn't too proud to ask for help when he needed it. He wanted each of his children to have their own bedroom. Because of the bickering that occurred between my brother Steve and me, this was more of a necessity for our parents than a luxury for their children.

My dad's engineering background, along with some occasional help, allowed him to renovate most of our basement into a finished state that was both attractive and practical. My bedroom was built next to the furnace room. It was private and secluded. It served to keep Steve and me apart and we fought less than we had before, once we were separated in this way.

One cold winter night, a friend of mine was visiting. I suggested he spend the night to avoid the bitter outside temperatures. Despite being in high school, neither of us had outgrown the fun of having sleepovers. I snuggled into bed as he climbed into a warm sleeping bag on the floor of my bedroom. There we talked about school, sports, and girls, until we fell asleep.

The smoke alarm awakened him in the middle of the night. He called out to me a few times, but I was a sound sleeper. Like the rest of my family, I slept on unsuspectingly. A little while later I responded to his persistent calls by asking him to remove the battery from the alarm so that we could go back to sleep.

After doing so, he went back to bed, but then said to himself, "Wait a minute, I can smell something burning." He wanted me to get up and persisted until I did so. I thought it best to alert my dad, who leaped into action immediately upon hearing our news. He told me to get Steve out of bed. I went to Steve's bedroom and explained what my friend had discovered.

Steve, like me, enjoyed sleeping in and he was difficult to get up. After a brief description of our situation, he wiggled back under the covers muttering something that downplayed our concerns. I informed Steve that something was burning, the house might be on fire, and we needed to get out. Steve, still in bed, asked if we had seen any flames. We replied that we had not. He again pulled the covers over his head. My friend and I stood at the doorway in amazement. I persisted with a greater sense of urgency, but to no avail. In an aloof tone, he said, "Call me if you see any flames."

I had to tell Dad. He stomped into Steve's room and yelled, "Steve, get the (beep) out of bed!" This worked.

Steve vaulted out of bed so quickly it appeared as if his legs were already running when they first contacted the floor. My dad then rushed towards the basement and shouted, "Call the fire department!"

I coughed through a short conversation after giving them our address. They told me to "Get everyone out of the house." I advised them that I would, then hung up. I updated my dad while he was still searching for the source of the problem in the ductwork next to my bedroom. The vents were very hot and creaking as the heat was causing them to expand forcibly against their supports and the wooden joists. This was visibly apparent in the exposed portion of the ceiling near the furnace.

Within only a few minutes, there was an ambulance, a few police cars, and many fire trucks, all directly outside of our house. It must have been a slow night. I stood on the front lawn in the snow half-dressed with my friend and my family. I joked that we should get off the lawn to provide room for a helicopter. I'm sure the neighbours were wondering what the Fearnley children had done "this time" in the wee hours of the morning. However, despite the sirens and coloured flashing lights, not one person came out to ask. Perhaps they only looked outside and realized the focus of attention was at our house and simply went back to bed.

In any case, my dad was being briefed about the firefighters' findings, while my friend and I were given oxygen by the ambulance attendants. The investigation into the cause of the burning smell revealed that our furnace had overheated. Normally, there's a device that independently shuts off the furnace if the thermostat fails to do so. This safety feature had been disconnected a few months earlier by an acquaintance referred to us for installing our new central air conditioning unit. For some unknown reason, this would-be contractor had cut the wires to the safety device to provide power for the air conditioner.

In addition to his error, the furnace fan had stopped working. Neither of these two problems are major issues on their own. Unfortunately, as if through some confluence of unpredictable providence, both problems occurred within a short period of time—the combination of which set the stage for a catastrophic outcome. Fire is the typical result in such a case because the furnace will not shut down—eventually igniting any flammable materials near the vents. This situation is extremely dangerous because many areas in the home can ignite instantly and simultaneously.

Fortunately, my light-sleeping friend, who accepted the last minute invitation to spend the night, acted on his legitimate concerns with persistence, and thankfully saved us all from almost certain disaster. The contractor's errors were countered by our friend's equally unpredictable actions…actions that clearly saved us all from a terrible fate.

I think my dad learned to have a licensed technician install the next major appliance. I know he worried about how many other homes this so-called contractor might have endangered.

On our memorable night, the cold air was contrasted by the 'hot' time my friend had experienced. Later, in school, I became the brunt of a running joke along these lines. Not surprisingly, this was my friend's first and last sleepover with me. He remains humble in his recollection of the events and has never acknowledged his actions as courageous. I have since lost touch with him, but my family remains thankful for his insistent efforts that night.

A true hero never thinks of himself as such.

∞ Counting Traffic ∞

My dad had an interesting approach to most things I would ask for in my teenage years. He would usually say I could have whatever I wanted no matter how much it cost—provided I paid for it. This was never the response I was looking for. He wanted me to understand the value of a dollar. Later, I remember my dad saying he felt proud of me when I had salvaged a lawnmower out of someone's garbage, overhauled it, and sold it for a profit. I was beginning to understand.

He has always welcomed news of me reaching one of my goals, whether or not he was involved. My dad has never been jealous of my ability to achieve some of the things he could not when he was the same age. To the contrary, he shares in my delight. His unselfishness also played out in the many odd jobs he offered me during my young adult life.

As a Professional Engineer who specialized in traffic planning and road design, my dad often studied traffic patterns. This would usually require counting the traffic, a simple concept. The job itself would entail sitting and observing traffic patterns and recording basic information. Typically, one would count how many vehicles entered an intersection, how many turned east or in another direction, or something like that. My dad would generally offer any traffic counting job to me, or one of my brothers, before advertising for such help through conventional means. At times he would also offer this temporary work to our friends as well.

Policing has been referred to as a profession in which one is not allowed to complain about being hungry, wet, or cold. The same can be said for counting traffic. But unlike policing, counting vehicles is so boring a task that the most challenging part of this job is staying awake. I can remember many a time when I was tempted to fall asleep in a lawn chair at the side of a road listening to the hum of the passing traffic while counting cars. Sometimes my mind would wander and I would calculate the money I expected to make that day instead of counting the vehicles that entered my view.

One time my dad needed more than just a couple of traffic

counters so I suggested he hire me and a few of my friends. On the day in question, my dad drove each of us to the survey locations. He dropped us off one by one and explained what was required.

It was an extremely hot summer day, and I thought some of my friends might abandon my money-making suggestion. My dad was to take turns filling in for each of us as we became hungry or needed a washroom break. Since the traffic had to be observed for the full day without interruption, there were no other breaks allowed. This was the only way to obtain accurate traffic counts, as opposed to estimating them.

My friends were placed at nearby intersections but out of sight from my location. By midday, the scorching heat increased my concerns about them quitting. All day I worried about them leaving my dad in the lurch through an early exit. Each time my dad came to bring me a cold drink, I would ask him about the others. Eventually, the counting had been completed and my dad gathered us all up and drove us home. We were sweating so much that we stuck to the seats in the car and to each other.

We were all fatigued from the brutal heat and mentally exhausted from our attempts to keep ourselves alert. Despite these challenges, I was relieved to hear that not one of my friends had even contemplated cutting out early. One of them told me about how he motivated himself by considering it an opportunity to get paid for getting a suntan. He was badly burned all over his body. He was wearing only his skimpy shorts and joked, "The white bits are the good bits."

I teased my sunburned friend, noting that when he had planned to sit in the sun all day, he should have bought a suntan lotion with an SPF greater than zero. I listened to each of my friends. I learned the ways they dealt with the heat and how they planned to spend their wages. I knew my friends had earned every penny and I appreciated them following through on their commitments to my dad, despite the discomforts of doing so. To this day, my dad still quotes statistics derived from that day's study.

Stick-to-itiveness is a work ethic that impresses even your friends.

Life's Lessons: A Successful Collection of Failures

THE
AMAZING RICK FEARNLEY

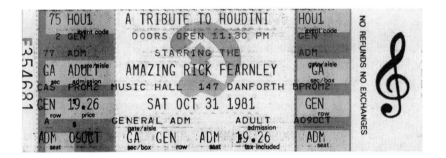

This next chapter is about my life in the entertainment business, a part of my past from which I learned many things. During this time I met many other up-and-coming performers and I always found that the circumstances surrounding their decision to enter show business could be as unique as their entertainment on stage. I trust this theory will hold true as I relay how my decision came about.

In the early 1980s, I was employed by a well-known Canadian catalogue store. I was in my late teens and held the position of Assistant Manager at a clearance centre in Scarborough, Ontario. I was promoted to this position after working diligently for this company in the previous year.

My retail sales career came to a sudden stop when a police officer greeted me at work one day. He placed me under arrest. Apparently, a new female manager who had just returned from maternity leave was upset with how well I was running "her" store. She accused me of stealing items from our employer. Strangely, the same management that had just promoted me suddenly embraced the concept. This jealous manager had convinced them that I had turned into a thief.

I have always believed that honesty is the best policy. So during the time I remained "before the courts," I looked for a new job and willingly told each and every prospective employer of my dilemma. I also offered to answer any of their questions. Throughout this time, no inquiries were made and no job was offered. This was extremely frustrating for my dad. He wanted me to "go out and find a job" but also wanted me to be honest and forthright. He believed I would be considered "innocent until proven guilty." Unfortunately, my candour was not enough to compensate for my predicament, as every prospective employer I approached appeared to hold the opposite belief—guilty until proven innocent.

My dad's frustration—which over the last twenty-five years or so has barely dissipated one iota—was compounded when I introduced him to a man who claimed to be a business manager of personal talent. This person had 'discovered' me while I was venting some of *my* frustrations in an onstage tirade during a talent night showcase at a local hotel. I was doing impersonations and able to throw the odd comical rant in the direction of any heckler. I have always had fun insulting someone with a compliment, and in this environment it was a helpful trait. In short, I could handle myself well in front of a crowd and this alleged talent scout recognized this.

My situation was not complicated. After vigorously 'pounding the pavement' for more than a few months, I was still without a single job offer. However, I did have a person who said that he believed in me, and that he could, "make me a star." It was at this crossroad in my life that I made a decision to become an entertainer.

Shortly after being 'discovered', I trained as an escape artist and performed as an illusionist. My alleged manager conned himself into believing that he could create an acting career for me using magic as a "stepping stone." He explained that many entertainers started this way, citing Johnny Carson as an example. I was billed as The Amazing Rick Fearnley and began my assault on the entertainment business with my first appearance as a 'professional' entertainer only weeks after making my decision to become one.

My manager thought that he could groom me into a seasoned professional through a series of "free shows." I understood the benefits of practicing in front of a live audience, but he seemed to thrive on the attention he received when providing my show for free. The first few months became a constant stream of steady performances that netted us diddlysquat. It was true that I had become well versed at executing the various illusions I performed on stage, but being paid for a show became the exception rather than the rule.

We had no budget for the stereotypical beautiful assistant; instead, his unkempt and unemployed son would have to do. He had come by this honestly, as my manager was a slob of dynamic proportions. My manager's other son would suffice as a one-man road crew when not in school.

The group of us would become excited if our leader actually managed to book us a paying gig. To us, the thought of being reimbursed for "gas money" was a high paying engagement. Even performances done in exchange for a "letter of recommendation" were treated as special occasions. After numerous appearances, for very little money, it was not long before we had captured the market on complimentary shows. When asked what type of show I offered, my wisecrack would be, "I'm the 'star' of a show, for people without a budget."

For the first few months, I practiced my art and delighted the hearts of many. From kids at birthday parties, to senior citizens at almost every retirement home in the city, yes, I was well on my way to becoming a household name. However, I had entertained primarily only people younger than eight or older than eighty for the first six months of my 'career'.

In time, I graduated to performing for people between these ages and progressed into stand-up comedy. After developing my show into something that was actually entertaining, I eventually worked with a number of name acts and entertainers such as

William Shatner, John Candy, Allan Thicke, and Eugene Levy to name a few. I also developed my comic routine into something marketable enough to be broadcast as part of a Toronto-based weekly radio program known as the CFNY Comedy Bowl. There were several live simulcasts. Jim Carrey was also one of those invited to participate in this show. At one point very early in our careers, a coin was flipped to see which one of us would open for the other. I don't think Jim does that any more.

After leaving "the business," I lost touch with most of the people I worked with. Of all the people I met in my short but memorable time as an entertainer, I only considered a few of them to be my friends. Jim was one of them. I met him during this time before he became an exceptional success. He still makes me laugh. For me, he will remain the funny but caring individual I knew him to be when he was my friend.

Virtually all of the events that are recorded in this chapter occurred while I was still "before the courts." In other words, they took place between the time I was charged with theft and the time I was found "Not Guilty" over two years later.

∞ Egg Salad Telethons ∞

While trying to build "The Amazing Rick Fearnley" into a household name, my manager never tired of booking my show for free. I have always been more comfortable in front of a crowd as opposed to a one-on-one situation. For this reason, I was more receptive to doing a freebie in front of a large crowd. However, having a cast and crew greater in number than that of the audience does not exactly build the ego of an up-and-coming entertainer.

Telethons were one of the few no-charge gigs that I enjoyed. They were always for a good cause and I enjoyed putting a smile on the faces of the children receiving the donations. It was usually a joint effort from our entire cast that provided me this opportunity.

Generally my manager's plan involved three co-dependent concepts. First, to justify my uninvited presence, I was to provide constant informal off-camera entertainment for all of the children in attendance. There were youngsters waiting to be interviewed on camera as part of the official telethon schedule. In addition, there were others that were simply roaming the halls because their parents were volunteering in some way. Everyone working at the telethons appreciated my efforts in this area.

Second, during any lull in demand for my first responsibility, I was to hang out, talk to, and have my picture taken with, as many of the well-known entertainers as possible. I preferred to spend time with performers I found entertaining, but my manager preferred that I only be seen with people the general public knew. This was so shallow.

Third, at each telethon, my manager would hang out at the main barrier. It was here that all of the excitement for my crew was created. This barrier separated the telethon's directors, hosts, and guests of the live broadcast from the general public. Spectators, including my manager, watched on from the other side of the restricted area. He knew there would be some difficult moments for the directors at various points in every live, three-day, continuous broadcast.

Life's Lessons: A Successful Collection of Failures

Moments such as a scheduled guest not showing up on time would require a filler of some sort. During these difficult moments for the telethon directors, my manager would casually suggest to them that "The Amazing Rick Fearnley" was ready, willing, and qualified to step in. I showed up for many telethons uninvited but almost always ended up with an on-camera appearance before it was over.

It was a lot of work to gain exposure this way. My manager would usually try to make things more bearable by talking the hosting hotel into giving us a small complimentary room for our entire cast and crew to crowd into. It would have been tight with just my manager, his two sons, and me, but the room was usually crammed with more than our four man team. My manager often insisted on bringing his girlfriend, which made things much more difficult to deal with in terms of space and privacy.

These awkward situations were compounded by other weighty factors. Aside from myself, only the son who was in school and my manager's girlfriend would shower regularly. Both my manager and my 'assistant' considered this a lower priority. We didn't have a lot of money, so fresh new clothes were never an alternative to the odour problem. In addition, the team effort to provide these on-camera opportunities for us was mentally and physically exhausting for all involved and made for a very tired and cranky crew throughout the weekend.

At one telethon, I stayed awake for over sixty hours, all in exchange for a three minute stint around four o'clock on the Sunday morning. Fortunately, the awkward situations in the room never became too great a problem since we were rarely in it. For the most part, we all remained close to the barrier focused on seizing an impromptu performance before the camera with the red light on.

Typically, we only went to the room to eat. Feeding five people for more than an entire weekend was a tremendous challenge to overcome without money. Normally, we could all pick at some of the sporadically donated food trays and this would tide us over until we got home at the end of the weekend. At times, my heavyweight manager would polish off an entire tray of goodies after diving into a food platter intended as appetizers for a large group of *official* volunteers. On one occasion he was so hungry that he turned snacks for all into a meal for him. He confused those providing the food and created a conundrum: how was it that all of the appetizers were gone and not one of the people they were intended for even got to see what they looked like?

We had an alternative meal plan that worked well at most telethons, and we stuck to it. It came about after attending a telethon that didn't provide any snacks or refreshments. We had to find our own food, and, we only discovered this after arriving late on the Friday afternoon. We pooled our money together and counted it. Only ten dollars and change between the five of us.

My heavyweight manager's first suggestion was to order a pizza and a couple of cokes and sort the rest out later. This was often the extent of his problem solving skills, and his catchall solution to most of our difficult situations. Each time he suggested this he would make his declaration in an excited manner as if he had just come up with an amazing solution to our problem. And, he would always make his pronouncement in a tone that implied he had never had this idea before.

Since the rest of us rarely got a chance to eat any pizza, this philosophy did not sit well with any of the crew, or me. So, I insisted we work this out together by collectively discussing our options until we found a workable solution. We had all deprived ourselves of sleep at previous telethons. On others we had managed to survive on very little food. However, we had learned through many difficult times together that we could not function well while being starved of both sleep and food. We could have given up and gone home, but we didn't.

Eventually, after some creative discussions, we arrived at an agreed solution to our hunger problem. My manager's girlfriend would purchase a few dozen eggs and as many loaves of bread as she could with the balance. She instructed the two boys to scrounge around all of the fast food restaurants in and around the hotel and gather up as much salt, pepper, and mayonnaise as they could in the free mini packets.

My manager obtained a metal knife from the hotel kitchen

staff and I prepared a place in our cramped quarters with which to prepare a ton of egg salad sandwiches. Water was always available for free so it became the default beverage.

We each ate egg salad sandwiches and drank water for every breakfast, lunch, and dinner at this telethon. At subsequent telethons, we would prepare our egg salad feasts at home, in advance, and take them with us packed in the same plastic bags the loaves of bread were purchased in. We were always able to smuggle them into our room, inside the magic equipment, since few challenged the secretive transport of such items.

There were only a few times during our survival stages that we could afford to splurge on "a pizza and a couple of cokes." These and other methods of survival became a way of life for me while I was chasing the dream of becoming a star. No doubt, many of those who have chosen such a calling have sacrificed in similarly gruelling ways. As awkward as these survival times were, they taught me that even enormous and overwhelming obstacles can be overcome—once this has become the goal. Therefore, I no longer ask *if* it can be done, but rather *how* it can be done.

Optimism is the ability to see beyond the problem.

∽ **Under the Canvas** ∽

Originally, my dad had fronted most of the costs for me to purchase our magic equipment. I say "our" equipment because my verbal arrangement with my manager was that we were effectively partners. We agreed that each of us would share in both the income generated and the expenses incurred from "The Amazing Rick Fearnley" shows. Since both of us were virtually broke, we also agreed to share in the debt to my dad. It had been many months and we had not yet made a payment. It was time we earned some money.

Although the promotional period of my entertainment life gave me the opportunity to polish my act, it never created any income. Probably because we never made making money a priority. It was for this reason that we took my packaged act on the road—literally.

My manager claimed that we could earn a living in the next step of cultivating my talent: join a carnival and travel with them. In this way, he felt we could say goodbye to the free show era of our lives and embrace what he described as a lucrative lifestyle passing around a hat at the end of a show, just like it was done in the Middle Ages. Also, in theory, we could do more than one show in a day and capitalize on the crowds created by the other attractions offered at the carnival. My business manager felt this was a great plan for us to create "unlimited income." I preferred to think of it as one step up from begging.

He called some of his contacts, and we joined a carnival scheduled to travel that summer. Boy, were we moving up. In no time, we were making much more than we had ever earned before. The problem was that we had never earned anything before. Sadly our wages were lower than those in the Middle Ages.

Basic lessons of "carnie" life had to be learned on the fly. Looking for a hat to pass around at the end of the show is best accomplished *before* the end of the show. Wind, for example, can tend to complicate even the most basic of illusions. Silk cloths used indoors remain motionless, whereas those used outdoors in near-gale airstreams require full-time help on stage to hold them in position as casually and as inconspicuously as possible. If an illusion requires a covering to remain in place until the magic moment but is blown away unexpectedly, the audience is never blown away by the illusion.

As well, sound does not carry well outside. Since we couldn't afford a sound system, the parts of our act that had to be whispered felt out of place as we yelled our lines at the crowd. As soon as we thought we had made all of the necessary adjustments to our new outdoor working environment—it rained.

The Amazing Rick Fearnley magic show used live animals, and all of them absolutely freaked if exposed to rain. One would think that an animal should be accustomed to such a natural occurrence. Next time it rains look outside and see how many animals you see carrying on as if nothing is happening. They all run for cover at the first clap of thunder, which incidentally is enough to turn any magic show that uses live animals into a demonstration of pure adversity.

Volunteers brought on stage to enhance the effect of some tricks were careful to bring the natural lubricant called mud onto the stage with them. Unexpected slips that result in tailbone injuries make it very difficult to maintain professional posture while the audience is laughing at you for falling on your butt.

All of these challenges helped us realize that we needed a tent for the balance of the season. We certainly couldn't purchase one with the limited funds we had earned in the first few weeks of the summer. But, my manager thought of a way we could acquire a tent made from the finest canvas and keep it for the entire season with a budget that ordinarily would have only covered the cost of renting one for a week.

Unfortunately, his idea was just as distasteful as our egg salad solution. I have always believed that the first step to solving any problem is to understand it. You simply cannot hope to solve a problem that you have not identified—correctly. My manager understood our problem quite well. We absolutely had to have a tent for the summer if we were going to make any money. Yet, we were pitifully penniless and unable to afford the luxury of performing "under the canvas."

However, my manager rented one of the finest tents available and arranged for me to pick it up from a large company in Toronto. He told them we needed to rent it for a week. He provided me with no funds but armed me with a cheque to cover the cost of the one week rental. We were back to that familiar place again—flat broke and miles from the closest egg salad sandwich. I paid for the tent, packed it into the van, and drove back to the small town where we were scheduled to perform next.

It was certainly better running the show from inside a tent. We found by limiting the number of exits, we could slow the people down when they saw us pulling out the hat. Unfortunately, the people who attend a carnival are far less generous than the patrons we had met inside classy hotel bars where we had performed for the almighty 'recommendation letter'. Although such a letter is a helpful asset to any up-and-coming entertainer, it is not edible.

Early into the second week, the tent company called for their tent. They were upset that we had not returned it on time and explained how there would be a charge for our tardiness. My manager's girlfriend was relaying these messages. She was based at home supposedly waiting by the phone for a call from someone who might want to book our show. I don't think we ever received one call for a booking during the entire summer, but she diligently stationed herself directly in front of the TV poised for such an occurrence.

It was most depressing to count the small change we received after a full day's work. We packed up and continued on our way with mixed emotions after each stop. We were always encouraged by the positive comments we received about our show in general. Unfortunately, the money we earned was not in line with the applause people offered. Our depressed state was occasionally suspended by the excitement of discovering that our next show was in a town that was big enough to be shown on a map.

Every time we had to pack up, my manager would take off and leave us to the task on our own. He claimed he was doing his part by ensuring the overdue rental tent remained in our possession. Originally, he did not elaborate on how this was done. I thought his calls were to the tent company, but in truth they were only collect calls to his girlfriend. After a couple of weeks beyond the scheduled return date for our tent, the rental company started making demands. The first of which was to call them back. To this, my manager simply instructed his girlfriend to ignore their messages.

Illogically, after a month of making a pittance above the money we needed to survive, the hope of making it big still remained. I was encouraged to concentrate on the larger venues we were scheduled to attend during the long weekends in the latter half of the season. With this, we were able to focus on the hope tomorrow would bring, instead of our dismal state of the day. Disappointments came often.

On one occasion, I couldn't figure out why the large main tent pole would not fit in the cube van after re-packing. With the exception of being packed about a foot higher off the floor of the van, it was in its proper horizontal position encompassing the full length of the vehicle. I could not push the pole forward enough to get the rear doors shut fully, so I grabbed the three-pound sledgehammer out of the toolbox and gave the end of the pole a smack.

Tap, tap, CSHHHH. I walked to the front of the van and discovered why the tent pole needed to be a foot lower. The short stub of metal on top of the large wooden pole was nestled firmly against the highest part of the front windshield. When I had decided to hit the other end with a sledgehammer, I smashed the glass windshield into an artfully decorative spiderweb of cracks, damaging it irreparably.

When my manager returned, we exchanged bad news. I explained how I had ruined his view to the next town. He advised me that the tent rental company had called. They were threatening to phone the police and have us charged with theft, if the tent was not returned promptly. Also, the cheque had bounced…and we were only halfway through the summer.

His solution to their fretful complaints was to do exactly what he had done in the past—nothing. In his mind, we had received a tent for the first month with this strategy. So, he felt it ought to work for the second month just as well. After a heated argument, I agreed to carry on as he had planned, only because he assured me that they would indeed get it back someday. I was worried that he might think he could just keep it until the police showed up and then return it without being questioned further.

This was not his plan at all. He told me that he intended to return it the moment we were done with it, and that we needed to keep the tent to earn the money necessary to cover the rental costs. I was not used to such paradoxical thinking. He reminded me that the tent was rented in his name, that it was his responsibility to return it, and that it was no concern of mine. He added that I could come with him at the time to ensure this if I liked. He seemed to think all would be well once it was returned but refused to elaborate or call the company and share this with them.

Unfortunately, we had only a marginally better take in the second half of the summer. I accompanied my manager to the rental company for the return of their tent. Our one week rental was now almost a season overdue. And, it was the only season people rent tents.

Strangely, everyone at the tent company was happy to see us. They were calling out to fellow employees saying, "It's back! It's back! I can't believe they brought it back!" The man in charge of the place came over to scold us, and to his credit, my manager listened to every word.

My manager's response was pure embellishment, with only pale reflections of the truth as he made detailed reference to every aspect of our difficult times. He claimed that for two months we could not get to a phone. He painted a picture of a mean carnival boss who made us work as slaves. He would turn to me for endorsement of his lame response on the few occasions he was able to recite a whole sentence without fabrication. I nodded from time to time in a stunned state as I watched the group of otherwise intelligent rental personnel listen attentively to his hard luck story.

The rental manager either believed this pack of lies or was so confused he was embarrassed to make any further inquiries. In the end, he didn't even ask for the late fee! In hindsight, my manager had worked two minor points into major advantages. First, he understood that the company would have likely written off the tent after not hearing a single word from either of us for over two months. Second, returning the expensive pieces of canvas unannounced meant that no one in the rental department had any time to prepare for a confrontation. In this way, my manager gained the upper hand.

We were still desperately broke with barely enough money to pay for gas to get us home. However, my manager's unorthodox problem solving skills had saved us from a major setback, had we been forced to pay the rental fee for the whole summer. On the way home, my manager suggested we celebrate by ordering "a pizza and a couple of cokes."

Finding something that was lost can be cause for celebration.

∞ Midnight Madness ∞

After taking our well-polished show on the road and learning that a carnival does not create "unlimited income," my manager and I had many meetings about other ways to make money. The problem as I saw it was that we were always dependent on someone hiring us and there were very few people that "needed" a magic show. Even in Toronto, a city of over two million people, there weren't enough opportunities to provide a steady income for an illusionist.

The frustration my manager and I shared was that a city of this size most certainly had a great number of people that would be willing to pay for a decent magic show. We decided we couldn't wait for a large group of people to come to this decision on their own. They needed our help. In other words, if we were to provide a bigger show at a large venue we might well fill the place with paying customers. To manufacture my big break, it would have to be well advertised.

With virtually no money, we would arrange interviews in the media, much like we had done for any prior show of significance. This type of promotion would only work if we had something newsworthy to share. A decision was made. We would produce, and I would star in, our own large-scale stage production. "If the mountain will not come to Mohammed, then Mohammed will go to the mountain."

The plan then required that we work out all of the details for the event before our planned Press Release. Now we needed that newsworthy item. Up until this point, the finalé for The Amazing Rick Fearnley show was a Houdini trunk escape performed in reverse to showcase my talents as an escape artist. For our special show, we decided to emphasize this with our own version of Houdini's death defying escape from a Chinese Water Torture Chamber. We felt this major undertaking would attract the attention of the press and the interest of the general public.

Typically, the Water Torture Chamber is a large tank full of water. Its lid is made of wood and has two halves. The inner edge of each half has two semicircles cut away to produce two small holes to lock the ankles of the escape artist as the halves are rejoined. Once both feet cannot be removed, the escape artist sits down and allows the lid to be hoisted into the air, carrying him upside down and underneath. He is then lowered into the water headfirst while volunteers from the audience securely fasten the lid with locks. A large glass window encompasses the top three quarters of the front of the tank. This allows the escape artist to enter upside down in full view of the audience and volunteers on stage.

While holding my breath, the volunteers are then quickly escorted a few feet away to allow a black curtain to be lifted from its prearranged position. It fully surrounds the circumference of the Water Chamber, with only a few inches of clearance around the tank, then, it is swiftly raised up. The volunteers are instructed to watch all sides of the curtain, including the rear, which is out of view from the rest of the audience. This is done to authenticate the fact that no outside help is provided. Once the black curtain reaches a height approximately twice that of the water torture chamber, it holds this position for a brief moment, then suddenly drops to the ground. At this point, I should be found standing on top of the tank posing like Superman, but dripping wet from my daring escape.

This was to be our new grand finalé. We had hoped that performing such a trick successfully would provide the necessary boost I needed to become a well-known public figure. Even if people only remembered me as the guy who escaped from the water torture, this would be a huge improvement to my feeble notoriety.

We decided to call our extravaganza "A Tribute to Houdini" and planned it for Halloween night in 1981. A suitable location would need to have a stage strong enough to hold the weight of our special aquarium, which would stand eight feet tall and would cover only a small three-foot square on the stage. Once filled, the water alone would weigh well over two tons. We searched all over town for a suitable location. Most of the larger venues had no problem with our proposal to grace their stage with our monstrosity. Unfortunately, all of the proprietors wanted to be paid. In addition, many of them insisted upon receiving a deposit to secure the date. We had no money for either. How disrupting this was to our plans. Our only hope was to find someone willing to accept a share of the door money as payment for the service. We were in no position to offer them any more than this.

Luckily, my manager came home one day and announced that he had procured a perfect location in which to hold our event. I was living at his residence at this point and his pronouncement refuelled our mutual hope to strike it rich. A popular music hall in the heart of Toronto would host our engagement on Halloween night, and the management had agreed to be paid out of the proceeds from our take at the door. As was always the case with my manager, this was not the whole truth—there was a catch. Apparently, there was a rock concert already booked there for the same night. My manager thought, "No problem. We'll start when they are done." In hindsight, agreeing to this probably eliminated more than three quarters of the potential audience we had set out to capture in the first place. Too bad I didn't come to this conclusion until the night in question.

I was told the rock band performing at this place would be finished around an hour or so before midnight. Guessing that this would be enough time to set up, we committed to a midnight start. We were also thinking that such a late start could be justified on Halloween night, especially since it fell on a Saturday that year.

It was official. "A Tribute To Houdini" was born and promptly scheduled. I was in charge of preparing for the show and my manager would promote it. I had to make myself available for many interviews with the press. I was also challenged with the task of making my manager presentable for such meetings. He was far from a well-dressed man. On one occasion, we had stopped at a local coffee shop on our way home to get some necessary promotional items for an interview with the press. He ordered chocolate milk packaged in a carton, and insisted on drinking it through a straw. While fixated on the straw, he poured the drink all over himself as he tipped the container forward. His idea of cleaning himself for the important meeting did not entail changing his clothes when we got to the house.

Life's Lessons: A Successful Collection of Failures

We arranged for the tickets to our event to be processed through one of the larger ticket companies in the city. While there, we noticed that most of the affairs they were selling tickets for were rock concerts. My manager decided it would be best to include some of the rock bands I had opened for in my recent past by inviting *them* to perform in our Halloween special as *my* opening act. Again the money thing got in the way. A complete lack of budget for any of the necessary expenditures meant there was no way to consider paying them for their services. The plan evolved from my one hour show to a two hour extravaganza that included three separate rock bands as opening acts. Without the lure of big bucks, the rather egotistical members of the rock bands insisted on setting up and playing on their own equipment. Like a fool, I accepted this. I also made such extreme concessions for everyone else involved, that *they* ended up dictating to *me* how the program would be run.

Ticket sales were not going well despite numerous interviews with the press. Radio interviews, newspaper articles, and television appearances all helped to get the word out but did nothing to bring the bucks in. In desperation, we called our friends and family, billing the occasion as a self-created "big break." If only we had every member of our families and all of our friends, we could pack the place. The problem was every family member and friend expected a free ticket. However, we needed to fill the place with paying customers to make money. Even if we could only bring in enough cash to pay the ridiculous charges I was running up on my credit cards, this would still break our record for the most amount of money generated by one of our shows. Gradually this dream gave way to a somewhat lesser hope. If we could only fill the place with people, the press might stick around long enough to review the performance and thereby help create the impression that I was a seasoned performer who could demand a fee for his *next* performance.

In the last week before the show we panicked, and reverted back to what we knew worked. We could pack them in—if the show was free. However, we failed to realize that packing a room in someone's basement for a child's birthday party was nowhere near the same as packing a theatre with over a thousand seats. Actually, I had been panicking for a much longer time than just that last week. I had been somewhat frazzled ever since the magic store indicated that they did not have a Chinese Water Torture Chamber in stock. Promises of six to eight weeks for delivery wouldn't accommodate our schedule. Oh, and there was one more thing. We needed to practice since I had never actually done this trick before.

Before the event, most of my time was consumed trying to build this ridiculously oversized prop. My manager had convinced some local glass supplier to take a post-dated cheque as payment for the enormous piece of glass we needed for the front of the tank. It was three quarters of an inch thick and took several people to move it. This rather heavy window was to be installed in the front of my solid steel one-man aquarium, which was later welded together. Once constructed, it took twelve large men to move it into our vehicle, which maintained a distinctive downward 'tilt' to the aft during transport.

My dad planned to attend our special night in much the same way he had shown up for my many hockey and baseball games when I was younger. Being an engineer, he had a greater structural intellect than I, and recognized the building of this device as a major undertaking. I lied to him, claiming that I had tested the thing earlier and had everything under control. Nothing could have been further from the truth.

The night went something like this. "The Amazing Rick Fearnley" cast and crew were all starving and fatigued after engaging in an overwhelming goal with an almost impossible timeline. We showed up at the theatre a couple of days before to set up what we could without disrupting the plans of the rock band that had booked the place long before us. I sincerely doubt more than a handful of the hundred or so people that had attended paid the full price of admission, which was significantly overpriced at $19.26 per person. A fee not established on fair market value, a research survey, or even a smattering of common sense, but rather on the year of Houdini's death. My manager thought that would be neat. It was neat. The midnight start eliminated most of our potential paying audience, and the ridiculous price neatly dismissed any hope of having the remaining balance of potential customers attend.

I wish we had started at midnight. We might have had a chance if each of the *three* opening bands did not insist on setting up their own equipment and doing their own sound check. When we were finally ready to start, the first band gave the cue to open the curtains as they began to play. We opened the curtains and they knocked over the lights on both sides of the stage simultaneously. It was the only coordinated action of the entire evening (sorry, morning). Both stands came close to injuring many of our limited number of guests. The emcee we commissioned for the night could not keep even my friends and family from falling asleep during the excruciatingly long breaks between the bands. There were surprisingly enthusiastic rounds of applause after some of the songs, only to be followed by audible groans every time a band began to play yet another tune. It was after two in the morning and only one more band to go—after they set up…did a sound check…and set up some more. Why did I agree to let them run the show?

In a desperate attempt to shorten the exceedingly long gaps between the bands, we made some last minute changes. I insisted the second band leave their cables in place and simply remove their instruments. This meant that the third rock band ran their electrical cables on top of those left scattered all over the stage by the previous band.

By the time the last group of rockers took to the stage, they were forced to strut their stuff over a multiplicity of unexpected wires and connectors. This significantly altered their originally planned gyrations as they circled the stage in frustration. No one was pleased. Not the theatre staff, stagehands, musicians, affiliates of The Amazing Rick Fearnley show, members of the audience, nor anyone from the press. There was not a happy person in the house.

Once all of the band members had finally cleared the stage that night (sorry, morning), almost everyone was awake for the first part of my show. It was not a bad magic show, but not exactly a captive audience either. Amazingly, most of the original crowd was still in attendance for the finalé. This was obviously the only reason the press hadn't left. They were all grouped together in one area while the stage crew prepared for the spectacular escape from The Chinese Water Torture Chamber. Just one more illusion and they could all go home.

We got out the heavy duty garden hose my manager had been careful to pack for this occasion. The tank was now being filled at a speed that would have almost ensured it was half full by daybreak. The audience groaned noticeably through this agonizingly slow process. Any suspense that may have been created up to this point was extinguished rapidly. In theory, the entire audience could have left and returned and missed nothing. Much like an intermission, but we had already had too many, and the theatre management had closed the snack bar long ago.

Our desperate situation required immediate action. Our pathetic state truly constituted an emergency as those of us on stage may well have been attacked by an irate group of ex-friends and family members had my manager not done something. Suddenly, my manager got an idea. He was emceeing my portion of the show as he usually did. A bunch of the rock band roadies were backstage near the fire hose encasement. Over the microphone my manager shouted at them in an overly dramatic manner, to "get the fire hose."

It was truly a shame that we never had time to fill the tank prior to this. Pulling out a smelly fire hose got the attention of most everyone present. Some of the people in the audience even sat up. The good news was that the fire hose was able to discharge water with incredible speed. The bad news came when the water first came into view and began to rise above the lowermost part of the large glass window at the front of the tank. In our haste, we never thought to flush the fire hose and no less than forty years of gunk came spewing out of the hose and into the tank. There was no way we dared test the audience's patience any further by attempting to drain the water and fill it again. Besides, I had forgotten to incorporate a drain into my original plans for this monstrosity.

Life's Lessons: A Successful Collection of Failures

At this point, I was psyching myself up for performing the escape in scummy water and hoped the amount of clean water that was now entering the tank would be enough to allow a somewhat clearer view of me. Of course, this would necessitate waiting a considerable length of time to allow the sludge to settle. This was not so much for the enjoyment of the audience but more for my safety. I had rehearsed signals that would tell my manager to remove me from the tank if required. In an emergency, I could signal him to break the glass. In addition, there were other signals that helped us coordinate the crucial timing of such a dangerous stunt. In any case, he needed to see me clearly.

It was at about this time our next major setback occurred. The tank began to leak. During construction, I had squeezed copious amounts of silicone into every corner of the tank. I had anticipated some small insignificant amount of seepage to occur so I brought a half a dozen towels to counter such a problem. Regrettably, this thing was spewing out water faster than a major attraction at a water park. The glass cracked and water sprayed over the entire stage. This was not only a concern for the theatre owner but also for those on the stage, which was still littered with unnecessary live electrical cables. It was mass pandemonium for all involved and no match for a group of bumbling idiots armed with only six towels. With the speed at which the Torture Chamber was now losing water, the fire hose could not keep up. The water flow was increased to full blast on the command of my manager.

Unfortunately, no one on stage had any training to handle a fire hose at full charge. My fearless crew were all desperately trying to grab this monster of a whip as it snapped back and forth soaking anyone who was daring enough to remain on stage. Luckily, this captured the interest of the people seated at the rear of the theatre to an extent not yet experienced during this evening (sorry, morning). Those situated in the front rows were not amused. This was not our planned Water Torture, but it was the closest anyone would get to witnessing torture by water that night. My manager eventually yelled, "Shut it off" with only a hint of defeat in his voice as it became apparent that my grand finalé would never come to pass.

Until this point, his babble, while he emceed my show, was somewhat excusable. Throughout the act, he fought to think of things to say to fill the many awkwardly dead moments. Sadly, he had now reached a point where he could no longer fill these lulls with rhetoric any more successfully than we had been able to fill the tank with water. There was a pregnant pause as he collected his thoughts and stared helplessly into what was left of the audience. It was almost as if he would have welcomed suggestions from them at that point. If he had, it would have been the first time since we had dreamt up the idea for our show, that he had welcomed a suggestion.

My manager had the audacity to believe that he could maintain the loyalty of all of our soggy patrons by assuring them that they would receive a "free" ticket (we still can't get away from this concept) for "Rick's *next* water torture show." Good grief. I was hungry, wet, and cold, and in no position to commit to my manager's whimsical promise made in desperation that night.

As the theatre cleared, I went to the van and collapsed in embarrassment. I awoke the next day without any recollection of the drive home or getting out of the van and into bed. Unfortunately, every painful detail from that show has remained engraved in my brain for life.

The only ones contracted and 'paid in full' were people who had agreed to work for free. The theatre management received their fifty percent share of the ticket sales as agreed in our contract. This was tabulated in very little time as it amounted to absolutely nothing. Fortunately, this was well within our budget. We settled our account with them before we left. Technically, it could be argued that had we paid them their half (of nothing) in advance, weeks before—on the day we signed the contract.

The biggest break I received that night was from my dad. He acknowledged that I had disgraced myself in front of our friends and family, and chose not to call me to task for lying to him. Well, not until later anyway. My road crew told me that they spent the balance of the weekend trying to clean up the stage after removing the dirty water from my Chinese Water Torture Chamber…without a drain. Now that's entertainment!

Shortly after, one of Toronto's national newspapers reported on their review of my show. The poor reporter who had been forced out of obligation to sit through the entire gruelling disaster commented that Houdini's ghost had haunted our production that night. Later, my manager took their quote and used it to our advantage. On my resumé it read: "The ghost of the master of escape"—*The Globe and Mail*. Once again he had turned a partial truth to our advantage. By doing so he managed to snag at least a dozen more free shows.

A free show is worth every penny.

∞ Carrey On ∞

If I could have capitalized on all of the mistakes I made during the production of "A Tribute to Houdini," I might well have become the most educated producer in all of Canada. After this enormous failure, I practiced my art with a far greater degree of commitment. Immediately following the disaster, The Amazing Rick Fearnley show was rehearsed thoroughly, with all of the cast and crew. We did not stop rehearsing until I was content that my show could not get any tighter. In other words, we virtually eliminated any moment that the audience was required to wait for something entertaining to happen.

Changes were made so that any unavoidable lull was offset with something more interesting happening on stage simultaneously. In some cases, we would pick a volunteer for an upcoming escape during the preparation for the illusion, rather than once it had been set up. At times, we would meld two illusions into a longer one to make the pace of the show quicker. The sound tape was changed to have accompanying music pieces start immediately after a previous track. In short, each of us improved our stage presence, and in turn enhanced the overall entertainment value of the show.

With this accomplished, my manager and I were both more excited about The Amazing Rick Fearnley show than either of us had been at any point prior to this. Then, I let my manager change the performance from illusions that were carried out for the purpose of amazing the audience, to illusions that were performed for a laugh. Unfortunately, once again I failed to take a stance with regard to letting someone else dictate to me how my show should be run.

This change meant that I had to concentrate more on the comic aspects of each illusion. The timing required to execute an illusion is much more forgiving than the timing required to pull off a gag during a live show. The toughest part of any magic trick is making it look difficult. Staging something funny is exactly the opposite—it cannot have even a hint of difficulty in its execution. My manager's change in the format of our show now necessitated that I focus on the crucial timing of our gags during the show, not the illusions. For this reason, I was required to perform every illusion in my repertoire, flawlessly and effortlessly, so I could concentrate on making the audience laugh.

In time, I found it more rewarding to receive a laugh in response to a funny part of my show, as opposed to applause for deceiving the audience into thinking I had performed something miraculous. I think the main reason for this is that most illusions use a gimmick or prop that makes the demonstration exciting. The only thing an illusionist can do is develop their showmanship to a level that complements the excitement of the trick.

I was now able to perform virtually any illusion with little effort and much showmanship. However, I was learning that making people laugh from a stage was quite different than telling a joke. A natural flow or transition to the quip, timing in the delivery, and confidence in the anticipated response, all play a part in procuring genuine laughter. Good comedy is serious business and the result of hard work. In any case, whether performed one on one, during a large stage show, or as a stand-up routine, comedy is an art—not a science.

The most difficult of these formats is stand-up. The entire audience is focused on a sole performer—the comedian. I was billed as "The Amazing Rick Fearnley" when I was performing as an illusionist, but I was also performing as a stand-up comedian. I always incorporated a few illusions into every performance of my stand-up act. These tricks would utilize relatively small props that I kept on my person for use at opportune times. They could easily be pocketed while maintaining the dialogue of my comedy routine.

Long before I met my manager, I had developed a sense of humour from my dad and various other members of my family. I had also trained with some reputable comedy troops like The Second City. This education proved to make me the least satisfied customer at any comedy show because I always saw the punchline coming.

To me, the richest soil from which to cultivate humour is the solid ground of our own real life experiences. In my opinion, a good comedian is one who can draw on real life experiences and portray them in a humorous light to get a hearty guffaw. I do not feel good comedians need to resort to crude themes and vulgar language just to obtain a laugh. I have witnessed some stand-up artists with great transitions from one joke to the next but make use of only mildly amusing points at best. Others have great one-liners but poor transitions to set them up. Some appeal to one kind of age group or audience but not to another. Simply put, anyone can be a comedian, but it takes a tremendously talented individual to be a great stand-up comic who can consistently amuse different crowds.

I began working the comedy club circuit after being encouraged to do so by Bob McBride. He had been the lead singer of a band called *Lighthouse*—a popular rock and roll group in the early 1970s. I met him while we were both performing at a place called Café on the Park, in Toronto, a few years after his band had broken up. We became good friends and during our time together it was always rewarding for me to hear him laugh after I had told him a funny story or two about my family's antics. Sadly, Bob died of a heart attack a number of years ago but long before this he was one of the first to suggest that I "write a book."

Another friend of mine in "the Biz" was extremely talented. He had great timing and stage presence, could think on his feet, handle any heckler in the crowd, and was genuinely funny. He was double jointed and multi-muscled in a few areas and could sing and dance. My professional relationships with other entertainers had taught me that almost everyone that ever "made it big" possessed all of these skills including the ability to sing and dance. This guy had all of this and more—he could make me laugh.

No matter how often I saw the same performance, he made me laugh every time. He was so original and quick thinking that he purposely interacted differently with each crowd to create ad lib opportunities. He would then seize these moments and capitalize on them by making funny comments that kept his act fresh, vibrant, and witty—even for those who had seen it before. I was proud to consider him as one of my entertainment friends.

The management of Café on the Park described my routine

as "a mixture of comedy and magic" on all of their promotional materials. My friend's act was also a mixture of sorts. He was billed as a comedian but his act was definitely not a typical series of jokes told one after the other. His routine involved impersonations of famous people and entailed an extremely accurate mimicking of both their mannerisms and voice—typically what most impressionists do. However, in addition to doing this very well, he was able to contort his face into an uncanny likeness of his subject complete with their unique features and expressions. Effectively, he created a four-dimensional entertainment experience for his audience, which included acerbic comments to various hecklers. Such side comments were as entertaining as his main performance.

I felt that he would definitely succeed one day and shared this with every family member and friend I had at the time. I encouraged them to come out and see his act—whether or not I was on the bill with him. When they did, the program read, "Jim Carrey—Canada's foremost singing comic impressionist." From the fall of 1981 to the spring of 1982, we each performed our comedy routines throughout the Southern Ontario comedy club circuit, and our paths crossed often during this time.

On several occasions, I caught his show and had my mom, dad, or a few of my friends see it with me. In early June of 1982, I had polished my comedy routine to a professional standard high enough to be offered a part as a regular on a weekly live comedy performance run by a local radio station. The show was called the CFNY Comedy Bowl, and was occasionally broadcast live from the Café on the Park—the same club where I had first met both Bob McBride and Jim Carrey. Bob had seen my act many times, so I asked Jim to come and see me perform for one of the live comedy broadcasts. Up until this point, he had only seen me perform the odd magic trick while hanging out together at some club. Jim readily agreed and attended with his manager at the time.

Jim's manager was the complete opposite of mine. Jim had a well-dressed, intelligent, mature young female who was articulate and preceded his arrival at important engagements. In my case, I dragged along an illiterate, older man who was an immature and uneducated slob. In fairness to my manager, he was surviving on only half of the revenue he generated from booking my shows for free. The expression, "you get what you pay for" held true in this case because I got my full money's worth. I do not mean to imply I was frustrated with his inability to make good business decisions for my career: I wish to state it outright.

The most frustrating thing my manager ever did was to insist that I change my comedy format on the very night I was to perform for my first live broadcast for the comedy bowl, and Jim Carrey. My manager chose to discard my well-established comedy routine—which landed me this regular spot on the comedy bowl—and instructed me to recite some other comedian's material. But Jim came to see me perform *my* material.

Copying some other person was not my style. Besides, reciting another comedian's lines might well be viewed as an impersonation of some kind. In an attempt to get my manager to change his mind, I jokingly told him that Jim was the only person in the place qualified to be doing any impersonations on stage that night. I wanted to share some of my funnier real life experiences, but like an idiot, I consented to my manager's ridiculous suggestion.

He was so convinced that I was talented enough to handle such a late change that instead of arguing with him, I put everything I could into an unrehearsed "mix of comedy and magic." Jim and his manager watched and listened attentively. Unfortunately, the illusions were the only part of my act worthy of anyone's attention. I completely bombed on the comedy front. Regrettably, wit was what people had paid for—not magic. I had wanted to impress Jim and his manager with my comedy routine. However, I must have looked like a simple magician who knew a few lousy jokes, rather than a multitalented charismatic performer who could captivate an audience.

To Jim's credit, he gave me his full attention while I was on stage. He steadfastly grinned during my act where most others would have slouched deep into their seats out of embarrassment for me. I am still thankful for the sympathetic smiles he kindly gave me during my one-of-a-kind performance. He was a gentleman throughout my entire routine. An insecure performer wouldn't have been able to maintain such sincerely encouraging looks during my 'comedy' stint, as Jim did for me that night.

Why did I listen to my manager? Why didn't I change gears and revert back to my original and proven material? Why did this have to happen on the one night Jim came to see my act? I played things over and over in my mind and agonized—I still do—as if in detention at the school of hard knocks. Virtually any record of my antics included in this book up until this point could have been shared with the audience that night, but I did not do so.

I had good material and had performed enough stand-up to execute a polished performance, but I let my manager talk me out of it. How disappointing. Unlike the situation with a 'tribute' to Houdini in which I let the opening acts dictate how my show would unfold, this time I was duped by my personal advisor. It was times like this that made me feel he was overpaid.

I had seen Jim continue on after being severely heckled by an unappreciative patron. I admired him for not leaving the stage and strangling the jerk (sorry, customer). In a similar way, I felt obliged to finish the routine I had started, since my manager was so insistent. Also, I felt that I might well have been told to do it again had I not completed it that night. I learned to forgive myself for this costly mistake. I reasoned that I had crossed my Rubicon once I had given my word to my manager that I would do the routine *he* thought was best for me. During the show I felt helpless as I sensed the crowd losing interest in my act, but by this time what else could I do but Carrey on.

Jim commented to me how much he had enjoyed my magic that night saying, "Just unbelievable." He allowed me to quote him formally and I used his comment in my resumé from that point on. Unfortunately, he had seen me perform many illusions before, and that night I was anxious to impress him with my comedic abilities—not magic. While my life in the entertainment business floundered, Jim's career started to take off. The only thing that contrasted more than our managers was the paths our careers took after this.

Jim became very busy performing as a "Comic Singing Impressionist." If he knew I was in the audience he would always visit and chat with my guests and me after his show…like the down-to-earth person he has always been. Jim and I both have been through many difficult times. However, in each of our cases I believe these experiences provided the fuel to drive us on to something better. Perhaps these hard knocks were the common ground that served to keep us in touch for a short time after—the time I remained in "the business."

__Most students from the school of hard knocks graduate with honours.__

❧ The Trial ☙

Originally, I began a career in entertainment because I had few other options available when the opportunity presented itself. I got into show business, not so much through a desire to chase the lure of stardom, but rather because no one from the conventional workforce was willing to hire me while I was before the courts.

The alleged victim was the clearance centre of a well-known Canadian catalogue chain where I worked. This store was one of only two that sold all of the damaged and discontinued goods for the entire company—Canada-wide. Supposedly, I had removed enough broken china and flawed jewellery boxes to account for this national company's losses for the year. This figure amounted to a sum greater than a quarter of a million dollars as calculated with the damaged value of said products.

They claimed to believe I was keeping the company from being profitable by storing the goods at my dad's house. My dad has been known to miss the odd detail or two in his day, but he is not the type to overlook a pile of retail goods in his house that would otherwise fill an Olympic pool. No one, including the police, stopped to calculate the implications of one jealous manager's claim. Later, when presenting this argument to the company's so-called loss prevention professionals, they changed their minds…and accused me of giving all of the stuff to my friends. It was flattering to think I had that many friends.

I was burdened in this state of limbo from the early spring of 1981, until my case was finally heard in June of 1983. During this time I plied my trade as an entertainer. Meanwhile, the emotional roller coaster the legal system bestowed upon us, by way of their various sporadic postponements and delays, significantly stressed my family and me. It took well over two years of being jerked around to have my voice heard by someone who possessed that rare quality known as common sense—a judge.

My trial took seven days to complete. I can tell you from experience, seven days at trial is enough to make one weak. Testimony from various witnesses on both sides was presented over the first six days, and the judge's findings were given after this. The first three days consisted of the prosecution's various witnesses taking the stand to testify for the Crown. After all of these witnesses had finished, my lawyer offered me some reassurance. He said, "A whole bunch of zeros still adds up to zero."

On the fourth day, I took the stand in my own defence, and reiterated the same facts I had stated over two years earlier to the arresting officer, the jealous new store manager, and anyone else who cared to listen. My lawyer questioned me and the Crown Attorney cross-examined me for about a day. The fifth day in court was filled with an examination in chief and the cross-examination of three former fellow employees who worked at the same store while I was employed there. They all testified in support of my 'claims'.

At the end of the fifth day, my lawyer had finished presenting our defence. The Crown Attorney pulled a fast one and announced he would be providing a surprise witness, who supposedly had only recently become available to testify. This became the sixth day of my trial. Ordinarily, the prosecution has to present their witnesses prior to the defence presenting theirs. I believe this alleged unavoidable occurrence was the Crown's underhanded effort to give them the last word. As I saw things, this didn't matter much, since the prosecution only had another zero to add to their sum of evidence.

We were reasonably sure of this fact, because we knew who this person was and how he was likely to twist the truth. This witness had been a former supervisor of mine that had spoken well of me in the past. But he had changed his tune once the company's head office personnel had contacted him. I knew what he was likely to say about me now that his position with the company was in jeopardy.

About two years earlier, my dad had paid a private investigator to look into the case since the police had never conducted any investigation of their own. The private investigator found that this company habitually fired any Assistant Manager, regardless of who they were or how hard they had worked, once a year just after inventory. Then they systematically blamed their losses on their chosen scapegoat. Their routine practice continued until they misjudged the willingness of one of their annual victims—me.

At the trial, my lawyer wanted to use a two-year-old *taped* conversation between my show business manager (pretending to be a potential employer of mine), and the "star witness" for the Crown. My lawyer urged my dad and me to transcribe this conversation and in turn provide him with a copy for use during cross-examination the next morning. My lawyer wanted to be fully prepared prior to the start of our scheduled proceedings. My dad and I knew that we could get the tape, but we were not confident that the transcription of the requested conversation would be helpful. At the time, my dad and I viewed my show business manager as an illiterate. All of his conversations demonstrated a butchery of what many have come to know as the English language.

My dad and I spent the night before the sixth day of my trial transcribing what we thought was possibly the worst conversation ever held in any English dialect. We had many favourable comments from this surprise witness on tape, but we feared it would be viewed as senseless babble. Despite this, we complied with my lawyer's request and worked through most of the night ensuring that it was recorded verbatim. We had to replay the tape several times. My manager-cum-potential employer had asked many poorly worded, long-winded questions. Pascal once said, "I have only made this letter rather long because I have not had time to make it shorter." My manager was not Pascal. When we handed the transcription of their full conversation to my lawyer on the morning of the sixth day, my dad said it sounded like, "two orangutans trying their hand at a conversation." How anyone could use such a sloppy exchange of grunts in such a formal setting was beyond both my dad and me.

Fortunately, the merits of my case were decided on fact and not grammar or sentence structure. The Crown Attorney examined the star witness, and then my lawyer cross-examined. I was tempted to laugh many times during this cross-examination, but I knew I had to maintain a serious demeanour. My lawyer used the transcript of the conversation to our extreme advantage. The witness was forced to explain why he made favourable statements concerning my work ethic but testified to the contrary only moments before while being examined by the prosecution. It was obvious to anyone in the courtroom that he had been pressured by the company to portray my actions in an unfavourable light.

The star witness was visibly agitated as his statements became increasingly contradictory. It was obvious that more and more internal friction was being created with each of my lawyer's probing questions. No wonder it is referred to as "the hot seat." My former boss squirmed while my lawyer forced him to give birth to the truth. Watching this was worth every moment of aggravation my show business manager had ever caused me in the past, and I had the best seat in the house. Evening came, morning came, and on the seventh day, the Crown rested, and it was good.

In the honourable Judge Matlow's verdict, he stated that he treated much of the Crown's evidence "…with the correspondingly appropriate weight." His verdict of "Not Guilty" brought an end to the trial. It had been well over two years since the ordeal had begun, but it took over six more to conclude the matter. It came in the form of a cheque after my dad and I successfully sued my ex-employer for wrongful dismissal.

We agreed to a settlement and received $15,000.00 as compensation for their actions, but this amount didn't even cover my legal costs. With no one left to blame for their large losses, the company went under a few years after I received their cheque in January of 1990. My family and I have since counted our blessings and put this painful part of our past behind us.

My ex-employer had taken me for some poor fool who would roll over and play dead because it was "easier" to plea bargain than fight false claims in our legal system. They were wrong. However, in the same way my ex-employer had underestimated me, I misjudged the potential help my show business manager was able to provide.

I had also made another incorrect assumption. The judge that presided over my trial was the one I feared most from the beginning. He had the power to change my life with his verdict, and significantly stress out my family in the process. At times during the trial I was very disappointed with some of the decisions he made regarding the material that he had allowed to be presented as Crown evidence. I had failed to understand his motives, but he refused to assume my guilt. This wasn't apparent until he gave his final summation. By allowing the prosecution exceptional leeway in presenting their case, the judge effectively eliminated any grounds for them to appeal his findings. Judge Matlow was the only one in the courtroom who was truly without prejudice.

My acquittal was not appealed and has remained uncontested by any of those involved. Although my family did not create the problem, they definitely paid a price. What surprised me the most was that everyone in the legal system assumed I would plead guilty to a crime simply because it was "easier" than going through a trial. It may very well have been easier, but standing up for what you believe in never comes easily…or without a price.

When you pre-judge a person, you never see their full potential.

∞ **Vertigo and Vomit** ∞

As of June 1983, the trial was officially over and I approached the upcoming summer feeling as free as a bird. It was a tremendous relief for me and my family. Overcoming such a problem made me think that I could do just about anything. The stigma of being "before the courts" was gone. And, at that point, the only thing I was interested in entertaining was the possibility of another career change.

Before this, I had made it clear to my manager that I was not happy with the income I was receiving from my show business career, which was significantly less than nothing and better known as debt. I advised him that I was contemplating a radical change and considering something the banks refer to as gainful employment.

I explained that we needed to start repaying my dad for all of the money we had borrowed to create and maintain our show up until that point. Over the summer, I took on odd jobs and made payments while still living at my manager's home. I performed for any *paying* gig he could book to help him pay the rent. It didn't matter if he booked my large-scale stage show of illusions with our full cast and crew, a solo stand-up comedy routine for me alone, or something in between. In any case, I was prepared to work so long as the end result was some money in our pockets. I desperately wanted to pay the bills that had piled up over the years, and I began by tabulating all of the money we owed.

By the fall of that year, we had amassed a debt of about twenty thousand dollars to my dad and an additional fourteen thousand dollars to others. This was a huge chunk of change to repay. There wasn't even a hope of having it disappear through work in the magic business. My new dream became earning money on my own through conventional work. I planned to do so passionately, and pay the entire amount off as quickly as possible. In turn, my manager would owe me for his half of the debts we had incurred.

In November, I drew up two Promissory Notes to document this. Ten thousand dollars for my dad, and seven thousand dollars for other people. He signed both documents with the same conviction he had shown when he rented the tent. Unfortunately, he adopted a similar payment plan—which effectively was "zero down, NSF in thirty days, and the balance when you catch me."

My manager was convinced that my odd jobs would hinder the entertainment work he still believed he could secure. For this reason, I agreed that any money raised through paid bookings would go to him alone. This was also meant to offset the cost of staying with him, and hopefully act as his incentive to book me for paying engagements.

I went through the motions each time my manager had a whimsical idea that he thought would bring me to the top of my entertainment career. In one such case, during the early part of the following winter, he encouraged me to attend a flying school that was looking to promote a relatively new type of aircraft. It was a place called Northern Microlites and they bought, sold, and taught people how to fly ultralight aircraft. My manager reasoned that he could arrange for them to sponsor us. They would provide an ultralight and short-wave radios for emergency ground to air communications, and in exchange, we would promote the versatility of their aircraft while I flew around Ontario and set a new "world record" for ultralight travel. Like most of my manager's plans, this one came up short on a couple of key points.

First, I didn't know how to fly. I hadn't flown any small aircraft or even been in one before. I was not at all familiar with a specialized, extremely light, and vulnerable-in-high-winds aircraft known as an ultralight. Second, I am extremely susceptible to vertigo. I threw up all over the instructor I was supposed to impress during my introductory flight. He was the only other person in the two seat flying machine. He made a valiant effort to maintain control of the plane while attempting to avoid my spewing vomit as he made an unscheduled landing in a farmer's field shortly after our take off.

Once we returned to the company's airfield, it took me well over an hour to regain my composure to the extent that I could sit up. It took about the same time for the cold and wet instructor to clean the aircraft, his clothes, and the snowmobile suit I borrowed from him to stay warm for the flight. The aircraft's open cockpit was good news from one standpoint, yet the rather forceful headwind pushed the involuntarily regurgitated food back into our faces with alarming force. I had no means of communicating verbally, and I didn't know the hand signal for "Hey buddy, put your goggles back on!"

The event blinded my instructor, taking him completely by surprise. I can still remember the sounds of my breakfast as it hit the propeller behind us while the prop efficiently painted the rear of the aircraft a new colour. My instructor was not impressed.

It was events like this that encouraged me to focus on living in the real world, and paying off my debts. On the way home, my manager told me that the aircraft dealer was willing to pay for all of my instructional costs and proceed with the promotion if I wanted to train to become an ultralight pilot. With his bizarre sense of problem solving, my manager went on to explain that people can build up a resistance to motion sickness. I thought he was crazy, but instead of saying so I offered to comply. I did this on the condition that certain criteria would be met. I purposely made stipulations that I did not feel he could meet. If he did, I felt that I could keep my part of the bargain, and at the very least learn to fly for free.

With my manager focusing all of his attention on such an enormous undertaking, I figured I could work steadily at my odd jobs. Also, if I maintained my live-on-nothing lifestyle and put my entire earnings towards paying off our debts, I believed that I could do so in a couple of years. I was wrong. I worked unceasingly and did it in less than one. By the spring of 1984, I was free from debt, and it felt great. I had finished my ground school and was qualified to receive in-flight instruction—if I could do so without throwing up. Nevertheless, I was preparing to formally sever the business ties with my manager.

I was very thankful for my manager's help with regard to his involvement in my court case and also the efforts he made to lead me in my entertainment career over the past few years.

Despite this, his "big plans" for my career would have to remain plans as I was intending on exiting 'stage right' for good. I had mixed emotions about leaving the business. After all, there were some fond memories I could take with me after three years of desperately trying to become an overnight success. It was not all pain and heartache, but it was close. At this point it didn't matter. I was about to leave the entertainment world for good.

At about the moment I was preparing to clear my throat and give my manager the news, something unusual happened. He explained that he too had been working, and had obtained corporate sponsorship from a number of large companies. I asked, "For what?" He said, "For your cross-Ontario, record-setting Flight for Pride." "My flight for what?" I asked. It still did not register. Then, my manager proudly stated that he had met all of my previously stipulated conditions that I had listed on that cold winter morning, months before, when I had been suffering from vertigo.

People tend to have poorer memories during times of nausea. As things started to sink in, I realized that he had been diligently working on my 'dream' while I was busy working to pay off our debts. He even recited a few bonuses that he had acquired for my added benefit. As he rhymed off all of the people and organizations that had come "onboard," I sat down and listened in a stunned state. He must have read my speechlessness as gratitude. He was so impressed with himself, if there had been a clap of thunder he would have run to the window to take a bow.

In a robotic state, I asked for further details as I tried to hide my disbelief. He had secured commitments from an airline called Nordair to fly all of our crew to anywhere in Ontario that we needed to go, both prior to and during, the summer trip. Our route was to begin in Kenora, Ontario, and wind up in Toronto—a direct trip greater than the distance from New York City to Miami, Florida. He planned for us to follow a scenic route along the Trans-Canada Highway to Ottawa, and then swoop south and head east, zigzagging through southern Ontario to cover an overall distance of more than three thousand miles. I was learning all of this for the first time.

Suncor Sunoco Group would cover our gasoline costs, and Cara Foods, who own Harvey's and Swiss Chalet, would compensate us for some of our food expenses. We received coupons from McDonald's plus eighty "Dinner for One" packs, and fifty "Family Buckets" from Kentucky Fried Chicken. Safety Supply Canada gave us all of the gear necessary to protect and equip our five person road crew for the specialized takeoffs and landings. Pepsi and Canada Dry donated a total of sixty cases of pop, and there was more, much more.

My manager's bonus was that he had booked me for a flyby at the Canadian National Exhibition (CNE) and my flyby was to be the official opening for their air show on the Labour Day weekend. Both the American Thunderbirds and the Canadian Snowbirds were scheduled to participate in the CNE's 1984 International Air Show. It was the chance of a lifetime and a dream come true for any pilot. Now, all I had to do was learn to fly.

With every lofty goal there are unique obstacles to overcome.

∞ Flight for Pride ∞

I was likely to receive significant exposure from my cross-Ontario, summer-long marathon, since The Muscular Dystrophy Association of Canada (MDAC) officially recognized our "Flight for Pride." In addition, I was scheduled to be one of the official hosts for the Canadian broadcast of the Jerry Lewis Telethon on the same Labour Day weekend that I would open the CNE International Air Show. There was more than an egg salad sandwich to look forward to on this gig.

Still, there were major concerns. The "pride" portion of our name came from two separate themes: pride in helping others, and pride in Ontario. The pride in helping others was tied to the donations we intended to collect on behalf of the MDAC. The pride in Ontario was tied into the Ontario Bicentennial, being celebrated that same year. The Bicentennial advisory committee, a government organization, had to officially sanction our endeavour before any sponsors would commit. It was imperative for them to do so within our timelines.

Not until the second week of June in 1984 did we get word that our official letter of endorsement from the Ontario government was forthcoming. With this commitment established, my manager quickly obtained the other commitment letters, and with them in hand, we collected the corresponding equipment, food, and other supplies necessary for our journey. In a few cases, the paperwork had to catch-up with our actions, but my manager eventually obtained all of our donated products in the week that followed. Every one of our sponsor's commitment letters came dated June 11, or later. Boy, was he cutting it close.

Meanwhile, I was busy with time challenges of my own. I had been spending all my waking moments learning a new trade—again. Not only was I still learning to fly at this point, but I was also learning the mechanics of how to fix every part of the aircraft. In fact, I had to be able to take the thing apart completely, and then safely put it all back together into an airworthy state. Our first scheduled appearance was to be on June 28, 1984, in Kenora, Ontario, and this was less than two weeks away.

Kenora is situated in the northern part of the province and would take a few days to reach in our cube van, which would be jam-packed with everything we needed for the trip—including the disassembled aircraft. It was not until June 14 that I completed my pilot and aircraft maintenance training. On that day I received an official endorsement letter from Michael Robertson, the president of High Perspective Hang Gliding and our sponsor, Northern Microlites. More importantly, I obtained the right to take my written pilot test with Transport Canada. Without my licence, there would be no flight.

Also, if I failed, I wouldn't be permitted to take the test again until well after my first scheduled appearance. To provide me with greater emotional turmoil and additional unnecessary stress, my manager and his sons had already eaten much of the food our sponsors had provided for us. Talk about pressure. Fortunately, I passed and received my licence on June 21.

I guess one could say I was cutting things close as well. However, I could now set out to raise money for the Jerry Lewis Telethon and the MDAC. I was very much looking forward to the exposure I would receive from this undertaking. We packed everything into our cube van and a four door sedan and headed north. I drove the cube van and my manager drove the support vehicle.

My manager was unfamiliar with any number above zero, and the rest of my crew was unable to add, so I felt I was the only one sufficiently capable to chart our road trip to our first scheduled appearance in Kenora. I familiarized myself with our route and plotted the stops. Based on my previous experience of travelling from my hometown of Toronto to the beautiful and popular Muskoka district, I calculated that our drive to Kenora could be completed easily within a weekend. My manager planned to make many sightseeing stops along the way. He did so early into our trip, making the first interruption after less than an hour into our two day journey.

All was going fairly well until we reached Sault Ste. Marie. This was a significant point in our road trip for a few reasons. First, the map of Ontario I was using for navigation had to be turned over to monitor the remainder of our trip northwest to Kenora. Second, because I was charting our progress at each fuel stop, I noticed a distinctly slower pace haunting us—despite our belief that we were now keeping our delays to a minimum and driving quickly.

For some reason, according to my plotting on the map, we were only moving at about two inches per hour beyond Sault Ste. Marie. This was in sharp contrast to the five inches per hour we had been progressing while I was monitoring our earlier progress through southern Ontario on the other side of the map. Something was amiss. It took me many stops to confirm that the map was wrong. After a few more stops, I realized that the map was fine. However, the scale used on the side of the map depicting northern Ontario was considerably different from that on the other side of the map. The difference was later calculated to be greater than a factor of two. This disparity was not in our favour.

My revelations were announced at the next 'tourist attraction'. I clarified our situation to the members of the road crew. We were a little behind but could still reach the airport before the Nordair flight carrying the rest of our crew would land. Now, all we had to do was drive continuously, at record speed, morning, noon, and night, for the balance of the trip. I went on to explain other requirements such as the need to grab something to eat—something of substance—because there would be no more time for meal stops. We would have to be content with fast food, picking it up while refuelling. Also, there was one last stipulation—we had to finish our coffee and be on our way within the next few minutes.

The required around-the-clock driving brought on a few challenges. My manager fought to stay awake while driving the sedan. I did the same in the cube van. And, somewhere between Sault Ste. Marie and Kenora, I saw my first Canadian moose. There were two actually. They were mating on the Trans-Canada Highway, at right angles to the centre line, and virtually blocking both lanes of the two lane highway. I thought this obstruction could best be dealt with by scaring them off the roadway. My plan was simply to drive straight at them without reducing my speed.

After reaching the point where it would have been impossible for me to stop, I changed my strategy. I was now close enough to see them much more clearly than before. I was looking into the eyes of a huge, rather unimpressed, male moose. It was the first time I had seen a moose this close. Although there was not a lot of time for admiration, I realized that hitting this monster would most definitely end the Flight for Pride, and possibly me. Luckily, I made a split second decision and managed to swerve towards the left shoulder into the oncoming lanes. The affair came to an abrupt end as the female headed quickly towards the right shoulder and came to an even quicker stop at the north ditch.

I had some warning and was in a large vehicle, but I was still scared half to death. I had narrowly missed the male moose on the centre line, paralysed in the afterglow of the moment, after they disengaged. My manager, on the other hand, was travelling close behind me. His perspective created a slightly different experience. He was startled because he received no warning; was driving a small car; and was forced to execute an impromptu thread-the-needle manoeuvre while swerving at full speed onto the right shoulder between the star-struck male and his departed lover, who was still stunned and panting by the north ditch. My manager later described his encounter as a significantly more traumatizing experience.

There was another reason Sault Ste. Marie represented a significant point of our trip. Suncor Sunoco Group—our fuel sponsor—didn't have any gas stations located beyond this city. Previously, I had downplayed this company's warnings about a disrupted fuel supply since my calculations of consumption were based on my incorrect interpretation of the map's scale for this part of our journey.

In the awkwardness of my revelation, my manager decided to use his girlfriend's credit card and obtain the necessary fuel to complete the first leg of our road trip. She had given it to him for "an emergency." She correctly defined an emergency as a life-threatening situation. She had made it clear that wanting a pizza and a couple of cokes did not constitute an emergency. My manager carefully considered our plight over the next few moments. I believe his mind was made up almost instantly, and he simply used the extra seconds to figure out how he was going to tell his girlfriend. He described our fuel shortage as a life-threatening situation, citing the repercussions from our sponsors had we decided to quit and go home.

We were still a few miles from completing our virtually non-stop trip from Sault Ste. Marie to Kenora. Our gruelling road trip would not be finished until we entered the outskirts and reached the airport. We were about thirty miles back when we caught sight of a plane. It was the only one in the sky, and right on par with the scheduled arrival time of the Nordair flight carrying my manager's girlfriend and the balance of our road crew. My heart sunk. My manager's girlfriend was expecting us to be well rested and organized. But instead, we were hopelessly late and extremely fatigued. We were supposed to pick them up and whisk them from the airport to a hotel my manager was to have already obtained by this time. From there we were to discuss the flight portion of the endeavour over a casual meal and then visit a small airfield where they would be introduced to our fully assembled and flight-tested aircraft.

The truth was what I called a 'photo-negative' of what they had hoped for. Instead, we presented them with a group of exhausted and dishevelled misfits who sheepishly informed them that we were already critically behind schedule and had not yet arranged for a hotel. There was no money for food, the cockpit of the plane was still neatly packed inside the cube van, and the wings tied to the roof of our van were more than significantly fatigued from flapping in the winds created by our excessive speed during our rushed home stretch into town. Oh…and there was one more thing. The only credit card in our group's possession belonged to my manager's girlfriend and it was nearly "maxed-out" and our many scheduled unpaid appearances meant that we would be in no position to pay her back—or even make a payment—for at least two months. Welcome to Kenora.

The three thousand mile flying portion of the Flight for Pride gave rise to numerous surprises that summer. The road crew was to venture on ahead to inform people about the upcoming arrival of the aircraft. However, prevailing west winds meant that my manager's girlfriend's hope of a casual sightseeing tour throughout northern Ontario was not to be. Alas, it became a continuous seventy-mile-per-hour race of passing transport trucks and other highway traffic just to arrive far enough ahead of me to set up a landing area before I ran out of gas.

On a serious note, I sincerely thought I was going to die on one occasion by the north shore of Lake Superior after flying through what I thought was "just fog," but what later proved to be thick cloud cover. I was so disoriented I wasn't even sure if I was flying over water or land for an unnerving amount of time. Fortunately, I did not panic and was able to keep negative thoughts from developing in that dark room called worry.

I survived only to crash-land the following day near White River, where the ultralight's engine stopped unexpectedly and I was forced to write off the first of two airplanes. A kind helicopter owner and pilot became an impromptu 'sponsor' by flying me on a makeshift Medivac flight to the hospital in Marathon, Ontario.

Prior to beginning the flight portion of our trip, we had eaten most of our donated food from those sponsors whose products we favoured. There were only a few other choices on which to gorge ourselves over the next two months. The balance of our meals would have to be filled with the remaining eighty "Dinner for One" packs, and fifty "Family Buckets" of Kentucky Fried Chicken. I believe even the Colonel himself would have been sick at the thought of being forced to eat only Kentucky Fried Chicken for breakfast, lunch, and dinner every day for two months. Talk about being super sized.

Fortunately, virtually every person with whom we came into contact was friendly, helpful, and appreciative of our efforts to raise money for the Jerry Lewis Telethon and the children it supported. During one of my many flights, I flew alongside a large hawk and we played together soaring over a farmer's field in unison. What a blessing. A few fond memories like that frame the many stories of adversity and survival from that summer's trip. In addition to the previously noted challenges, there are enough memorable adventures from my flight to fill another book.

Life's Lessons: A Successful Collection of Failures

Upon joining the entertainment business, I had set many goals for myself. The sum of these was to be featured in various newspaper articles, radio interviews, and television shows. My manager had indicated I would someday need full-time staff to handle the overwhelming flood of fan mail. Typically, he was overly optimistic. To date I have received only one note. It was from a very nice woman who had seen my magic show and enjoyed it enough to write and encourage me. Eventually, I did reach every one of my goals while in show business—including enough media coverage to ensure there was no hope of ever obtaining a copy of all the published reports. The plane crash did this for me.

I even attained a goal that I did not set for myself. I was honoured with a featured exhibit in the Houdini Hall of Fame in Niagara Falls, Ontario, and it remained there, on display, for a number of years.

Sadly, I had misjudged the potential for such accomplishments to produce revenue. It has been said that there is no such thing as bad publicity, but I strongly suggest that there is *poor* publicity—the kind that produces no income. This was my specialty.

I was beginning to realize the emptiness of my shallow goals and I was becoming increasingly uncomfortable with my sleazy lifestyle. I felt unfulfilled after the Flight for Pride had been completed, despite it being a giant accomplishment. My thoughts of leaving the entertainment business were motivated from the stark contrast between my expectations of a public life…and reality.

By Labour Day Weekend, the Flight for Pride was over. However, I still needed to coordinate my appearance in the International Air Show—the finalé for the 1984 Canadian National Exhibition. I flew into the Toronto Island Airport very early on the morning of the day before I was to open the event. I received permission from the control tower to fly one circuit so that a reporter for *The Toronto Star* could take pictures of me flying the ultralight with the city's skyline in the background. Once I had landed again, I opened a bottle of bubbly while he interviewed me and snapped a few more pictures.

This national newspaper actually stopped the presses to replace an existing article on their second page—with this reporter's story about me—for their afternoon edition. This made me feel like I was newsworthy for the first time since I had been in show business. Later that evening at the official pre-show briefing, the organizer introduced me to the man who was going to pilot the Concorde at the end of the show. We, in turn, were invited to speak to the other pilots about our plans to fly the smallest and the largest aircrafts that would appear in the show. I opened the CNE's 1984 International Air Show and he closed it. What a thrill.

My dad says that next time I take on a mammoth undertaking, I should work up to it. The Flight for Pride was my longest non-paying gig, but it was over. And suddenly I felt—for the first time in my career as an entertainer—I was a success. But…strangely, almost instantly after I had reached my goal, I felt as if I could now, finally, leave the entertainment business if I felt so inclined.

Incidentally, immediately after completing the official opening flyby for the air show on that windy day, I returned to the island airport and landed. Just before I was able to tie the ultralight airplane down, a gust of wind blew it over and severely damaged one of the wings.

That day I made a decision to literally 'take off' in another direction—real life. After co-hosting the Canadian Broadcast of the Jerry Lewis Telethon throughout that Labour Day weekend, I left the entertainment business for good.

It takes a long, long time to create an overnight success.

Life's Lessons: A Successful Collection of Failures

LIFE AFTER THE ENTERTAINMENT BUSINESS

It has been said that everyone is likely to experience fifteen minutes of fame. If this is so, I apologize to the few who won't get any as a result of me receiving more than my fair share. This next chapter involves my life immediately after I refused to accept the sacrifices necessary for such an experience.

After I stopped paying for the privilege of performing as an illusionist and a stand-up comedian, I experienced many pressures during my transition from working for free, to life with a paying job. Fortunately, my mom and dad were both able to help me. They did so willingly, but unlike before the trial and during my entertainment years, they did so from different homes. I lived with my mom for the most part but visited my dad often.

I began full-time work with a small sound and lighting company. I was not quite out of show business entirely, but I had made a significant change. I had moved from an unpaid role on stage to a paying position behind the scenes.

One of the things I had learned while entertaining was that a microphone should be set up at a height that does not require adjustment when the performer first arrives on stage. Contrary to common practice, a microphone should not be set up on a stand at a height convenient for the shortest member of the crew doing a sound check. The moment a performer arrives on stage is a crucial time in which he or she must capture the audience's attention, and hold it.

Generally, just before their entrance, an entertainer has spent some time psyching themselves up for the show and into an optimum state of mind for their performance. Routines of even the best entertainers can be disrupted if the newly introduced performer is forced to hold the microphone with one hand, and adjust the stand with the other—just to get the audience to hear what they're saying. My experience has taught me that such unnecessary fiddling tends to take the performer out of their emotional high—especially if they are trying to palm a rabbit at the same time.

Apparently, this frustration and many others I experienced when I had been performing on stage were common. However, the knowledge of these problems and the ability to provide solutions for them proved to be an asset in both acquiring and working at my new job.

For the most part, this chapter encompasses my experiences off stage in a new profession—stage production. My onstage experience helped me obtain my new job with a small production company, but I was in no way an expert simply because I was familiar with sound and lighting. There were just as many tricks of the trade to be learned from the other side of the curtain.

I have since come to adopt the philosophy that one should always make plans based on a "worst case" scenario. The next chapter focuses on my work during this new phase of my life, the lessons I learned, and the reasons for such a belief. The accounts of my experiences during these times support Murphy's prime law—"If anything can go wrong, it will."

∞ Egg Nog ∞

My birthday is a few days before Christmas, and each year of my youth, both of my parents would make a point of keeping it separate from any of our Christmas celebrations. I appreciated this immensely. Many others would send one present and offer it as both a Christmas *and* birthday gift. I felt shortchanged, but as I grew older all that mattered was getting together with my family.

My mom invited me for a visit on my twenty-third birthday. Being the guest of honour, she offered to cook any meal I chose. She makes an awesome roast beef dinner, and I opted for this with all of the fixings. For dessert, I chose her homemade angel food cake covered in whipped cream and topped with fresh strawberries. Given the choice, I would rather have my mom's cooking than that of most restaurants.

My birthday fell on a Saturday but I had to work that day. My mom agreed to postpone dinner until I arrived, but I didn't know exactly how long the job would take. My employer was under contract with a hotel to run power to various convention rooms from their main power supply. In technical terms, this was known as providing "power drops." I was scheduled to oversee a Christmas party in this hotel, which had been arranged for the children of its executives. They wanted us to provide a power drop, set up the sound system, and later disconnect the power once they were finished their party.

The hotel had arranged for new carpet to be installed in time for this celebration. A huge Christmas tree was purchased, and I had to run one large power cable to it so that all of its lights could be plugged in without any extension cords dirtying the new carpet.

All of the kitchen staff were dressed in their new uniforms to impress the executives and their wives. There was an open bar for the adults, and a special table with coffee, tea, non-alcoholic Christmas beverages, and treats for the children. One of my duties was to keep the children away from any of the power cables. Everyone was to have lunch, then Santa would enter and hand out gifts. After this, my helpers and I could 'tear down' and go home. The afternoon went very smoothly. I called my mom to say that I would be there in an hour or so.

As the children finished opening their gifts, things were dragging on, and from my perspective, taking a lot longer than necessary. The executives offered lunch to the employees of our company from the leftover food. Accepting such an offer is not a normal practice, but it was Christmas and things were a little more relaxed than usual. With my road crew all enjoying a tasty meal, the only way I was going to be on time for mine was if the executives decided to pack up their families immediately and head home. Instead, they decided to provide one more round of drinks for their employees, and the children audibly welcomed the extra time to play with their new gifts.

No one—not even my helpers—were motivated to go home anytime soon. I was becoming a little impatient and looked for ways to hasten my departure. Not much could be done in terms of disassembling the sound, lights, and power, until all of the guests had cleared out. I figured I would help the hotel staff move some things into the kitchen to speed things up. I gave up on this thought when it became apparent that none of them spoke English very well.

The bartender had begun to disassemble the bar, so I decided to offer my services in this area. I was preparing to move one of the tables out of the celebration room and into the kitchen—the one set up for the children. A fellow employee was finishing his meal from behind this table and helping himself to his favourite non-alcoholic beverage—eggnog. He was not at all enthusiastic about packing up just yet—especially things that were not even our responsibility to move.

In my rush, I insisted that this co-worker assist me in my efforts to save some time. I asked him to help me move the special serving table. We removed the coffee pots and placed the balance of the few remaining treats on the floor as I encouraged him to stop quibbling in front of the hotel staff. I neglected to remove the skirting from the large table even though it was apparent that the non-English speaking waitresses disapproved.

I motioned these helpers out of the way, but they seemed to be indicating that they would take care of moving the table themselves. I was behind schedule and required a faster pace than the kitchen staff was accustomed to moving. I therefore tried to drag the table along the floor on my own, but was unable to do so. As soon as my co-worker finished his meal, I instructed him to "grab an end."

We demonstrated our strength as we attempted to move the table lengthwise towards the kitchen. We were still noticeably being held back by something underneath. We lifted it a good distance off the floor and applied brute force to the problem, which broke like a dam when we prevailed.

Our celebration of accomplishment was overshadowed instantly with the outpouring of the hotel's entire holiday supply of eggnog—all over the hotel room's new carpet. I was quickly informed by an irate executive that we had knocked over a forty-five gallon drum of the stuff. It had been—until recently—stored in a huge stainless steel container specially shaped to fit underneath the hotel's serving tables. My helper and I still held the table in surprise while the yellow beverage took a few seconds to finish spreading into the room.

People rushing to help fought to keep their balance as they navigated in and out of the areas of the carpet that had been overly saturated. Children remarked on the "waves" as the mass of thick liquid bounced off the fixed walls and returned into the centre of the room. The language barrier eliminated any chance of forewarning the unsuspecting hotel staff who soiled their new uniforms when they slipped and fell as they entered the room. Despite the noble attempts of my co-workers to "dam up" our leaking function hall with the 'handy' linen tablecloths, excess amounts of the holiday drink permeated under the temporary partitions and into other rooms. It was not well received by other holiday guests attending unrelated Christmas functions.

Everyone was laughing at me, with the exception of the hotel executives. Their attention had been drawn to the puddles in the deepest parts of the room. Some of these pools displayed a picturesque mass of bright coloured fluid, with contrasting live black power cables half submerged from the spill. Although quite colourful, this presented an electrical hazard that, for me, was second only to the one created in "Midnight Madness."

The two owners of the small production company that employed me were both present on that day. Fortunately, they were more understanding than the executives at the hotel. Had it not been Christmas time—and my birthday—I likely would have been fired for my lack of patience. I was dismissed from my duties for the day. Ironically, this allowed me to get to my mom's house only fashionably late for dinner.

Later, my superiors confessed that part of their decision not to fire me was because they had not laughed so hard during the tear down of a show in a long time. Besides, they reasoned, how much worse could things get? In their defence, they had no way of knowing how many titles would be in this chapter.

Brute force doesn't always work.

LIFE AFTER THE ENTERTAINMENT BUSINESS

∽ Could You Give Me a Push? ∽

While I worked at the sound and lighting company, packing was one of my specialties. I could cram more gear into a van than my average co-worker could get into a small truck. I received this gift from my dad. His persistence (read stubbornness) has always motivated him to "get everything in" whenever we travelled in the family car. If not for his efforts, every member of my family would have had to travel a little lighter during our getaways together.

A good student always surpasses his teacher. I treated every opportunity to help a customer get something into their vehicle as a personal challenge. It did not matter if a pastor had come to pick up a one-thousand-watt spotlight for his Christmas presentation in a Volkswagen beetle, or a lady came to pick up a smoke machine on her bicycle. I welcomed the opportunity to get each client loaded up and on their way. I found the only thing most people lacked while packing items into their vehicle was the will to do so. It was proof of the old adage, "Where there's a will, there's a way."

On one rather memorable day, our company had been expecting a large truck to pull up to our loading doors to receive a sizable theatrical lighting rental. It was a complete package and included a dimmer, control board, many lights, and miles of cable.

The dimmer is a very large and extremely heavy device that allows numerous powerful lights—usually thousands of watts each—to be dimmed from a remote location such as a control booth. This is done using a low voltage cable and control board. All are usually packaged tightly in road cases for their protection during transport. The lights are focused and fine tuned before leaving the shop, and like the dimmer, they are also sensitive to bumps during travel. Therefore, they are usually packed in road cases as well. The heavy-duty extension cords, known as cables, also weigh a lot, but unlike most of the other gear, are relatively rugged. For this reason, they can be placed up against the large caster-styled wheels of a road case, to stop it from moving around on the floor of a moving vehicle. In roadie jargon, this is called "keying in" the load. I believe this term comes from the significance of removing such an important item *first* when unpacking. It's like a key that unlocks the puzzle from which all other items can be removed. Regardless of how the term came to be, the last step of packing a vehicle properly will usually include a few cables laid around the wheels of the road cases to key in the load. This stops *all* of the other items from rolling around inside a vehicle.

When our naïve customers arrived for their major lighting rental, two guys showed up in a rented cube van. They were subjected to ridicule from some of my less sympathetic colleagues. My co-workers were making jokes about how inadequate the vehicle was for the items they had rented from us. Many unwelcome comments were directed in jest towards these rather uneducated customers. An owner of our company came to the loading dock to ask how our customers felt they were qualified to set up the equipment and take care of it, if they didn't even know what it looked like. Our clients explained that they were simply volunteers who were asked to transport the lighting equipment to their community theatre located in a small town well north of Toronto.

After the paperwork had been completed, I began to load their cube van while the other employees participated in a conversation concerning the possibility of an off-hour pickup for them. It took almost an hour before I figured out a way to get most of the rental equipment into the back of their truck. I took all of the lights out of their cases and hung them on the ceiling supports of the cube van's boxy area, in much the same way they would later be hung in the theatre. Effectively, this gave me a complete second floor of storage without placing additional heavy equipment on the sensitive gear below. This was so much better than the client's suggestion of strapping the other more expensive and heavier pieces of gear to the roof. Besides, I felt uneasy about entrusting another pound of product to the already overstressed roof supports.

I was pleased with myself for cramming most of the rented gear into their van, but they still weren't satisfied. They wanted us to drive whatever we couldn't get into the van to their theatre many hours away. My two superiors felt no obligation to do so. This was creating some friction between them and our clients, so I asked the drivers to get into their van. I continued stuffing lights, cables, and other equipment into the cab of the truck while they 'discussed' the matter with our company reps. After our two customers had each taken their seat in the cab of the truck, I continued packing and piled the remaining lights around them. The back of the truck and the cab was now filled to the brim. I had to ram the front doors shut and squeeze the two man crew in between the various rows of lights to get everything in. This somewhat unorthodox but otherwise extremely efficient packing job had been completed in just over two hours.

As we made our final exchanges, I thought they should have been happy because I had safely jammed them inside with everything they required—just as they had insisted upon. Instead, they were now whining about something else. In my first attempt to see them off, I took a few steps back from the driver's door and a pathetic protest of discomfort came from the man in the passenger seat. He explained that he was not "comfortable," but I addressed his physical state rather than the issue of an overloaded van. It was true that I had used their bodies to 'key in' the load, but given that this was in line with their previous demands, I saw it as more of a creative solution to their problem rather than something they had the right to complain about.

The driver began relaying a series of his own issues, starting with, "But I can't see out of my windows." Still trying to excuse myself and get them on their way, I asked if he could see out of the front window and into each of the two rear-view mirrors. He said that he could but highlighting this point was not enough to get him to adopt any amount of confidence. He was also concerned about getting a ticket.

I offered my reassurance. I said something to the effect of, "Don't worry, to get a ticket for an obstructed view, the officer has to witness the obstructed view from your position. Since I've been careful to pack the equipment around you in the driver's seat—to the point you can't get out of the van without moving the equipment—the cop can't get into your position and 'witness' your view without altering it." This, I explained with confidence, would eliminate the possibility of any officer making such a claim.

He persisted with other statements of concern regarding the extremely unusual angle of the van, and the weight on the rear wheels. I gave a serious response to each of their complaints but never once acknowledged that we should rethink things and opt for another solution. I assured them that, "Once you get out of the inclined loading area and top up the tires, you'll be fine." When they finally agreed to drive away, I had to keep my laughter in check as I waved goodbye and headed back into the building. They looked like a couple of unwilling test pilots for some sort of new rocket van that was a little short of air in the back tires.

I went back into the shop and everyone in the place was laughing. Once I had finished giggling, we all got back to work but our discouraged drivers were honking in a pattern that implied they wanted our attention. Apparently, they were unable to get the van up the incline of the loading dock to get on their way. They were thankful we had heard them honking; they feared opening the door and getting out of the van would certainly damage any lights that were bound to fall out upon their exit.

Apparently, even though the driver had floored the accelerator, the weight in the van was so great that it prevented the vehicle from moving up the loading dock's small but steep hill. I was determined to get them home in one load. I gathered up everyone from the shop, and together we helped push the cube van (from the side) until they made it up the hill. They were about to stop and thank us for the push, but I encouraged them to continue without stopping as they made a rather wide turn out of the parking area. I was reasonably sure that they would make it home safely—provided the rear axle did not break beneath them and the roof didn't cave in from above.

Once their show finished its run, it took three trips with the same vehicle and drivers to return all of our gear. When they arrived with their last load, I was in the shop and asked the drivers how their show went. They explained that their theatre production didn't possess as much drama as the trip to get there. Apparently, the front wheels of the cube van didn't always steer in the direction the driver turned. Strangely, there wasn't enough weight in the front of the vehicle (read too much weight in the rear) to provide the front wheels with sufficient purchase to effect proper steering. The driver went on to describe in great detail the extremely unnerving delay he experienced with each turn. I didn't want to get into another lengthy discussion with them, so I simply said, "Good thing I loaded up the cab as much as I did."

The heavier the load, the more difficult the journey.

Life's Lessons: A Successful Collection of Failures

∞ The Chandelier ∞

Sales are a very important part of any business. The small production company I worked for was especially dependent on the income from their equipment rentals. During one of our tougher times, management made a decision to formally branch out into sales. Rather than just selling theatrical lighting and accessories such as that in our own rental department, the owners felt we could easily broker any other product from our existing suppliers as well. In other words, they reasoned, why buy only theatrical lighting from our manufacturing suppliers if they could sell us many other lighting products and offer the same retailing discount to our company.

Most of the staff would have preferred to stick with the familiar lighting fixtures. Nevertheless, we embraced our new calling enthusiastically and learned about many more lighting products. If our supplier carried it, we familiarized ourselves with it. Eventually, we were known for selling anything from dance floor disco lights to outdoor neon signs.

This was relatively easy work. Anytime we didn't know something about a product, we simply called up the particular supplier and got the answer. Back then there were a lot fewer buy-direct-and-save stores than there are now. Twenty years ago, the average consumer was happy to pay a middleman as long as the retailer provided reasonable service. In our case, we provided installation. The more specialized the light, the greater the benefit to our customer. Since we catered to a theatrical lighting market, any additional products were offered with an option to have one of our specialized lighting technicians install them. Our willingness to service what we sold complemented our product sales, and in a short time the sales department grew to gross more than our rental department.

Our suppliers manufactured the products they sold to us. On one occasion, a major supplier called to say that they were pleased with our increased purchases. During this conversation, they casually offered to make any custom lighting fixture if the need arose. This gave one of the partners of our company an idea.

Rather than fine-tune what was working, he felt that it was best to branch out once again. This time we were expanding into the manufacturing of custom lighting. There were no pamphlets to read or specs to go over. We needed only to adopt the position that we could make any type of lighting fixture—for the right price.

Only a few days after getting the word out, we received a call from a very reputable national lighting chain. They had heard how we were willing to make virtually any lighting fixture provided the customer's pocket book was in line with their imagination. The representative from this chain store contacted us with a referral. However, he wanted assurances from our company that we would treat his valued customers—a well-to-do couple—with the same attention to detail that they were accustomed to receiving from him. He assured us that there would be no problem with this husband-and-wife team paying for anything they ordered.

I was appointed to meet with them for the purpose of defining their needs. I went to their well decorated home and entered in awe. The husband introduced me to his wife and we entered the dining room to hear how they had dreams of designing their own chandelier. Their dream, as they described it to me, was to work with a company such as ours and help create a customized chandelier that would be unique, extremely attractive, and stylish enough to command attention as the focal point of an already elegant dining room. It was not to be a traditional one with many hanging pieces of crystal illuminated by a few standard light bulbs. It was to be the complete opposite of what any dinner guest might anticipate.

They wanted thousands of extremely tiny light bulbs, interconnected with the option of dimming some or all of them, in patterns that would accurately reflect the stars and their celestial patterns in the sky—all sunk individually into the ceiling of this grand room. They both wanted their new lights to be virtually unnoticed until the other lights in the room were dimmed and these special lights were turned on. I knew of an exceptionally small low voltage bulb that was about half the size of a grain of rice. It came with two extremely thin insulated wires that exited a sealed bottom and required connection to a transformer to be illuminated. I warned them that what they were asking for was extremely expensive. I refrained from saying that it wasn't worth it, because this was obviously a dream of theirs. Quite likely, it was one that they had shared for some time as their input and answers to my questions weren't debated between them. They simply responded excitedly as they relayed what they had envisioned.

I discouraged them as best I could, knowing that their concept would have to be carried out using an incredibly sophisticated assembly of lights. Since this was our first meeting, I had no idea how many transformers would be required. I did know that there would be a significant amount of tedious manual labour necessary to craft the connections between the exceedingly fine wires of the numerous bulbs and their power supply from an unknown number of transformers.

In addition, I shared with them how the bulbs would have to be wired in the space between the ceiling of the dining room and the floor of the room above. This plan wouldn't be practicable in any house—especially theirs. In addition, I wasn't sure how to compensate for the group of equidistant and parallel two inch wide straight lines of blank spaces on sixteen inch centres that the joists would inevitably create in what was supposed to be a free-form display of God's creation.

There were also a myriad of other problems, none of which I had begun to address. Could the ceiling maintain its structural integrity after our electric drills had honeycombed their drywall? Were there maps available at a scale of four light-years to the inch for designing the portion of the sky that was going to be portrayed? Could the Internet be advanced quickly enough to be thrust into the public domain twenty years prior to its scheduled arrival?

This would have been a major undertaking for any lighting manufacturer. Since this was our first attempt to boldly go where no other lighting company had gone before, and in truth into a completely different lighting dimension, I felt that I should just decline, go home, and rest my brain. Their response was to offer me "any amount of money" that could make their dream a reality. To this I replied, "Uh…I'll see what I can do."

After I returned to the shop, I briefed the two owners of our small lighting company about the meeting. The type of custom light this well-to-do couple was asking for wasn't one that any of our manufacturing suppliers were willing to make. All of them were unfamiliar with the type of bulb required and the work necessary to complete the job. When we pushed them to provide a quote anyway, they offered ridiculously high figures to compensate for "too many" variables and unknowns.

One of the two owners of our company—the visionary—was excited about the idea anyway and actually suggested that our firm create the spectacle ourselves. In his mind, we only had to calculate the cost of the materials and labour involved, and then add double our usual profit. He justified his suggestion by clarifying that we deserved two healthy markups—one for designing the effect, and the other for building it. Our other owner—the guy who had to design it—was less excited. As he saw things, our company was experienced in selling someone else's lights, not making our own.

After a collective effort, we calculated the cost for this special lighting effect. We arrived at figure of over five thousand dollars. Putting things in perspective (perhaps for the first time), to that date our most expensive household lighting fixture sold for about two hundred dollars.

I was elected to break the news to our clients. I think they mistook the five thousand dollar price tag as one that reflected something of value rather than a series of labour intensive tasks to assemble a batch of expensive parts. Nevertheless, they excitedly handed over a large cheque as a deposit. One owner—the guy who had to build it—was almost immediately overwhelmed by the task at hand.

We should have advised our customers that recreating an exact replica of our galaxy was not within our world of expertise. I was faced with asking them to change their criteria but warned them that we were not in a position to lower the price for such a compromise. Appealing to their egos, I suggested that a random motif of theirs would translate into a more personalized custom fixture and reflect more of their own 'design' than a simple reflection of someone else's. I added that there would be no extra charge for such a service. They humbly agreed.

The children's picture books of the Milky Way were immediately discarded in exchange for a meeting to obtain the husband's 'design' for the new placement of the bulbs. He was not an artistic man, nor was he prepared for such a creative moment. I had to keep putting the pencil back into his hand and diplomatically discourage him from putting the lights too close together so that he didn't blow our predetermined budget for bulbs.

There were many other complications associated with bringing his ideas to fruition. Sadly, there was no way to assemble the parts on site. It became apparent that we could not incorporate the design into the area above the ceiling. The only way we could hope to illustrate a modicum of talent was to build a separate fixture and fasten it directly to the ceiling. The joists that had previously presented a design problem were now being considered an asset in the installation of our very heavy 'chandelier'. The reason was primarily because of the many transformers necessary to provide power for the numerous low voltage bulbs that were part of our modified design. However, the framework needed to house the many transformers was a monstrosity all on its own.

This dainty behemoth had been designed after a revolutionary afterthought—whatever entered a room had to be smaller than its ceiling. Not only was the size of the contraption limited by the dimensions of the largest doorway in the home, it was also restricted by the layout of the hallways and the size of the exterior doors. We elected to make a dozen or so standalone fixtures each composed of a separate wooden frame about three feet square and having their own transformers for separate control. For added elegance, we selected two-by-six pine lumber as the construction material of choice. Unfortunately, at this point, the only way to justify keeping our customers' deposit and continuing with the project was to finish manufacturing these large awkward pieces of the whole and later assemble them on site in our clients' dining room.

Our clients granted a further concession to the design team. They allowed us to decrease the overall dimensions of the fixture. The finished size would no longer incorporate coverage of the full ceiling. It would now be modified to cover all but a two-foot space around the perimeter of the room. Supposedly, this was to create a symmetrical surround that would frame the lighting display and complement its splendour. Instead, this recessed portion of the ceiling acted more like an out-of-place margin that focused a guest's attention towards our maladroit wooden box of tiny lights—the 'chandelier'. Fortunately for our budget, a good number of bulbs were successfully scrapped from this most recent evolution of the project. Still, no discounts were offered.

One owner of our company—the guy who had to install it—was constantly frustrated by the never-ending challenges he faced as the overall project consumed him for more than a month. It took three men the better part of a week to permanently affix our culmination of effort to our customers' dining room ceiling. Once assembled, this giant fixture was greater in size than any light pictured in any of our suppliers' catalogues. Each separate square had its own opaque white plastic panel that held our miniature bulbs in place but allowed the outline of every internal transformer to be seen when the lights were illuminated. Shadows of other innards were also evident but not distinctive enough to define what they were to any first time observer. The only splash of light that resembled anything elegant was the unplanned seepage that escaped from the top of the units where they did not meet the finished surface of the ceiling squarely.

Oh, and there was one more thing. Each time this eyesore was turned on, any illumination was accompanied by a discordant "thdnngggg" generated from the numerous transformers, each struggling for their own share of the available power. Loud dinner music was almost essential to drown out the constant hum of their existence. It was enough to prompt any returning guest to bring a safety helmet to the next dinner function. The chandelier was probably considered most presentable during power outages.

After the installation was complete, I was once again elected to meet with the client. This time, I was to collect the balance owed. At their home, I picked up the much needed funds for our cash-strapped company. A strained parting conversation gave way to some kind words of post-justification from the classy couple. As we reviewed the confusing course of events, we wondered how their magnificent concept had manifested itself into such a vile piece of junk. To their credit, they were a forgiving couple, too refined to even complain. Perhaps they had understood our pathetic state better than we had ourselves.

The dream of masterfully recreating the heavens in light, to be enjoyed with their guests at each formal meal, was not to be. Instead, the rather forgiving couple would have to be content with accommodating an unwanted blemish permanently lag-bolted to their dining room ceiling. In truth, had they been able to remove it, they could have placed it in a garage sale without any loss of potential value. It would most certainly have fetched enough cash to purchase the latest copy of a real lighting manufacturer's catalogue. Talk about the need for a public apology.

Stargazing can cloud your judgment.

∞ Neon Lights ∞

The small production company I worked for had only a few employees when I started. At the company's peak, we employed about a dozen people and grossed just over a million dollars of total revenue in one year. The years previous and afterward, each only grossed about half of this amount in annual sales. Interestingly, the net profit from all three of these years was about the same. Not proportionally, but the actual dollar amount of profit was similar in each of these three years. Since I held positions of responsibility in virtually all areas of the business, I grew to understand something about cash flow and profit—including the subtle but distinct difference.

In our best year, we had branched out into sales beyond our already established theatrical lighting market. We were providing rentals for everything from trade shows to laser light displays. We were also selling virtually any type of light available from our suppliers. We felt that by bowing out of the manufacturing end of lighting, we could ensure only top quality products and services, especially since we were no longer making 'chandeliers'.

Although still able to produce and install other custom lighting fixtures, we chose to remain focussed on our traditional sales. Our company actively promoted our established lighting products by making local designers aware of our unique product line. Our company's relationships with these well-known professionals were very profitable for both the designers and ourselves. Each designer received our advice about the effects our unique lights could produce as well as the realistic life expectancy of the associated specialty bulbs. Our experience had come from replacing the bulbs on a contractual basis for various bars and dance clubs. We, in turn, had our lights specified in their drawings and designs. This helped increase our sales considerably.

One day, one of the rather flamboyant interior designers invited me to his apartment, which was located directly above his office in downtown Toronto. After a tour of both, he explained how many of his meetings involved entertaining his clients informally in his apartment after a formal meeting in his office had been concluded on the floor below. In the early 1980s, the entertainment business commonly referred to this wooing of a potential customer as "schmoozing." His apartment was high-tech and had the feel of a cozy local pub more than that of a bachelor's residence. It was well suited for schmoozing.

He had overheard me talking about neon lighting one day when he was in our showroom. This gentleman asked for my advice. He wanted some sort of bright light to be installed in the ceiling, high above the main area where he talked with potential clients. He envisioned four lines of blue neon light, which together would form a large square directly above the centre of the hardwood floor in his dining room. This area was often used as a dance floor when formal meetings turned into impromptu entertaining. After his budget was established and he gave us the almighty deposit, I contacted our neon supplier and placed the order.

This supplier was a one-man-show, but considered to be the highest local authority on neon lighting because he had extensive experience installing many different neon signs. He was quite good at this, but our indoor project was somewhat different from his usual line of outdoor work. A basic outdoor neon sign consists of a metal box with a message contained on a plastic face, the focal point of the sign. The message is stencilled over the frosted plastic and the intense neon lights from inside the box illuminate the message—even in daylight.

More expensive versions consist of stand-alone letters that have only one colour of frosted plastic but their metal boxes are formed into the shape of the individual letters. These are effectively a group of individual signs spelling out the message or the name being advertised. In such a case there are *many* awkward metal boxes—the crude forms of which remain relatively unnoticed next to the bright illuminated message. In either case, none of the electrical connections are visible to the onlooker since they are all inside the sign or letter.

My supplier came to take measurements, since all orders for neon lights had to be manufactured to a custom length in order to fit the dimensions of each individual job. It took over six weeks to make four simple straight lines of neon. Once the lights were completed, my supplier returned to my designer's loft to install them into the agreed square pattern above the dining room floor.

Unfortunately, my ambitious supplier had ripped out most of my designer's ceiling in preparation for running the specialized wire needed for the installation. He was careful to fasten the neon tubes securely before he asked me how he was going to hide the high voltage connections. I told him that I didn't care where they went, as long as they were hidden.

Unfortunately, he explained that according to the electrical code, no connection can be hidden above a ceiling or inside a wall. Every single electrical connection must be made inside an accessible junction box. Puzzled, I asked how he was allowed to hide them inside his signs. He told me that the sign itself was considered to be a junction box because it had a removable cover and all of the electrical connections were accessible once this cover had been removed.

In short, my installer was telling me that the thick high voltage wires had to be connected inside an approved (ugly) metal box that he thought would be best fastened to my customer's ceiling, with large unsightly wood screws. As we discussed more suitable possibilities for solving the problem, it became exceedingly obvious that we were not on the same page. I couldn't get him to understand that this was someone's home, and that these lights were meant to be the centre of attention in the elaborately decorated entertainment area *inside*.

This guy must have gone to the same school where they teach the phone man to install your phone. You know the school…the one where the students fail unless they expose and staple as much phone line as possible to any nearby wooden part of your home—including but certainly not limited to handcrafted baseboard and antique trim. This school still accepts applicants from your local cable company so that their 'cable guy' can destroy the exterior of your home with similar flagrant disregard to any structural or artistic design. Four large ugly gray boxes, surface mounted beside each of the fancy and expensive neon lights, was not a solution—despite his offer to "paint" them the same colour as the stylish ceiling.

This was the first time I realized that the high-tech lighting we had ordered was being installed by a low-tech contractor. I didn't have a clue how I was going break this news to my designer friend. I consulted the installation team working at my company, who were equally stumped. With the sole exception of one custom chandelier, our installation work until this time had taken place above a stage or dance floor with an open ceiling which enabled us to dress the cables neatly along the black framework of each application.

My client and I met with the fearless neon sign installer for a much needed chat at the designer's home. My soon-to-be ex-customer was horrified when he first viewed the many wide cavernous holes in his textured ceiling. To his credit, he was able to appear relatively calm. However, throughout the discussion, he agitatedly fiddled with the many golden charms that were habitually dangling from his neck, exposed by his fully unbuttoned shirt. My confused contractor stood in his stained overalls, still failing to grasp what I had just learned. Indoor neon lighting is art—outdoor is not.

It was agreed that it would be best if the sign man went home…and took his sledgehammer, crowbar, and his four gaudy neon sticks with him. Our company agreed to refund my client's deposit. An *indoor* neon lighting company manufactured and installed what had been ordered in the first place. My employer then paid for the much needed repairs to the ceiling.

The best advice does not always come from the highest authority.

∞ Fit for a King ∞

My employer was forever biting off more than it could chew. We were continually behind in our financial obligations. Most weeks, the imaginative partner would make optimistic assurances to our clients, and promise that their projects would be "ready for the weekend." Meanwhile, his conscientious colleague would regularly scramble to meet these corporate responsibilities. Our company was in a constant battle with money and we fought every week just to make payroll.

In the theatre business, we learned the true meaning of a deadline. In our terms, you were *dead* if you crossed the *line* with regard to being late. It is simply not excusable to be found still taping down loose cables with gaffer's tape across a stage when the curtain opens on opening night. Such tardiness is regarded as complete failure in any facet of show business.

Although the meaning of the word may appear obvious, missing deadlines is quite acceptable and at times the norm, depending on the line of work. Construction, for example, is a trade in which deadlines are more of a goal, a direction, a hope, or an impossible dream. A contractor, regardless of specialty (electrician, plumber, or painter, etc.) may completely fail their client in terms of having something ready on time. However, for some unknown reason most consumers forgive the contractor's broken promise and demonstrate this through their complete and immediate acceptance of a new 'deadline' from the same bonehead. The tradesman need not put much thought into how this date is arrived at. In fact, if the day of the week suggested matches an actual date in time, this is usually sufficient. Thus, the only tool any contractor truly requires is a calendar. Everything else can be worked out after this—and, as I am sure most have experienced—even after the newly revised deadline if need be.

In reality, this is why most contractors are well versed in the phrase, "It's almost done." The operative word "almost" makes this common proclamation about as assuring and on par with "It's not done." As he reaches for the calendar, you pray that he continues working on your project before he really starts thinking ahead and quotes some other job creating yet another black hole of promises with someone else.

These tidbits of reality are why no contractor is ever hired to work on a trade show. Trade shows are like theatre work. A deadline is a deadline. It is not a plan. In this trade, you need more than a calendar and a pencil in your ear to participate. That is, more than once.

Our sound and lighting company knew how to meet a deadline. We made a habit of always finishing our work on time. Our desperate need to cover the previous week's payroll drove our concentration to complete projects in a timely fashion. Writing cheques was never a problem—cashing them was. We welcomed any suggestion on the customer's part to increase the value of their job, even though it might have meant less time to have things "ready for the weekend."

We were always playing catch-up.

On one particular project, a trade show customer of ours was hosting a royal visit. Our client was a large Swedish corporation operating in Aurora, Ontario. The owners of this company had been promised a visit from their royal family. We were doing trade show work for this corporation on an ongoing basis and were in the process of setting up a large-scale presentation of employee awards inside the plant. I was in charge of coordinating and accommodating all of our client's requests.

On the morning of the awards ceremony, it was confirmed that the King and Queen of Sweden would be dropping by, not only for the planned tour, but also to participate in the presentations. This last minute update was difficult to service because seating for the King and Queen had to be provided. Two special chairs were required. They had to be suitable for monarchs, a matching pair in the colour scheme of the company's logo (blue and yellow like the Swedish flag), and purchased and delivered *within a couple of hours.*

When first apprised of this update and the corresponding requirements, I asked for a few minutes to gather my thoughts. The biggest obstacle, of course, was our payroll. The reality of our company's cash flow predicament became a weighty factor in every decision we made—we could never afford to say no. I accepted the impractical request and treated it as a personal challenge to exchange a couple of makeshift thrones for some much needed cash.

Rather than ask for suggestions as to what might be appropriate, I chose to pursue my own initiative and headed straight for the local discount furniture store. My belief is that if one adapts, one will overcome. I was hoping that my clients and the Swedish royal family would embrace my philosophy.

Had I presented a couple of simple wooden chairs with blue fabric and asked my client to approve them as their offering for the royal bottoms, I am sure the plainly padded pine seats would have been flatly rejected. However, my ploy was to show up and place them into position only moments before the start of the event—just as they were needed. This is precisely what I did.

They came. They sat. They went. These thrones-for-the-day got a 'warm' reception, but not from my clients. Instead, the owners of the company hosting the royal family gave me looks of disappointment. I thought for a moment that they might even refuse to pay their bill. I tried to smooth things over by highlighting some of the chairs' features: they were "royal" blue, a matching set, had "yellowish" wooden frames, and were procured from a Swedish furniture manufacturer. These lame attributes did little to raise their spirits, but this was all that could be said in defence of my actions.

Fortunately, if they had refused to pay for the chairs, we would not have lost any money. I had managed to secure the furniture free of charge. I had explained to the manager of the furniture store that the chairs would be returned in pristine condition if he allowed me to "use" them for a short time. It is against their store policy to replace a "used" item and return it to the floor for resale as a new one. However, I was able to overcome his resistance. I explained that these Swedish chairs, from their Swedish store could be sold at a premium because they were to be 'used' by Swedish royalty.

If anyone reading this is perturbed by the thought of a well-known furniture outlet agreeing to put a used chair back into their stock and later selling it as a new product, remember this: the chairs were fit for a king. Not only did this benefit the furniture store, this arrangement allowed me to meet all of the company's cash flow goals—for the week anyway.

Sometimes it is easier to receive forgiveness than to get permission.

∞ **The Laser Show** ∞

In the years that followed my stint in the entertainment business, I was climbing my way up the corporate ladder at the sound and lighting company I had been with for a couple of years. Promotion with this employer was limited as my boss was one of the two owners. My title grew only by nature of how many people were hired to work underneath me. This made my corporate ascension like riding a merry-go-round on a ladder while being permanently affixed to the second rung from the top.

In the last story, I explained how I had gambled on a seating solution for a special event involving Swedish royalty. Originally, my efforts did not sit well with the management of the firm. (The pun is very much intended.) However, in time, this company's management came to accept my impromptu solution as creative. A few months later, they gave our company another chance to impress them.

This time our client wanted us to provide entertainment for a group of dignitaries from various other Swedish firms. After an all day pitch on the advantages of being associated with their company, our friends planned to entertain them at a special dinner. This was to take place at the world famous Ontario Science Centre in Toronto. Supposedly, this was the perfect place to host an evening in which the theme for the day was to be "high-tech" advancements. This company had experienced many challenges when they first began work in Canada and some of their more innovative solutions were to be highlighted throughout that day at various locations.

My boss and I were asked to design a show that could be enjoyed during the dinner meal. It was to be the grand finalé after this company had spent a full day of patting themselves on the back in front of these dignitaries. When we met with our client's key representatives to discuss the possibilities, my boss made a confident statement. He said that our company could develop a "high-tech" show to top off their special evening, and did so without the slightest thought as to how this would be accomplished. He always said, "Get the job first, and worry about the rest later." I believe he viewed this opportunity as a chance for our company to redeem itself with this major corporate giant. We were hoping that one day we would be the exclusive source for all of their trade show and production needs.

On the way home, I asked my fearless leader what he had in mind. He stated that this would be solved on our next trip to New York City together. We got back to the shop and arrangements were made to meet with various other production companies in the Big Apple.

While in New York, we viewed many dance club lighting fixtures, all of which consisted of many flashing coloured lights that spun and changed direction at various intervals. Some would illuminate in sync with the beat of the music while others could be flashed and moved around with manual remote controls. Unfortunately, any of these lighting pieces would have made the dinner setting seem more like eating on the dance floor of a disco.

Later, on the same trip, we stopped at a production company that boasted laser light shows as their specialty. The owner of this company was on hand to describe some of the unique features that only a laser could offer. In just a few minutes, he had set up a makeshift demonstration in which he captured our company logo in his scanning machine, and within moments projected it in fluorescent green as it twirled and spun in all different directions, including three dimensional twists that created new, never-before-seen images of our logo. We were very impressed.

If this guy could do this with no time to prepare, imagine what he could do if we gave him a few weeks to create something special. It was difficult for my boss to contain his excitement while he inquired about the possibilities of subcontracting this New York lighting company. The laser expert described many options for a well-polished show, which he delivered with paralleled finesse during his pitch. We asked the owner to prepare a quote and told him we'd be in touch once we had a better idea of our client's budget.

Subsequent meetings with our client led us to hire the laser specialist, and I quickly began making arrangements to bring him to Canada for the special evening. Our contract with this New York City production company was many pages in length and extremely unfair from what we understood. It was so one-sided that virtually anything could have happened—like rain—and our laser man could have refused to do the show and been entitled to full pay. The fact that the show was to be held indoors didn't persuade him to allow us to cross this part of the contract out. In fact, he stated that any change to his standard contract would eliminate the possibility of him preserving our scheduled time slot.

Supposedly we were paying him for the work he had to do to prepare a special show that fit into the high-tech theme of our client. Since this is what our client was paying us to do, we simply decided to accept his ridiculous fee for the time being and approach our client with the price before signing anything. With only a slim markup on our part, we had to charge a thousand dollars per minute for a ten minute laser show.

I was apprehensive when I approached our European friends with the price, especially since they often prided themselves in creating economical solutions to their problems and weren't used to paying megabucks for anything—let alone a few minutes of fun for a group of strangers. At the time, $10,000.00 was a significant amount of money—still is actually—and it would probably equate to more like five times this amount today. Nevertheless, the Swedish executives accepted the cost without any specifics being discussed.

When this news reached the two owners of our company, one was thrilled I had secured the contract. The other was thankful that I had been able to do so without disclosing our complete lack of knowledge in terms of what was to take place. Apparently, my sincere response of "I don't want to spoil it for you," only served to increase their excitement and fuel their imagination of what was to come. I think my comment was interpreted as a concerned and confident endorsement of their upcoming customized laser show.

On the day of, my boss's partner and his crew were busy working throughout the city on a number of smaller contracts related to the high-tech day. He was to meet us at the Science Centre around 4:00 so my boss and I could introduce him to our laser hero. There, we could all view a test run of the show and my boss's partner would be on hand with his crew to work out any of the kinks after the much-anticipated preview.

The laser lighting crew from New York City were to drive though the night and arrive first thing in the morning at the border crossing where our broker was. This detail seemed to be missed by our lighting expert as he showed up at the wrong bridge. It took him until noon to get to our broker. Laserman had allowed himself to fall behind schedule considerably. He had barely enough time to drive to Toronto and set up in time for the owners of our company to witness the test run of his lighting creation.

Around the time I had originally scheduled to leave the shop and head to the Science Centre to coordinate the load-in, I received a call from our broker indicating that the laser show creator we had hired was not legally allowed to work in Canada. Apparently, he required official government endorsement. In addition, his rental truck full of specialized equipment was being held indefinitely and wouldn't be allowed to cross the border into Canada without said approval. My broker requested I write a well-worded letter to the Canadian Government, making all encompassing statements that would affect everyone involved. He wanted me to send him a copy as soon as it was written.

I had no time for any of this. This was great, just great. My key lighting man and his rental truck full of laser gear was all tied up in red tape, and I had less than six hours until showtime. Worse still, laser boy had absolutely no motivation to help me solve the problem since he had already been paid in full.

In frustration, I asked to speak to our contracted helper. I became extremely discouraged as he began to offer half-hearted apologies as if he had already embraced an early return to his hometown, pocketing our fee and leaving us to face our client without a trace of laser gear in the country. My mind raced. Then, with the same blind faith my boss had displayed when he first sold the idea of a laser show to the Swedish executives, I assured this alleged professional that he would be working in our country, with his gear, and that he would be doing so in time for dinner at the world renowned Ontario Science Centre. I thought to myself, "No big city slick-talker is going to take *me* to the cleaners."

In my desperation, I threatened to place anonymous calls to customs on both sides of the border and hint that his truck was full of drugs. I stated with unjustifiable authority that Canadian officials practiced thorough and meticulous anal cavity searches in such cases. I turned my head slightly away from the mouthpiece of the phone and pretended to talk to my boss, asking something to the effect of, "Maybe we shouldn't respond at all and he'll be forced to remain in custody at the border indefinitely." I'm not sure which one of my desperate attempts to persuade him changed his mind, but eventually he accepted the concept that "The show must go on."

I quickly educated myself about the specifics of our problem with the government employee that was pressuring my broker. Luckily, this person was in Toronto and only a few blocks away from where I was standing. I got in my car and sped to the employment office that governed such activities. There I convinced (begged) a kind female manager to issue our company a temporary permit allowing the lighting 'specialist' to work for one day in our country. The issue was that any person coming into Canada was not allowed to work if there is someone else anywhere in the country that is capable of performing the same duties.

It was awkward explaining to her how this highly skilled laser lighting technician was unequalled in talent by any other individual in all of Canada, while simultaneously asking her to hurry up because he was hopelessly behind schedule due to a number of his oversights.

Once the paperwork was signed, I had her call my company's broker at the border to release him and his truck full of gear. I didn't leave until I had heard that they were on their way. My next step was to get back to the shop and pick up my boss in hopes of getting to the Science Centre before the other owner got there and freaked out. My boss's partner was the type that took comfort in eating. Anytime he was stressed, he ate. The more he was stressed, the more he ate. If we didn't arrive before him, and our laser was nowhere to be found, we ran the risk of finding him in the venue's only kitchen devouring the dinner meals intended for the VIPs.

On the way to the Science Centre, I pulled our company truck onto the only highway that heads north out of the heart of the city. It was just after 4:00 and the show was scheduled to begin in less than two hours. Travelling in rush hour ensured this time crunch would be even more difficult to overcome. Rush hour in Toronto produces stop and go traffic for hours—assuming there are no accidents, construction sites, or other common complications along the way.

As I edged our truck onto the highway and into the bumper-to-bumper traffic, I noticed a rental van creeping up to a position directly beside us. It was our American lighting team. Although it was comforting to know that they were in the right city, it was just as disturbing to be so blatantly reminded of how far behind schedule we were. I had an overwhelming feeling of lateness, second only to watching the Nordair flight on final approach to Kenora during my "Flight for Pride."

My boss and I arrived only moments before his eat-to-reduce-stress partner showed up expecting to see everything set up and ready to go. Nothing had even been started. There would be no test run to witness, no one to complain to, and there was no unmanned kitchen that he could run to. It was even close to dinnertime but to his credit he didn't lose control and offered to help in any way he could. There was simply too much riding on this show to do anything else. Within moments, he was helping coordinate the power drop with the in-house electricians for the massive amount of electricity the laser needed.

The young woman from the Swedish company came over to instruct us to begin, and we were all running around like contestants on a senseless game show racing against the clock. Since I was the one who had officially 'sold' the show to them, she apprised me of the final arrangements. The plan had been for the president of the Swedish firm to introduce the laser show, and creatively tie the high-tech theme of the day into the company's history of innovative problem solving and progress. This was supposed to justify dragging a couple hundred dignitaries across town in rush hour. Instead, after I informed her we weren't ready, an announcement was made that the overly anticipated high-tech laser show was delayed due to "technical difficulties."

Our employees managed to help get the American laser team set up in record time. This collective effort allowed us to be only slightly late for the scheduled start of the long-awaited laser show. I informed the Swedish company representative that we were ready. After catching up with her, I proudly stated, "We're good to go." Her relieved look was comforting and she smiled as she told me how much she was looking forward to seeing the show herself after all of the hype. She went on to say how she had reserved a special seat for herself in a position that would be sure to catch all of the excitement.

Feeling like I had just summited Mount Everest, I headed back to our laser specialist. I walked with a proud confidence like the mountain climber who has just reached his pinnacle. With a similar sense of achievement, as if scaling back down the mountain, I hustled to the control area to give the signal and start the show. It was at this moment that my lighting liberator confessed to me that he had planned to "design and create" the customized show once he was on site. All of those watching had imagined a spectacular light show was about to take place. The truth was he had done nothing to prepare. No wonder his contract was stacked in his favour. The only thing he was prepared to do was a few twists and spins with the Swedish company's logo—for a full ten minutes.

In complete blackness, the theme from the movie "2001" began to play. Then, out of the darkness came a great light. It was the Swedish company's logo in a bright green colour, twisting and spinning on a huge screen rented specifically for this occasion. This was only the second time in my life my attention was given to a twirling and spinning logo and I feel I can say with certainty, that it is no more interesting the second time round, even if it is with a different logo. No one else in the room other than my boss had seen this sort of thing before and for the first fifteen or twenty seconds it captivated the entire audience. Sadly, their interest dwindled rapidly as they began to realize that the show would be nothing more than an incessant repetition of the first few seconds.

Within the opening minute or so the groans of frustration became noticeably audible. The final nine minutes was completely redundant and people were whispering loudly and pointing at me. My contact at the company was trying to get my attention. I presumed she wanted to pull the plug. I feared stopping it before the ten minute mark would allow her to claim that her company should only be liable for the time it played. At a thousand dollars a minute, they might well have been happier with a nine thousand dollar refund. Having prepaid for the service ourselves, we simply couldn't afford to risk such a reduction in our customer's price. Therefore, I deliberately ignored her desperate attempts to gain my attention. I stared at the screen, pretending to be enthralled by the show. This was perhaps the only time I was able to benefit from my professional acting abilities…another free show.

When it was finally over, I looked around for support. However, my boss and the not-so-bright laser butcher both ran for cover—away from the woman who had hired us. The other partner darted to the kitchen to eat. I gathered my thoughts. Being the salesman responsible for this atrocious display of high-tech entertainment, I chose to do exactly the opposite. I rushed towards her asking with an excited tone, "Wasn't that great?"

I knew she was not impressed…nobody was. But I also knew that the manner in which one asks a question, will, to a large extent, determine the response. So, with enthusiasm in my voice and a bounce in my step, I led her in conversation about the performance. She didn't complain, but she did ask if we had both witnessed the same show. Puzzled by my apparent willingness to celebrate undeniable mediocrity, she pressed further, querying if it was indeed the show I had quoted her—for $10,000.00.

In the end, persistence had paid off, sort of. The eating partner had polished off three full course meals in less than ten minutes. It took our company considerably longer to be paid in full. Predictably, we never did any other work for this Swedish company again—thanks to the New York City bonehead who billed himself a laser lighting specialist at almost a thousand dollars a minute.

Some time after, still frustrated and disappointed, the two owners and I were discussing our company's policies concerning the reselling of other peoples' products and services. In reference to the laser show, my boss's partner asked, "Why didn't you guys take the time to view it first?"

We had spent weeks hyping something that was no more impressive than a basic screen saver and disgraced a major corporate client in front of their valued customers and prized business associates. My boss's partner was looking for some kind of explanation that would help him cope. My only response was that sometimes our imagination gets the better of us. Together we learned that imagination without reality is pure fantasy.

Anticipation is often more exciting than the experience itself.

∞ Concert Time ∞

Most people have heard the adage that we learn from our mistakes. In truth, I believe that we fail our way to success, provided of course that we are indeed learning from our mistakes along the way. Although I had learned earlier that I shouldn't let anyone tell me how to run my show, I didn't have the courage to apply it until I was asked to quote on a large trade show concert for a group of Ford executives.

I was asked to estimate the total cost of producing a show featuring Linda Ronstadt. Her performance required a rather sophisticated set-up. Providing sound for the thirty-six piece orchestra accompanying her was only half the battle. The other half was coordinating in-house follow-spots and elaborate stage lighting for both her and the opening act.

By this time I had produced a number of large stage shows successfully. I was making a name for our company in terms of coordinating and executing complex, full-scale performances. The management company that took care of Linda Ronstadt's production needs was aggressive in terms of both the demands they made for her, and the manner in which they made them.

I had allowed many a show in the past to be compromised by letting other less experienced people call the shots or influence my decisions. Just because someone has "been in the business longer" doesn't automatically mean that they are more experienced. Generally, we're taught that qualifications reflect competency. This is simply not the case in most lines of work. These terms are not synonymous in any field and this paradox is often confused, especially in the entertainment business.

Although it was exciting to receive a chance to bid on a name act that would most definitely put our company on the map, we were already busy with other shows scheduled around the same time. So, to simplify my workload, I quoted high. I did this for two reasons. First, I wanted to discourage the management of Linda Ronstadt's show from chewing up a lot of our company's time and energy with requests for subsequent and more detailed quotes, only to be told "no" in the end. Second, by quoting high, if we did get the job, we could be motivated to do the extra work for the higher price, even if we were too busy to do it from a practical sense.

The philosophy of "get the job first and worry about it later" can be successfully applied only when sufficient markups have been included to accommodate mass quantities of overtime to account for the unexpected. The price I quoted for the gear and the manpower to set it up and run the show was over $70,000.00, a significant price to pay for less than a two week rental. Even more so, considering this took place in the mid-eighties.

The day had come when it was time for the management company to make a decision about who was supplying Linda Ronstadt with equipment for her show in Toronto. Her management team had spoken to me on the phone a number of times on this pivotal day. They kept asking for more and more things to be "thrown in," citing their large budget. But this time I stuck to my instincts, and my boss allowed me to make the final decision. He wanted desperately to have his company on the proverbial map. We all knew that this show would do it for us, but he trusted my judgment. Everyone at our company wanted to be able to boast, "We did Linda Ronstadt." I confidently hung up the phone after reiterating to the aggressive negotiators that if they wanted more, they had to pay more, and added that this principal did not change based on who they were representing.

In doing so, I truly believed that I had saved our company from almost certain financial death by declining their "final offer." I remember trying to console my boss and his partner by saying, "Maybe we can be just as proud saying, we *turned down* Linda Ronstadt." Almost immediately after I made this statement, the management company called back. The shrewd man at the other end of the line had somehow now turned quite friendly. He congratulated me on receiving the contract and agreed to pay our higher price. I was ecstatic.

When I hung up the phone, I explained why the process had seemed like such a battle. The management firm's mind games were in fact a test. My contact had explained that American firms did not believe that most Canadian companies could perform to their standards. Indeed, many cannot. He went on to explain that the questions and answers over the previous weeks were designed to give them a feel for how devoted we would be in honouring their ongoing requests during the weeks in question. His inquiries were not designed to see how well we evaluated costs to provide these services. In other words, they didn't care about the price—provided Linda would be well accommodated.

Hearing this boosted my confidence. I was so proud of myself for sticking to my beliefs and not letting someone less experienced talk me out of my decision. I got on the phone and called my dad to share the sweet taste of success and flaunt the fact that I had taken the show away from a major American production company. My dad was pleased with my accomplishment. I invited him and Nancy to see the extravagant show.

I invited them to one of the performances later in the week because I wanted to be sure the show was running smoothly before they came to see it. The first show went well and the others that followed throughout the week had no major issues. There were minor kinks that had to be worked out during the first week, but overall, there were no more problems than one would expect from a show of that magnitude. The night my dad arrived with his soon-to-be second wife, they were both dressed formally. I met them out front of the venue to escort them in.

I had forgotten to tell them that this was a "closed" show, which meant that it was not open to the general public. Only people with Ford nametags were being allowed in through the main entrance. My plan was to sneak them up via a service elevator. One of the two was filled with our road cases. So, I had them follow me to the other one—the food service elevator.

No cologne or perfume could overpower the stench that surrounded us as we entered the building between the scattered industrial garbage bins. The smell of rotting vegetables permeated inside this service elevator. We had to step over spoiled meat caught in the tracks of the elevator doors. All of us slipped on a variety of spilled juices in the hallways, before we managed to make our way through a maze of "restricted access" doors. My efforts to impress my dad and his better half were further reduced when we passed by a jumbled mess of squished desserts. Eventually we entered the large entertainment room hosting the event.

A little later, Dad and Nancy declined the appetizers being passed around the venue that night. For some reason they weren't hungry. The entertainers executed the show flawlessly and Linda closed with the song *Desperado*. It was a memorable night for all in attendance. The highlight of the "free" show for my dad and his date was being allowed to leave through the normal exits along with the rest of the crowd.

On that night, before he left, my dad shared with me one of the two things he learned from the experience. He said that you can pay for things in many ways. I have since modified his observation to a philosophy along the same lines. "Cash, hide, or pride, we pay for everything we receive in some way." As for the other lesson my dad learned that night, it is reflected below.

If you want to go to a fancy show, buy a ticket.

∞ The Dimmer ∞

I have worked with many different kinds of musical groups and enjoyed talking to various band members over the years. I found each musician to be as unique as their music. But, whether from a Rock and Roll, Pop, Progressive, or Country group, they all had one common complaint. Since I was in the sound and lighting business, each one would have his or her own style of introducing their displeasure in not being able to find affordable lighting rentals for their band.

Although there are a number of similarities, the lighting rental market is not the same as the sound rental business. The main difference is that the demand for lighting is significantly less. Few establishments can accommodate the power requirements needed for even a small light show. The result is that only the more popular bands working the larger clubs have lights, and the up-and-coming bands working the smaller clubs do not. To some, this implies that a band with lights has reached a greater level of success than the band without.

In truth, this is only a general indication, but like anything else it has a few exceptions. One day over some drinks, I was talking with one of my friends who was in a rock and roll band. He desperately wanted lighting for his group. Through our discussions, I got the idea of renting a lighting system to them on an ongoing basis. The agreement was that I would purchase a complete stage lighting package suitable for their needs, and they in turn would rent it from me personally, to justify my outlay of capital for the system.

They asked for twelve one-thousand-watt lights, with enough stands and trusses to hang them from. Various sheets of gel, the tinted plastic that goes in front of the fixtures to produce a coloured beam of light, were also included along with the necessary gel holders for each light. A hundred foot cable for each fixture was provided to connect them individually to the heart of the system—the dimmer. This extremely heavy and expensive electrical device was mounted on wheels, as it was impractical to carry. Various other accessories were also packaged with the system. For example, a long low voltage cable was necessary to connect the dimmer to a lighting board for remote control of the stage lights from any area within one hundred and fifty feet of the power supply. With borrowed money from the 'Bank of Dad', I bought the system.

My boss gave me a "great deal" because there were no guarantees being offered, and he accepted my promise that I would not attempt to resell the items to his company's clientele. Despite this, the lighting equipment still cost me megabucks. Based on my calculations, I concluded that I would break even once my friend's band had rented the equipment for a year and a half. Any rental income produced after that point could be considered profit. Before delivering the goods to the excited band members, I had custom road cases made for all of the equipment to protect my investment. This additional expenditure changed my prospectus and meant that it would now take two years of continuous rental to recapture my investment.

Around the time the final rivet was being snapped into place for the last road case, the band broke up. This left me sitting on an enormous heap of specialized gear, all well packed into a series of matching road cases in accordance with the needs of a band that no longer existed. Because my employer was also in the business of renting lighting gear, I didn't feel comfortable trying to rent my personal equipment to any of my would-be business clients. My boss echoed the feeling when it became apparent that I had inadvertently created a conflict of interest for myself. As if I had not caused him enough grief already.

If I chose to pursue renting the equipment to someone else, I was taking business away from my employer, the owners of which were more like friends, and typically struggled each week to clear my paycheque. Since I was not prepared to do this, and I had nobody willing to rent the lighting package, I decided to sell it. The lack of response to my advertisements meant I had to store it. When I couldn't find anyone to store it for me, I decided to do what any young adult generally does. I took the problem home and dumped it on my mom.

I decided not to tell her about it at first, thinking I could obtain forgiveness easier than permission, a lesson I had learned earlier. I figured the best way to work these large pieces of unwanted equipment into the basement of my mom's townhouse was to move the heaviest but smallest item in first—the dimmer. This was no easy task. I solicited the help of my cousin, Dave. He is the type of guy that would encourage any police officer to call for backup if he were pulled over. This isn't because he has ever been in trouble with the law, but rather because of his intimidating stature.

I needed Cousin Dave to help me carry it down the stairs and across the floor of my mom's basement. It was so heavy even pushing it along her floor would crumple and disfigure the wall-to-wall carpet. Once it was in place, it would soon become obvious to my mom that it was too big and heavy for her to move. Moreover, it would be completely unrealistic for her to expect me to remove it on my own. So, as a result, I hoped my mom would let me keep it in her basement indefinitely.

On the day of the momentous move, Dave was repeatedly warned not to comment on how heavy the dimmer was and my reasons for keeping this information from my mom. It was a struggle to get it out of the truck and into the townhouse. At the top of the stairs to the basement, I reminded him once again. In a quiet voice I whispered, "If my mom gets wind of how heavy this is, there's no way she'll let me keep it here." With coordinated focus, we applied a determined grip to each of the four available handles. Each of our hands squeezed a handle with distinct purpose. I had placed my weightlifting relative on the basement side of the dimmer. This gave him the heavy side of the load. I felt if he could manage to hold the thing high enough to keep it level as we walked down the stairs, I would be able to maintain a steady grip of the lighter side. This was serious business. Any slip would likely result in the thing crashing down the stairs and almost certainly give my mom an excuse to refuse my 'needs'.

We began a slow controlled lift. Dave—who has never had trouble lifting anything in the past—had difficulty getting it off the floor at first. The expression on his face as he prepared for his first step indicated he was suppressing his grunting. With the exception of Dave's muscle shirt stretching in the process, we completed the lift in absolute silence. However, as we took our first steps downward onto the creaking stairs and left the landing, my mom cried out from a floor away, "That sounds awfully heavy to me!"

We had just passed our Rubicon and Dave began to laugh inwardly. This was not good. His laughter was contagious and further innocent inquiries from my mom caused both of us to lose our focus. We had no choice but to complete the decline quickly before our giggles affected our ability to hold onto the handles. In one continuous motion we made our way down the stairs, over the floor, and into the laundry room.

We managed to contain our laughter until the dimmer was carefully set down onto its wheels. It was almost as big as the washing machine and we were looking for a place to position it. I thought we could make room by moving some of the many boxes that were stacked up in this area. As I considered the possibilities, Dave began to laugh again. This time he wasn't able to control himself. When I inquired as to what was so funny, all he could do was point. He directed my attention to a group of boxes stacked nearby. Every single one was labelled, "Not Pictures."

I began to laugh hysterically as the rationale of such a labelling system was beyond me. If laughter was an indication of bewilderment, Dave was still struggling to grasp the concept as well. Just then, my mom entered the room. I tried to divert the attention away from my dimmer and focus it on my mom's unorthodox method of identification. I asked her how anyone could possibly know what was in "that box" for example, as I pointed to the one farthest away from my dimmer. Without hesitation, Mom explained, "It's probably books." Simultaneously she pointed to my dimmer, and said, "WHAT'S THAT?" I began to clarify (beg) about how I needed a place to put the dimmer. Meanwhile, Dave was busy investigating my mom's claims by retrieving the box in question. He wanted to see what was inside. Upon opening it, he exclaimed, "I can't believe it, there's nothing but books." Mom looked at him as if to say, "I know, I just told you."

With disbelief, both Dave and I questioned my mom further and in each case she was able to detail the items in each of the boxes labelled, "Not Pictures." On the way up the stairs, Dave was still in a state of confusion and muttered to me, "Your mom should work for the CIA decoding surveillance messages."

Apparently, when my mom and dad had split up, a lot of her boxes were full of pictures and only a few contained other items. In her trying time, the only boxes that were labelled were those that were "not pictures." After my mom moved into her own home, the boxes that contained books, clothes, games, or whatever, were never relabelled. My mom's chosen strategy to memorize the contents of the cardboard cartons rather than simply relabel them still perplexes Dave and me. However, it worked for her, so we let it be.

Some of the items were things she had purchased because they were a "great deal." Others were keepsakes that had sentimental value. I think she sympathized with my situation since *my* great deal was not needed at the time and I was desperate for a place to store my dimmer. It took a few years to sell the lighting package, but my mom let me keep it at her place until I sold everything—piece by piece. Wasn't she wonderful?

She still is.

It isn't a deal unless you need it.

∽ Rush Hour ∾

My cousin Dave and I are very close. One of the reasons is the common love we share for the game of hockey. We've played together for more than twenty years. From outdoor makeshift shinny in the winter to indoor organized leagues in the summer, we play as often as we can. One season when we were both single, we were playing together five nights a week and took turns driving each other to our games.

Our Wednesday night league was located in the northwestern part of the city. Typically, we would commute together to these games as we were both working in downtown Toronto. The sound and lighting company was located near Dundas and Parliament in the east side of the downtown core in Toronto. Dave was working for a company situated on the west side known as the financial district. Generally, on this night of the week, he would take the public transit system to my workplace—a two-mile stretch—and I would drive both of us to the arena in my car.

Our games started anywhere from 6:30 p.m. to 11:30 p.m. and our team had about an hour of ice time for each game. Dave usually finished work at 5:00 whereas I finished around 5:30. One day when we were scheduled to play the early game at 6:30, rush hour traffic was so bad Dave elected to *run* all the way to my workplace. Talk about a pre-game warm-up. He reasoned that he could catch his breath and relax in the passenger seat of my car while I drove to the arena. The trip from my workplace to the Wednesday night rink typically took about forty minutes to complete in light traffic, but on this night having an early game meant travelling in rush hour. Dave expected to have about an hour's rest in my car on the way there.

He was sweating and exhausted when he arrived, but dry and well rested by the time my boss let me leave work that night. Dave was extremely frustrated with the situation and quite disappointed in me for letting him down in terms of getting him to the rink on time. It was around 6:00 p.m. before my boss finally let me go. I ran down the stairs to where Dave greeted me with a look of hopelessness.

As I whisked him into the car, he followed with body language that clearly indicated he felt all was for naught. Certainly with less than thirty minutes before game time, he had a right to think we had lost any chance of playing hockey that night. Nevertheless, my goal was still to get to our game on time.

I raced my little car out of the parking area on our way to the arena. In an effort to restore his hope, I asked him to help me calculate the average speed we had to travel to reach the arena in time for our game. As he started thinking about this, I began to set a series of goals for myself to meet along the way. Mentally, I planned how I needed to reach given intersections within specific times. I shared this with Dave and encouraged him to help evaluate our progress. I was even prepared to go a little off course because I believed that maintaining forward movement would make him feel better than if we were standing still.

Dave told me that he thought my new time schedule was "unrealistic." His faith appeared to be directly proportional to the speed we were travelling. Each time I sped up I could sense his optimism increasing, but every time I hit the brakes I saw the look of despair in his eyes. Unfortunately, the first traffic light we came to presented us with a fresh red light. We were stopped at the light in westbound traffic behind a taxi. This was particularly frustrating since there was only one car in front of us and we needed to turn right and head north in order to stay ahead of the northbound congestion. Any experienced pizza delivery man knows the importance of staying "ahead of the pack."

I beeped my horn with a friendly short tap to encourage the cab driver to pull up a little. I knew if I could get him to pull forward even slightly, I could squeak by his right side and make the turn. He crept up a foot or so but there was still no way of making the turn.

I had a fleeting thought of cutting the corner and letting my right wheels mount the curb, but I decided against it. I sounded my horn a second time and the taxi driver responded by once again pulling forward slightly. Still not enough room. I hit the horn again, for the third time in less than twenty seconds.

As I did this, the driver stared at me through his rear-view mirror in confusion. Motioning with my hands, I tried to explain my keen desire to get by. Struggling to understand, and once again in an effort to accommodate me, he began to creep forward further into the intersection.

Dave focused his attention on the curb to our right. I maintained eye contact with the driver of the cab through his rear-view mirror. I anxiously encouraged him to move forward by continually sweeping my hand in a manner similar to a helpful person assisting a truck driver in reverse. Suddenly there was a loud crash. The cab driver's attention was quickly taken away from my hand and immediately affixed on the northbound vehicle that had just smashed his front driver's side quarter panel.

This completely unplanned stroke of luck benefited me in two ways. First, the impact had been significant enough to push the taxi in a clockwise rotation that created enough space for my vehicle to now make the turn. Second, the unsuspecting driver of the northbound vehicle was now engaged in a heated dispute with the helpful cab driver.

The combination of these two recent developments allowed me to make the turn. I continued in traffic significantly reduced by the two vehicles now blocking the intersection. Good manners are always appreciated so I willingly gave the cab driver a grateful thank you with the proverbial double tap of my horn as I turned right and headed north. I have deliberately omitted the precise intersection in an effort to avoid potential lawsuits. I strongly feel no public apology would suffice in this case.

My unexpected good fortune allowed me to make my first checkpoint on time. However, other strategic manoeuvres, such as passing on the wrong side of the road, travelling though empty construction sites, and driving backwards into oncoming lanes reasonably free of traffic, were also employed to ensure we maintained my so-called unrealistic time schedule.

We were nearing the end of the northbound portion of our car ride when we passed the Downsview Airport, not far from the arena. A giant dirigible was hovering closely overhead distracting drivers. When Dave brought it to my attention, I had an inadvertent moment of carelessness and just about hit the car in front of me. I jammed on the brakes and brought my car to a screeching halt…but the screeching sound continued. We looked back. The driver behind me was having trouble bringing his vehicle to a stop as well. It came to rest about a pencil width from my back bumper. Another coat of paint on either of our vehicles and all of my efforts to this point would have been for naught.

We needed to head westbound, but the left-turn lane was so backed up it seemed "unrealistic" to get into. I asked Dave to watch out the window to our right and look for a break in the traffic. I planned to avoid the line-up by staying to the right and turning eastbound at this last major intersection before we reached the arena. From there, I had hoped to make an immediate and abrupt U-turn and go westbound towards the rink.

Suddenly a space in the left-turn lane appeared and I felt I could get into it and turn westbound directly from our northerly heading. I cranked the steering wheel hard to the left. This sudden change of direction forced Dave's face and fingers into the passenger window of the car squishing them both into the glass.

As we pulled into the arena's parking lot I explained to him that I felt there was enough room to make the sudden left turn, but only if it was made quickly. Dave suggested that this was only possible because I was headed due west in the northbound lanes travelling "sideways" through traffic. He was noticeably overwhelmed from the many navigational calculations I had forced him to make throughout our trip.

Inside the arena, the last team member to leave the dressing room was locking the door as we approached in a hurried manner with our gear in tow. We asked our teammate to notify the others that we had arrived and would be out shortly. Our adrenaline was pumping so fiercely that we were able to dress in record time. We were slotted into the second line and we didn't miss a moment of ice time.

As I lined up to take the faceoff with Dave just to my left, I motioned to the referee to hold off dropping the puck for a moment. I turned to Dave and said, "Where are we?" I felt compelled to ask this question because it seemed as if we had been so rushed during our trip that our minds had still not adjusted. After the game, I thought about the poor cab driver who was probably still waiting for the police to arrive.

On the way home, Dave advised me that my aggressive driving did not score any points with him. A trip that typically would have taken forty minutes to complete in light traffic had been completed in less than thirty minutes—during rush hour! He referred to my low level flying skills as a pile of garbage. I tried to lighten him up, justifying our haste by claiming it was "all in the name of hockey."

When he finished his rant, I challenged him, saying that he could have spoken up during the car ride. He took a deep breath before he responded, and in a controlled tone said, "I didn't have time."

One man's garbage is another man's goal.

∞ Belts in the Bush ∞

By the mid 1980s, I had given up the pipe dream of becoming a well-known entertainer along with the sleazy lifestyle that had been introduced to me by my so-called personal business manager. It was true that some of the more respectable skills I had acquired during this time of my life had led me to a rewarding position with the sound and lighting production company immediately thereafter. In addition, the stage management experience I gained while working for this company was more than just interesting. At times it was very exciting. I was doing well financially, but something was missing.

A change in my life led me to divest myself of a rather extravagant toy, the ultralight aircraft I had purchased after my cross-Ontario charity flight for the Jerry Lewis Telethon. After the telethon, I mounted it on pontoons and tied it down on a beach near the government dock of a small lake in southern Ontario. I wanted to take every one of my friends for a memorable flight in my two seater flying machine before I sold it. Besides, the by-law enforcement officers in the Muskoka area were 'encouraging' me to move it from where I was "storing" it.

It was a very light and extremely simple aircraft. The cockpit was completely open, no cabin—just seats fastened underneath the wings. One time when I was learning to take off and land on the water, an excited passenger stood on the front support that joined the two pontoons. His weight flipped the tiny craft forward and upside down into the drink. It took more than a dozen high-powered boats—all pulling in different directions in the middle of the lake—to flip it back over and onto its floats.

I had to remove a number of drenched parts, dry them, and reinstall them into the plane. Then, after the water had been drained out of the motor, it was rebuilt. Five hundred dollars later, I was flying again. I learned from Michael Robertson—the best when it came to in-flight training and ground schooling. He ensured that the maintenance portion of my training included being taught to "expect surprises."

For example, a good ultralight pilot is taught to keep a

potential landing site within gliding distance—at all times in flight—in the event that the engine should fail. These controversial aircraft have a history of having problems in the air, and one's safety is largely dependant on the ability of the pilot to land without power. This type of occurrence is known as a forced landing. This is not a terribly difficult procedure for any experienced ultralight pilot, as normal landings in this type of plane are usually done with the engine powered fully back to idle and with no thrust. There is, however, one main difference. On a forced landing, you only get *one* chance to land the aircraft safely.

This assumes that the pilot in question has not relaxed his willingness to follow the most paramount safety habit of all—remaining well within a safe gliding distance of a suitable landing area at all times during any flight. In such cases of neglect, a single chance to land without incident is significantly reduced to no chance at all. These unfortunate instances, although still technically classified as 'forced' returns to earth, usually turn out to be what is commonly known as a crash landing. And you wondered why it's called "final" approach.

One weekend, I planned to follow this simple safety guideline and visit my cousin Dave by flying to see him at a family cottage near Honey Harbour on Georgian Bay. It was about thirty miles due west of where my ultralight was moored. I looked forward to taking him and any other willing guest for a flight once I had arrived.

I made some calculations before taking off. Travelling through the air at thirty-five miles per hour, with only a slight headwind of say five miles per hour, I would have achieved a groundspeed of thirty miles per hour (35 mph airspeed - 5 mph headwind = 30 mph groundspeed) and likely reach my destination in approximately one hour's time. I called Dave just before leaving and went over this, and thereby effectively registered my "official flight plan" with him. I am not sure he understood or cared about the math as he simply replied, "See you when you get here."

The same trip by car takes over an hour and a half and is by no means a direct route. I filled the plane with gas and remember thinking about how lucky I was. The route I was about to take was literally "as the crow flies." For the most part, all of my flight would be directly over water. I thought about how amazing it would be to enjoy the scenery along the way, and the overall experience. There was just one caveat. Just after I had let Dave know I was on my way, the wind picked up considerably.

A more disciplined pilot would have cancelled or at least postponed the trip. I did neither. All I could think about was the fun I would have taking everyone for rides once I had reached my destination. With pontoons instead of wheels, I would be able to land and take off from directly out front of the cottage in Honey Harbour. Besides, what was the worst that could happen if I remained true to my plan and flew over open water at all times?

Run out of gas, that's what! Unfortunately, I had used an optimistic allowance for the headwind when I made my first calculations. On the day in question, the prevailing west wind had escalated from five to almost twenty-five miles per hour.

Forgive me, but let me do the math for you one more time to illustrate how wrong I was and how much difference my mistake made. Travelling through the air at thirty-five miles per hour, with a significant headwind of twenty-five miles per hour, I achieved a groundspeed of merely ten miles per hour (35 mph airspeed - 25 mph headwind = 10 mph groundspeed). This requires considerably more gas, and I would not reach my destination for at least three hours. In other words, the flight would take three times as long as I had originally estimated. My hosts would be worrying unnecessarily for at least two hours.

On top of this, I now had to stop for gas. It was quite unnerving searching from the air for a gas station that could accommodate my needs. Have you ever realized you had a desperate *need* to find a gas station but had only hopeless thoughts about the prospect? On this part of my flight, this is exactly how I felt. Miraculously, I spotted a marina on the shores of the Severn River, precisely on course and not far from Honey Harbour.

It was an awkward landing but an even more challenging ride taxiing over the waves towards the marina in the extreme wind. The most memorable part of the stop was the mesmerized look I received from the gas pump attendant. I shut off the motor and coasted into the dock. As I approached, I maintained a heading directly into the wind and immediately began hurling somewhat hurried instructions at him in an attempt to get him to hold the plane close to the dock and refuel it while I remained in the pilot's seat. I dared not risk getting out and removing my weight from the front of the floating aircraft. Without the engine's thrust to compensate for the strong headwind, I feared that any sudden gust would flip my flying watercraft over backwards and into the river. I could afford neither the time nor the money to correct such a problem.

Gassed up and with the headwind dying down, I finally approached Georgian Bay. My direct flight had taken more than twice as long as the indirect route by road.

After a delicious dinner I took every interested party for a ride. Dave's mom, my aunt Thel, was not one of them. It was getting dark so we thought it best to leave in the morning, once it was decided I would drive Dave home after our flight. Besides, I was now being offered free beer around their campfire and who could resist a few belts in the bush with family and friends.

That night, instead of telling traditional campfire stories, our conversation was more of a question and answer period about the airworthiness of my elaborate toy. I took great delight in addressing everyone's concerns. My aunt Thel asked a few questions of her own. I remember explaining one of the safety features of my ultralight to her. The driveshaft, I said, is connected to the propeller with *four* drive belts! As I held up my beer I joked, "That's more belts than anyone needs." My confidence, and willingness to share the reasons for it, seemed to outweigh her doubts. I think we all retired for the evening with everyone much less worried than they had been when I first showed up—more than two hours late.

Dave and I arose very early the next morning. After breakfast and a refreshing swim in the bay, Aunt Thel loaded us up with additional clothing (it's cold up there), along with an extra five gallons of gas in a portable plastic gas tank—just in case. I strapped the gas container to the framework of the plane on my side of the cockpit to offset Dave's heavier weight on the other.

It was a beautiful day and the calmness led me to believe that it would likely be an hour's flight home, barring any unforeseen difficulties. Again, I planned to fly over water to be safe. The night before, I had gone to great lengths to explain why this was so important and how it was my habitual practice. I did not dare deviate from what I had promised my aunt Thel, to take good care of her son. As we boarded my small plane, I made a last-minute attempt to calm the once-again concerned guests who were bidding us farewell. In a half-serious tone I told them, that I had had many opportunities to practice the art of forced landings. For some reason their anxiety was not reduced.

We took off without incident, waved to the other guests, and headed home. It was a relatively uneventful flight. That is…until we got out of earshot. Almost precisely at the point that our hosts could no longer hear the loud whining sound of the small engine, one of the belts to the propeller broke. Unfortunately, it was the upwind one and the air rushing past it pushed it into the other three. Within less than a second, we had gone from having an enjoyable flight to having an on-board crisis.

We were just north of the lake called Gloucester Pool. With no belts left on the propeller, there was no thrust and consequently we were on our way back to earth for Dave's first experience of a 'forced' landing. This time I had enough gas to make a return trip, but sadly we wouldn't even make it one way. Since the engine was not contributing any thrust, I shut it off to avoid the distraction. I also wanted to hear the wind to help me determine its precise direction. I quickly turned directly into the wind and began gliding quietly towards my intended landing spot on the water. It was a picturesque but short glide down. To Dave's credit, he didn't panic.

We scared the bejeebers out of a lone fisherman who was quite startled to hear "Good Morning" as we silently floated past his boat in the middle of the lake without a hint of our approach. The kind man invited us back to his island cottage to use the phone and allowed us to tie up our disabled craft in the centre of his U-dock. He graciously moved his fishing boat out of its usual home to make room for my grounded plane.

I elected to call and explain our trouble to Aunt Thel. I figured it would be best if I answered the inevitable questions, rather than have Dave struggle to describe our predicament. I feared that if the word "crash" was used, Aunt Thel would be sent into a tizzy. She had obviously been listening to my explanations about groundspeed the night before. There was absolutely no way we could have reached our destination by this time. With a faltering and more than curious tone, she asked, "Where are you?"

We had a short conversation. Instead of blasting me for putting her son's life in jeopardy she thanked me for saving it. Although Aunt Thel was not close by, she offered to help. As it turned out, the owner of the cottage where she was staying had a friend on Gloucester Pool not far from where we were stranded. Within a few minutes of my aunt's orchestration, this friend picked us up.

I thanked the helpful cottager and made arrangements to return at a later date with the four replacement belts in hand, and fly the aircraft back home. Aunt Thel acted like a dedicated rescue worker. She volunteered to cut her weekend short, pick us up from our rendezvous point, take me back to my car an hour and a half away, and drive Dave home from there—all before she could unpack from her weekend getaway. Wow!

On the car ride back, my aunt Thel explained that she was not mad. She was a little anxious, but not mad. Apparently, my aunt had a very busy schedule that week and helping us was not part of it. In the conversation that followed I learned that if you want something done quickly, it's usually best to give it to a busy person—because the job with the greatest sense of urgency will always be done the quickest by the person who has the least time to do it. My aunt Thel and her pending schedule provided a perfect example of this principle. She also displayed a perfect example of unselfish love in her willingness to help both Dave and me.

Later, after purchasing the necessary replacement belts for my plane, I returned to install them and flew it home. My weekend of fun had turned into a two week adventure. But I will never forget how helpful and considerate my aunt Thel was.

You can never be too far away to help.

∞ Night Service ∞

I was living with Cousin Dave and a mutual friend in a three bedroom house that we rented in North York, Ontario. The house was scheduled for demolition and had always reeked of furnace oil from the day I had moved in. Each of us had our own bedroom, but everything else was shared.

During the pursuit of a new career, and living with these bachelors, I learned to appreciate how well my mom and dad had treated me in my days of dependence. These experiences also helped to reinforce the longing I had for a wife and children to love.

While I was single and living in this smelly house, I believe I demonstrated a few unique characteristics that helped define me as a typical bachelor. On the downside, I was still learning skills related to filling the refrigerator. I remember one day returning from the grocery store after purchasing ripe bananas that I had carried back to our rented home in a plastic bag next to a few cans of frozen orange juice. The three of us agreed that anyone who shopped could present the others with a bill and the other two would each reimburse the shopper with their third of the cost. This was designed to be an incentive for the one doing the shopping, since he was privileged to pick what *he* wanted. This served as sufficient motivation to help keep our icebox well stocked. However, on the day I brought the blackened bananas home, my fridge filling privileges were revoked.

On the upside, we alternated by helping to move food in the opposite direction by the three of us each taking turns with the cooking. As a result, we all learned a few things about each other's culinary skills. I believe that every bachelor has at least one special meal they can prepare. Without it, they would have died of starvation shortly after beginning life away from their parents. I consider myself to have been a stereotypical male in my single days because I generally did not like to 'waste' time preparing food. I can remember pausing to contemplate eating the goldfish after returning home from a long day at work. I believe my special 'meal' is perfect for any bachelor because it takes very little time to prepare, is tasty, provides a nutritious entrée, and produces very few dishes. Sound too good to be true? For the benefit of any starving bachelor, forgive me while I boast.

I take a handful or two of any pasta and throw it into a pot of water. While bringing the water to a boil, I open a large tin of my favourite spaghetti sauce, pour myself a glass of milk, and set the table with one fork. Then, once the water has boiled away—usually in less than ten minutes—I pour the cold sauce onto the steaming pasta and stir it with my fork. The extremely hot temperature of the pot and its tender contents heat the cold sauce. Or if you prefer, the sauce at room temperature cools the hot pasta. Either way, osmosis ensures that the entire serving is el dente in only a few stirs and can be readily consumed directly from the pot with said fork. This limits the number of things that will need cleaning to a mere three—the pot, the fork, and the glass. Anyone not thirsty can reduce this number by one third. As an added bonus, or in cases of extreme apathy, the fork can be safely stowed in the pot with any uneaten pasta to be placed in the fridge as 'leftovers'. This further reduces the number of items requiring a wash, to nil. Behold, my special dish. Serves one lazy bachelor.

One night I arrived home late from work and the smell of heating oil in the house was so strong I lost my appetite. Or, maybe I was just too tired to 'cook'. Either way, it was the coldest night of the winter and I wanted nothing more than to get into a nice warm bed. Unfortunately, there was no heat in the house. It was so cold I can remember seeing my breath. I joked that I was going back outside to "warm up."

Fortunately, our roommate had already called the twenty-four hour service line of the home comfort company that regularly filled the tank with oil. The weather forecasts that had previously warned of these extremely low temperatures meant that the oil company was completely booked throughout the night. To their credit, they kindly offered to engage the area's serviceman earlier than he was typically scheduled to start work the next day. They were able to confirm this with him because he was still out servicing our neighbourhood when we called. They told us that they would "slip us in." A technician willingly accepted the overtime as he was nearing retirement and welcomed the extra income.

Huddled together on the thin mattress of the pull out couch on the main floor, three hungry and tired single men lay waiting for morning in the ever-plummeting temperature. On the makeshift bed in the living room, we tried to sleep—side by each while fully clothed including winter jackets, mitts, and boots. We sprawled about and coughed from the strong oily smell all night long.

When the serviceman arrived very early the next day, we were already awake. There was no need for any alarm that morning. His arrival found us in an appreciative but very groggy state. The near freezing air temperature that welcomed us as we exited the shower served to combat our drowsiness from a virtually sleepless night.

The repairman was our first guest to enter the home and not ask what the terrible smell was. He was an older, balding man dressed in a clean uniform, unspoiled for the day's work ahead. His sparse light gray hair covered his noticeably receding hairline. Despite being cold and cranky from our lack of sleep, all of us responded to his soft-spoken seemingly pointless questions about the furnace.

He was rambling on about some reset button which none of us had been able to find, despite being spoon-fed its location by the oil company on our phone call to them the night before. All we cared about was getting the heat turned back on. It took a few minutes of casual conversation before our new friend finally decided to investigate the problem firsthand by entering the basement to fix the furnace. None of us knew much about the maintenance of the home. Also, since the house was scheduled to be demolished, even the owners were unconcerned over proper upkeep.

Apparently, this type of home heating system generates heat by burning small controlled quantities of flammable heating oil inside the furnace. Usually, when the furnace stops producing heat it's because one of two things has happened. Either the fuel tank is empty or the pilot flame has gone out. In a case were there is no flame, a safety device typically shuts off the oil flow from the holding tank to the furnace. This occurs to prevent mass quantities of the flammable oil from entering the furnace and thereby ensures that only a small amount of the heating oil is ignited once the burner's flame is "reset."

The methodical maintenance man marched into the basement with the intent of simply lighting the pilot light and restarting the furnace. As luck would have it, there was no flashlight in the house. Fortunately, our friendly soon-to-be-retiree smoked, and had a lighter as part of his customary tool set. He peered into the firebox through a tiny peephole that was covered with a small iron shield. This cover can be lifted to peek inside and inspect the burner, and when necessary, relight the pilot light without having to dismantle the lower portion of the furnace. However, the small portal does not provide a thorough view of the inside.

I remained on the main floor at the top of the stairs to the basement as he began his inspection. We were all waiting with anticipation. Through the open door, I heard him trying to spark his lighter in an effort to see. I distinctly remember hearing, "Chick…Chick…*KAPPOW!*" The whole house shook violently with that last sound. It was akin to someone launching a rocket from the basement and felt as if the house was about to take off.

Our older but spry serviceman was knocked over but immediately got up and ran up the stairs, shouting, "Shut it off, shut it off!" Before he had reached the top of the stairs, the short but intense blast was beginning to quieten. He revised his plea for help to a calmer, "I think you better call the fire department." We replied, "What do you mean you *think?*" as we all knew that this was something of which one should be relatively certain.

Eager for our own update, we inquired as to what had occurred. The stunned serviceman took some time to calm down. Due to some happenstance, a faulty ignition switch had combined efforts with the failure of our much needed safety shut off valve. This allowed the oil to drip continuously and accumulate into a pool of unburned oil in the bottom of the furnace. Had the old ignition switch been working properly, the flowing oil would have been ignited and would never have created the small pond of flammable fluid lying in wait for ignition. Unbeknownst to any of those present that day, oil had been dripping into the bottom of the furnace for many hours prior to our first call for service. This excess oil was a fire hazard and should have been fully drained before restarting the burner but none of us knew it was there. At the time of his crude ignition, all of the oil that had accumulated over the last day detonated in what seemed to be a millisecond.

When he dragged us into the basement to express his complete displeasure with his near-death experience, he called our attention to the main vent leading from the furnace into the ductwork of the house. This, he explained with a pointing sooty finger, had turned "red and then white hot" as he lay on the floor watching helplessly. He explained that if it had melted—which it surely had come close to doing—the entire house would have caught fire in a matter of minutes. His lecture mentioned that the furnace was not designed to contain this magnitude of instantaneous combustion, part of which was forced to escape out the conveniently ajar peephole. Its small size acted as an opportune exhaust for our permanently affixed basement rocket. Our furnace friend indicated that quite a long flame had come through that hole but had missed him entirely "through some stroke of luck."

He brought our attention to where the flame had discharged from the furnace and shot towards him. Dave and I noticed a perfect circle of fresh black soot on the wall several feet behind the peephole. We returned to the main floor marvelling at our close call. Seemingly unscathed, yet visibly shaken, he asked us to call his office so that he could talk to his dispatcher. Our oilman was heard to say something to the effect of, "I don't think I'll be making the next call on time…in fact…you may as well go ahead and cancel all of my calls for the rest of the day."

Later, in a calmer mood upstairs, and in the considerably better light, we noticed his thin off-white hair. Earlier, it had been neatly combed back in the style of his youth but now featured a sooty stripe from the centre of his forehead straight to the back of his skull. The path of the fireball that exited the peephole had burned a narrow line of complete baldness over the top of his head. When I first noticed this, I blurted out,

"Your hair!" The unnerved serviceman calmly brushed his hand through his once glorious locks, looked down at the black soot now on his hand, and mused, "Well, I guess I got a little singed."

While he was recapping his adventure to our roommate, we all took turns looking away so as not to laugh. It was evident that the trauma from the situation had accelerated his aging process considerably. We sensed he was about to have his stress level increased dramatically when he discovered the shortage of wispy strands of gray hair, which up until recently, had been 'swept' across his scalp in a vain attempt to disguise his obvious balding. Sadly, these few but significant hairs had all been sacrificially lost in a heartbeat…and removed from his life for good. The poor man would have to be content spending his retirement without them.

To this day I cannot picture his frazzled state and his burnt hair without laughing out loud. We didn't allow him to use the washroom before he left, claiming that it was out of order due to the cold. In reality, the three of us were nervous about him seeing himself in the mirror, and as a result demanding some sort of compensation. Another public apology is offered here.

Comforting comments were given to our rankled repairman in an effort to help him cope with his recent ordeal. It would be fair to say he had aged considerably—especially in his appearance. As the oilman left the house, we encouraged him to count his blessings in a backhanded way. The traumatized technician received a parting reminder from our roommate. "Remember that *I* have to *live* with them."

Our roommate later commented that he "…had lived in a house beside a railway track for twelve years but had never been in one that shook as much as ours had that fateful day."

The oilman doesn't ring twice.

Life's Lessons: A Successful Collection of Failures

FAMILY AND FRIENDS

Virtually all of the narratives in previous chapters took place before I met my wife Annette. This chapter is the first to introduce her and is composed primarily of occurrences that happened in our life together. In some cases, she is the main character, and in others simply an important part of the situation.

She is truly a blessing. She is the manifestation of the habitual closing to my prayers during my single life: "…and Lord, please grant me a good Christian wife." Annette was not a gift from God *to* me: she is my Master's gift of grace despite my failings.

I first met Annette at a bible study, early in her career as a frontline police officer, working for the largest force in Canada. However, my dad was not at all pleased when he first heard I was dating a police officer.

Since both my dad and I have been subjected to what we believe to be unfair treatment from two different police forces in our past, this news was not well received. However, in short order Annette had restored a great deal of our lost respect for the profession. Her integrity and policing skills impressed him and continues to do so, just like she does with the other members of my family.

Before we were married, I remember washing dishes in the kitchen of the house I was renting with my Cousin Dave. I had been sharing how I felt about Annette. At the time, I was dating others, but coming to realize the importance that Annette held in my life. I was puzzling over my future and turned to my cousin for some advice, asking, "What do *you* think?" His response was a simple sardonic statement: "Don't disappoint the one with the gun."

His mind-searing remark was so pointed that I have never forgotten it. Nor has Annette, because on our wedding day I had Dave relate his comment, and the context of it, during our reception.

I used to say that she quit a career in policing to accommodate our family's needs once our third child had arrived. Every time I use the word "quit" in the same sentence as her name, she objects—citing this as an unfair indication of her general attitude and outlook towards life. She is by no means a quitter.

Annette prefers to think of herself as "retired." However, to me retirement implies some sort of residual income. She does have a pension coming to her, but not for another twenty years or so when the value will have dropped considerably. The annual pension reports always contain a number of platitudes with respect to the 'security' her pension will bring. However, the administrators of the plan continually fail to present their numbers in future value.

At the time of this writing, we have been married for more than nineteen years. We have survived the supposed seven-year itch. Perhaps twice, depending on how one calculates things. I can truthfully say with great conviction that I love her dearly, and love loving her. She has since brought three beautiful children into the world for us—for which I will be forever indebted to her.

Although our children are mentioned a couple of times in this chapter, the relationship that Annette and I share with each other and with our friends is the main focus. All three of our children have a section of their own in the next chapter in which they each have their turn at centre stage. They are only referred to as our daughter or our son in this chapter as the case may be, to keep the focus of this chapter where it belongs—on Annette.

∞ A Tale of Two Ties ∞

One significant part of my life has not been discussed in this book: relationships with young women before I met my wife. This isn't because I want to hide anything from her (she already knows) but rather that these relationships aren't worth discussing. Any relationship I had prior to meeting Annette was one of great frustration and internal stress.

The young women I was involved with in the past did not possess the qualities Annette does. Annette is logical, decisive, determined, and beautiful. To put this in strictly guy terms—she has both beauty and brains. However, this phrase alone still does not do Annette justice since the benefits of her love go far beyond this. It's difficult to put into perspective, but I feel Annette maintains a perfect balance of her gifts. She's logical, but open minded enough to listen and even try strategies of unconventional thinking. She can make a decision yet is not stubborn. She is strong-willed but at the same time willing to compromise. Annette is a devout woman, whose love for her family is demonstrated in her daily sacrifices for each of us.

Annette does, however, possess an attribute common to all women I have met. My somewhat limited personal experience has led me to believe that women are subtle when it comes to the signals they send to men. It was only a short time after we were married when I realized this. I was putting on a suit that I had worn a few times when we were dating. I laid out two neckties at the foot of the bed. They were both gifts from Annette given to me during our engagement. I felt that either one would match well with my suit.

I asked Annette for her opinion. I wanted her to recognize that I was only considering her two gifts and that I valued her opinion. Her response was, "Both of them look fine, pick one." I rephrased my question. She replied the same way. I feared picking the 'wrong' one so I asked a third time. I clarified that I was seeking her input because I wanted to wear whatever one *she* wanted me to. I walked over to the bed and pushed my knee out towards them, indicating my need for greater attention.

Her answer was the same. I walked around the room deep in thought trying to understand what she was thinking. I didn't want our first argument to be about such a frivolous thing as choosing a tie. I could only justify arguments over important issues—like what sport is the most fun to watch on TV. I purposefully walked back to the bed and grabbed the thin end of one tie. Picking it up seemed to create more interest from Annette than anything I had done up to this point. Before the fat part of the tie had left the bed Annette asked, "What's wrong with the other one?"

I was shocked and didn't know what to say. I don't think I even answered her. In a confused state, I returned the tie in my hand to the closet, and chose to wear the "other one" that evening.

It's never too late to change.

∞ New Clothes ∞

Buying new clothes is something Annette and I usually do together. I like to have her opinion (read approval) of anything I select for myself. This comes from my complete lack of skill in selecting clothes that match. This lack of talent might be because my mom always had my clothes laid out for me on the end of my bed when I was younger. Children do not tend to become skilled in any task if they never have to do it themselves. Despite my mother's intentions, the love she displayed while providing this service has not served me well. However, I am tempted to cite Freud or any psychologist who would support me in blaming this shortcoming on my mother.

When Annette is shopping for clothes, I like to tag along. I know that if she comes home with two newly purchased outfits, I'll usually be fond of one and not as pleased with the other. I simply know what looks good on her. I'm not claiming that I could design something or play with different garments and come up with a mix that suits her—oh no. I cannot tell her what to pick out, or why one outfit looks better than another. I can only tell *if* someone looks good, not why. Perhaps one could say my opinions are based more on intuition than on any sense of fashion.

To me, Annette looks amazing in just about anything she has on—or off—as the case may be. I love to go out with her on my arm. Whether to the beach or on a formal night out, it is always a better occasion if she is with me. So, from both of these perspectives, I prefer to be with her when she shops for her own clothing.

One time when Annette needed a new bathing suit, I insisted on accompanying her. She either comes home with ones that are unflattering or ones likely to induce drool from any nearby male. I was determined to ensure that the next one she bought would be somewhere in between these two extremes.

We headed to the local department store. Annette had selected a few to try on and prepared to take them off the main floor and into the change room. The female clerk with the door keys reminded us of the rules, which meant I had to remain outside the change room area. I was anticipating that Annette would return to model the bathing suit that she felt looked best. Assuming I agreed, we would be on our way shortly.

I was in a hurry and grew impatient as I waited for Annette to come out. It seemed to me that she was taking an unusually long time. I couldn't imagine her being embarrassed. I waited and waited for her to surface. For some unknown reason, she had failed to exit the change rooms.

Eventually, the clerk gave up and left. Seeing this as an opportunity to speed things up, I decided to sneak into the main hallway of the private area and out of sight from the other shoppers. My thought was that I could view her in each of the proposed swimsuits, make a quick decision, and save her a trip into the main part of the store. In this way, I reasoned, I could put us back on track and on time for the other things we had planned to do that day.

As I entered the forbidden area, I called out to Annette and she casually asked me to hold on. I was bothered that her response and tone lacked the sense of urgency I felt was required given the circumstances. I didn't want to be caught inside the women's change room for any reason, and the female clerk was likely to return at any moment.

I hastened towards the locked cubical and knocked loudly on the door. My wife immediately began to laugh. I confidently asked, "Come out and show me what you look like." I waited a full two or three seconds and then with greater firmness added, "I want to see you now." My wife continued laughing, a distinctive, quiet laugh that typically gets anyone in a giddy mood to laugh all the more, but in this situation, it was adding to my frustration. I told her to "Stop laughing." She continued her irrepressible giggling as if she had lost control. "Let me see them," I repeated in an irritated manner. My frustration grew and I suggested with a threatening demeanour that I would force my way in and help her change if she didn't open the door and, "Let me see them." I was exasperated to the point I had tunnel vision, as I remained focused only on the locked door that kept me from getting to my wife. Annoyed, I rattled the door.

Just then, Annette struggled to open the door—the door *next* to the locked one I was rattling! Nearing collapse from laughing so heartily, she waved some piece of clothing as if this was all the energy she could muster whilst peeking out from behind her door. My actions had brought on a surplus of laughter and had weakened her to the extent that she was unable to speak. I stood there stunned, but focused, on the door in front of me—the one I was shaking. In a confused state, I remember thinking, "How did she get over there?" When her door swung open and she motioned me towards her, I noticed all of her clothes and the three bathing suits in her little room.

Slowly, I began to understand why Annette was laughing so hard. I had mistakenly assumed that she was the only one in the change rooms because she was the only one I saw enter. Just as I had realized this, a slight, middle-aged woman opened the door in front of me and left in a hurried fashion. My wife was desperately trying to explain my mistake between bursts of helpless laughter. A few pieces of clothing dropped from the small but agile woman's grip as she exited her cubical, brushed me aside, and darted for the exit.

I felt the need to explain my actions to this poor victim but she left without saying goodbye. The last glance she gave was a mixture of disapproval towards me, and that of heartfelt sympathy towards my wife—presumably for choosing me as a mate. Annette explained quickly how each of my previous statements to this unsuspecting female could have been taken as if I was some sort of pervert who fancied threatening women into exposing themselves. No wonder my promises to leave once I had, "seen everything" were not comforting.

My wife was taking this all in stride, knowing the situation was not what I had intended. However, I was not anxious to explain my actions to any person of authority. Besides, according to my plans, we were falling behind schedule for the day. I weighed this with my urge to find and apologize to this frightened female. My wife and I decided to do what any reasonable people would do given the circumstances—we promptly left.

The swimwear was left in the change rooms without another

thought and we literally laughed all the way home. We still laugh when we think of this poor person and the look she gave us when she made good her escape. If by some fluke she reads this some day, I do hope she now understands and accepts my public apology for causing her such unnecessary grief.

Like other times in my life, the harder I tried to resolve the conflict, the worse it got. In hindsight, had I *asked* for my requests to be fulfilled, the other woman would likely have responded audibly and with conviction. Since I chose to demand instead of ask, I was doomed from the start. A demand rarely gets better results than a request.

> ***Rather than demanding something of your wife,***
> ***better to ask—better still, ask HER.***

∞ Cottage Road ∞

Annette and I purchased a cottage in 1989, with the intention of flipping it shortly after. The thought was to ride the wave of the increasing waterfront property values, sell the cottage, and use the profits towards the purchase of our first home.

Unfortunately, the trend of rising property values stopped abruptly on or about the day we closed the sale. Within a year, it was worth so little that attempts to sell it for two thirds of its original purchase price did not even fetch a single offer. After consulting with real estate agents and other advisors, Annette and I realized we were faced with a difficult choice. Either reduce the price further and sell the cottage for about half of what we paid for it, or keep it until the market recovered.

We opted for the latter because we simply could not afford to take the loss. Unfortunately, ten years later the market had still not recovered to the point that the property could be expected to sell for what we had originally paid for it. The good news was that by this time, Annette and I had almost paid for it, and its market value was no longer such an issue. During that time period we bought our first home. We managed to keep the cottage by renting it every chance we could.

For more than ten years, Annette and I diligently maintained the cottage in a state of good repair and used the funds from the rentals to offset the mortgage costs. Despite fulfilling all of the responsibilities to maintain a second home, we sacrificed the benefits of ownership for over ten years. Often people will remark, "Y*ou* have a cottage, must be nice." I usually respond in the tone of a shallow but enthusiastic salesperson making a comment about how they could "have one too."

After peaking their curiosity, the listener generally loses interest when they hear the part about not visiting in the summer for at least the first decade, except to mow the lawn for the next renter. If I'm still feeling particularly misunderstood, I may throw in a statement or two about a previous renter, or explain about the guy who thought I would forget that the fishing boat had a motor on it when I rented it to him. Simply put, when a few of the sacrifices Annette and I made are brought to the forefront of the conversation, no one asks for me to outline our plan so that they can "have one too."

Annette and I do not regret the decision we made years ago to keep the cottage, but we still become frustrated when people unthinkingly say, "Must be nice." Some choose to continue muttering this comment in envy despite having a myriad of cottages available for them to purchase and do exactly the same thing. Annette and I have even offered to help and guide others through the process so that they would not encounter all of the same difficulties…but no one asks.

The problem as we see it, is that most people who continue to make this statement want the rewards of our collective sacrifices but are not willing to make the same sacrifices themselves. All of the struggles Annette and I have had along the way are not listed here, but in truth, they have taught us much about ourselves, and about each other.

Renting became a way of life for us. Regular trips to see renters in and out were common and necessary. Each week in the blazing hot sun, one of us would have to check things over to ensure that the previous week's renters had not destroyed our place. This required a two hour drive, settling their accounts, cleaning up inside and out, and seeing the new renter in before we could begin our two hour car ride back. We called this process "seeing in the renters."

Early one summer, Annette and I made the trip together with our one-year-old daughter in tow. She was in the back seat affixed to her car seat. There were many buttons, straps, clips, and belts with which to fasten her in. It looked as though the creator of this seat was a wannabe space shuttle designer for NASA. Only people with an aptitude for engineering could possibly have fitted a child into this contraption in the manner in which it was intended. Getting her in and out was a major production. I was running behind schedule, perhaps because of the many attempts made to place her into the seat and still allow her to breath. Annette was a frontline police officer and always insisted on children being properly transported in a vehicle—especially her own. I decided to make up for some of the lost time on the way home by speeding along our twisty cottage road.

Within the first mile or so of our turny cottage road, our first born threw up. She managed to cover every single clip, button, and belt of her car seat as well as dousing the rear seat of the car. Knowing that I simply cannot deal with vomit, Annette volunteered to clean up the mess and I willingly assisted—at a distance—by unloading the trunk of the car until we found various things that could be used for the clean-up. Getting our daughter out of the restraining device and cleaning up took an unbearable length of time. We simply were not prepared for this. It took a long time to get back on track that day and my attempts to speed things up only served to slow things down.

With Annette and I both working shift work, the times we travelled together for such a trip were few and far between. If one of us was working, the other would have to make the trip. If we could not find a babysitter, our daughter came along for the ride. It wasn't until much later that our shifts once again provided another opportunity for all of us to go to the cottage together and see another set of renters in. After doing so, I was eager to get home, but in an uncanny set of circumstances running a bit late… again.

On our way back, I focused my attention on my responsibilities at home. I systematically planned each task out in my mind hoping to save myself time upon arrival. I mentally prepared myself for my next shift at work. I was in a hurry and Annette casually said, "Remember what happened last time." I nodded, without giving her my full attention. Once again she reiterated the point with the exact same statement. This time I believed Annette was looking for more than a nod, so I replied, "Yeah, bummer, wasn't it." I continued along the winding cottage road concentrating on the task at hand—getting home. For the third time, Annette repeated the same words but added my name at the beginning of her comment, presumably for greater effect.

Strangely, in about the same place of the bumpy cottage road where my daughter had had her first bout of carsickness, she threw up…again. This time my wife gave me a look as if to say, "You get the wipes and I'll take care of the baby." At least that's what I thought she was trying to convey. She wasn't. Annette refused to clean up the vomit, insisting I do so, citing this as my fault and claiming, "I told you three times to slow down." In sincere puzzlement, I replied, "You never told me *once!*"

This difference of opinion was disputed aggressively—by both sides—all the way home. It was only interrupted briefly when I stopped at the first house that had a hose. I got our little one out of the car seat faster than Houdini could have, and carried her like a contaminated football directly to the hose at the side of the house. Simultaneously I said to the homeowner, "Mind if I use your hose to clean off my daughter?" I did so in a tone that clearly would not accept "no" for an answer. The confused owner watched as I sprayed my little one in much the same way someone would clean their car at the car wash. Being a hot summer day, I saw no problem with wedging her back into her special seat wet and half naked for the journey back to the house. I joked about how the water on our baby's skin acted as a lubricant against the vinyl parts of the seat, helping me to "slip" her into our sophisticated car seat. Annette was not amused.

On the way back to our house, Annette and I argued for the entire trip over her claim that she had told me to "slow down." Although I completely accept that this is what Annette meant, I sincerely had not taken it as such. Also, I had no problem with the concept of listening and accepting any of her requests, but we did not come to an agreement until only a few miles from home. We agreed that despite her making a comment that anyone else in the world would have understood, I was such a *literal* person, I truly had missed the implications of her request. Our truce was this: Annette *should not* have to be so literal when communicating her thoughts to me, *but* if she expected me to understand what she was saying, being literal was the only hope she had.

Every car trip from the cottage to the house takes us over the twisty, turny, windy, bumpy cottage road. I liken this to the stages of our life together. Rough at first, smoother in the middle, and in the end, a unique comfort like returning home. Although both of us were reasonably well versed at communicating with others, we were still learning how to communicate and understand each other. We learned the most about ourselves during the earlier times of our married life.

In truth, it would probably be fairer to say that Annette learned how to deal with the bonehead she vowed to take as a husband. However, I still believe if you can't mean what you say…you should at least say what you mean.

If you want your listener to take action, they must understand what you're saying AND feel what you're feeling.

∽ A Shot in the Dark ∽

Annette and I have experienced many financial difficulties together. I imagine that they are not unlike problems many others face. One time, during an awkward cash flow position, I succumbed to the temptation of a get-rich-quick scheme. It contained all of the typical claims. Do very little, receive a lot, and enjoy the rest of your life in financial comfort.

The gimmick promised to find your fortune in the so-called "untapped" mailing list market. I had never heard of anyone making money with a mailing list. (There is a reason for this.) The only story I had heard similar to the one being proposed was about a man who put an ad in the paper that read, "Send me a dollar and a self addressed postage paid envelope in the mail, and I'll send you a way of making a million dollars that worked for me." Anyone who answered his ad supposedly received the man's secret. "Put an ad in the paper, exactly like mine." As the story goes, he couldn't be sued for false advertising or prosecuted for fraud, since he followed up each response with a written comment and had indeed made a million dollars out of his scheme. Supposedly, this justified his claims. It was probably just another urban myth.

Either way, I did not subscribe to the lottery mentality of thinking someday I might actually win. Nor did I frequent the local casino with similar hopes. Annette and I have gambled a few times in the past, but only with a predetermined amount of money for the evening. In other words, we do not risk our survival money, or use our investment money for unsupported ideas with unrealistic hopes. Well, not after the mailing list anyway.

The scheme looked promising and the total investment was only five hundred dollars. I thought it was worth a shot. What could I lose? The answer to this profound mathematical conundrum is, precisely five hundred dollars. After following the program's suggestions and not changing any portion of their "recommended" plan, this was exactly what I lost. I have often referred to mistakes as having to be paid for in cash, hide, or pride. I usually say this with a pronounced rhythm to anyone who would care to listen. I believe my ditty to be a catchy statement with painful results for those that learn it for the first time. This was my first time I had made such a mistake—with my family's money.

Inasmuch as this scheme was a total disaster, we did not lose a large sum of money. Annette was very understanding. Also, she didn't mind reminding me that her predictions were right. Annette has a very trusting nature and I am grateful that she allows me to 'invest' our money. After the mailing list failure, we agreed to look for more practical ways of supplementing our income.

The most important lesson I had learned in math class during my school days was that the answer to any mathematical problem had a formula for the solution. However, understanding the formula is only half the battle. Calculating the answer requires every number in it to be correct. It only takes one incorrect number entered into a perfect formula to produce an incorrect answer. Perhaps the most gruesome example of this was learned when a single entry in an otherwise flawless mile-long mathematical calculation blew up a space shuttle.

In simpler terms, salesmen with marketing ploys have often taken advantage of their prospective customers by applying this principle. I have seen hypothetical mathematical scenarios that illustrate how an unusual amount of money can be made with very little effort. The problem with this type of presentation often lies with only one incorrect number. Everything else is plausible. And, who could fault them for making only one mistake? This is done on purpose. We tend to excuse people who aren't perfect. Therefore, criticizing one wrong number after scrutinizing all of their other assumptions seems harsh. Be careful: this is their ploy.

Replacing this one incorrect figure can be enough to change their entire projection from realistic to something outside the box called reality. I fell for this once when I bought a vending company. The owner appeared to be more of a salesman than anything else. He had illustrated how it was possible to make $11,250.00 per month! He laid out the number of machines (50), times the number of "vends" (cans of pop sold) per day (10), times the number of days in a month (30), times the amount of gross profit (75¢) for each vend. I did some quick calculations: 50 x 10 x 30 x $0.75 = $11,250.00 gross profit per month, just as the owner had claimed.

This money-making projection easily justified paying $50,000.00 for a vending route. In theory, such profit would cover ongoing expenses for gas, wear and tear on our van, miscellaneous costs along the way, and still provide tremendous additional monthly revenue. Not a bad monthly income for working one to two days per month. Or so I thought.

I was excited by what the numbers represented and purchased the route with borrowed money from the good old 'Bank of Dad'. Then, about one week into my five-month plan, I noticed a major discrepancy in the numbers. The owner had inflated the number of "vends" to such an extent that any used car salesman would have been green with envy. It turned out to be about one vend per day—not ten vends. This was not even enough to justify pluralizing the term! Thus, I received a tenth of what had been hoped for—an undisputed *gross* income of approximately $1,125.00 per month. And, it was a far cry from the $11,250.00 the owner had demonstrated with his math formulas. Had I looked well into the matter and done the math with the actual figures this guy was proposing, I would have realized that his scenario required 625 *cases* of pop. All of which had to be purchased and refilled into the machines—each month.

Such a task would not be a part-time undertaking but rather a full-time job. Also, this amount of pop would require a freight truck for transport. Using my passenger van "like everybody else in the business" as the con artist had suggested, would simply not work. Besides, we don't have enough dentists in the world to compensate for such consumption.

Over the years that we were in the vending business, I learned that most vending machines are doing well if they are receiving one vend per day. This is why you see vendors driving around in their passenger vans and not transport trucks. The only people in the business with transport trucks are the employees of companies that make the pop.

It took many years for the vending route to earn enough income to pay back the loan I borrowed from my wonderful dad. He allowed me to change my hopes of paying him back in less than five months to just over five years. The sad part is that both financial pufferies—the mailing list and the vending business—were indeed long shots.

Oddly enough, our vending machines, which cost one hundred times more than the mailing list, still outperformed the "untapped" mailing list market. The vending route eventually came to make money and the mailing list only ever reaped the loss of five hundred bucks. The only response I received after my mailing blitz to over one thousand would-be customers was one pathetic twit who actually expected *me* to buy mailing lists from *him*.

Perhaps the anguish felt after learning any tough financial lesson is designed for our protection by helping us to remember the pain…so we "never do it again." But then again, if time were able to erase the agonizing memory, there is always your wife.

If you're playing the long shot, place your bet at the casino where there is at least a chance of winning.

∞ Tennis Anyone? ∞

The road to our cottage is defined as a three season road. During the spring, summer, and fall, we can drive to the front door. In winter, we can cross over the frozen lake to visit. However, the ice is not passable for about a six week duration both immediately before and after winter. During the times when the ice is unsafe to cross, there is usually unplowed snow on the road and absolutely no way to get to our cottage unless you have a small helicopter. Fortunately, the low season in the travel market is precisely when we are unable to visit our cottage.

Not all of our married life has been burdened with financial difficulty. Annette and I have enjoyed the odd vacation somewhere other than at our cottage. On one occasion we travelled to the Bahamas, with our children in the care of others. Annette and I met up with Steve and his wife in Freeport after checking into our oceanfront rooms.

We had hoped to lie in the sun, drink, and join in the activities available. We especially looked forward to participating in various sports and games because most of them would not have been practical if our children had been with us. We relaxed much of the time but still took part in the many activities offered by the hotel.

Steve and I ensured we were on time for each archery lesson. There's nothing like the thrill of shooting something so powerful while 'under the influence'. Both my brother and I are reasonably well coordinated and usually pick up any new sport relatively quickly. Archery was different. We were always anxious for another opportunity to have the young female instructor put her arms around each one of us and forcibly demonstrate how to move with the bow.

She was of German descent and well endowed. Her accent was enough to make even a sober man melt. Standing only a few inches shorter than Steve or I, she would tenderly reach around us to 'help' with our lesson. All this in a bikini, which was so sparse, I'm sure it could have easily been stored in a thimble. There was no line-up for those confident enough to venture off to the other target area a few feet away. The line-up was only for those wishing to be 'helped'.

About halfway through the week, our wives went for a walk together. They were intent on satisfying their mutual curiosity as to why Steve and I had taken a sudden interest in archery. Also, they were confused as to why it was the only event for which we refused to be late. Luckily, Steve and I saw them coming. We moved out of the line-up for 'help', and over to the target area for practice.

Unfortunately, the other guys in the group standing nearby started asking questions. Loud inquiries like, "How come you guys are over there today?" destroyed our chances of getting away with anything. This, along with the bubbly reception our wives received from the young female instructor, eliminated the hope of citing only innocent interests in our new hobby.

With strong 'encouragement' from our wives, Steve and I agreed that it would be best if we stuck to games where we were all involved, like tennis for example. Steve and I could smack the ball with force, enough to let out some of our frustrations. As well, our wives could keep a closer eye on us. Besides, no instructors were needed since all of us were proficient tennis players and took the game very seriously.

Usually I gauge my level of improvement in the sport by the distance my brother throws his racquet in frustration. If, for example, he threw it twenty feet into the net one time, and then forty feet clear over the fence the next, I could safely conclude that I was performing twice as well as at our last meeting. A 'safe' conclusion, however, was only possible when I kept my head up after winning a point, and, never ever turning my back on my opponent. It is truly ironic that I was the one with the bad temper when Steve and I were children but later in our adult lives things are completely different. The tables have turned a full 180 degrees.

That week, our tennis games turned into more of a regulated competition. One time it would be the men against the women. On another, the couples would play as teams, and later my sister-in-law and I would take on Annette and Steve. One night, we managed to schedule both of the only two tennis courts available for the same time just after dinner. The plan was for the ladies to use one and the men to use the other. Our wives did not enjoy Steve and me rushing our dinner or take kindly to the insinuation that the game between us could be more important than the game between them. They are both earnest tennis players.

The hotel was strict about who used the courts and how those using them behaved. So strict in fact that if you were playing on the wrong court, they would make you switch. Games played after dinner required the court lights to be on if anyone hoped to see the ball. Our scheduled time indicated that we had both courts to ourselves. Steve and I were lucky since our court was free, and we began to warm up by hitting the ball back and forth to each other. Our wives were surprised to see people still on their court.

Steve's wife sat down and remained seated for much of what was to come. Annette decided to allow the foursome to finish their game before taking over the court. This is a basic courtesy or tennis etiquette for amateurs such as ourselves. The four adults on Annette's court were many years our senior and were taking their match very seriously. It was as if they were considering themselves professionals when they distinctly motioned to Annette to wait.

They appeared to be disputing each point while yelling in a language we did not understand. One of them seemed to be claiming Annette was in the way as she stood unusually close to the sidelines attempting to make *her* point. I think they were of German descent. In any case, they had staked their claim. Annette had become somewhat aggressive but it appeared warranted from my perspective. It did not look like the usurpers were going to leave until they were done—regardless of how much their obstinate actions reduced our wives' playing time.

As a police officer, Annette has no problem confronting someone she feels is in the wrong—whether on duty or on vacation. The lights on the court in question were fully illuminated. This intense group had had them turned on earlier to ensure an uninterrupted flow of their match as night fell. However, this foursome was about to get it with both barrels. As Annette's frustration became obvious to Steve, he suggested she switch on the lights to our court and have the four of us play together once the lights warmed up.

This would be about a ten minute wait. These special lights used mercury and required this time to become fully lit after being switched on, and the same time to cool down when turned off. I agreed with Steve's suggestion, feeling it best to let these rather uncooperative people have their way, but Annette would have none of it. She was in the right, they were in the wrong, and it was that simple.

Annette—now in a very agitated state—began a warm-up routine in a pronounced manner that was more of an attempt to annoy the occupiers into giving up and leaving. Annette unzipped the cover of her racquet and started swinging her racquet around in large circles. At the side of the court, she did jumping jacks and bounced balls into the air and against the ground. All the while, the foreigners kept playing and failed to retreat. Their refusal to leave infuriated Annette to the point that she yelled her final request at them with sweeping hand motions designed to get them to understand. Nothing worked.

She later made various other comments towards each of them but they are not included here in this family book. Steve and I reiterated our offer for our wives to join us. Annette grudgingly agreed to comply. In complete disgust and frustration, she marched to the electrical shed to turn on the lights for the court where Steve and I were now having trouble seeing the ball in the darkening night. Annette was hoping to see the hotel security at some point and have them enforce the obvious, but they were nowhere to be found. At this time, jokes about "where's a cop when you need one," would not have been well received.

The greatest frustration for Annette was not being able to have those who had commandeered the clay understand what she was requesting, and indeed, what she was later demanding and thinking. I believe she had hoped to obtain some kind of peace with them even if unable to persuade them to leave. I am also sure that if Annette had been able to communicate her position, she would have been more than willing to listen to what they had to say. The language barrier prevented any of this from happening.

Annette finished her hundred-foot strut to the electrical shed and promptly flicked the switch. Normally, it would have been a ten minute wait. In this unique set of circumstances, we noticed an immediate change. Inadvertently, Annette had turned off the lights at the court where the Europeans were still playing. The electrical shed did not have things well marked on the panel. Realizing her mistake, she began to laugh uncontrollably. Steve and I followed suit, thinking she had intentionally dreamed this up on the way to the breaker panel. Annette was innocent, but it did not appear this way to her rivals, or to Steve and I at the time. However, she was quick to explain her mistake once she had managed to stop laughing and catch her breath.

The Europeans' tennis match turned into a yelling match as the stubborn foursome began to fight amongst themselves. Their disputes somewhat paralleled the way I had regulated our week of tennis competition. First, there were arguments between the men, then the ladies, then the group, and later between the spouses.

Their game stopped the instant the lights went out, unlike their comments in their mother tongue—which continued well after they left the court. They marched past Annette with much to say and could still be heard ranting farther along the path closer to the hotel. Obviously they realized that they were in for a long wait before the special lights could be turned on again. It was immediately apparent that they would not be able to continue later with the same intensity. Being forced to cool down before resuming play would have increased their stress level significantly. Their game was over and they knew it.

I am sure they were convinced that this had been Annette's plan all along. Despite her innocence, not even a prominent lawyer would have been able to successfully defend Annette's actions. The opportunity for an agreement had been lost. There was little chance for any meeting of the minds since Annette was doubled over with laughter and still struggling to stand next to the electrical booth when the angry group passed by on their way to the showers. When Annette finally made it back to the courts, Steve and I were noticeably handicapped from our own laughter, which was still fighting to be fully released.

We giggled through every game and laughed throughout the night. Later, I suggested to Annette that we play less tennis and make archery our sport of choice, but my suggestion did not receive spousal approval.

***The more light you shed on an issue,
the greater the chance for peace.***

∞ Call Waiting ∞

During one of our family visits to our cottage in winter, my daughter and son had invited a mutual friend from church to tag along. They were typically invited to each other's birthday parties and other get-togethers.

He was quite young, attending an earlier grade of elementary school at the time. This was his first overnight stay away from his parents, and they had prepared Annette and me for a homesick little boy.

We felt that being friends with both of our two children at the time would help him adjust quickly. Also, we had hoped tobogganing, skating, and going for a ride on a snowmobile would tend to help him forget about being away from home. Besides, he had visited us before with his family.

We managed to get through the first night by changing the subject each time he asked for his "mommy." In an attempt to comfort him on the second night, Annette suggested calling home and talking to his mom at bedtime. He could tell her all of the things we had done during the day and focus his attention away from the forbidden subject—"I miss my mom." Despite this, he was able to slip this theme into his conversation a few times when Annette was not able to anticipate his abrupt changing of the subject.

Most of the boy's commentary went something like this:

"I went tobogganing today and I *miss* you."

(Annette interrupted and encouraged him to relay other activities of the day.)

"I went skating today and I miss *you and Daddy.*"

(Annette interjected again with similar persuasive tactics.)

"I went for a snowmobile ride today and I miss you and Daddy *a lot.*"

Each interjection was prefaced by the same comment from Annette, "Tell your mom about…." But, with each of his unsuccessful attempts to elicit sympathy from Annette, she interjected with greater enthusiasm. My wife was more interested in putting the whiny kid to bed and getting on with our important evening of watching TV. The poor child was struggling to convey his innermost feelings while Annette was anxious to prevent any such thing.

In fairness to Annette, there was no practical way of taking our little guest home. All of us would have had to pack our things, drain the water, shut off the electricity, and perform other necessary tasks to shut down our cottage in winter. In addition, a daunting trek across the ice in the dark would not have been welcomed as a 'warm-up' for the two hour drive home. The child likely would have fallen asleep long before we got on the highway, and getting him to fall asleep was the reason Annette called his home in the first place.

At the end of a rather lengthy conversation, he handed Annette the phone and walked away with an air of resignation. He was truly homesick but this had been anticipated and was therefore not overly disconcerting for us. Besides, movie time was fast approaching.

Annette took the receiver from our little guest and was welcomed to the conversation by an irate female who quickly and adamantly stated, "I am not his mother." Annette had made an innocent mistake, again. This time, she had dialled the wrong number.

Apparently, the woman at the other end of the line was so frustrated that she chose to wait out the conversation until the bitter end. Possibly to ensure that she got a chance to express her intense displeasure with Annette interrupting *her* TV program. If it had not been for the frustrated mom's extreme need to tell us what she thought of us, she may well have hung up at the beginning of the call, and likely we would have never found out that Annette had dialled the wrong number.

Annette re-lived the conversation in her head and I laughed each time she paused in embarrassment as she relayed it to me. We never did make another call to his home. By the time we had mentally sorted things out for ourselves, our little friend was in bed…and almost asleep. Also, it was movie time.

You can't do the right thing with the wrong number.

∞ The Life Preserver ∞

Every once in a while Steve will call from Atlanta to invite our family on a trip. Usually we can't afford the expense of what he has planned. His suggestions are always accompanied by generous offers to help. Generally, Annette and I prefer not to borrow money for a vacation. We subscribe to the theory that one should work first and play after, rather than playing first and working to pay for it later.

One time Steve proposed that our families embark on a four-day white water rafting trip on the Colorado River in the Grand Canyon. He went on to explain how we could make it a one week vacation and spend a few days in Las Vegas after our time together on the river. Since this required return airfare into one of this city's seven airports, we could experience some of the nightlife it had to offer for an additional cost of only three nights at a hotel. Upon further investigation, we noted that children under the age of ten were not allowed on our white water rafting trip. Since we had offers from others to take care of our children for the week, I was left with only one major concern—getting seasick from the unpredictable movement of the rubber raft.

Annette and I had not been on a trip without our children for almost five years and felt at ease with the thought of leaving them at home. It was fun planning for our adventure to the Grand Canyon. In preparation, we ordered a video from one of the tour operators being considered. We learned there were many rules on such a trip. Apparently, there are only a few operators licensed to conduct tours of white water rafting expeditions on the Colorado River.

Originally, one of Steve's friends sent out an email inviting people to join him on this excursion. His hope was to fill both of the eighteen-person rafts used for a typical tour, thus the reason for our invite. Steve and Jamie, along with Annette and I, made up four of the thirty-six people who responded to his invitation.

We took a short but turbulent ride into the canyon in a small twin-engine plane and landed at Whitmore Airport. This was my first aerial view of a desert and it was truly barren land. The first night in the canyon, we slept in a covered wagon at a ranch that was eighty miles from the closest paved road. In the morning, groups of about six people per trip lined up for the helicopter ride down into the canyon to the riverside 4100 feet below.

Gathered on the shore of the river, we watched as others from our group got out of the helicopter. On our first briefing from our tour guides we all received the rationale behind the rules previously noted in sales pamphlets. There were very large rapids to be navigated and it took teamwork to traverse them safely. Our guide explained how rapids are ranked on a basis of one to five and that all other rapids in the world are rated in comparison to those found on the Colorado River. This was what the Grand Canyon had in store for us.

The guides maintained a serious tone throughout their detailed talk. They explained that our life jackets had to be worn at all times while on board either of their two rafts. To counter the macho men in our group, they cited a relatively small number of people who had had their lives saved by a life preserver after inadvertently falling overboard. Sadly, there had been casualties.

Aside from their cautions of common sense, the rules they listed mainly concerned the environmental preservation of the canyon. For example, absolutely nothing was to be left behind on land—including human waste. A portable toilet was to be carried onto land each time we stopped. This was the only legal method of containment for solid human waste and it was to be stored for sanitary disposal at the end of the journey. The extensive flow of the icy cold water and its natural aeration through the rapids ensured that any urine in the river would be appropriately broken down. This method of disposal is the only environmentally acceptable routine for dealing with liquid human waste. We were told that it would take over one hundred years of average rainfall in this desert area to compensate biologically for the damage one could create in a single urination on land. I was on vacation but it felt more like I was attending an ecological lecture. Actually, I had been. However, I felt that the entire message could have been summed up into one simple statement: poo in the loo, and pee in the sea.

Unfortunately, stops on shore were only planned for mealtimes. The schedule would only accommodate one brief stop at lunchtime, and one more when setting up camp at the end of the day. This would not be a major challenge for most.

We had received casual warnings about becoming dehydrated from our hosts at the ranch the day earlier. The official tour guides reminded us about this, adding that we were a long distance from a hospital, and their policies required that anyone who hurt themselves in a non-life threatening manner had to endure the pain until the end of the trip—without exception. The thing that worried me the most was their caution about not drinking enough water to avoid dehydration and nausea. It was suggested we could avert such a problem if we each drank five gallons of water per day. When I first heard this I became fixated on preventing such a sickness.

My mind raced. Over and over I went through the math in my head. I was calculating how many litres of water were in a gallon and then converting to American gallons, which fortunately were slightly smaller than Canadian ones. In basic terms, I eventually deduced that I had to drink a gulp of water almost every other breath to keep up with their recommendations. I had purchased a special water bottle at the ranch the first night we were in the canyon. It had a lid with a strap attached to it, which I wrapped around my neck to keep the bottle close by. We received a mini lecture about pop and beer being diuretics—taking water away from the body. Pre-instructions limited each paying tourist to twelve tins of pop, and twelve cans of beer. However, the tour company provided enough water and lemonade for all aboard to combat the effects of dehydration.

For the most part, I spent the entire trip with a water bottle tied around my neck in fear of puking for three days straight while strapped onto a raft in one of the roughest stretches of water known to man. What was I doing?

Attempts to consume five gallons of water per day had me urinating frequently and in such unusual patterns, the group nicknamed me "pee boy." On one occasion, a sick-minded individual timed me as I relieved myself off the end of the raft during a calm stretch along the river. After a few minutes, he abandoned his project, possibly thinking he could have been the brunt of the next set of jokes had he stared at me for any longer. Nobody else was having this problem. But then again, nobody else was as susceptible to motion sickness, or as concerned about nausea, as I was. Also, the group was generally more interested in drinking beer and having a good time, rather than worrying about water consumption.

    Each night, the two rafts would come ashore and we would set up camp for the night together. Night fell quickly in this part of the country. It went from hot, bright, and sunny to cold, dark, and quiet in less than an hour. In this time, the temperature would drop from over one hundred degrees to about sixty degrees Fahrenheit. It was therefore prudent to set up your bed inside your tent as soon as the boat was tied up. We also tended to our group responsibilities while the official guides went about theirs.

    Everyone was responsible for some group task in addition to addressing their own personal needs. One group would set a fire, while others would hang community clotheslines. The paid help carried out other necessary duties. For instance, the portable toilets needed to be set up once the boats had been moored, then be securely shut and fastened to the boat for transport to the next stop each time we packed up. The crew took this task upon themselves, but not solely for the convenience of the passengers. One spill could have resulted in the tour company losing their licence to operate on the river, and the livelihood of many would have been lost. Therefore, the operators of each craft took this job very seriously.

    There were two transportable toilets unloaded at each stop until one of them had reached its capacity—making the other the most important asset of the trip. The protocol was to place the portable toilet somewhere out of sight and downwind from the main camp with a life jacket in an agreed spot nearby but en route to the loo. In this way, privacy could be extended to anyone using the facility provided they took the life jacket with them. The missing life jacket signalled anyone travelling towards the portable toilet that it was in use. Further, this privacy rule was followed so strictly that no one would even approach the loo if the life jacket was not there. Once finished, the occupant would place the life preserver back in its appointed spot while exiting the area. This was a signal to the next person in need that it was acceptable to enter the private grounds.

With thirty-six people plus tour guides and crew for each boat, line-ups were a common occurrence for this service. Urination breaks could be spent at the side of the river. Of course, I was at the river's edge more often than anyone else on the tour. The trick as I saw it was to visit the loo for number two when the line-up was short. My strategy entailed moseying on to the boat last, thereby ensuring an earlier exit at the next stop. In this way I could choose a location for our tent, nearer the facility than most. It was not long before the people from the other boat had heard about my nickname and the stories that tended to justify it. The first night on the river, everyone teased me.

Each morning, we were awakened for an early start. One morning, after the night of teasing, I was up earlier than the others. I used the portable toilet, remembering to bring the life jacket along with me. This room with a view was so spectacular, my mind wandered. I thought of the many sights to be seen that day, the glorious weather we had been blessed with, and pondered peaceful thoughts. I didn't think about the importance of returning the same way from which I came. Later I joined my wife for breakfast. Scrambled eggs, bacon, toast, and tea down by the water was my kind of roughing it. It felt good to relax.

Others joined us at our informal meal and the conversation ranged over many topics. Discussions about the picturesque pathways, the shoreline, the various cliffs, the water, and the beauty of this natural setting continued for some time. My thoughts once again began to wander. I casually mentioned the steady decline in the number of people lining up for breakfast. After this, Annette and I returned to our tent—the one closest to the entrance for the portable loo.

Annette commented on the fact that there was an unusually long line-up for the official resting place. It seemed as if more than half of the crew and passengers were in this queue. Then the lightning hit. Up until this point, I had been completely oblivious to the plight of those still needing to use the loo. None of the relevant conversation I had been involved in during breakfast had jogged my memory. Now, I needed help. With Annette still commenting on the line for the loo, I hushed her in a panic and explained why they were still in line—*I had forgotten to return the life jacket to its properly appointed place.*

Everyone believed that someone was having a rather difficult morning. The majority of our group was still patiently (read painfully) waiting in line for their turn. Snorting in disbelief, Annette helped me figure out a way to avoid the two of us being purposefully left behind on this desolate shoreline, had I confessed.

Annette would distract those in the ever-lengthening line-up while I attempted to return to the loo via my unauthorized exit route. I needed to retrieve the jacket and return it to its designated position, unnoticed. We both understood that during the 'mission' laughter from either of us would create undue attention. After I got Annette to stop laughing, we began our coordinated approach. She distracted: I skulked.

The plan worked flawlessly until the first man in line spotted me exiting the loo. He sprinted towards me with a waddle in a half-seated position as if preparing for the inevitable point of no return. There was no time to place the jacket on the tree as it was handed off in a split second, perhaps faster than a baton in any Olympic relay race. I was holding my laughter in check while he fought to prevent his bowels from exploding. I'm not sure who was having more trouble keeping things in. I casually continued out the proper exit path with the calmness of one who would normally take well over an hour for his first movement of the day.

I received a special look from those still confined to the line-up—the look of pure unadulterated relief. They couldn't lecture me, for I was like a child receiving a hug after purposely staying away from home for too long. Annette later commented about how quickly the queue cleared once the life jacket had been re-commissioned. Unbeknownst to them, in an ironic twist of fate, these partners of pain became the first group of people to have their lives saved by a single life jacket while standing on solid ground.

Later that evening around the campfire, those who had been dancing in line relayed their experience. They mistakenly believed that I had a bowel problem in addition to my already established plumbing problem. Laughter that came from Annette and I was misinterpreted as that of embarrassment. The joke was truly on them; it was only a memory problem at best. They didn't know that I had become their personal life preserver by returning to the scene of the crime to correct the situation.

When I first told this story to my dad, he said, "You're lucky you didn't soil yourself while you were laughing." We've discussed the possibility of addressing awkward issues by including apologies in this book. We've even joked about gathering them together in one chapter entitled Public Apologies, of which the one offered here would most certainly be included.

I had taken the authoritative tour guide's warning literally without questioning it. In hindsight, I realized he was exaggerating in jest, but this comment was given in the midst of many other serious statements and I—being a *literal* bonehead—accepted it willingly. He just didn't want anyone in the group to become ill substituting water with pop and beer.

Five litres, or quarts, would have been more than adequate as daily water consumption in the desert. However, the guy in charge of the tour assumed that everyone already knew this. He was mistaken. I continue to pay with my pride for this misunderstanding because my irregular peeing traits have remained, and my wife still teases me about them.

A life jacket is only helpful when used properly.

Life's Lessons: A Successful Collection of Failures

∞ **The Birthday Party** ∞

Annette and I have various different arrangements when it comes to our day-to-day life. I believe this helps maintain harmony between us. In many situations, it's clear who will handle a given job as it comes up. One of our arrangements is how we've set out the household duties at our home and cottage. Generally, Annette takes care of anything on the inside and I take care of anything on the outside.

Most of the time, Annette manages all aspects of our home life well. She competently attends to the needs of all our children, and demonstrates her love for us through her daily life. I am content to sit on the sidelines and focus on my own responsibilities unless she asks for my assistance. For this reason, it's easy to motivate myself to help when a part of her daily routine requires my input.

Sometimes I get the urge to help her with something that I believe if not handled well, will cause her—and me—grief down the road. I am of course not speaking in terms of a literal road since Annette has proved herself far more clairvoyant than I when it comes to…a cottage road, for example.

One year, I had been observing Annette as she filled out invitations for my daughter's birthday. Since she was born about a month before Christmas, this typically busy season is more hectic for our family. Primarily because we want to celebrate her birthday as a separate event from our family's other holiday plans. I wanted to participate in the scheduling, so I worked my way into a conversation between my wife and daughter. There were a couple of dates considered and after the three of us had discussed the matter, one was set. My wife clearly did not appreciate my input at the time, claiming that I had only served to confuse the situation. She added that she would have been fine on her own.

I agreed that things had become confusing, but once the date had been agreed upon, I was content to step away from all of the other details. Invitations were sent out and everyone invited had responded positively. My daughter's excitement grew as my wife coordinated when they would pick up the children for the planned outing. One of these guests was the homesick little boy who spent his first night away from home at our cottage.

Opportunities to get together with family and friends this particular Christmas were significantly limited. Annette and I were both working separate rotating shifts, which provided for only seven days off together in a total of five weeks. During this festive season, we visited other families and entertained guests as our schedules permitted. Occasionally, our visitors would join us for dinner. On the Saturday before my daughter's birthday celebration, another family was seated with us around our dinner table when we received a phone call just as we sat down.

It was the mother of the homesick child. My daughter answered the phone but Annette asked her to take a message since we had just sat down to eat. Insistence at the other end of the line prompted her to hand the phone to Annette. Church mom was upset with Annette for being late in picking up her son for the birthday party. Annette said calmly, "You have the wrong date." She did so with a sense of urgency in her voice as our dinner guests listened.

This church mom's frustration increased dramatically as Annette tried to hurry her off the phone. Church moms rarely yell and scream. She was adamant that the wrong date had been written on her son's invitation. Annette was tied up at the time and reminded the caller, "I'm a little busy right now with dinner guests." Annette tried to focus the attention on happier thoughts, reminding her that the boy had not missed the party and he could still join in all of the fun exactly one week—to the hour—from this day.

This did little to comfort those at the other end of the line. Church mom explained that she had cancelled a weekend getaway for her entire family so that her son could attend our daughter's birthday party. Her exasperation must have lasted all week, since the following Saturday she presented Annette's incorrectly-dated invitation immediately upon my wife's arrival to pick up church mom's patient son. To her credit, church mom equipped our little guest with a high-quality birthday gift for my daughter and has never held a grudge.

I'm not sure how church mom ended up with the only invitation that had a different date. Perhaps I was to blame. Maybe I had confused Annette when I interrupted her making the birthday plans with my daughter. In any event, Annette still faults church mom and only accepts half of the blame for the misunderstanding. She maintains that if anything is unclear, one should *ask* for clarification—*before* making (or cancelling) other plans. Annette has since been able to forgive church mom for her error.

Any important message deserves a response...do you copy?

∞ The Laundromat ∞

Annette and I have owned pop and snack vending machines over the years. Servicing the various routes taught us that money could be made in the vending business. Often we would service the machines together. The most frustrating part of owning any vending route is not the monthly duties: it's the agony of showing up at a location ready to service the machine, only to find it moved or unplugged because someone has decided it's no longer welcome there.

It is a major undertaking to move any full-sized pop or snack machine. Worse than this, it often has to be moved twice. It has to be moved out of the unwelcome spot, into a storage area, then later from the storage area to the new location. Finding new locations is the most difficult challenge with any vending route. Finding *profitable* locations is also a challenge. Any written contract designed to eliminate the most difficult challenge usually requires compromising any hope of making a profit.

Locations that are stable *and* profitable are not common. This conundrum was difficult to overcome, but I had an idea about how I could ensure never having to struggle in these areas again. The concept was for Annette and me to open our own laundromat. We wouldn't have to allocate any more time towards the common problems of a vending route. This plan would require no greater time commitment from either my wife or myself. Also, I would no longer have to worry about machines being kicked out. The challenge would then become finding a good location for our laundromat.

Pedestrian traffic near a vending machine is usually directly proportional to the amount of profit one can expect to make from that machine. There is one caveat—its location. As the popular saying goes, the three most important things in real estate are: location, location, and location. There is no difference in the vending business. I had learned that low-income residential areas produced greater profits than machines located in well-to-do districts. This paradox seemed to complement the new avenue of vending I was pursuing.

My plan was to find a fair rent in a suitable neighbourhood. Once I had secured a rental unit, I planned to finance the equipment over a number of years, and then, tend only to the basic duties of vending. With such a plan in place, servicing the machines would only require ensuring they were in proper working order, and emptying the money collected in the machines on a regular basis. Without worries about machines being kicked out, I could focus my attention on developing and serving a client base.

One day while looking through the paper, I noticed an ad for "used" laundromat equipment. After responding to the ad, I found most of the equipment offered for sale was in good repair. I made an offer for the lot, to which the seller laughed. However, after bringing the disadvantages of having to store this awkward and heavy equipment to the forefront of his mind, he agreed it would be better to sell it to me for considerably lower than his asking price. We made a deal.

I was delighted knowing that I needed every piece of it. It was comforting at the time to have purchased the entire package for less than the interest costs would have been on a loan for new equipment. I reasoned that the "used" items had to last only one year for the deal to have been worth my while. Also, if the location was poor, I would have risked much less money learning another life lesson.

Thus, I began my hunt for the ideal place to rent. Later, I continued in my search, willing to settle for a good location. Near the end, I tried to find any dump I could work with. Finally, I gave up looking altogether, and I put the assortment of specialized equipment into storage—abandoning my original hopes of building a laundromat.

I placed an ad in the paper hoping to sell everything as a single lot. Later, I continued in my search for enough people to buy everything by allowing the various washers and dryers to be separated into smaller lots. Near the end, I tried to find anyone who would buy even a few pieces of the industrial products. Finally, I gave up hoping that anyone would buy a single piece of my mix-matched batch.

Of those who answered my ad, no one wanted just the

equipment. Everybody asked if I was able to install it in *their* laundromat. I was willing to entertain the thought, but I couldn't complete the task personally. I tried to hire various contractors but none were interested. I followed this up with various calls to manufacturers of this type of machinery, but they would only install their own "new" washers and dryers.

Eventually, I found a private individual with related experience who agreed to do the work. With my new asset, I was able to incorporate the sale of my equipment into a purchase agreement with a small group of local Sri Lankan businessmen. Unfortunately, my new *ass*et turned out to be nothing more than half of that. It took considerably longer than quoted to complete the project.

I had learned a valuable life lesson through my earlier experience with "The Dimmer": "It isn't a deal unless you need it." It took me over two years to get rid of the laundromat equipment I 'needed'. I didn't make any money on the overall venture, and it was beyond a shadow of a doubt the longest non-profit endeavour I had ever taken on. I did, however, manage to build on a previous life lesson.

It isn't a deal unless you need it—NOW.

MY THREE CHILDREN

In an earlier chapter, I explained how I had accumulated a lot of debt during my stint in the entertainment business. After paying off these debts, I took a trip to the United States to celebrate. I planned to enjoy a holiday filled with wine and women. Instead, my vacation turned out to be a life-changing experience.

When I returned, I boldly stated my new beliefs. Everyone who knew me was shocked to hear that I had become a "Born Again Christian." I had made a decision to accept Jesus, the Christ, as my Lord and Saviour and shared this news with anyone who would listen.

At the time, my friends and family considered my interest to be nothing more than another phase I was going through. However, to their surprise, I became more focussed on the everlasting God and less concerned with worldly, temporal possessions.

I read the Bible, and the missing piece of my life's puzzle was found. I learned quickly that I had been viewing the world from an extremely selfish perspective and that there was much more to living than I had previously understood.

The meaning of my life was transformed. Indeed, it could now be summed up in a single sentence: God wants to bless me so that I can bless others. I fail every time I forget that the second part of this equation is the reason for the first. My Christian walk gave rise to a new life for me in all aspects: new friends, new home, new career, and a totally different lifestyle. I began to pray for the things I needed as opposed to craving the things I wanted.

When I was single, I had always dreamed of being married. When I married Annette, it was a dream come true. The two of us were ridiculously happy. Yet, I began to imagine how much more complete life would be with children—especially with a wonderful wife.

Rachel was our first. Andrew followed a little more than two years later, and Jaclyn arrived about five and a half years after that. Rachel, Andrew, and Jaclyn all have their own section in which they each take centre stage. The beginning of each section introduces the featured child.

Most of the stories that follow have enriched my life considerably, despite being quite frustrating for both Annette and I at the time. However, we now treasure these memories with fondness. We continue to love our three children dearly and they, in turn, continue to present us with new challenges—daily.

SECTION ONE: RACHEL

Annette and I were married about three years before we were blessed with the birth of our first child. As Christians, we wanted to give her a biblical name. Annette and I settled on the name Rachel, long before November 23, 1992, the day she was born. Her name came to us while reading about the biblical Jacob and the great lengths he took to make a girl named Rachel his wife. The biblical Rachel's attributes were also in line with those we hoped our Rachel would one day have as her own.

While Annette and I were still parents-to-be, we enrolled in a prenatal class. We chose one at the local hospital where Rachel would be born if all went according to plan. The course was an effort to educate and prepare its students for the coming events. The hospital staff encouraged participation in this course because it answered a number of awkward questions that would be best addressed well before a woman's patience has been fully spent dealing with the pains of labour.

When this day came for Annette, there was great pain. I say

Annette, and not Annette and I, because I agree with the comment Robin Williams made about childbirth in one of his comedy routines: "Unless you're passing a bowling ball...you are *not* participating in the birth." The hospital taught men in the class how to help their mate concentrate on breathing, and how they could 'participate' in the birth.

Annette's very first contraction lasted over forty minutes before I decided to call the hospital for advice. They told us to get to the hospital right away, but didn't indicate that both Annette's and the baby's lives were at risk. I was shocked to find the on-call doctor who lived much farther away from the hospital reporting for duty within minutes of our arrival. I was thinking about how I could comfort my wife, believing that I would be beside her for the birth, but the doctor motioned me out of the way as the nurses wheeled Annette into the operating room. The doctor looked me straight in the eye and said, "We should be able to save your wife." This was her way of telling me she didn't think the baby would make it.

The doctor and all of the nurses working at that time went into a small, well-lit room. I looked up at the hospital clock and noted the time. It was 2:30 in the morning and all was not well. I didn't have time to worry. At 2:33 a.m. I heard a baby cry. It took a moment for this to sink in —I had just become a father. One of the nurses rushed out, handed Rachel to me, and then rushed back into the operating room. I held Rachel in my arms and admired her. She stopped crying and looked around the room, seemingly frustrated with the bright things around her. The same nurse returned to update me with Annette's condition and commented on how alert our baby was.

Apparently, Annette had had an abruption. The placenta had come away from the inside of her womb. In many cases the baby dies and this in turn increases the risk to the mother. The doctor performed an emergency C-section. Not a planned or routine C-section, but something quite different. This was not something that was discussed in a typical prenatal class—including ours. Since our prenatal course had taught me to slow my wife down and encourage her to take her time on the way to the hospital,

I had lengthened the time before the doctor could operate on Annette. I had unknowingly increased the risks to both Annette and our baby.

Later, when Annette and I were at the doctor's for a follow-up visit with our newborn, we confronted our doctor. We asked why she had to be so impatient with Annette and dramatic in her statements to me. She replied in a sombre tone that one week prior to Rachel's birth she had been involved with another patient who had also had an abruption. In this case the baby died and the mother was still suffering from the inherent complications. Shockingly, this is a typical outcome if the operation isn't performed within *ten* minutes after the abruption occurs.

In our case, over an hour had lapsed by the time the doctor had even had a chance to examine Annette. The doctor confessed that she was surprised but not optimistic when she heard the baby's heartbeat during Annette's initial examination on that memorable night. Annette and I had learned in the prenatal course that a baby's heart rate should fluctuate between eighty and one hundred and forty beats per minute, but not stay at any one speed for any length of time. The first reading of the baby's heart rate was 170, and it did not fluctuate—indicating that the baby was in great distress.

The doctor explained that had Rachel not been strong-willed, firm, unwavering, and determined, she would not have survived. The words the doctor used on that day to describe our first child are the same words Annette and I use to describe Rachel today. We are truly blessed.

∽ The Milk Train ∽

Rachel was just over two years old when her younger brother was born. She welcomed him into the family as eagerly as her mom and dad. The novelty of having a baby brother lasted many years, and the two of them did not begin their sibling rivalry until he was old enough to speak for himself.

My son had an inner ear problem when he was born and this affected him to the point that he was unable to articulate clearly when most babies begin to talk. He was plagued with ear infections, had many tests, and at least one ear operation during his first few years. Rachel always understood him well, and at times was able to translate his baby talk into words and phrases Annette and I could understand. This benefited the entire family and in turn drew him closer to Rachel as he relied on her to do much of his talking.

Rachel became accustomed to speaking for him and enjoyed the process. With this status came a feeling of confidence that she soon realized could be applied to influence her parents as well as her baby brother. She learned to manipulate a conversation to her advantage and recognized the control she had over him. By the time Rachel had reached the age of three, Annette and I had to monitor this as we sensed Rachel was 'feeling the power'.

The relationship enjoyed between Rachel and her younger brother was not entirely made up of situations where Rachel dominated, nor did she have a thirst for supremacy over him. However, there were many instances where it was clear that she enjoyed being in control.

One such instance occurred when she was feeding him his bottle. She loved to do this and was excited every time we trusted her to sit on the couch and carefully hold him in her arms. She had done this enough times that she knew how to burp him and could easily lift him up to do so.

Our confidence in her completing a feeding meant that Annette and I would often take short breaks from supervising her and run to do another errand elsewhere in the house. On one of these occasions, we came back to find Rachel in the hallway kneeling in front of him with his bottle in her hand. He was pulling himself along the floor in a crawling motion to get to the bottle. Rachel was forcing him to stretch out his neck to get to the milk. In a sweet but dominant way, Rachel would move a couple feet back and he would yell out with a whiny cry. Rachel would then lean towards him to entice him into moving forward with the promise of letting him reach the bottle. Then the little guy would stop moaning and eagerly crawl forward to suckle once again.

Rachel could not resist the temptation of repeating this process and continued to do so many times. She would also move back slowly, keeping the bottle in his mouth and staying close enough to him to ensure he never stopped the sucking motion. She exercised an assortment of entertaining manoeuvres that demonstrated clearly who had the upper hand. She was truly milking it.

Annette and I thought of scolding her for teasing him in this way but decided it would be best to discuss the matter after we got the camera and took a few photos. See if you can "get him to stick his neck out further" my wife would ask Rachel with camera in hand. My input was something like, "Get him to crawl over here into the light where Mom can get a better picture." Rachel was more than willing to oblige us both. The incident was over within a few minutes and the attention her little brother received as a result was all that was required to make the sweet, playful interaction an enjoyable experience for him as well.

Our son has since grown out of following Rachel's lead and she is no longer able to dominate him to the extent she once did. It's as if there comes a time when the influence of an older sibling wanes and one realizes that if annoyed, a younger sibling can give them a whale of a fight. Teasing eventually becomes no longer worth the risk. Rachel has since learned to appreciate this and her influence has dwindled to other persuasive incentives. She has, however, maintained her ability to talk at great lengths for him—or about any other topic for that matter.

Dominance is not permanent.

✐ **The Cutting Edge** ✐

I believe every parent would be better off if their children were able to get along. I'm not suggesting that children have to agree with their siblings or support the other's beliefs, but I strongly feel a home experiences greater happiness when the children are not at odds with each other.

Personally, the conflicts of yesteryear that I shared with my two brothers produced an incredible amount of frustration during my adolescence. At times, I can remember feeling so mad at Steve for embarrassing me in front of others that I wanted to hurt him. Jamie was eight years my junior when he was born (still is actually) and there were only minor bouts of sibling rivalry between us. Despite our quarrels of days gone by, I have wonderful relationships with both of my brothers in my adult life. I am thankful for my relationship with Jamie primarily because we can boast we never really fought. Oddly, Steve, the brother I feel closer to in my adulthood, is the one I fought with constantly in my youth.

If the amount siblings fight when they're children is any indication of how close they'll be when they're older, Rachel and her brother will eventually become the best of friends. Their aggression towards each other began early and has gained momentum though the years. One minute they're playing a game and the next they're yelling and screaming at each other. Fortunately, the yelling and screaming rarely turns into pushing and shoving.

Perhaps this is because they both learned early on—when Rachel was about four and her brother around two—just how quickly one can get hurt when things turn physical. One winter afternoon when Annette was at work, I was home 'taking care' of Rachel and her brother. I was working at the kitchen table nearby with regard to the sale of some surplus film I had in our cold cellar. They were standing near me, talking amongst themselves and I was on the phone giving directions to our house for a would-be customer. The conversation between Rachel and my son quickly turned into an argument of some sort.

Rachel, in her disgust at one of his comments, pushed him head first into the outside corner bead of the wall in the archway between the kitchen and the family room. Blood spurted from his forehead. Rachel stood motionless. He cried out only for a moment and then moaned. He was struggling to tell me how much it hurt as this was around the time Rachel did most of his talking for him. Rachel remained silent.

When she saw the blood, it appeared as if she instantly understood what had been done, and that it was wrong. Like most little girls, she would get quite upset at the sight of blood but usually only when it was her own. In any case, I do not think she had ever seen that much blood come out of anything. Even before my son started crying, she was showing signs of remorse and fear of Daddy's discipline.

The sound of his head hitting the wall was like a coconut dropped on a concrete floor. I don't think it was the echoing sound that made her so uneasy. It was the speed at which her whimsical act had created physical pain that would obviously stay with him for some time.

It has always puzzled me as to why contractors ensure that the metal corner bead is placed on the corners of every room in a house to ensure injury upon contact—all in the name of saving a bit of plaster. Nevertheless, I placed my boy on the kitchen counter to remove the bits of plaster from his wound and checked him out. The cut was very deep and even with my basic first aid training, I knew right away that it would require a couple of stitches to be closed properly.

I was reluctant to just hop in the car and take him to the hospital, so I called 9-1-1 and asked for an ambulance. "Place a clean rag over the laceration and press firmly until the bleeding stops" came the voice from the other end of the phone.

Rachel, although very young at the time, had taken it upon herself to clean the floor to occupy her time while we waited for the ambulance and the medics. By the time medical help arrived, she had cleaned up most of the evidence of her assault, perhaps so that her police officer mommy would not see it upon return from her tour of duty.

Life's Lessons: A Successful Collection of Failures

After treating him with basic first aid, the emergency crew left my injured young son in my care, entrusting that I would take him to the hospital on my own and have him stitched up. Moments after they left, there was a knock at our front door. It was the two female university students I had talked to on the phone earlier. They were making their own low-budget radical flick and had decided to buy some of the super-eight film I had for sale. They had no trouble finding the house and offered to wait outside while I got the reels. I encouraged them to wait inside out of the cold, reassuring them that my wife worked for the police. They went on to explain how they were in a rush and felt a bit uncomfortable after dark inside the home of a male they didn't know.

After some reassurances, they grudgingly came in and waited close together just inside the front door while I went downstairs to fill their order. During the money exchange, there was some discussion about whether or not I would reduce my price further. Just then, Rachel—my beautiful four-year-old daughter—came into view holding a bucket with a mop that bounced off the walls in the hallway. She solemnly said, "I finished cleaning up the blood in the kitchen, Daddy." To which the already uncomfortable teenaged girls queried, "Whose blood?" They asked the question slowly, as if hoping it wouldn't be answered.

Rachel's guilty response of, "my little brother's" sounded more like that of a despondent child whose daily chores included cleaning up blood. If my clients were apprehensive about coming into my house only a few minutes ago, this was not helping. When my son walked around the corner with a gaping hole in his head greater than any makeup artist could produce for their upcoming movie, they both began showing signs of absolutely terror. They chose not to pursue further negotiations to receive a cheaper price for their film.

Feeling the need to explain, I relayed what had happened in the last few minutes and how this misunderstanding was really my four-year-old daughter's fault. Their few reluctant laughs gradually turned into comments of sympathy and offers to help. We joked about how truly gory my son's head looked. We could all see the muscles moving underneath the skin of his forehead each time he winced in pain. His lack of ability to express himself with clear wording added even greater effect.

In my typical thirst for detail and constant need to explain things thoroughly, I felt it would be best if I had the benefit of a picture of my little boy's gruesome looking noggin to show Annette. We took pictures with all of us taking turns holding him and positioning his head for the best camera angle and dramatic effect. The university students left with the film they had purchased, along with more than one or two ideas for their upcoming flick. I took my injured boy to the hospital. With Rachel looking on, he received only a few stitches—after the needle for freezing had been administered and he stopped dancing from the pain.

Rachel's lecture never came. As I looked into her eyes immediately after the accident, she gave me an all-knowing look. Nothing more needed to be said.

Some of life's lessons are learned without a word being spoken.

∞ Listen to Your Mommy ∞

Rachel has always been a sweet child. She is usually polite and well mannered. In her infancy, Rachel was so regularly well behaved and extremely calm that Annette and I had concerns that she may have received some kind of brain damage after the ordeal with her dramatic birth.

Her logical arguments and persuasive negotiations with Annette and me in her later years have caused us to abandon any worries of this nature. She is truly a bright child and both her mom and I are very proud of her—usually.

She can have her moments. There have been many occasions in which, like me, she can be quite literal. This often results in some sort of frustration for those close to her. Generally, Rachel does not try to give anyone a hard time, but is often mistaken for doing so when she processes information in a literal way. In these cases, she requires direct and explicit explanations if the person communicating with her hopes to gain any resolution. Rachel has come by this honestly, and it is *not* my wife's fault.

On one unique day in which Annette and I were both home spending time with the kids, I intervened in a conversation between Rachel and her mom. Annette was trying to get Rachel to share something with her younger brother and I was in the background listening. I shouldn't really call it an exchange because to the untrained ear it would have appeared as if Rachel was rudely ignoring Annette.

Rachel had been asked several times in various tones to give one of the toys she was playing with to her brother so that he could play as well. There was such a complete lack of response from Rachel that Annette thought Rachel was having trouble hearing her. Other topics were quickly discussed to prove that Rachel could indeed hear Annette. In each case, Rachel would always reply politely. This confused us further.

Annette looked at me as if to say, "What is Rachel's problem?" She tried for a few more minutes to get Rachel to respond to her wishes, patiently interacting with her on other levels. Annette was being careful to place the emphasis on different words with each repetition of her same request. Still no audible response. Not a grunt or a groan from Rachel, nor even a look from the corner of her eye…nothing.

At this point, I addressed the issue with a firm fatherly voice. "Rachel, listen to your mommy." Rachel continued to ignore Annette and failed to respond with any word or gesture. The statement was made a second time, "Rachel, *listen to your mommy*." With each successive command, my voice got deeper and possessed an even greater tone of authority. After five or six repetitions of exactly the same request, I was becoming more and more frustrated. I thought Rachel might have the gumption to ignore one of us, but not both. Eventually, I looked her straight in the eye and asked, "Did you hear what I said?" "Yes," she replied in a matter-of-fact tone. In one last desperate attempt to solicit an informative response from Rachel, I yelled, "Well, why aren't you listening?" Rachel finally replied, "I *am* listening. I don't want to do it."

She said this in such a confused state it was clear to Annette and I that Rachel felt we were the ones who didn't understand things. She was right. If either Annette or I had re-worded the statement into a *question*, Rachel simply would have answered it, and likely done so in the same polite way she did with all of the others that were asked during that time.

It has been said that if you want a better answer, ask a better question. This was one example of how true this is. Children are literal beings who make their own decisions.

A child may hear exactly what you say and not know what you mean.

∞ The Move ∞

When I was very young, I was playing on the driveway of our home. A moving man arrived and walked directly into my house without acknowledging me. I tried to stop him, explaining that strangers weren't allowed into the house without my mom or dad inviting them in. He discounted my objection, stating that he was a mover and that my family was moving. I knew nothing about this.

I was confident that if we were moving I would have been told. I explained this to the man, but he didn't waiver in his beliefs or actions. So, I followed him into my home and asked my mom to explain to him that he was mistaken. To my complete surprise, my mom sided with him. She stated that we were indeed moving, and that the man was there to move our things. She attempted to comfort me by saying that the moving man would be bringing everything, including my toys, to our new home. I was devastated because of the tone in which both the moving man and my mom had spoken to me. It was as if I was not significant enough to be informed. This stung terribly. I was very young but I remember it vividly and I swore I would never risk doing anything to make anyone feel as I did that day.

Throughout my life I have been plagued by the need to explain. As a result, I'm often told to "lay off," "get on with it," or "shut up." Despite this, I usually continue. In my married life, my wife and I came to terms with this part of my personality. Eventually, she allowed me to use the expression, "Humour me." In other words: I don't care if you're uninterested, if this has no significance to you, or even if it's completely irrelevant. Please just listen and "let me explain" anyway.

Only then do I feel I am able to stop. On an *intellectual* level, I know in most cases my listeners don't care, or at times are even becoming increasingly agitated while I continue. My problem is that on an *emotional* level, until my explanation has been completed, I am not at peace internally. I think I feel my long-winded explanations excuse me from being accused of creating the same emotional pain to another, similar to that which I experienced as a very young child on that hurtful moving day. I say, "think" because I just realized why—a revelation that had not manifested itself until I was *writing* this story.

One time when Annette and I were moving to another home, Rachel was about the same age as I had been when I experienced the trauma of a family move. Rachel was a young child but I felt she was old enough to understand our situation. I told her, "Mommy and Daddy are moving." I made a point of explaining the various facets of our move to her. I went into great detail explaining where we were going, when we would be leaving, and the reasons for our move. I even specified the times and dates emphasizing the fact that there would be no strangers helping us. She appeared to accept this.

As moving day drew nearer, Annette and I noticed that Rachel didn't seem very excited. We packed our belongings from the four bedroom house with a large basement, in preparation for our move into a three bedroom home without a basement. The smaller house forced us to put many items into storage. Even Rachel's younger brother had fun helping to make the necessary decisions. Rachel, on the other hand, still seemed somewhat upset.

The day before we moved, Rachel was on the verge of tears and appeared withdrawn. In an attempt to cheer her up, I merrily asked, "Aren't you excited that Mommy and Daddy are moving?" In a controlled but extremely sombre tone, she innocently asked, "*Who's* going to take care of me?"

I was more devastated than I had been when I was a child. All of my efforts to eliminate the possibility of a misunderstanding were for naught. I had specifically taken time to explain things to Rachel so that she *wouldn't* feel insignificant or left out. My attempts to protect her from the negative feelings I experienced with *my* first move had failed. Unfortunately, the outcome was exactly the opposite. Unknowingly, I had created greater anguish for Rachel than I had ever experienced as a child.

I dropped to my knees and whisked her into my arms. I lovingly hugged her and kissed her repeatedly. I continually reassured her that I would never abandon her. I did so until I felt she had been thoroughly comforted. In her inimitable spirit, Rachel has never held my blunder against me. With this account, I am only able to express a pale reflection of the stress I still feel from my childhood experience. Imagine how I now feel having created greater torment for Rachel.

She didn't feel what I was feeling, so she didn't understand what I was saying. I should have given her enough time to ask questions after I explained the situation to her. It wasn't until I felt what Rachel was feeling that *I* understood *her*.

Even the most thought-out, well-intentioned explanations can fail.

SECTION TWO: ANDREW

Annette and I talked about many things before we had children. In our younger years, I was good at math and Annette did well in English. We would laugh, sharing how we hoped our children would have my math skills and her talents in English rather than the other way around.

One philosophy we share about children is that they should be taught things the correct way the first time. For example, we did not use "ta" for thank you. As the popular song goes, "Get it right the first time, that's the main thing, get it right the next time, that's not the same thing." We also believe that parents should lead by example.

After being blessed with a girl for our first child, we naturally hoped for a boy as our second. In fairness though, after the drama that accompanied Annette's first bout with childbirth, we would have been happy with any healthy child.

Being born ten days before Christmas Day was not something I enjoyed while growing up. I appreciated my parents' effort to distinguish between my birthday and Christmas by ensuring that I received separate gifts for each. I swore I would never have a Christmas baby. Unfortunately, in mid March of 1994 I had a momentary lapse in my commitment to myself, and my second child. I have since apologized to my son for placing his birthday a week closer to Christmas than my own.

My wife has always considered my past to be that of an ongoing battle with bad luck. I have always considered myself blessed, and her single life somewhat sheltered, almost boring. Nevertheless, we both agreed that our hope for our children was to inherit her qualities and attributes rather than follow in my family's footsteps.

Rachel was just over two years old when Andrew was born, and up until this point our luck seemed to be holding. Rachel's disposition continued to strengthen both of our families' belief that Annette's calm demeanour had somehow prevailed over a lineage of frantic Fearnleys—that is until Andrew was born.

Andrew has been described as a busy boy. Anyone who has met him would tell you that this expression falls somewhat shy of describing his temperament. However, if "busy" could mean a tornado damaging everything in its path, and "boy" could mean a short male Tyrannosaurus Rex, then I suppose "busy boy" would suffice as an introduction.

When Andrew was two years old, one of our neighbours nicknamed him "Tas" likening him to the cartoon character of a Tasmanian Devil—at full speed.

In fairness to Andrew, he was plagued with numerous ear infections from birth until he was around three years old. On one occasion during an all-night car trip when Andrew was about two, I was looking for ways to pass the time.

I decided to measure the length of time he slept without awakening. His record during the night was only forty-three minutes. Sadly, this was typical for him. The poor child never enjoyed an uninterrupted sleep for longer than that until he was well into his fourth year.

My mother keeps telling me that it's much easier to tone down a spunky child, than to motivate a listless one. If this is truly the greater task, Lord help the parents who have children with no energy. This next section illustrates that my handsome Andrew is a perfect example of how a good student will always exceed his teacher.

◈ Gone Fishing ◈

When we were engaged, Annette and I bought our cottage together—much to her parents' chagrin. I believe they thought it wasn't wise since we weren't yet married. Later, they became more at ease with our decision, and have since focused their disappointment on another one—to get married.

They both gave my wife her love for fishing. Most of their family enjoys this pastime. Also, over time, a love for fishing has been passed down to Andrew through Annette. When I first met Annette, I wasn't fond of the activity. I was only able to land small fish and it seemed somewhat of a waste. To Annette, fishing is both a relaxing challenge and an exciting hobby. She views it as a sport that can be enjoyed in virtually all kinds of weather and throughout every season when approached with the right attitude.

In our newlywed phase, almost anything we did was fun if we did it together. So, we made a deal with each other that I would try to enjoy fishing once again, if she would try to rekindle her interest in waterskiing. This agreement proved to be beneficial for both of us since we each came to gain a greater love for these sports as we saw them *once again* for the first time. The benefit was not just the promise of sleeping with the teacher after the lesson, but rather that the teachers were both qualified *and* competent.

Annette soon taught me how to reel in the big ones and I taught her a number of waterskiing skills. Our deal has always been a win-win situation. That's the way we prefer things. If both sides stand to gain from a relationship, then it's far more likely to withstand the test of time.

Over the years, we made many deals where we felt both of us won. Some, I am unable to share with you in this family book. We have one such arrangement pertaining to my inability to deal with vomit. Simply put, I am a sympathetic vomiter, if there is such a thing. Even the slightest look or smell of it and I'm off to the bathroom to offer my sympathy, so to speak. Our agreement is that Annette deals with the family vomit whereas I must tend to the other end.

We have never had a well on our cottage property. The lake is our only source of drinking water as there is no town service on lakefront properties in our area. So we've taught all of our children and those that visit not to piddle in the lake. Because, "We may be making dinner with the same water."

When Andrew was teething, he was also being toilet trained. He was keen to pee against any tree on our cottage property and soon learned the benefit of doing so upwind. When it came to number two, he would often wait too long before alerting Mom or Dad for their assistance. For this reason, and for convenience, Annette and I placed one of his port-a-potties outside, closer to us at the water than the bathroom in the cottage.

Andrew was such a busy boy he had trouble sitting still for any reason—even this. One time Annette was headed up to the cottage for a drink or something and noticed that Andrew had "missed." What caught her attention was not so much his business but rather a shiny object gleaming from the mound at the start of the trail. Since this type of clean-up is my responsibility, Annette called me over.

Her findings were clear. The smooth piece of foreign matter was half of a rubbery fake minnow lure. A joke came to mind. "What's worse than biting into an apple and finding a worm?" I focussed on the punchline: "Half a worm." Then it hit me, the other half of Andrew's lure—the half with the hook—could well be stuck somewhere deep inside our son. Hoping to find evidence to the contrary, I went 'fishing' for a hook. I gave up after his droppings had been thoroughly strained by hand—a gross but necessary task.

Annette poked fun at me each time she walked past, whether on her way to the cottage to get a drink, or to the lakefront to enjoy a swim. I think she was glad I was finally making good on my part of our agreement because up until Andrew's toilet training, I had "gotten off easy." The only thing that kept her from laughing out loud was her concern for Andrew's health.

Of all the fishing expeditions I had been on, this one was truly the most disappointing in terms of being skunked. Annette always teases me about how her life was "normal" until she met me. Hoping that Andrew would poop out the other half of the lure—along with the hook—without any internal problems, was not something we were about to leave to chance. A decision was made. The entire family would pack up and go home early, so that I could take Andrew to the hospital for x-rays.

Andrew was too young to notice the funny looks or understand the subtle snickers from the others in the waiting room listening to me explain our plight to the triage nurse. My hesitation in answering some of the more awkward questions only added to their entertainment. It was agreed that x-rays were in order, as any metal hook could easily be discovered. When the doctor lifted Andrew's x-rays onto the lighted board, he asked, "Now, what are we looking for?" "A fishing lure," I replied. The look he gave me is not easy to describe. It was sort of like, "You've got to be kidding."

After explaining about my wife's recent discovery, the doctor agreed an x-ray was necessary. As he placed all of the negatives onto the lighted board he joked, "If it's in there, this will be the first time I go fishing for just a hook."

To our complete surprise, it wasn't there. What a relief. However, the doctor couldn't resist poking fun at me once more, suggesting maybe Andrew didn't find the hook as tasty as the wiggly part of the lure. Although other small objects appeared on the x-ray, the doctor assured me in a jovial manner that he did not think even the squishy other half of the lure was swallowed since its outline would have shown up on the x-ray. Just in case, he went on to give me advice about watching out for Andrew passing the second half of the lure. The doctor and I agreed to let things work themselves out naturally without consulting Andrew.

With the need for major abdominal surgery no longer a worry, I felt I had only good news to report back to Annette. Once at home, I relayed how the doctor wasn't worried about Andrew's predicament. I tried to make light of the situation, and said as I have often done…"At least it's another funny story for the book." To this, Annette gave her usual response: "We have enough."

On that day, I more than caught up on my part of the double-ended arrangement that I made with my wife earlier. The triage nurse had a short snicker. The other patients had a good giggle. The doctor had a chastising chuckle. And eventually…Annette and I learned to laugh at this as well.

Many things will work themselves out in the end.

∽ Bumping Heads ∽

While my dad and I were still discussing the layout of this book, I suggested that we group all of the accidents into one chapter and call it Head Injuries. After all, almost every member of our family has sustained at least one. This was later abandoned in exchange for the current semi-chronological format.

In the last section, I talked about how Rachel was quite literal. Over the years, Andrew has proved he can be just as much of a pain in the butt—sorry, just as literal. The following incident occurred when he was still a young child. He had hurt himself and I was trying to console him. I was also trying to figure out how he had injured himself.

He had managed to bump his head on the curved, smooth portion of the wall in the hallway of our home. Big sister Rachel was not around to translate, so I was struggling to understand Andrew's description of what had happened. I asked how he did it...many times, but to no avail. I started with short simple questions like, "How did this happen?" Sensing his frustration, I rephrased the request to, "Show me how this happened."

I assured him that Daddy would "not be mad" if he would just open up to me. I thought he was worried about me keeping such a promise as he looked to me for reassurance. "I promise you Andrew, Daddy will not be mad if you just show me what happened." Believing that his reluctance was due to his lack of confidence in my promise, I pushed on.

Rather than lock horns with him, I explained why I needed to know. He was still whimpering from the pain and shaking his head, indicating no interest in complying with my request. I detailed that it was necessary for me to understand the specifics of his head injury to be able to treat him properly.

I'm sure he sensed that I was becoming more impatient with each of his successive refusals. Perhaps he thought I wasn't about to comfort him further unless he obliged me. In my latter attempts, I was almost begging. However, it must have seemed more like a threat as I reiterated my request for the last time.

Andrew finally agreed to show me what had happened. At

full speed, he took a run at the wall, striking his head against it with great force and re-injuring himself in the process. I was dumbfounded. He had taken my use of the word "show" literally, and demonstrated how he had tripped while running, which had resulted in him landing head first into the wall—twice now, thanks to me.

I felt terrible and picked him up to console him. I tended to his wounds and reassured him that I loved him unconditionally. I didn't let him go until we had enjoyed a long cuddle, and until I felt he understood it was never my intention for him to relive the accident or the trauma.

Children always think you say what you mean…
and mean what you say.

∞ Tuberboy ∞

The cottage has always been made welcome to anyone who wished to enjoy the wilds of nature with us. All members of our family invite friends to visit from time to time. When whole families visit us, there seems to be a preponderance of girls. There are only a few young boys Andrew's age on the lake, whereas the girls in the 'hood' are mostly Rachel's age. Sometimes we feel nearly overrun by young girls. Anytime boys of Andrew's age are visiting, it's a special occasion for him.

During the summer of 2003, Steve had joined us along with two other families for the lake's annual regatta held on the July-August long weekend. Andrew was thrilled to be part of the gender that held a majority on this weekend. On the days before the regatta, the children were all in the water practicing their swimming skills for the coming races.

Included in the fun was the opportunity for every person to go for a run behind my family's ski boat. Some chose to water-ski, while others preferred to kneeboard, or wakeboard. As an added bonus, we offered rides in our newly acquired triple-tube, specifically designed for three people to ride side by side. Passengers of this monster tube only required two skills. They were experts in the sport if they could simply sit down and hold on. The novelty of this new toy, combined with the ease of riding in it, proved to make tubing a very popular pastime. On that weekend, the only thing faster than our two-stroke 130 horsepower outboard motor was the speed at which money was being poured into our gas budget. Consequently, these triple-tube trips were considered to be a treat for both the young and adult children.

Everybody had a choice as to what device he or she wished to use as personal transportation for skimming across the surface of the water. After the chaos of the group quarrelling over the water-skis, kneeboards, wakeboards, and tubes had ended, we all climbed into the ski boat, taking turns riding and spotting. For the most part I drove, only deviating from my appointed position on rare occasions when I got the chance to go for a barefoot run.

For this to happen, the planets had to align and produce calm waters and even calmer psyches amongst all participants. Despite being the driver of choice, this did not preclude me from being criticized by virtually every rider. The nattering ranged from "my bump wasn't big enough" to "he got more spray" to "how come she always gets the left side of the tube?"

By late afternoon, every guest had experienced each type of ride imaginable. However, Andrew was not satisfied. He was complaining that his ride wasn't long enough, didn't have enough bumps, and lacked speed. His turmoil resulted in challenges to just about everything except the quality of the rope. In true fed-up-fatherly fashion, I placed him alone in the tube positioned in the middle seat and got everyone else into the boat. I wanted him to ride solo because I planned to give him a high-speed trip with enough bumps, waves, and spray to eliminate any further complaints.

I chose the longest bay on the lake in hopes of tiring him out. Also, I had firmly stated previously that we would be returning to the cottage after his ride. Later, once we had reached the far end of the bay, this produced a series of other complaints. Andrew frustrated me to the point where I decided to just get his ride over with as quickly as possible, and race back to the cottage as fast as the boat would go, fully trimmed in.

With spotters in position and rope taut, I accelerated quickly and the tube soon reached its highest possible speed on water. I know this because it left the water and headed off into the sky. The altitude was only limited by the towing rope remaining attached to the ski boat. Andrew could have flipped over but with the rope still attached, and him still holding onto the tube, he made a somewhat graceful return to earth. Mentally, he was really high. Together we had managed to turn Andrew's afternoon of disappointment into a thrill and a lifelong memory.

With time and practice, Andrew and I, along with the assistance of his helpful sisters, perfected his stunt. Later, we had his uncle Steve make a video of Andrew flying down the lake—literally. That summer many neighbours enjoyed watching and one in particular stated how it was the most interesting spectator sport on the lake. At one point in our very first video, the sky can be seen clearly above the tops of the trees on the shoreline hills and *below* the bottom of Andrew's flying tube. Andrew does not make his next appearance on film until just before landing safely.

Since that time, many neighbours on the lake have tried to duplicate Andrew's success, but to no avail. Our record for distance travelled over the water in one continuous flight was about 220 feet. We recorded our speed at thirty miles per hour and timed the flight at just over five seconds. His record height, gauged by the boathouses we passed on the lake, has been estimated to be about fourteen feet from the surface of the water. Although now too heavy for a re-entry into his thrill ride, Andrew still remembers his first flight and each successive trip with great excitement and fondness.

I will never forget his unique talent in this sport. To this day he enjoys reminiscing about his experimental flights and has since chosen the name tuberboy for use in his email address.

Success wrought from chaos makes the memory that much sweeter.

∾ Hooked on Fishing ∾

Annette and Andrew often enjoy fishing together and both manage to bring home large fish after an outing. Andrew *can* be very patient. He will regularly assemble puzzles with hundreds of pieces and not ask for help. I have witnessed him fishing as he tolerated a most avid fisherman nagging him to "give it up" in the middle of the day, only to find Andrew reeling in a big one while the nagger watched on in envy. Unfortunately, Andrew is usually quite impatient at almost every other activity known to man. Perhaps, fishing is a time for him to rest. I know that it is mine.

Late one hot afternoon in the summer of 2004, he wanted to go fishing and try out one of his impressive new lures. Annette decided to join him and do some fishing of her own. It was approaching the best time of the day to fish. Annette asked him to wait for her arrival on the dock. The day before, he had been casting rather carelessly. For safety, Annette wished to be around so that he didn't hurt anyone.

Andrew no longer fancied the soft spongy minnow type lures with a single hook like the kind he chewed during his teething. He had matured into a fisherman who now fancied hard-bodied lures with multiple tri-hooked contraptions. When a fish bit into one of these babies, you could be sure at least one of the nine hooks would find its way deep into the flesh. The barbs were also quite sharp since his lures were new.

Andrew changed from one lure to the next, but with each one he had a renewed vigour as he began casting it out into the water. Annette tried to encourage him to take more time reeling it in, joking that the lure has to be in the water to catch anything. Andrew disregarded his mother's advice and continued to cast *his* lures *his* way.

Had I been on the dock, I would have been shouting at him to slow down. Annette's approach is usually something that leans towards the opposite. However, her casual approach to Andrew's actions didn't serve her well on this day. Within a few minutes of Annette's arrival, Andrew had snagged his largest catch ever—my wife. Hooks from his lure had embedded themselves into her leg after bouncing off the lower part of her bathing suit. The deepest of which came to rest next to her bikini bottoms well inside her upper left thigh. Had she been fishing in the nude, she may well have been injured in ways I could not describe in a family book.

Andrew had learned one of those life lessons that occur without a word being spoken. Annette now danced on the dock in much the same way a fish does after being hooked in the water. Inasmuch as her calmness towards Andrew had failed to prevent this from happening, it was now saving Andrew from almost certain retaliation. Besides, two hooks were now digging their way into Annette's private area and she needed Andrew to help her get them out.

Luckily, the drag had been on a low setting and the first hook was easily removed once Andrew stopped running away and put the fishing rod down. Its barb had not drawn blood like the other one as it was not fully under the surface of the skin. The damage was minimal. The pain was not.

The second hook presented a greater problem because it managed to pierce the skin fully but failed to resurface. The point of the hook could be seen (and felt) a short distance from where it had first entered. The leading edge of the hook was still far enough below the surface of my wife's tender skin that only two logical options for removal existed. Both options included freezing the area as any method of removal was expected to be quite painful.

Option one was to hold the shaft of the hook and pull backwards, forcing the barb in her flesh out, in the opposite direction to its entry path. Option two entailed snipping the shaft of the hook, pushing the barb forward through the flesh, and pulling the barb and the remaining part of the shaft out—thereby minimizing the tearing of flesh.

After managing to find a bearable position to drive, Annette headed to the hospital with Andrew in the front seat. On our twisty-turny-windy-bumpy cottage road, Annette met a neighbour and in an embarrassed tone described what had happened. Her husband is a doctor and they're both friends of ours. Annette showed our neighbour her wound as discreetly as possible. This neighbour called her husband on her cell phone and described the situation to him. He preferred option two, but advised going to the hospital. A tetanus shot was required in either case. Taking his advice, Annette and Andrew continued on their way.

After arriving at the hospital, Annette psyched herself up for option two while she waited. However, doctor two preferred option one. To add to the embarrassment of having nurses and fellow patients laughing at her situation, doctor two had a young sidekick in training who appeared to welcome new challenges.

Unfortunately, no matter how many times Annette and I reflect on their decision, it still seems somewhat peculiar—especially since both chose to support the procedure that maximized the tearing of flesh.

We're still mystified as to why doctor two chose option one. Any fisherman knows how to take out a hook. To extract an embedded hook, point first is best. Obviously doctor two and his lackey had not done much fishing.

This is likely not the first time a doctor has forgotten to consider their patient's pain. By the time Annette and Andrew returned home, the optimum fishing time had long since passed. However, despite the agony, the experience has not lessened their love for fishing—even with each other.

Some doctors just don't get the point.

Life's Lessons: A Successful Collection of Failures

SECTION THREE: JACLYN

When it came to naming our children, Annette and I have always felt it best to give each one of them a name that was spelled as it sounded. Our belief has been that children should always learn a rule before they learn the exception to it. Since their name is one of the first words they learn to spell, we only considered simple names, or to put it in Annette's terms—"normal ones."

This is not to say that parents who choose special names with unique spellings have done their children a disservice. Rather, Annette and I simply believe that each child is special and unique in their own way and their name does not add to or take away from how special they are.

On Victoria Day, when Rachel was seven and Andrew five, our third wonderful child was born. We named her Jaclyn, and she arrived with a red mark on the left side of her chest. It was diagnosed as a strawberry haemangioma. Annette and I have always felt that the truth is something that can and should be shared with young children, so we answered her questions about this mark when she asked. She learned to pronounce this word by the time she turned two, with emphasis on the correct syllables, and all the inflection of an enthusiastic pediatrician.

With the age gap between our children being what it is, Jaclyn is always trying to keep up with her older siblings. As well, she can be just as literal. She has been known to play with dolls but more often can be found doing something more challenging. By the age of four, she could water-ski, swim, snorkel, and drive an All Terrain Vehicle all on her own. Her sweet but strong-willed disposition adds to the dynamics of our family and she continues to be an inspiration for most of our relatives.

From her earliest days, she sucked one thumb and would grab anything silky to rub between her fingers with her other hand. Although she has since stopped sucking her thumb, she has yet to show any desire to stop calming herself with various silky materials. Her memory is more like that of a sharp adult as she can remember unrelated items like "groundhog" and "hotel" from an alphabetical game we played in the car a year prior. She plays with calculators for "fun." At bedtime, she can't sleep without having her pillow turned face up and positioned precisely square with the headboard of her bed. She is my child, and my wife reminds me of this every time Jaclyn has to have things a certain way.

∞ **Mother Beware** ∞

Guests had been invited to our cottage for a weekend visit and we were all enjoying an evening meal. The children were seated at the kitchen counter on bar stools to make room for the adults at the main table, who were reminiscing in our typical family fashion. Our family stories were being shared in much the same way we described at the beginning of this book, but in this case without recognition of any lessons learned.

The conversation at the table was competing with the chatter from the children. Jaclyn was only four years old, but being just as vocal as her older siblings, she was gabbing away with the others in the bar stool club. They were exchanging stories about their life at home, school, and various other topics of interest.

It is common for children to pick up various sayings from school and outside of the home. Often such jargon is unfamiliar to the parents. These comments can be surprising if used in the correct context when first uttered. One such example occurred at this get-together.

Annette was in the middle of negotiating with Jaclyn concerning too much talk and not enough vegetable consumption. In this case, a conditional and traditional threat of no dessert and an earlier bedtime was being stipulated. Annette paused briefly after identifying the problem, but before she had a chance to specify the consequences, Jaclyn interrupted her with an animated pronouncement: "Don't go there girlfriend!"

This was a saying that Jaclyn had picked up from her older siblings. Even though she was only four years old and not yet in school, Jaclyn was adept at mimicking such schoolyard jargon and mannerisms. Her remark was fashionably stated with an abrupt ending, accompanied by her hand being swept to a commanding *stop* position for effect.

Everyone at the table was trying to suppress their laughter. It only took one member of the family to snicker for the dam to break. Some of us couldn't get our laughter out fast enough. We were all laughing so hard that Annette couldn't continue and she forgot what she was going to say.

A prime rule of parenting is to refrain from laughing at a saucy response. On this occasion, we all had failed to respect this. Jaclyn knew that it was her comment that made everyone lose control. She also realized that it had halted the lecture. In doing so, she learned that laughter can stay almost any family punishment in our home.

Sometimes laughter is not the best medicine.

∞ **Table for Ten** ∞

Our favourite family pastime is entertaining guests at our cottage. We asked Steve and his family to join us for a July-August long weekend. They had all flown up from their home in Atlanta, Georgia, and were eager to partake in the festivities of our lake's annual regatta.

Our dinner afterward was special because all of the visiting cousins had participated in the day's events, and not one of them was without a medal for their accomplishments. Even the adults teased each other about who beat whom in various races. It was wonderful that everyone could take home a souvenir they had earned through their efforts, rather than the pathetic little "participation" ribbons I was prepared to dish out if things had not worked out so favourably. Everyone in the place had played a part in making this day full of memories.

At four years old, Jaclyn was the youngest one present. But, as always, she wanted to be part of whatever the group was doing. Annette was making an effort to include her in the dinner preparations and had suggested to Jaclyn that she set the table. The kitchen was full of people helping and Jaclyn willingly accepted. There were ten place settings to be set around the table. I handed her various items and the necessary utensils. There was ten of each, except for the steak knives. I gave her enough to give one to everybody—except her.

It was cute watching her take her time to place the cutlery just so. Once she had 'placed' all of the knives I had given her, she appeared puzzled and looked around the room. In a similar tone she said, "Where's the other knife, Daddy?" This caught the attention of others in the room and their eyes looked to me to see how I would respond. I didn't want her to cut herself so I told her she wasn't having any food that needed one. My ploy did not work.

She saw right through my attempted diversion. When Jaclyn looked at me askance, all the eyes on me shifted to her. It was the same expression a knowing teenager presents to a parent who has just decided to sit them down for a talk about sex. She tilted her head as if to explain a topic I was unfamiliar with. In a mature tone, Jaclyn said, "I'm old enough to handle a knife, Daddy." Everyone laughed. The astuteness of her retort was in sharp contrast to my lame attempt to avoid discussing the issue. She made me look like a dummy and enjoyed the razzing I received from the other listeners as a result.

My beautiful little Jaclyn, the youngest member of the Fearnley family, had made a comment that would be remembered fondly for many years, by everyone there that day. I felt it worthy of noting and committed it to memory; including it here as part of our family's chronicles in much the same way my father did for me…so many times…for so many years.

The knowledge of a child is often underestimated.

CLOSING: PART TWO

Jaclyn and Rachel

Rachel, Andrew, and Jaclyn have all proven to be blessings in my married life. It is my hope that they will grow up to become blessings for others as well. At this point though, I would settle for them just growing up. In addition to nurturing, children also have a need for self discovery uninfluenced by parental experiences. I believe we are better parents if we leave some secrets unrevealed, some treasures undiscovered, and some words unspoken, so that they can encounter memorable life lessons on their own.

Rachel has always proven herself to be a kind and considerate person. Her generosity exceeds that of many adults I know. She has learned that love is displayed and measured by the sacrifices we make towards others. Not long ago, Jaclyn told her that Rachel was her mentor. Where my youngest daughter picked up this term I do not know. Regardless, I commend them both.

In my view, Andrew is the most likely to continue in my footsteps in terms of pushing the limits of each and every situation presented. He has a phenomenal amount of energy. So much so that his pediatrician prescribed a diet of solid foods and soft cereal when Andrew was only ten days old. Mother's milk simply was not enough for a child with his vigour. Many of the pictures I've taken over the years are of situations that people would not believe without the benefit of a photo.

I still laugh at a picture I took of him standing at the age of four months. He was not really standing per se. The picture was taken when Andrew was in the habit of letting out his frustrations by going completely stiff and stretching out his body into a straight position as if he were a soldier standing at attention. The problem was he could only do this on the floor or in someone's arms, as he had no sense of balance.

One day while visiting Steve, I demonstrated Andrew's peculiar talent by ignoring Andrew's temper tantrum and propped him against Steve's couch in the family room of his house. I refused to acknowledge Andrew's fussing and left him leaning like an oversized wooden toy soldier. As long as I disregarded his antics, he continued his tantrum and remained stiff. He did so long enough for us to get a camera and get everyone out of the way. I positioned myself directly in front of him so as to create the appearance of him standing all on his own. The angle at which he was leaning was less apparent from such a viewpoint. His mom's willingness to play along by dressing him up like a toy soldier added to the effect.

By eight months, Andrew could stand on his own. He certainly had the strength, and he had had over four months to develop some balance. His determination to walk allowed him to do so early in his ninth month. His balance was still not fully developed, possibly because of his ear problems. By the time he was a year old, he could run at the speed of a child twice his age—but with the grace of a rhino. On my wife's 39th birthday, Andrew placed 39th in a long distance run of one and a half kilometres (just under a mile). To qualify, he had to place in the top four boys in his grade at his school. Boys from more than fifty other schools participated. Not a bad finish, considering he was racing against many boys who were nearly a year older. Despite any professional aspirations, his speed and agility have always proven to be of benefit when running away from his older sister—and not necessarily because "she started it."

As for my wonderful wife, Annette, she has often remarked, "Sometimes I think I don't know you." This has been her usual response after first hearing a story from somebody else—about my past—which she had not heard before. Hopefully, after reading this book of my family's chronicles, she'll never feel this way again. With my luck, I doubt things will turn out that way. But, one can always hope.

Our nineteen years of marriage has been full of adventure and truly without a dull moment. The only regrettable part is the sibling rivalry between my three children, which continues to puzzle and frustrate me. I've tried to find an explanation that would allow me to stop worrying about their relationship...and their problem. However, I still feel responsible, as though this is my problem in some way, since they're my children after all.

I wonder if the rivalry starts when we first approach our oldest child to announce Mommy and Daddy plan to bring a little brother or sister into their family. Children are not always enthusiastic about the idea. Imagine telling them, "I love you so much that I just have to have another." As if to comfort them, we say things like, "I hope they're just like you." We think such comments will be well received. However, think of how this would feel if your spouse approached you with the same concept and this statement, "I love *you* so much I want another one just like *you*." Saying something like this to a child could well be what sparks a never-ending jealousy towards their new sibling.

I wish I had some magical advice for every parent. A special recommendation that could be applied and typically solve all of the infighting between our children. If one wonderfully profound but simple statement could solve the problem, I'm sure it would remove the mountain of guilt and anguish that most parents feel when their own children cannot live in peace together.

If I had such knowledge, I would have applied it in my own family long ago. Unfortunately, the regular bickering between my children has ensured I'm not even close to such a miracle find.

Sadly, I have no solution on the horizon. Despite this, I continue to love my children and in time cherish every moment that they bring to us as a memory. Some incidents require more time than others—but with humour administered as an antidote, I tend to cope much better.

As one of God's children, I shake my head in embarrassment watching the so-called adults of this world at war over some of the most inconsequential issues. Sometimes I feel we are no better in His eyes than our children are in ours. I believe if His children could learn to live in peace with each other, the world would be a better place.

Such harmony is only possible when we look at things through the eyes of a child and put aside our so-called sophisticated issues. Maybe this paradox is our Maker's own sense of humour at work. Or perhaps humour is His gift to us to endure the hardships of this world until we see him face to face in the next.

In any case, my hope is that this book gives each reader at least a few more laughs than they might have had without it.

EPILOGUE

Andrew

As mentioned earlier, a significant part of writing this book was the "sign-off" phase. This involved visiting our family and friends to share our first draft and various other edits of each story. We wanted to incorporate their suggestions and contributions so that each story would be more than just the authors' understanding of the truth. Our hope was that this process would be an enjoyable one for all involved. Unfortunately, this was not the case.

Both of us added one more mistake to our list of many, when we naïvely assumed that this phase could be completed without stirring any emotions. During the sign-offs, we spoke with one of the owners from the sound and lighting company mentioned in Part Two. Although we laughed many times throughout that evening, this man read the stories of which he was a part and made a perceptive comment.

He noted that we had only included stories that made everyone look like we were nothing more than "a bunch of dummies." This was not our intent. Later, we decided that we would be remiss if we failed to include a statement about some of the many more successful shows this company was involved with. There were indeed far more successful shows than troubled ones.

However, this book is not about perfection. It is about mistakes. We accept the old adage that "We must learn from our mistakes." And, this is precisely why we believe that we must fail our way to success. This is exactly what the production company did. Simply put, it is not by avoiding failure but rather by overcoming it, that makes our life's lessons worth the pain of each experience.

Humour often helps to grease the gears of self-forgiveness. Fearing failure is the first roadblock that must be passed on every road to success. To us, challenges are the continuing series of forks in the road of life. Although we may never know which one we should have taken, once a course has been set, there is no way of determining what might have been. However, regardless of what has taken place in the past, we feel there is a mindset we can use to brighten our future path.

We believe that time is a great healer. It gives everyone the opportunity to reflect on more aspects of an experience than that which was initially apparent. There are always two diametrically opposing views to the outcome of the same action. We have a choice.

Just as beauty lies in the eyes of the beholder, truth is in the memory of the storyteller. And just like "there are two sides to every plate," there are two sides to every story. Our love for life has taught us this many times—both together, and on our own—and we often refer to this paradox as a "double-edged sword." We liken the blade that cuts sharply and simultaneously on opposite sides, to the contrast between both humour and pain that is buried in every past life experience. If one has the courage to dig deep enough, they can find both. Some must dig hard for the pain, others for the humour, but either route has the potential to improve the future.

There are advantages and disadvantages to every action we take, and the author of the actions does not always know how they will be understood. Any lawyer will tell you that evidence presented in court can affect a case either positively or negatively, depending on how it's interpreted. If we are to create a brighter future by overcoming the negative aspects of our past, we must revisit them armed with a double-edged sword.

The process of writing this book has led us to believe that if there is a saving grace for all of humanity, it is the ability to recognize humour in a painful past experience...and *remember* it in that way.

This, with time, has helped transform some of our family's most awkward situations into enjoyable memories. As authors of our own experiences, we are able to reflect upon our own actions and reactions, those of others, and the poor souls who had the misfortune of being part of our stories.

Now that some of our memories have been recorded, it is our hope that they can be shared and enjoyed many times over. Stories like these continue to occur in our family and contribute to our love for life. We are sure that many of our readers will have had similar experiences and encourage those of you with any unique memories to write them down so that they too can be shared. Perhaps you could even send us a copy so that we can enjoy them also.

Uncle Ted and Aunt Pearl at Puck's Lodge

INDEX OF LIFE LESSONS

Ted, Cleo, and Greg mowing the Croquet Lawn at Puck's Lodge

-A-

A child may hear exactly what you say and not know what you mean 431

A free show is worth every penny 290

A life jacket is only helpful when used properly 411

A threat misses its mark if the person being threatened welcomes the suggestion 7

A true hero never thinks of himself as such 263

Although a dog is man's best friend, it is possible he is working as a double agent 217

Anticipation is often more exciting than the experience itself 351

Any important message deserves a response...do you copy? 414

Anything or anybody can snap under enough stress 177

Anything shared increases in value; those who share increase in worth 200

Appearances are secondary 94

As in all great moments in sport, only the winning team readily accepts the decision of the judges 77

465

-B-

Bad news travels fast…even amongst small animals 97

Before any record is broken, a goal has been set 242

Brute force doesn't always work 322

-C-

Children always think you say what you mean…
and mean what you say 443

Cockiness is the point at which we stop learning 111

Consequences are the rewards for our mistakes 208

Contractors are rarely finished on time,
even when YOU are the contractor 52

-D-

Dogs will find a way 215

Dominance is not permanent 425

-E-

Even animals have to account for their ups and downs 41

Even the most thought-out, well-intentioned explanations can fail 434

Even young children have an instinctive desire to
understand where we come from 143

Every pet deserves a special place in your home 32

Every problem has more than one solution 120

Every smoker's life is reduced by at least one life lesson 13

-F-

Few things improve when you get to the end of your rope 213

Finding a simple solution is the trick to resolving difficult problems 54

Finding something that was lost can be cause for celebration 280

For faster service, shower before ringing bell 99

-H-

He who laughs last, laughs best…but he who laughs inwardly
can laugh longer 16

Help comes in many forms 141

INDEX OF LIFE LESSONS

Humour is like a life lesson...it can only be enjoyed after it is understood 57

-I-

If by accident you expose your friend's skull, take the time to tell his mother 123

If you are going to build a tunnel to your friend's place—START THERE 35

If you are going to try emulating Native Canadians, talk to one first 90

If you ask a question, take the time to listen to the answer 87

If you know the consequences, why bear the pain proving the point? .. 147

If you want to go to a fancy show, buy a ticket 355

If you want your listener to take action, they must understand what you're saying AND feel what you're feeling 392

If you're drinking to forget, remember—too much sauce can ruin anything 183

If you're going to have a chat, take the time to find out who you're talking to 128

If you're going to lose your temper, put the knife down 118

If you're going to play hooky, don't do it for a full week 30

If you're playing the long shot, place your bet at the casino where there is at least a chance of winning 396

Inasmuch as our children often underestimate the value of our words, we, as parents, often overestimate them 20

In England, always carry a letter from your mom 185

It is unwise to start any project without approval from the appropriate authority 79

It isn't a deal unless you need it 360

It isn't a deal unless you need it—NOW 417

It takes a long, long time to create an overnight success 315

It's never too late to change 383

-J-

Just because your sibling lets you call the shots
doesn't mean you won't get stabbed in the back 240

Justifying something to yourself does not make it right 22

-L-

Later is better than never, but on time is better than ever 196

Learn to take direction from your instruments 92

Life in the wild is fraught with surprises 96

Love is…swallowing your pride for the sake of others 129

-M-

Making a point is not worth making an enemy 134

Making the best of any situation creates warm memories 46

Many things will work themselves out in the end 441

Most students from the school of hard knocks
graduate with honours 297

-N-

Nature will find a way—even at the most awkward of times 106

No lesson is complete unless we learn something about ourselves 165

No one has a fond memory of the flu 26

No passion for poison ever has a happy ending 221

Nobody is your friend when you're full of gas 255

Not every great idea will get off the ground 43

Not every St. Bernard is a work dog 69

Not every trouble melts away 145

-O-

One can treasure what others long to throw out 153

One man's garbage is another man's goal 365

Optimism is the ability to see beyond the problem 274

Our passion shapes our destiny 45

INDEX OF LIFE LESSONS

-P-

Parents should be cogs in the wheels of justice 198

Patience is more than a virtue; sometimes it is a necessity 205

People not as sharp as their implements are often considered tools 71

-R-

Rather than demanding something of your wife,
better to ask—better still, ask HER 387

Recovery is a sweet gift for more than the one who was sick 223

-S-

Slow down; impulsive acts reveal our true selves 163

Some conveniences are inconvenient 67

Some doctors just don't get the point 449

Some of life's lessons are learned
without a word being spoken 429

Some old gems never lose their lustre—they are
preserved by being shared 105

Sometimes childhood fears return to haunt us through our children 9

Sometimes it helps to listen with more than your ears 5

Sometimes it is easier to receive forgiveness
than to get permission 342

Sometimes laughter is not the best medicine 454

Sometimes resolving one problem makes another one worse 161

Sometimes the best discoveries are those that are re-discovered 126

Sometimes the better things look, the less likely they
are to meet your expectations 82

Spelling always counts 191

Stargazing can cloud your judgment 334

Stick-to-itiveness is a work ethic that
impresses even your friends 265

Success wrought from chaos makes the
memory that much sweeter 446

-T-

Taking a break helps to provide a fresh perspective 55

Tempered self is stronger than tempered steel 173

The art of survival calls for creative strategies 49

The best advice does not always come
from the highest authority 338

The best recipe for success is one that has
room for failures along the way 11

The bigger the secret, the harder it is to keep under your hat 169

The finest compounding interest is that which
we invest in others 260

The heavier the load, the more difficult the journey 327

The knowledge of a child is often underestimated 456

The longer away from the comforts of home, the more
they're appreciated upon return 101

The more light you shed on an issue,
the greater the chance for peace 402

The oilman doesn't ring twice 377

The power of positive thinking works—even for dogs 219

There is always an opportunity to change when
something is broken—especially for people 18

There will always be greater challenges just around the corner 251

There's only so much a parent can do 193

To live in the hearts of those we love is not to die 62

Two day trips are better than one—even on the same day 48

-U-
Understanding is a medicine that cures 59

-V-
Vacuums without a dust bag really just suck 38

Venting is communication from the soul 181

INDEX OF LIFE LESSONS

-W-

What you sow, you can't always eat 10

When you pre-judge a person, you never
see their full potential 302

With every lofty goal there are unique obstacles to overcome 307

Without experience, danger can be mistaken for adventure 73

Worries increase until you face your fear 237

-Y-

Yielding to temptation can be a dead end on the road of life 150

You can never be too far away to help 371

You can stop the blood, but "truth will out." 244

You can't do the right thing with the wrong number 404

You need not rush to enjoy the slow pace of reel life
in the great outdoors 108

About the Author
Ted Fearnley

Born in 1932, Ted spent his younger years getting in and out of trouble. After graduating with a degree in Civil Engineering from the University of Toronto, he spent a few years in structural design. Later, he designed highways and other roads for a major Toronto consulting firm. Then, in 1971, he formed his own consulting business and worked as a specialist in traffic, and road planning and design. For over thirty years Ted wrote technical reports concerning highway routes and traffic analyses and never once succumbed to the temptation of inserting a humorous comment.

He pined away writing normal, detailed, boring reports despite a secretive career-long desire to write a humorous traffic report. This was probably his most impossible dream—doomed to failure because of an incompatible approach to a mundane subject.

Ted gave up Civil Engineering for a career in sales as the Canadian representative for an innovative American company that sells Camera Lowering Systems and other unique roadway safety products. This new line of work has proven to be more interesting and much more rewarding.

Ted's three children along with his wife's two boys have given them eight grandchildren. Ted and his wife, Nancy, live on their own with their dog Titia, in Toronto, Ontario, and are enjoying their retirement years together…although Ted's version of retirement is working full-time.

About the Author
Rick Fearnley

After high school Rick became an entertainer and took to the stage as an illusionist in a large scale Magic Show. He was billed as The Amazing Rick Fearnley. Later, he transitioned into stand-up comedy and shared the stage with many notable comics such as John Candy, Eugene Levy, Andrea Martin and Jim Carrey.

Rick has worked as an Air Traffic Controller, been involved with major theatrical productions, and used his experience in retail management to help him run various businesses from vending routes to sound studios.

He now works as a 911 operator and Police Dispatcher for The Toronto Police Service. He is often asked for his editorial comments concerning manuals and documents produced by the unit responsible for training 911 personnel. Recently he was honoured with the highest award in his profession—Communications Operator of the Year (2005).

Rick has been married for nineteen years and lives with his wife, Annette, and their three children in Aurora, Ontario. Together they attend church and spend much of their free time entertaining guests at their cottage in Muskoka, Canada.

CONTACT US

Thank you for taking the time to read about our Life's Lessons. As we indicated in our Epilogue, we would be thrilled to read any family story that you may have. If you wish to send us one or more of your stories, please do so through our website. We also encourage your comments.

In addition, both of the authors can be contacted through our website at: www.lifeslessons.ca

Therefore, if you wish to:

- Contact Ted Fearnley,
- Contact Rick Fearnley,
- Order more copies of this book,
- Comment formally about our book,
- Read more about the Author Ted Fearnley,
- Read more about the Author Rick Fearnley,
- Find the closest bookstore that carries this book, or
- Offer your story for consideration in a future book of ours…

Please visit us at www.lifeslessons.ca

(Apologies to Lynne Truss for omitting the apostrophe in our website name.)